T0234898

Lecture Notes in Computer Science 9976

Commenced Publication in 1973
Founding and Former Series Editors:
Gerhard Goos, Juris Hartmanis, and Jan van Leeuwen

More information about this series at http://www.springer.com/series/7408

Franz Wotawa · Mihai Nica
Natalia Kushik (Eds.)

Testing Software and Systems

28th IFIP WG 6.1 International Conference, ICTSS 2016
Graz, Austria, October 17–19, 2016
Proceedings

 Springer

Editors
Franz Wotawa
Technische Universität Graz
Graz
Austria

Mihai Nica
AVL LIST GmbH
Graz
Austria

Natalia Kushik
Télécom SudParis
Evry Cedex
France

ISSN 0302-9743   ISSN 1611-3349   (electronic)
Lecture Notes in Computer Science
ISBN 978-3-319-47442-7   ISBN 978-3-319-47443-4   (eBook)
DOI 10.1007/978-3-319-47443-4

Library of Congress Control Number: 2016954192

LNCS Sublibrary: SL2 – Programming and Software Engineering

Printed on acid-free paper

This Springer imprint is published by Springer Nature
The registered company is Springer International Publishing AG
The registered company address is: Gewerbestrasse 11, 6330 Cham, Switzerland

Preface

This volume contains the conference proceedings of the IFIP 28th International Conference on Testing Software and Systems, which was held October 17–19, 2016. The International Conference on Testing Software and Systems (ICTSS) addresses the conceptual, theoretic, and practical problems of testing software systems, including communication protocols, services, distributed platforms, middleware, embedded- and cyber-physical systems, and security infrastructures. ICTSS is the successor of previous (joint) conferences TESTCOM and FATES and aims to be a forum for researchers, developers, testers, and users to review, discuss, and learn about new approaches, concepts, theories, methodologies, tools, and experience in the field of testing communicating systems and software.

In 2016, the conference took place at the main building of the Technische Universität Graz, Austria. Conjointly with the main conference, three workshops were organized as part of the ICTSS workshop program, namely: the 4th International Workshop on Risk Assessment and Risk-Driven Quality Assurance (RISK), the Workshop on Digital Eco-Systems, and the Workshop on Quality Assurance in Computer Vision (QACV).

ICTSS received 41 submissions from 24 countries, which were evaluated in a rigorous single-blind peer reviewing process by a Program Committee including 53 experts and ten external reviewers. From the 41 submission, six were desk rejected because of substantial deviations from the submission requirements and lack of acceptable content. For the remaining 35 submissions, we received 105 reviews. Based on the reviews, of the 41 submissions, 13 (32 %) were accepted for inclusion in theses proceedings as full papers, and eight (20 %) were accepted as short papers. From the short paper's authors decided to retract three papers from these proceedings.

We wish to thank all Program Committee members and additional reviewers for their great efforts in reviewing and discussing the submissions during the reviewing process. The outcome of the review process shows the effectiveness of the selection process and the commitment of the Program Committee to continue the high-quality standards of ICTSS.

The ICTSS 2016 program also included three keynotes given by distinguished scientists. Special thanks go to Gordon Fraser, Arnaud Gotlieb, and Jeff Offutt for their thought-provoking keynotes and their active participation in discussions during the conference.

Last but not least, we want to thank everyone who helped make ICTSS 2016 a success. This of course includes all authors, Program Committee members, Steering Committee members, reviewers, and keynote speakers, as well as the organizers, reviewers, and authors of the workshops. In addition we want to sincerely thank the participants of ICTSS, without whom a conference would never be a success.

October 2016

Franz Wotawa
Mihai Nica
Natalia Kushik

Organization

General Chair

Franz Wotawa	TU Graz, Austria
Mihai Nica	AVL, Austria
Natalia Kushik	Telecom SudParis, France

Steering Committee

Rob Hierons	Brunel University, UK
Andreas Ulrich	Siemens, Germany
Ana Cavalli	Institut Mines-Telecom/Telecom SudParis, France
Khaled El Fakih	American University of Sharjah, UAE
Nina Yevtushenko	Tomsk State University, Russia
Mercedes G. Merayo	Universidad Complutense de Madrid, Spain
Cemal Yilmaz	Sabanci University, Turkey
Hüsnü Yenigün	Sabanci University, Turkey

Publicity Chair

Ingo Pill	TU Graz, Austria

Local Organization

Jörg Baumann	TU Graz, Austria
Petra Pichler	TU Graz, Austria
Elisabeth Orthofer	TU Graz, Austria

Program Committee

Bernhard K. Aichernig	TU Graz, Austria
Fevzi Belli	University Paderborn, Germany
Gregor Bochmann	University of Ottawa, Canada
Kirill Bogdanov	The University of Sheffield, UK
Ana Cavalli	Institut Mines-Telecom/Telecom SudParis, France
Byoungju Choi	Ewha Womans University, Korea
John Derrick	University of Sheffield, UK
Khaled El-Fakih	American University of Sharjah, UAE
Gordon Fraser	University of Sheffield, UK
Angelo Gargantini	University of Bergamo, Italy
Sudipto Ghosh	Colorado State University, USA

Jens Grabowski	Georg August University of Göttingen, Germany
Klaus Havelund	Jet Propulsion Laboratory, California Institute of Technology, USA
Rob Hierons	Brunel University, UK
Teruo Higashino	Osaka University, Japan
Dieter Hogrefe	Georg August University of Göttingen, Germany
Thierry Jéron	Inria Rennes - Bretagne Atlantique, France
Ferhat Khendek	Concordia University, Canada
Hartmut Koenig	Brandenburg University of Technology, Germany
Victor Kuliamin	Institute for System Programming, Russian Academy of Sciences, Russia
Natalia Kushik	Telecom SudParis, France
Bruno Legeard	Smartesting, France
Stephane Maag	Institut Mines Telecom/Telecom SudParis, France
Patricia Machado	Federal University of Campina Grande, Brazil
Wissam Mallouli	Montimage, France
Wes Masri	American University of Beirut, Lebanon
Radu Mateescu	Inria Grenoble - Rhône-Alpes, France
Karl Meinke	Royal Institute of Technology (KTH) Stockholm Sweden
Zoltan Micskei	Budapest University of Technology and Economics, Hungary
Edgardo Montes De Oca	Montimage, France
Tejeddine Mouelhi	ENST Bretagne – GET, France
Mihai Nica	AVL, Austria
Brian Nielsen	Aalborg University, Denmark
Manuel Nuñez	Universidad Complutense de Madrid, Spain
Alexandre Petrenko	CRIM, Canada
Andrea Polini	ISTI – CNR, Italy
Ina Schieferdecker	FU Berlin/Fraunhofer FOKUS, Germany
Holger Schlingloff	Fraunhofer FIRST and Humboldt University, Germany
Adenilso Simao	ICMC/USP, Brazil
Dimitris E. Simos	SBA Research, Austria
Miroslaw Staron	University of Gothenburg, Sweden
Uraz Cengiz Turker	Gebze Technical University, Turkey
Andreas Ulrich	Siemens AG, Germany
Cesar Viho	IRISA/University of Rennes 1, France
Tanja E.J. Vos	Universidad Politécnica de Valencia, Spain
Neil Walkinshaw	The University of Leicester, UK
Farn Wang	National Taiwan University, ROC
Stephan Weissleder	Thales Deutschland, Germany
Burkhart Wolff	University of Paris-Sud, France
Franz Wotawa	TU Graz, Austria
Hirozumi Yamaguchi	Osaka University, Japan
Hüsnü Yenigün	Sabanci University, Turkey
Fatiha Zaidi	University of Paris-Sud, France

Additional Reviewers

Abbas Ahmad	Easy Global Market, France
Gulsen Demiroz	Sabanci University, Turkey
Patrick Harms	Georg August University of Göttingen, Germany
Steffen Herbold	Georg August University of Göttingen, Germany
David Honfi	Budapest University of Technology and Economics, Hungary
Jorge López	Telecom SudParis, France
Diego Rivera	Telecom SudParis, France
Urko Rueda	Universidad Politécnica de Valencia, Spain
Wendelin Serwe	Inria Grenoble - Rhône-Alpes, France
Paolo Vavassori	University of Bergamo, Italy

Keynotes (Abstracts)

Gamifying Software Testing

Gordon Fraser

University of Sheffield, Sheffield, UK

Abstract. Writing good software tests is difficult and not every developer's favourite occupation. If an activity is so difficult, boring, or otherwise unattractive that people do not want to engage with it, then gamification offers a solution: By turning the activity into a fun and competitive task, participants engage, compete, and excel. In this talk, I will explore how this idea can be applied to software testing. Our ongoing work with the Code Defenders game demonstrates that players engage with testing, and perceive it as a fun activity. At the same time, by participating in the game, players produce test suites that are far superior to anything automated testing tools generate. This illustrates the potential of using gamification to address some of the many problems that we are facing today in software testing. There are, however, many challenges ahead, and I will outline some of the challenges and research opportunities related to gamifying software testing.

Constraint-Based Test Suite Optimization

Arnaud Gotlieb

Simula Research Laboratory, Fornebu, Norway

Abstract. Test suite optimization is a crucial topic in software testing which was recently boosted by the contributions of constraint programming and search-based algorithms. The increased complexity of testing procedures and the combinatorial nature of the underlying testing problems, namely (multi-criteria) test suite reduction, prioritization and scheduling requires the usage of advanced techniques which have been developed in other contexts. In this talk, I will review some of these advances and their application to real-world testing problems that we address in Certus, the Norwegian research-based innovation centre dedicated to Software Validation and Verification.

Beyond Test Automation

Jeff Offutt

George Mason University, Fairfax, USA

Abstract. Many software testing researchers have the goal of making their research valuable to industry. For example, STVR's tagline is "Useful research in making better software," and a common exhortation is that software engineering research should "help real engineers make real software better." If so, then improving test automation is certainly an effective strategy. Increasing test automation is currently one of the most important and pervasive changes in the software industry. This talk will overview the key elements of test automation, summarize some of the recent research advances in test automation, explore how this change is playing out in industry, and present some current challenges in test automation. The talk will conclude by asking a simple question to go beyond test automation: "why are my tests so dumb?"

Contents

Practical Applications

Short Contributions

Testing Methodologies

Conformance Testing with Respect to Partial-Order Specifications

Gregor von Bochmann[✉]

School of Electrical Engineering and Computer Science,
University of Ottawa, Ottawa, Canada
bochmann@uottawa.ca

Abstract. This paper deals with the testing of distributed systems. An implementation under test is checked for conformance with the properties defined by a reference specification. Since distributed systems usually have multiple interfaces, the reference specification will not define the order of all pairs of interactions taking place at different interfaces. Therefore a specification formalism supporting the definition of partial orders is required. Different such formalisms are compared in this paper, including MSC-Charts (or Interaction Overview Diagrams). A variation of this formalism, called Partial-Order-Charts (PO-Charts) is proposed which makes abstraction from the exchange of messages. It concentrates on the specification of partial orders between local actions in different system components. It is shown that the partial-order testing approach introduced for a single partial order specification can be adapted to testing PO-Charts which define various combinations of different partial orders which are sequenced by strict or week sequencing, including loops. Various examples are given to compare this testing approach with state machine testing methods which can be applied for **bounded** PO-Charts for which one can derive an equivalent state machine. The testing complexities and fault model assumptions of these two approaches are compared.

1 Introduction

Conformance testing is an activity where an implementation under test (IUT) is checked for conformance to a specification. For this purpose, input interactions are applied by testers at the different interfaces of the IUT and the outputs provided by the IUT are observed by the testers and are compared with what is expected according to the requirements defined by the specification. For distributed systems, the order of interactions taking place at different interfaces are often irrelevant for the defined behavior, furthermore, it is sometimes difficult to control the order of inputs at different interfaces, and to observe the order of outputs at different interfaces. For this reason, state machine models for the specification are not appropriate, since they precisely define a total order for all interactions. As a consequence, partial-order specifications have been proposed for describing the required behavior of distributed systems. A well-known example of a partial-order notation is Message Sequence Charts (MSC, or UML Interaction diagrams).

F. Wotawa et al. (Eds.): ICTSS 2016, LNCS 9976, pp. 3–17, 2016.
DOI: 10.1007/978-3-319-47443-4_1

In order to test partial-order specifications, [Haar] proposed the concept of Partial-Order Input-Output Automata (POIOA) and discussed how to derive conformance test suites from such specifications. A POIOA is a state machine where each transition involves in general a set of input and output interactions for which a partial order is defined for their execution. However, each state of the POIOA represents a global synchronization point involving all the distributed interfaces. This enforces strict sequencing between the execution of subsequent transitions, that is, an interaction of the next transition can only occur after all interactions of the preceding transition have been completed. In real distributed systems, one often rather wants to impose weak sequencing which means that sequencing is enforced locally at each interface (or each component of the distributed system), but not globally.

Concepts for specifying control flow in distributed systems with partial orders including strict AND weak sequencing was proposed in [Castejon]. These concepts are quite similar to the more formal definition of MSC-Charts given by Alur and Yannakakis [Alur]. In a few words, an MSC-Chart is a state machine in which each state is associated with an MSC to be executed and the transitions between states are spontaneous. We modify this concept as follows and call it Partial-Order Chart (PO-Chart) by specifying for each transition whether it represents strict or weak sequencing, and by associating with each state a partial order of actions (including inputs, outputs and local actions) where each action is placed on a vertical "swim-lane" ("process" in MSC, or "role" in [Castejon]). Such a partial order is very similar to an MSC, but the arrows represent a partial-order dependency, and not necessarily exchanges of messages (as in MSCs and MSC-Charts).

We discuss in this paper how a test suite can be derived from a given PO-Chart specification. The main point is the fact that the partial-order test derivation from [Haar] can be applied to execution paths involving several PO-Chart states (corresponding to several transitions in the POIOA model). For limiting the length of the test suite in the case of loops in the PO-Chart, we adopt the approach that is common in software testing: assuming regularity of the IUT (as explained in [Bouge]), which means that one assumes that there exists an integer k such that, if a loop has been executed k times, then no further fault would be found if one executed the loop more than k times.

The paper contains many examples to illustrate the discussion. For the testing of an IUT in respect to a PO-Chart the partial-order testing of [Haar] is compared with state machine testing methods based on an equivalent state machine model. However, often the PO-Chart specifications are not **bounded** [Alur], which means that no equivalent finite state model exists.

The paper is structured as follows: In Sect. 2, an introduction to POIOA testing is given, as well as a formal definition of partial orders. In Sect. 3, we discuss the different notations for defining the reference specification for testing. In Sect. 4 we show how the partial-order testing of [Haar] and state machine testing can be applied to PO-Charts. In Sect. 5, we provide some comments comparing the specification formalisms of POIOA, collaboration ordering, MSC-Charts and PO-Charts. We also compare the complexity measures for partial-order and state machine testing, as well as the underlying fault models. Section 6 contains the conclusions.

2   Preliminaries

2.1   Testing POIOA

The testing of POIOA was introduced in [Haar]. A POIOA is a state machine where each state transition involves possibly several input and output interactions for which a partial order is specified for execution. When all interactions of a transition have been performed, the machine enters the next state and is ready to execute another transition. One normally assumes that each transition starts with a single or several (concurrent) input interaction(s). An example of such a transition is shown in Fig. 1(a). This transition starts with the single input i1 which is followed by two concurrent outputs o1a and o1b, each followed by a sequence of input and output, i2 followed by o2 and i3 followed by o3, respectively.

When testing an implementation for conformance with a POIOA specification, one has to verify the following two aspects:

1. The partial order of interactions specified for each transition is implemented as specified.
2. Each transition leads to the correct next state.

For the second aspect, traditional state machine testing approaches can be used, such as Distinguishing Sequences [Bochmann a] or the HIS method [Bochmann c]. For this purpose one needs state identification sequences for each state which are applied after the execution of a transition, and which should be checked for validity on the implementation. We do not discuss these issues further in this paper.

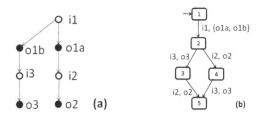

Fig. 1. (a) A partial order with two roles. (b) An equivalent state machine

For the testing of the partial order of input and output interactions defined for a given transition t, the following **partial-order test** has been proposed (see for instance [Bochmann a]). For each input i of t, perform the following test (where it is assumed that the implementation is already in the starting state of the transition):

1. Apply all inputs (different from i) that are not after i in the partial order of t (in an order satisfying the partial order), and observe the set of output interactions, called O1.
2. Apply i, and observe the set of subsequent output interactions, called O2.
3. Apply all other inputs of t (in an order satisfying the partial order), and observe the set of output interactions, called O3.

If one of the output sets is different than what is expected from the specified partial order, we have detected a fault in the implementation. We have a guarantee of fault detection under the assumption that the transition t is realized in the implementation as a single transition and in the form of a partial order. For the example transition shown in Fig. 1(a), we obtain the following test suite (where the tested input is written in bold, and the expected output sets are given in { }):

- For testing i1: <{ }, **i1** {o1a, o1b}, i2 {o2}, i3 {o3}>
- For testing i2: <{ }, i1 {o1a, o1b}, i3 {o3}, **i2** {o2}>
- For testing i3: same test case as for i1.

In [Bochmann a], it was also explained that the tests for several inputs can be combined into a single test case if one of the input comes after another one. For the example transition, we are left with the two test cases given above.

In this paper, we limit our attention to quiescent states of the IUT, that is, states in which no further outputs are produced by the IUT unless further input is applied. The above partial-order test goes only through quiescent states, since the next input is only applied after some time-out period to ensure that no additional output is expected. An interaction sequence is called a quiescent trace [Simao] if each input is applied when the IUT is in a quiescent state. For example, the sequence <i1, o1a, i3, etc.> is allowed by the partial order of Fig. 1(a), but it is not quiescent. The testing of non-quiescent traces is discussed in [Bochmann a].

It was noted that the length of the resulting test suite for testing a single transition using this method is much shorter in the presence of many concurrent inputs as compared with traditional state machine testing. For the example transition shown in Fig. 1(a), the corresponding state machine (showing only quiescent states) is shown in Fig. 1(b). State machine testing (without state identification) yields for this state machine the same two test cases above. However, if there are more concurrent inputs, the number of states of the corresponding state machine will blow up exponentially (see also Sect. 5).

The notion of POIOA has been criticized because it assumes that there is global synchronization (involving all interaction points) in each state of the automaton. It was argued that this is not realistic if the behavior of the POIOA is supposed to represent the behavior of a distributed system where interactions take place at different inter-action points distributed over several system components. To avoid this criticism, we consider in this paper the concepts explained Sect. 3, which allow for strict sequencing of transitions (as in the case of POIOA), as well as for weak sequencing (which is more natural in distributed environments).

2.2   Formal Definition "Partial Order"

Given a set E of events, a partial order on E is a binary relation < of events which is transitive, antisymmetric and irreflexive. If <e1, e2> is in <, we say that e1 is before e2. Often we characterize an order by the event pairs that generate all pairs in the order by transitivity closure. We call these the generating event pairs of the order. For instance, the arrows in Fig. 1(a) correspond to the **generating event pairs**, for instance the pair

<i1, o1a>. However, the partial order defined by this figure also includes pairs such as <o1a, o2> which are obtained by transitivity.

In order to deal with a situation where the same type of event occurs several times, one usually considers a Partially Ordered Multi-Set (Pomset). Given a partial order $(E, >)$ where some events in E may be of the same type, a Pomset on $(E, >)$ is obtained by adding a labeling function $L: E \rightarrow V$, where V is a set of labels. For a given event e ϵ E, L(e) represents the type of event e. In fact, the names given to events in our figures represent the type of the event shown. For instance, the first event in Fig. 1(a) is of type i1.

We call **initiating** event any minimum event of the order, that is, event e ϵ E is minimum if there is no event e' ϵ E such that e' $<$ e. Similarly, we call **terminating** event any maximum event of the order. In the remainder of this paper, when we talk about a partial order, we always mean a Pomset where the set of labels V is often partitioned into two subsets: the set I of inputs and the set O of outputs.

3   The Concept of PO-Charts

3.1   Collaborations

Concepts for describing the behavior of distributed systems in a global view have been proposed in [Castejon]. First, the UML concept of collaborations is used. A collaboration identifies the different roles that the components of the distributed system may play in a given application. However, this UML concept does not talk about the dynamic aspect of the behavior. For describing the dynamic aspect of the behavior, it is proposed to decompose a given collaboration into several sub-collaborations (each involving possibly a subset of roles) and indicating in which order these sub-collaborations are performed. Using the sequencing primitives of UML Activity diagrams (sequence, alternative and concurrency) an Activity-like notation is proposed, however, with the following modifications to the semantics: (a) a single Activity – called a "collaboration" – would normally involve several parties (roles – or swim-lanes); and (b) sequencing between successive collaborations may be in strict sequence (as in UML Activity diagrams, where any sub-activity of the second collaboration can only start when all sub-activities of the first have been completed), or in weak sequence (where a role may start with its activities of the second collaboration when it has completed its own sub-activities for the first).

A simple example is shown in Fig. 2 (this is Fig. 3 from [Castejon]). This is a simplified model of the execution of a medical test at the patient's premises in the context of tele-medicine. There are three roles in the system, as shown by the UML collaboration diagram of Fig. 2(a): **dt** (doctor terminal), **tu** (test unit), and **dl** (data logger). Figure 2(b) shows the dynamic behavior of the Test collaboration: A *Test* starts with the *DoTest* sub-collaboration which is followed by the *LogValues* sub-collaboration. This may be repeated several times until the *GetValues* sub-collaboration is performed. The whole may be repeated several times.

The *Test* collaboration shown in the figure can, in turn, be used as a sub-collaboration in a larger context of tele-medicine, as discussed in [Castejon]. This

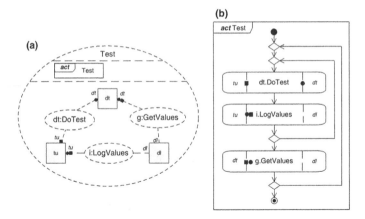

Fig. 2. The Test collaboration: (a) UML Collaboration diagram, (b) behavior definition containing three sub-collaborations

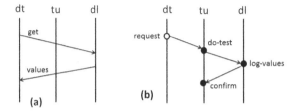

Fig. 3. (a) MSC defining the *GetValues* collaboration. (b) Partial order with roles defining *DoTest* and *LogValues* combined

notation, therefore, allows for writing hierarchically structured behavior specifications. At the most detailed level, the behavior of a collaboration can be defined in the form of a Message Sequence Chart (MSC, also called UML Interaction diagram). A very simple example is shown in Fig. 3(a) for the behavior of the *GetValues* collaboration included in Fig. 2(b).

However, in the context of this paper, we prefer to define the behavior of a basic, unstructured collaborations in the form of what we call a **partial order with roles**. This is a notion very similar to an MSC. Like in MSCs, the roles involved in the behavior are explicitly shown as vertical line. Actions performed by a role are indicated by dots (events) with their names (event labels) and the partial order between these events is indicated by arrows. However, these arrows do not necessarily represent messages, as in MSCs. An example is given in Fig. 3(b) for the behavior of the two collaborations *DoTest* and *LogValues* combined (see Fig. 2(b)).

The semantics of the sequencing primitives that define the order in which sub-collaborations are executed are defined in [Castejon] informally, based on the semantics of Activity diagrams (with modifications). A formal definition, using partial orders of events, is given by Israr [Israr] where, in addition, performance aspects are considered.

3.2   MSC-Graphs

In their article of 1999 [Alur], Alur and Yannakakis consider model checking of MSCs. This paper contains several discussions that are useful for our purpose:

1. The paper formally defines the semantics of an MSC (basic features only) based on partial orders.
2. The paper formally defines the notation of **MSC-Graphs** which correspond to the UML notation of Interaction Overview Diagram (see for instance Fig. 17.27 in [UML]). An MSC-Graph is an oriented graph where each node represents an MSC and each edge represents the sequential execution of the pointed MSC after the initial MSC. It is assumed in [Alur] that all edges either represent strict sequencing (called synchronous concatenation) or weak sequencing (called asynchronous concatenation). However, in this paper we assume that for each edge the type of sequencing can be specified separately (similar as in the collaboration notation discussed in Sect. 3.1).
3. The paper formally defines **Hierarchical MSCs** which is an extension of MSC-Graphs were a node may also represent another MSC-Graph or Hierarchical MSC. However, it is assume that there is no recursion in this dependency. It is shown how a Hierarchical MSC can be flattened in order to obtain an equivalent (more complex) MSC-Graph. As this notation does not introduce any additional power of description, we do not further discuss this notation in this paper.
4. The paper defines a subset of MSC-Graphs, called **bounded MSC-Graphs** which have the important property that the defined behavior is regular, that is, it can be represented by a finite state machine. Therefore, such MSC-Graphs can be model-checked (which is further discussed in [Alur]), and also, for such MSC-Graphs state machines testing methods can be applied. – An algorithm for determining whether a given MSC-Graph is bounded is also given. Essentially, it proceeds as follows: (a) The **communication graph** of an MSC has nodes corresponding to the roles (processes) of the MSC and an arc from p1 to p2 if role p1 sends a message to p2 in the MSC. (b) Given a subset S of nodes of an MSC-Graph, the communication graph of S is the union of the communication graphs of all the MSCs in the nodes of S. In such a graph, the roles that receive or send a message in some MSC of the graph are called the active processes of the graph. (c) An MSC-Graph is bounded if for each cycle c in the graph, the communication graph of the nodes on this cycle (after eliminating all non-active roles) is strongly connected.

3.3   PO-Charts

Inspired by the definition of MSC-Charts, we use in this paper the notion of PO-Charts. These charts are defined like MSC-Charts, except that each node, instead of containing an MSC, contains a **partial order with roles**, as defined in Sect. 3.1. **Hierarchical PO-Charts** and **bounded PO-Charts** can be defined as described for MSC-Charts in [Alur].

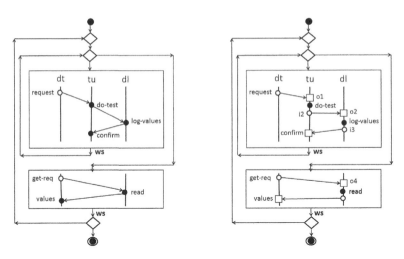

Fig. 4. (left) PO-Chart representing the *Test* collaboration. (right) The same behavior with additional input-output interactions for testing.

The main difference with MSC-Charts is the fact that for each edge representing the sequential execution between two partial orders with roles, it is indicated whether sequencing is weak or strict. Weak sequencing (abbreviated "ws") means that sequencing is enforced for each role separately. Strong sequencing (abbreviated "ss") means that the initiating events of the second partial order may only occur after all terminating events of the first partial order have occurred. This means that a strong synchronization point is introduced at this point during the execution.

We note that Hierarchical PO-Charts are an alternative notation for defining the behavior of collaborations as discussed in Sect. 3.1. We prefer this notation because it has a formally defined semantics, however, it does not support directly concurrency. An example of a PO-Chart is shown in Fig. 4(left): This chart defines the *Test* collaboration already shown in Fig. 2(b) – with a small change of control flow.

4 Conformance Testing with Respect to PO-Charts

4.1 General Testing Assumptions

Test Architecture. For distributed systems, the test architecture has a big impact on testing. For testing a system that has several interfaces, one often uses the distributed test architecture where a local tester is associated with each interface of the system. If the local testers cannot communicate with one another, there are usually synchronization problems for controlling the order of inputs to be applied to the system and difficulties to observe the order of outputs at different interfaces. Therefore an architecture with local testers without mutual communication provides usually incomplete testing power. – In the following we assume a test architecture with local testers that can communicate with one another by message passing.

Architectures for testing distributed systems in respect to specifications in the form of MSC were described in a recent paper [Dan]. In this context, it was assumed that the processes identified in the MSC can be classified as system or user processes. Then the user processes are replaced by local testers (that may, or may not communicate with one another). These testers exchange messages as specified by the given MSC.

We take a slightly different approach for testing distributed implementations in respect to PO-Chart specifications. We assume that each role of the PO-Chart may have a local interface to which a local tester can be attached. We assume in this paper that these local testers can communicate with one another by message passing. We assume that, at each local interface, the local tester communicates with the implementation of the role behavior through input and output interactions. These are synchronous inter-actions between the tester and the role implementation, without queuing. This is similar to the interactions of POIOA, although the interactions of PO-Charts are associated with a particular role.

Let us consider the example PO-Chart of Fig. 4 (left). In order to define a suitable test architecture, we have to determine which of the given actions are input or output, or whether they are local actions that cannot be observed by the local tester. It may also be necessary to introduce additional input or output interactions in order to increase the power of testing. For this example system, we propose the enhanced PO-Chart of Fig. 4 (right) which contains a few additional interactions with the local testers. Non-observable local actions are represented by dark dots, inputs by white dots, and outputs by white rectangles.

Test Suites. Since usually no finite test suite provides the guarantee that all possible implementation faults would be detected, Bougé et al. [Bouge] suggest to consider a sequence of test suites TS_i ($i = 1, 2, ...$) with increasing complexity, such that all faults detected by TS_i would also be detected by TS_{i+1}. Then one can talk about **validity** of such a set of test suites, which means that for any possible implementation fault, there is a test suite TS_i (for some i) that would detect this fault.

Fault Models. [Bouge] also stresses the point that there are always some assumptions that are made about the tested implementations. These assumptions are often called **fault model**. The fault model defines the range of faults that should be detected by the given test suite. And at the same time these assumptions also state what properties of the implementation are assumed to be correctly implemented (and therefore need not be tested).

In this context, [Bouge] mentions the following types of assumptions that are important for justifying the selection of particular test suites:

- **Regularity hypothesis:** This is an assumption about the structure of the imple-mentation. Assuming that we have some measure of the complexity of each test case, the regularity hypothesis states that there is a value of complexity k such that, if the implementation behaves correctly for all test cases with complexity less than k then it behaves correctly for all test cases. – In program testing, for example, one typically executes loops only once or twice and assumes that if no fault was detected then further executions of the loop will not lead to undetected faults.

- **Uniformity hypothesis:** This assumption justifies the practice in program testing where the domain of input parameters is partitioned into sub-domains and some random values are selected in each sub-domain for testing. It is assumed that, if the implementation behaves correctly for some value in a sub-domain, then it will behave correctly for all values in that domain.

How do these considerations apply to the testing of PO specifications? – The uniformity hypothesis applies to the variation of parameters of inputs to the implementation. In this paper we assume a finite set of distinct inputs where parameters can be ignored. – The regularity hypothesis takes on a particular form in the context of FSM testing methodology. The typical fault model of state machine testing assumes that the number of states of the implementation is not much larger (if not smaller or equal) to the number of states of the reference specification. Under this assumption, the test suites with test cases of bounded length can provide the guarantee of fault coverage.

For testing PO-Charts, we propose to use a regularity hypothesis similar to what is used for program testing. A PO-Chart defines possible control flows from the initial MSC-node to the final MSC-node. This is like the control flow in a program. As in program testing, we propose to test a PO-Chart by executing the different control paths through the chart, possibly using the well-known All-Branches or All-Paths criteria and executing loops typically once or twice.

4.2   Testing PO-Charts

For a bounded PO-Chart, there are essentially two approaches to test suite selection:

- The partial-order testing method proposed in this paper: The test designer should select a number of control flow paths through the PO-Chart, concatenate the partial orders of the nodes in the order of the path, using weak or strong sequencing as defined by the PO-Chart. The resulting partial order of inputs and outputs is then tested using the **partial-order test** described in Sect. 2.1.
- The state machine testing approach (with all its different test selection methods): Derive the state machine that has the same behavior as the PO-Chart, and then use one of the state machine testing methods.

If the PO-Chart is unbounded, the second approach is not applicable. As an example, we first discuss in the following the testing of a very simple bounded PO-Chart, and then consider an examples of unbounded PO-Charts.

4.3   Example of a Bounded PO-Chart

We consider the PO-Chart shown in Fig. 5(a) which contains a loop with node A containing the partial order of Fig. 1(a) with an additional ordering constraint indicated by the dotted arrow. All sequencing between nodes are week sequences, although for this example this is equivalent to strong sequencing. Figure 5(b) shows the corresponding state machine.

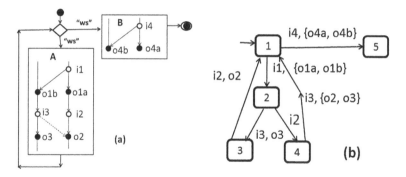

Fig. 5. (a) Example of a PO-Chart. (b) An equivalent state machine

State Machine Testing. The state machine of Fig. 5(b) is a partially defined machine. We recall that many state machine testing methods assume that the machine is fully defined (that is, in all states for all inputs). Let us assume that input messages received by the system are stored in a message pool until the system gets into a state where the input can be consumed (this is called "full reordering of messages" in [Castejon], Sect. 3.1). This is advantageous in distributed systems for avoiding race conditions [Bochmann b]. If we assume this for the state machine of Fig. 5(b), then in all states all inputs can be accepted – inputs for which no transition is defined in the current state will provide no output, however, the state of the system changes since the content of the pool changes.

Under this assumption, the state machine of Fig. 5(b) has unique input-output (UIO) sequences of length one for all states, except for state 5. Let us assume that we ignore the possible implementation fault that the i4-transition leads to one of the states 1, 2, 3 or 4. A test suite with fault detection guarantee for implementations built as state machines with not more than 5 states would first include the test cases for validating the UIO sequences. These tests would already include the test cases <i1, i2, i3, i4> and <i1, i3, i2, i4> which cover all transitions of the state machine.

Partial-Order Testing. This PO-Chart allows for an infinite number of execution paths p(n) – for n = 0, 1, 2, … where p(n) consists of n repetitions of the partial order of node A followed by one execution of node B. If we only test the path p(1), using the **partial order test** described in Sect. 2.1, we obtain the two test cases <i1, i2, **i3, i4**> and <i1, i3, **i2**, i4>. For the path p(2) – shown in Fig. 6(a) - we obtain the following test cases (where the dependencies of the bold inputs are determined): <**i1**, i3, **i2, i1**, i3, **i2, i4**> and <i1, i2, **i3**, i1, i2, **i3**, i4>.

4.4   Examples of Unbounded PO-Charts

Let us consider the PO-Chart of Fig. 5(a) again, but now without the dashed dependency. This chart is not bounded because there is no dependency where the right process has to wait for the left process. In this case, the right process may execute a second i1 input before an i3 input is applied to the left process, and this may repeat after a second i2 input is applied to the right process.

14   G. von Bochmann

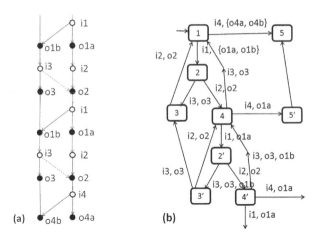

Fig. 6. (a) Partial order of path p(2) based on the PO-Chart of Fig. 5(a). (b) Part of the infinite state machine equivalent to the PO-Chart of Fig. 5(a) without the dashed dependency.

With partial-order testing, we obtain for testing the path p(2) the following test cases: <**i1**, i3, **i2**, **i1**, i3, **i2**, **i4**> and <i1, i2, i1, i2, i4, **i3**, **i3**>. For state machine testing one may want to test an initial part of the corresponding infinite state machine. Such an initial part is shown in Fig. 6(b).

Another example of an unbounded PO-Chart is shown in Fig. 4(right). The shortest execution path goes through the partial orders of the two nodes only once. In this case, the **partial-order test** gives rise to the following test cases (again, the inputs for which the dependencies are tested are written in bold): <**request**, get-req, **i2**, **i3**, **i5**> and <request, i2, i3, **get-req**, i5>. The realization of a correct implementation for the behavior defined by this PO-Chart is not straightforward, as discussed in [Faleh]. An implementation using messages for the order dependencies shown in the PO-Chart does not work because in the case that the doctor terminal (dt) sends a *get-req* message immediately after the request message to the test unit (tu), the former message may arrive at the *data-logger* (dl) before the *o2* message arrives, which means that the data value returned does not include the last test measurement. Such a fault would be detected by the first test case. A well-known solution for a correct implementation is to count the number of times that the first node of the chart is executed, and include this information in the messages sent to the *data-logger* [Faleh].

We note that this implementation fault would possibly not be detectable if there was no testing interface at the *test unit* system component. On the other hand, the observation of the *confirm* output at the *test unit* is not useful for fault detection. We note that the first test case requires some coordination between the local testers at the doctor terminal and the *test unit* in order to make sure that the *i2* input is not applied before the *get-req* input at the doctor terminal and all resulting outputs (in this case none – a timeout is assumed after each input in the test case) are observed.

5 Discussion

Specification Formalism. The POIOA specification formalism has been criticized for assuming strong synchronization points in each state of the machine. This corresponds to PO-Charts in which all sequential edges between different nodes (partial orders) have strict sequencing. In contrast to the partial orders associated with POIOA transitions, the partial orders associated with a node of a PO-Chart indicates for each interaction the role (process or interface) where the interaction takes place. This additional information allows us to define weak sequencing between different nodes of a PO-Chart.

One could possibly introduce an extension to POIOA where the sequencing of incoming and outgoing transitions at each state could be explicitly specified by indicating for each initiating event of an outgoing transition what are the terminating events of an incoming transition for which this initial event must wait before proceeding (if the state was reached by that incoming transition). If it has to wait for all terminating events, then we have the situation of normal POIOA where the incoming transition must be completely terminated before an outgoing transition may start. Weak sequencing could also be specified if the roles of the events are known. However, we are not convinced that such a generality of defining the sequence of transitions is useful – we prefer the addition of the role information (as defined for PO-Charts) which automatically defines the semantics of weak sequencing (if this is the desired form of sequencing).

Testing Complexity. It was argued in [Bochmann a] that the **partial order test**, as discussed in Sect. 2.1, is of much lower complexity than state machine testing when applied to systems with concurrency. This does not show up in the simple examples discussed above. But it is clear that the number of states of a state machine that is equivalent to a partial order grows exponentially if the degree of concurrency in the partial order increases. With the number of states of the reference specification, also the length of the test suite will grow accordingly.

As an example, we consider here a variation of the partial order of Fig. 1(a) where we assume that three inputs i2, i3 and i4 are enabled after the input i1 (see Fig. 7(a)).

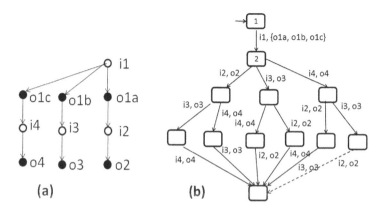

Fig. 7. (a) A partial order with roles. (b) An equivalent state machine.

The corresponding state machine is shown in Fig. 7(b). The state machine testing approach requires at least 6 test cases to cover all the branches of the state machine. With the partial order approach, we obtain the three test cases <**i1**, i2, i3, **i4**>, <i1, i3, i4, **i2**>, and <i1, i2, i4, **i3**>.

Different Fault Models. One may suspect that the lower complexity of the partial-order tests implicitly implies that their fault coverage is lower. This is in fact true. The fault model for which the partial-order tests provide fault coverage makes stronger assumptions about the tested implementation than the fault model used with state machine testing.

It was shown in [Bochman a] that the partial-order test method provides complete fault coverage under the assumption that the tested implementation has the behavior that can be defined by a single partial order (without alternatives). That is, a transition of the POIOA model is implemented as a single transition in the implementation POIOA. An example of an implementation that does not satisfy this assumption would be an implementation that has the behavior of Fig. 7(b) with a single output fault in the dashed transition. Such a fault is not detected by the test suite given above, and this faulty implementation cannot be described by a single partial order.

6 Conclusions

For describing the behavior of distributed systems with multiple interfaces, one needs the notion of partial order for the interactions at the different interfaces, since there is no total order defined for all the interactions of the system. We have compared different notions of partial-order specifications, including POIOA, ordering of collaborations, and MSC-Charts (also called Interaction Overview Diagrams). We propose the use of a variant of the latter, called Partial-Order-Charts (PO-Charts). We have shown that for the testing of distributed systems in respect to such behavior specifications, the partial-order tests of [Haar] can be used.

In the case that the PO-Chart is bounded, one can also derive an equivalent state machine and use FSM testing methods. We provided in this paper a preliminary comparison of testing complexities and fault models for these two testing approaches (partial-order tests and FSM testing methods). For systems with much concurrency, the partial-order tests are advantageous if one can assume that the fault model of partial-order testing is satisfied. This is presumably the case when the implementation uses message passing between the different system components to implement the order dependencies defined in the specification.

Acknowledgements. I would like to thank Guy Vincent Jourdan for many fruitful discussions on testing POIOA.

References

[Alur]   Alur, R., Yannakakis, M.: Model checking of message sequence charts. In: Baeten, J.C., Mauw, S. (eds.) CONCUR 1999. LNCS, vol. 1664, pp. 114–129. Springer, Heidelberg (1999)

[Bochmann a]   von Bochmann, G., Haar, S., Jard, C., Jourdan, G.-V.: Testing systems specified as partial order input/output automata. In: Suzuki, K., Higashino, T., Ulrich, A., Hasegawa, T. (eds.) TestCom/FATES 2008. LNCS, vol. 5047, pp. 169–183. Springer, Heidelberg (2008)

[Bochmann b]   von Bochmann, G.: Deriving component designs from global requirement. In: Baelen, S.V., Graf, S., Filali, M., Weigert, T., Gerard, S. (eds.) Proceedings of the First International Workshop on Model Based Architecting and Construction of Embedded Systems (ACES-MB 2008), Toulouse, CEUR Workshop Proceedings, vol. 503, pp. 55–69 (2008)

[Bochmann c]   von Bochmann, G., Jourdan, G.V.: Partial Order Input/Output Automata: Model and Test, unpublished document

[Bouge]   Bougé, L., Choquet, N., Fribourg, L., Gaudel, M.C.: Test sets generation from algebraic specifications using logic programming. J. Syst. Softw. 6(3), 343–360 (1986)

[Castejon]   Castejòn, H.N., Bochmann, Gv, Braek, R.: On the realizability of collaborative services. J. Softw. Syst. Model. 10, 1–21 (2011)

[Dan]   Dan, H., Hierons, R.M.: Conformance testing from message sequence charts. In: Proceedings of 4th International Conference on Software Testing, Verification and Validation (IEEE), pp. 279–288 (2011)

[Faleh]   Faleh, M.N.M., von Bochmann, G.: Transforming dynamic behavior specifications from activity diagrams to BPEL. In: Proceedings of IEEE 6th International Symposium on Service-Oriented System Engineering, Irvine, California, pp. 305–311, December 2011

[Haar]   Haar, S., Jard, C., Jourdan, G.-V.: Testing input/output partial order automata. In: Petrenko, A., Veanes, M., Tretmans, J., Grieskamp, W. (eds.) TestCom/FATES 2007. LNCS, vol. 4581, pp. 171–185. Springer, Heidelberg (2007)

[Israr]   Israr, T., Bochmann, G.v.: Performance modeling of distributed collaboration services with independent inputs-outputs. In: Proceedings of 5th International Workshop on Non-functional Properties in Modeling: Analysis, Languages and Processes Co-located with 16th International Conference on Model Driven Engineering Languages and Systems, Miami, USA, 29 September 2013

[Simao]   Simao, A., Petrenko, A.: Generating asynchronous test cases from test purposes. Inf. Softw. Technol. 53, 1252–1262 (2011)

[UML]   OMG Unified Modeling Language, Version 2.5, March 2015. http://www.omg.org/spec/UML/2.5/PDF/. Accessed June 2016

Back-to-Back Testing of Self-organization Mechanisms

Benedikt Eberhardinger$^{(\boxtimes)}$, Axel Habermaier, Hella Seebach,
and Wolfgang Reif

Institute for Software and Systems Engineering,
University of Augsburg, Augsburg, Germany
{eberhardinger,habermaier,seebach,reif}@isse.de

Abstract. When developing SO mechanisms, mapping requirements to actual designs and implementations demands a lot of expertise. Among other things, it is important to define the right degree of freedom for the system that allows for self-organization. Back-to-back testing supports this hard engineering task by an adequate testing method helping to reveal failures in this design and implementation procedure. Within this paper we propose a model-based approach for back-to-back testing. The approach is built on top of the S# framework and integrated into the Visual Studio development environment, enabling the creation of executable test models with comprehensive tooling support for model debugging. By applying the concepts to a self-organizing production cell, we show how it is used to fully automatically reveal faults of a SO mechanism.

Keywords: Adaptive systems · Self-organization · Software engineering · Software testing · Quality assurance · Back-to-back testing · Model-based testing

1 Introduction

The increasing complexity of current software systems has led to an increase of autonomy of software components that are resilient, flexible, dependable, versatile, recoverable, customizable, and self-optimizing by adapting to changes that may occur in their environments [11]. Self-organization (SO) has become a keystone in the development of autonomous systems, allowing them to adapt their behavior and structure in order to fulfill their goals under ever-changing environmental conditions. Mechanisms of SO are built on top of the concepts of classical feedback loops (cf. [9,16]). Therefore, the environment and the components are sensed and controlled, using the feedback to adapt the behavior and/or structure of the components. Different architectural concepts were developed to engineer SO mechanisms, e.g., the *MAPE Cycle* [9] or the *Observer/Controller Architecture* [16]. As an important part of the development of SO mechanisms, testing needs to be integrated in order to achieve the required quality level of the system.

F. Wotawa et al. (Eds.): ICTSS 2016, LNCS 9976, pp. 18–35, 2016.
DOI: 10.1007/978-3-319-47443-4_2

This paper presents a thorough approach for supporting the engineering of SO mechanisms by *back-to-back (BtB) testing* [19] of feedback loop-based self-organization mechanisms. In our experiences in developing SO mechanisms, mapping requirements to actual designs and implementations demands a lot of expertise. Among other things, it is important to allow the system the right degree of freedom to enable self-organization. Back-to-back testing supports this engineering task with an adequate testing method helping to reveal failures in this design and implementation procedure. In order to supply BtB testing for SO mechanisms, we are faced by the following challenges:

1. *Supplying test oracles* that are able to cope with the unbounded decision space formed by different possible configurations of the systems controlled by the SO mechanism(s) as well as the huge state space of the mechanisms themselves.
2. *Systematic test case selection* is needed since exhaustive testing is not possible due to the unbounded state space. Additionally, most SO algorithms are based on heuristics, making their behavior quite non-deterministic and their state space non-uniform. Thus, common test case selection strategies relying on structured program behavior cannot be used.
3. *Automation* of test execution and evaluation is a keystone for the success, since this is the only way to execute the large test suites.

We address these challenges in a model-based approach for BtB testing where the test model mainly consists of two parts: (1) the model of the system controlled by the SO mechanism, i.e., the environment model, and (2) the model of the intended behavior of the SO mechanism, i.e., the test model. The latter is based on our concept of the *corridor of correct behavior (CCB)* [7] that describes the intended behavior of the system as a set of constraints. The concept of the CCB is used as part of the test oracle by evaluating the constraints on the current state of the model resp. system [3].

The model of the system to be controlled by the SO mechanism is used for test case generation as well as for their execution. This is possible due the S# modeling framework used by our approach: With S#, executable model instances can be composed together with a high degree of flexibility in order to test different system configurations. Furthermore, it is possible to integrate the concrete SO mechanism(s) under test into the execution environment provided by S# and to map the mechanism's state back into the model instances for evaluation within S#. The evaluation is based on checks whether the current state matches the constraints made in the model of the intended behavior.

Overall, the following main contributions will be presented:

1. A *model-based BtB testing* concept for SO mechanisms that is fully integrated into Visual Studio.
2. An approach for *systematic test case selection* for BtB testing of SO mechanisms.
3. *Automated evaluation* of test results within our test model which is based on the concepts of the CCB.

The paper is organized as followed: The next section embeds the approach into our overall testing concept for self-organizing, adaptive systems. After the introduction of the case study (Sect. 3), Sect. 4 gives an overview of our S# modeling framework and the BtB testing model. Section 5 describes model of intended behavior of the SO mechanisms. Section 6 shows how test cases are generated and executed. Section 7 evaluates the approach. We consider related work in Sect. 8 and conclude in Sect. 9.

2   The Corridor Enforcing Infrastructure

Our approach for testing *self-organizing, adaptive systems (SOAS)*—and consequently for testing SO mechanisms—is based on the *Corridor Enforcing Infrastructure (CEI)* [3]. The CEI is an architectural pattern for SOAS using regio-central or decentralized feedback loops to monitor and control single components or small groups of components in order to ensure that the system's goals are fulfilled at all times. The CEI implements the concepts and fundamentals of the *Restore Invariant Approach (RIA)* [7]. RIA defines the *Corridor of Correct Behavior* (CCB), which is described by the system's structural requirements, formalized as constraints. Concerning a self-organizing production cell scenario the CCB is formed by the constraints describing valid configurations of the system. The conjunction of all these constraints is called the *invariant* (*INV*). An exemplary corridor is shown in Fig. 1: The system's state is inside the corridor if *INV* is satisfied; otherwise, the system's state leaves the corridor, indicated by the flash. In that case, the system has to be reorganized in order to return into the corridor, as shown by the transition with a check mark. A failure occurs if a transition outside of the corridor is taken, like the one marked by a cross, although a transition back into the corridor exists.

The CEI implements the RIA either with centralized or decentralized pairs of monitors and controllers, as proposed by the MAPE cycle [9] or the Observer/Controller (O/C) architecture [16]. Figure 2 shows a schematic view of one possible implementation of the CEI based on the O/C architecture where the essential parts are the system under observation and control (SuOC), i.e., single agents or groups of agents; the observer (O), i.e., the component monitoring the state of the SuOC (in- or outside of the CCB) and providing information to the controller; and the controller (C), i.e., the SO algorithms controlling the SuOC.

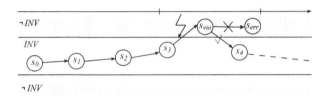

Fig. 1. Schematic state-based view of the corridor of correct behavior; *INV* is the conjunction of all constraints of the system controlled by the CEI [3].

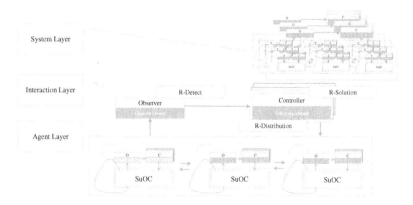

Fig. 2. Schematic view of one *CEI* implementation and its different layers for testing (agent, interaction, and system layer) [2].

Note that the CEI consists of sets of nested feedback loops controlling the entire system. Figure 2 further sketches the different layers for testing to cope with the complexity of the system: agent, interaction, and system layer.

The reorganization by the controller is performed by one or more SO algorithms resulting in a new system configuration. Such a system configuration has to satisfy the constraints describing a valid organizational structure. The concrete choice of the SO algorithms and their constraints has no impact on our approach. Since the system behaves like a traditional software system inside the CCB, traditional test approaches can be used to ensure the quality of the SuOC. The CEI, by contrast, enables self-organizing and adaptive behavior of the system and demands new concepts for testing to cope with the challenges described in Sect. 1.

In order to grasp SO mechanisms for testing, we need techniques to stepwise examine the CEI and its mechanisms, covering the following responsibilities of the CEI: correct initiation of a reorganization if and only if a constraint is violated (monitoring infrastructure, R-Detect); calculation of correct system configurations in case of violations (R-Solution); and correct distribution of these configurations within single agents or small groups of agents controlled by the CEI (R-Distribution). In this paper, we focus on revealing SO mechanism failures which relate to (R-Detect) and (R-Solution), extending our approach of isolated testing of SO algorithms presented in [2].

3   Case Study: The Self-organizing Production Cell

Future production scenarios demand for much more flexibility [4] than today's shop floor design to cope with the trend towards small series production, individualized products and the reuse of production stations for different tasks. This flexibility becomes possible due to the increased automation and data exchange in manufacturing technologies. These future cyber-physical systems will integrate self-organization mechanisms to resolve the tasks of decentralized decision making, to optimize the systems structure, and to autonomously react to component failures at runtime increasing the system's robustness. We envision self-organizing production cells, where the production stations are modern robots equipped with toolboxes and the ability to change their tools whenever necessary (self-awareness). They are connected via mobile platforms (carts) that are able to carry workpieces and to reach robots in any order. Thus, the production cell is able to fulfill any task which corresponds to tools (capabilities) available in the cell. This is possible due to the SO mechanisms that reorganize the carts and robots in a way that the tools are applied to the workpieces in the correct order. Finding a correct allocation of tools to robots and according routes to carts (system configuration) constitutes a constraint satisfaction problem. Any violation of the calculated configuration (represents a state of the system within the CCB) at run-time triggers the SO algorithm calculating and distributing a new system configuration. A tool-supported approach to systematically model and analyze these kind of systems is shown next.

4   Building the Environment Model of SO Systems

The self-organizing production cell is an instance of the system class of self-organizing resource-flow systems; a metamodel [18] for this system class based on CEI is explained by Sect. 4. The case study maps to the metamodel as follows: The robots and carts are Agents monitored by the Observer/Controller. The carts transport workpieces, i.e., Resources, between the robots, which have several switchable tools, i.e., Capabilities, such as drills and screwdrivers that they use on the workpieces. A Task requires a workpiece to be processed by a sequence

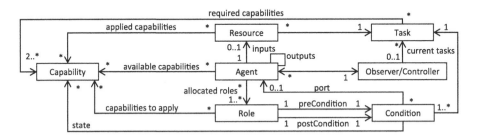

Fig. 3. A UML class diagram giving a simplified overview of the metamodel for self-organizing resource-flow systems (according to [18]): Resources are passed along a set of Agents, each applying certain Capabilities in order to conduct a step towards the completion of the Resource's Task. The Observer/Controller—encompassing the SO mechanism—monitors the Agents and assigns their Roles such that all Resources are eventually fully processed with the correct order of Capability applications. Such a resource flow is specified by the Pre- and PostConditions of all Roles within the system, as well as the inputs and outputs of the Agents that establish their interconnections.

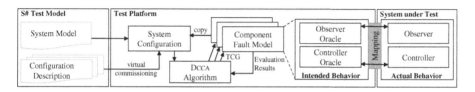

Fig. 4. Our approach is divided into three parts: the first part consists of the S# test model as well as corresponding configuration descriptions (cf. Sect. 4). The second part is the test platform that instantiates a system configuration as the basis for the test case generation with DCCA; the component fault models represent the test cases that are evaluated (cf. Sects. 4 and 6) and provide the test oracles for the observer and controller (cf. Sect. 5). The third part represents the actual behavior of the SO mechanism which must be mapped to the intended behavior after each execution for evaluation purposes (cf. Sect. 6).

of tool applications, e.g., by applying the drill, insert, and tighten Capabilities. Therefore, the robots and carts are responsible for processing incoming work-pieces in a given sequence of tool applications. The Roles assigned to each robot and cart indicate which tools they apply on the workpieces or which robots the resources are transported between, respectively. The Observer/Controller forms the SO mechanism of the system; it is responsible for reconfiguration in order to compensate for broken tools, blocked routes, or to incorporate new tools, robots, or carts, for instance (Figs. 3 and 4).

The case study is modeled using the S# modeling and analysis framework for safety-critical systems [8]. As its modeling language is based on the C# programming language, the metamodel shown in Sect. 4 can be directly represented by a set of C# classes, with two additional classes RobotAgent and CartAgent derived from Agent encapsulating the production cell-specific parts of the model. Even though the S# model of the case study is represented by a C# program, it is still a model and not the actual implementation; for instance, it completely abstracts from any distribution concerns, executing all modeled agents locally to simplify modeling and analysis. S# also allows the composition of a model to be automated: Arbitrary C# code can be executed to instantiate system components and to connect them together in order to build up the overall model, thereby providing meta-constructs for model creation. These capabilities are particularly useful for the creation of different system configurations when testing the case study; model instantiation with S# is illustrated by Listing 1.

```
CreateWorkpieces(5, produce(), drill(), insert(), tighten(), polish(), consume());
CreateRobot(produce());
CreateRobot(insert());
CreateRobot(tighten(), polish(), tighten(), drill());
CreateRobot(polish(), consume());
CreateCart(new Route(Robots[0], Robots[1]), new Route(Robots[0], Robots[3]));
CreateCart(new Route(Robots[2], Robots[3]));
```

Listing 1. Parts of the S# instantiation code for a configuration of the case study consisting of five workpieces that require the task PDITPC to be carried out on them. Four robots are created with some minor redundancy in available capabilities. The two carts connect all four robots via bidirectional routes.

S# executes the models as regular C# programs, taking care of potential non-determinism in the models such that all combinations of non-deterministic choices are fully analyzed. It is also possible to spawn additional processes during model checking, enabling the integration of other tools into the models and the analyses: For the case study, for example, a constraint solver is used to model the SO algorithm within the Observer/Controller. Whenever a reconfiguration is required, the S# model encodes the current system configuration for the constraint solver, requests a solution from it, and applies the returned solution back onto itself.

5 The Test Model for the Intended Behavior of the SO Mechanisms

S# integrates, as shown in Sect. 4, the complete testing framework, including test cases derivation, test cases execution, as well as test case evaluation and logging. In order to enable the evaluation of test cases, the overall model needs to be extended by the test model. The extension encompasses a definition of the intended behavior of the system under test within the S# model, as shown in the right part of Sect. 4. Within the BtB testing approach, we propose this one important step: to co-develop the intended behavior of the system and check it against the actual behavior. Thus, the co-development of the intended behavior is used in order to check whether it corresponds to the actual behavior. The intended behavior is modeled in two parts, consisting of (1) a description of valid system states, i.e., the *INV* of the CCB for the SO mechanism, as well as further constraints concerning the form of the results of the SO algorithms itself and (2) an evaluation mechanism that is able to state whether there is a possible configuration for the current system state in order to spot whether the SO algorithm missed a valid solution.

Valid system states are determined using one of the major advantages of the CCB for testing SOAS: *INV* is a way to distinguish between correct and incorrect actions of SO mechanisms—as described in Sect. 2. A failure occurs if a violation of the CCB is not detected (R-Detect), the computed solution does not lead to a system configuration inside the CCB (R-Solution), or a correct solution is distributed incorrectly (R-Distribution). The approach of this paper focuses on the first two aspects. As a basis for the evaluation, the constraints that form the CCB are developed separately—an important step of co-development in BtB testing—and integrated into the model. Listing 2 shows how parts of the production cell case study's CCB constraints are specified in the S# model.

The constraints that form the oracle are divided into two parts, one for the observer and one for the controller (cf. Sect. 4). The observer part describes all violations of the CCB that have to be detected by the observer. The constraints of the observer oracle are evaluated after the observer decided whether to reconfigure or not and the oracle judges this decision. Afterward, the controller might be activated—in case of an activation by the observer—and the result is evaluated by the controller oracle. Note that for both evaluations, the mapping

```
agent.Constraints = new List<Func<bool>>() {
    // I/O Consistency
    () => agent.AllocatedRoles.All(role => role.PreCondition.Port == null ||
        agent.Inputs.Contains(role.PreCondition.Port)),
    () => agent.AllocatedRoles.All(role => role.PostCondition.Port == null ||
        agent.Outputs.Contains(role.PostCondition.Port)),
    // Capability Consistency
    () => agent.AllocatedRoles.All(
            role => role.CapabilitiesToApply.All(capability =>
                agent.AvailableCapabilites.Contains(capability))),
    /* ... */
}
```

Listing 2. Partial S# model representing a subset of the constraints defined for the oracle.

between the actual SO mechanism has to be establish with the test system, i.e., the results need to be interfaced. For the evaluation of the controller a set of the constraints needs to be evaluated that is part of the controller oracle. In most cases there are overlaps between the two constraint sets, however, mostly the set of the controller oracle is a superset of the constraints of the observer oracle, however, it also might be vice versa. The additional constraints in the oracles might be due to the fact that additional requirements are necessary to fully check the results of the different parts of the SO mechanism. In our case study, this is the case for the controller oracle. The additional constraint concern the assigned roles for the robots and carts: they must be connected in the correct order for any task after reorganization so that they are applied the right way (for instance, drill, then insert, then tighten). This constraint would not be checked by the observer, since no environmental influence would change the role definitions; only the tools within the roles are affected, for instance.

The satisfiability check of the oracle focuses on another obligation for the SO algorithm: if a solution for a new system configuration is feasible on the current system instance, the SO algorithm must find it in order to find a valid configuration for the running system. If we do not check that second part of the solution we would neglect faults resulting from too strict restrictions made as a design decision in the development. Indeed, in the BtB testing approach, we aim at revealing such errors. For this purpose, it is necessary to search in the configuration space for possible configuration(s) of the system that fulfill all requirements resp. constraints considered in the previous paragraph. We use a search algorithm that systematically checks every given configuration for validity; if one is found then a solution is possible and the SO algorithm has to find it. Algorithm 1, for instance, shows a search algorithm that evaluates whether a reconfiguration is possible for the case study of the production cell: It starts by checking whether all capabilities needed for the tasks that should be applied in the system are available, e.g., if a task requires drilling at least one robot must be able to drill. If that prerequisite is satisfied, the algorithm checks whether the robots with the necessary capabilities are connected by carts such that work-pieces can be transported between them in way that the tasks can be fulfilled. Such an algorithm, if one exists at all, might be expensive in time and space. But this is acceptable due to the following facts: the check has to be performed only occasionally during the testing process as it is only executed when no solution is

---

Algorithm 1. Checks whether a reconfiguration is possible for a given set of robot and cart agents as well as the tasks to be carried out.

Input: robotAgents, cartAgents, tasks
Output: a Boolean value indicating whether a reconfiguration is possible
1: $m \leftarrow$ GetConnectionMatrix(robotAgents) // transitive closure of all connected robots
2: **for all** $t \in$ tasks **do**
3:     **if** $\neg \forall c \in t$.Capabilities: $\exists a \in$ robotAgents: $c \in a$.AvailableCapabilities **then**
4:         **return** false
5:     **end if**
6:     $A \leftarrow \{a \in$ robotAgents $\mid t$.Capabilities[0] $\in a$.AvailableCapabilities $\}$
7:     **for** $i = 0$ to $|$task.Capabilities$| -1$ **do**
8:         $A \leftarrow \{a \in m[a'] \mid a' \in A \wedge t$.Capabilities[i + 1] $\in a$.AvailableCapabilities $\}$
9:         **if** $|A| = 0$ **then**
10:             **return** false
11:         **end if**
12:     **end for**
13: **end for**
14: **return** true

---

found by the SO algorithm; when the SO algorithm cannot find a solution, the configuration space is small in most cases.

6   Generating and Executing Test Cases with S#

A necessary prerequisite for deriving and executing test cases is to instantiate the model with a concrete configuration, e.g., the numbers and kinds of robots in the production cell. Within one such configuration the number of different test cases are determined by the different possible environmental events the system has to adapt to. Since the number of different configurations is unbounded, a concrete configuration is chosen for testing. Subsequently, test cases for a chosen configuration are defined by triggering environmental events that are modeled as S# *component faults*, e.g., a tool breaks, a path for carts get blocked, and so on. All of these events result in reconfigurations, i.e., executions of the SO mechanism. The huge number of configurations and component faults make exhaustive testing impossible, thus, we follow a two-part test selection strategy. d latter adding the concrete observer to a tested SO algorithm.

6.1   Test Case Generation for SO Mechanisms

The test strategy we purpose is based on the ideas of virtual commissioning and boundary interior testing. On the one hand, we only consider one concrete configuration and use the concepts of *virtual commissioning* to check other configurations on demand; on the other hand, the concepts of *boundary interior testing* are applied to SO mechanisms to find relevant test cases more quickly.

Virtual Commissioning of SOAS Systems for Test Case Reduction. The concept of virtual commissioning is mainly applied in the field of large manufacturing systems where a virtual manufacturing system is built in order to simulate individual manufacturing processes for optimization and validation purposes [10]. Within this virtual environment, the real controller is executed on the virtual plant enabling to test, tune, or initialize it for a specific configuration of the plant. We adopt this concept for the reduction of possible configurations of the system to be tested. The idea is to base the tests on only one configuration, namely, the one which should be rolled out afterward. Indeed, there will be changes at run-time, e.g., new robots are integrated, new tools are added, or tasks change. Before such a change is rolled out to the running system, the model instance must first be updated and the tests have to be re-run on the new instance. Since the change of the current configuration of the system is due to a human intervention—we assume the system not to extend itself by other components or similar—it is possible to run this test-first-deploy-after strategy at run-time. Thus, we select only the configuration for testing that is crucial for the deployment and have the ability to test new configurations on demand. This is possible due to the generic S# test model in which it is easy to instantiate new configurations (cf. Listing 1) and to automatize the testing process.

Boundary Interior Testing for SO Mechanisms. For test case selection within one configuration of the system we adopt the concepts of boundary interior testing, where the idea is to select test cases at the boundary of expected behavior changes. The boundaries of SO mechanisms are states of the system where reconfiguration is rarely possible, i.e., where only few solutions are still possible. Reconfigurations, as we consider them, are mainly driven by changing environmental conditions that force the system to reorganize itself. In our test model, we define these changing conditions as *component faults* of the controlled system such as a robot being unable to apply its tools in the production cell case study. The component faults are part of the S# model.

In order to find the component faults that bring the system to its boundaries, we use *Deductive Cause-Consequence Analysis (*DCCA*)*. DCCA is a fully automated model-based analysis techniques integrated into S#, usually used to assess the system's safety by computing all minimal cut sets for a hazard [8]. Minimal cut sets are combinations of component faults that can cause a hazard, characterizing a cause-consequence relationship between component faults (the causes) and the hazard (the consequence): a set of component faults is a cut set for a hazard if and only if there is the possibility that the hazard occurs and before that, at most the faults in the fault set have occurred. DCCA has exponential complexity as it has to check all combinations of component faults. In practice, however, the number of required checks usually is significantly lower, as the cut set property is monotonic with respect to set inclusion. DCCA can also be used to compute the boundaries of SO mechanisms: the hazard is simply defined as the inability for further reconfigurations. To compute the boundaries, the combinations of component faults are checked in order to determine whether such a set does or does not have the potential to cause that hazard. DCCA

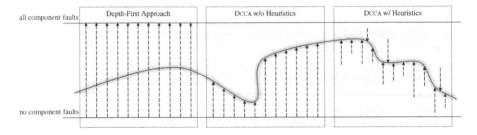

Fig. 5. The three boxes represent different test case generation strategies. The x-axises of the graphic shows different system states for a particular SO mechanism under test that are formed by the possible different configurations and settings of the system under control. The boundaries of the SO mechanism relative to the number of component faults activated is shown by the black line. The idea of boundary interior testing for SO mechanisms is to stay inside and at the boundaries for testing. The left box represents a naïve depth-first search whereas the middle box shows the boundary interior approach with the standard DCCA and the right box it extension by heuristics.

automatically chooses the next set of component faults to be activated, i.e., the next test case, and executes it. S#'s standard approach for DCCA checks the fault sets by increasing cardinality, thus the approach also includes test cases for inner boundary tests. The concepts of boundary interior testing for SO mechanism is exemplified in Sect. 6.1. The left box refers to a naïve approach where test cases are selected in a depth-first attempt and the boundaries of the SO mechanisms are not taken into account. That implies that many negative test cases are executed where less faults are expected to be revealed; in our evaluation no fault has been detected by these negative tests. The middle box of Sect. 6.1 is representing DCCA for boundary interior testing and covers the interiors and boundaries. The right box shows an extension that is currently under development and evaluation where only the boundaries are considered by conducting DCCA with different heuristics for selecting sets of component faults. They optimize the search of the boundaries by selecting component fault sets first where more faults of the same kind are activated and subsumption relations between component faults are exploited (Fig. 5).

6.2 Test Case Execution with S#

In order to achieve significant results, we advocate to integrate different parts of the SO mechanism step-wise: first isolate the SO algorithms, which form the controller, and afterward hook up the observer part. That enables to assign possible failures to the different parts, e.g., if a test suite is re-run after it has passed for the SO algorithm with a hooked up observer, the failure is most likely due to a faulty observer. In order to unhook the observer, the controller is triggered after every execution step, causing the system to continuously reconfigure itself. This leads also to a reduction of failure overlapping due to a missing activation of the controller by the observer. Since S# models are fully executable, the generation and selection of test cases, their execution, and their evaluation are automatically performed together. Additionally, it is also possible to manually execute or re-execute given test cases. The integration of S# into Visual Studio lets the development and execution of the test model benefit from the whole tool support of Visual Studio, e.g., the debugger. Thus, it is possible to step through every test case to monitor and control the execution and the state changes, making fault localization and test model development much easier.

7   Evaluation

For our evaluation—whose implementation is fully available at http://safetysharp. isse.de—we addressed the following four research questions:

R1. Is the proposed approach for testing SO mechanisms applicable to real scenarios?
R2. Is the approach able to reveal failures in SO mechanisms?
R3. Do real faults reflect the ideas proposed and exploited for test case generation (i.e., occur faults at the boundaries of the SO mechanism?)?
R4. Does the mechanism for reaching these boundaries outperform a naïve approach?

For the evaluation, we co-developed a SO mechanism for the self-organizing production cell, described in Sect. 3. However, the test cases and constraints are applicable to the whole system class of self-organizing resource-flow systems and in particular, the concrete implementation of the SO algorithm can be replaced by any other implementation. In the case at hand, we used MiniZinc[1] as a constraint modeling language with *FlatZinc* as the low-level solver. The system constraints have therefore been translated into a MiniZinc model that describes valid configurations for the production cell; the MiniZinc input for a system configuration is shown in Listing 3. Thus, it is possible to feed the SO algorithm with a specification of a task, the number of agents (carts and robots), the capabilities, and the routing table. If satisfiable, the SO algorithm returns a solution that assigns each tool needed for the task to some robot and that routes the carts between the robots accordingly. This SO algorithm has been plugged into S# via an interface that provides the specification of the problem to be solved by the SO algorithm and that parses MiniZinc results. The constraints of the observer of the SO mechanism—originally developed in *Java* for our implementation of the production cell based on the multi-agent system *Jadex*[2]—have been converted to C# in order to integrate them into the S# model. This completes the integration of the developed SO mechanism into the S# model and shows that real scenarios are realizable with our approach *(R1)*.

For evaluation purposes, we analyzed different configurations (cf. Table 1) of the production cell. The configurations differ in the number of agents (robots

---

[1] http://www.minizinc.org/.
[2] http://www.activecomponents.org/.

```
task = [1,2,3,4,5,6]; noAgents = 6;
capabilities = [{1},{3},{4,5,4,2},{5,6},{},{}];
isConnected = [|true,false,false,false,true,false
               |false,true,false,false,true,false
               |false,false,true,false,false,true
               |false,false,false,true,true,true
               |true,true,false,true,true,false
               |false,false,true,true,false,true|]
```

Listing 3. The input model for MiniZinc describing a task, the available capabilities of the robots, as well as the connection matrix based on the carts' routes, corresponding to the configuration instantiated by Listing 1.

and carts), the average number of capabilities per robot, the number of tasks, and the number of routes established by the carts between the robots.

One main achievement of the evaluation is that we were able to reveal the following faults with the implementation of the SO mechanism; each fault is annotated with the responsibility of the SO mechanism where the fault was detected (cf. Sect. 2):

F1. The fault affected route handling: the MiniZinc implementation interpreted transitive routes as direct ones. Its computed configurations included direct connections that were not available, e.g. $0 \to 2 \neq 0 \to 1 \to 2$ (R-Solution).
F2. The fault was that the SO algorithm expected the routes to be unidirectional while they were in fact bidirectional. The failure manifested itself as overlooked solutions even though at least one existed (R-Solution).
F3. The fault was a wrong implementation of the interface for the SO algorithm. The interface expected first the capability of a designated agent, but got the first capability of the task assigned to the designated agent (R-Solution).
F4. The fault was a wrong format for the mapping of the solution from the SO algorithm to the system model concerning the pre- and postconditions of a role (R-Distribution). The pre-/postconditions contained the state of the workpiece in form of the remaining part of the task, e.g., for task $[D, I, T]$ the precondition contained $[D, I, T]$ and the postcondition $[I, T]$ if D had been performed. But the mapping should lead to states of the workpiece representing the part of the task which already had been done, e.g., for task $[D, I, T]$ the precondition should contain $[]$ and the postcondition $[D]$ if D had been performed (R-Distribution). This fault was detected even though the testing approach was initially not focused on R-Distribution.
F5. The fault was a too narrow restriction in the SO algorithm that did not allow to use intermediate robots that apply no tools since the maximum length of concatenated roles was restricted. Thus, Listing 3 was mistakenly considered to be *unsatisfiable* instead of returning the following solution, for instance: agents $= [1, 5, 4, 6, 3, 6, 4, 5, 2, 5, 4, 6, 3, 6, 4]$; workedOn $= [1, 0, 0, 0, 2, 0, 0, 0, 3, 0, 0, 0, 4, 5, 0, 6]$ (R-Solution).
F6. The fault was a missing constraint with the observer, namely the I/O-Consistency constraint checked in the oracle of Listing 2. The failures occurred after activating a component fault that deactivates a cart that is part of the active task (R-Detection).

Table 1. Statistical data concerning the configuration used in the evaluation, the number of test cases generated and executed, the demanded time. Note that all detected faults have been removed and the time is used for complete testing of the interior and boundaries. Note that the runs within our framework are deterministic, i.e., there is no need to consider mean values or standard derivations.

#robots	#carts	#capabilities per Robot	#capabilities per Task	#routes	#test cases	time (in min)
4	3	2.75	6	6	131,000	570
3	2	1.67	5	4	49	0.2
3	2	3.67	5	4	26,763	69.25
3	2	1.67	5	6	157	0.78
3	2	1.67	8	4	47	0.38
5	2	1.6	5	5	1,577	6.88
3	4	1.67	5	5	369	1.08

The faults F3, F4, and F6 have been detected in all investigated configurations. Indeed, F1, F2, and F5 mainly depend on the routing structure used in the configuration, e.g., smaller configurations would not be able to reveal the faults. F6 mainly depends on changing the active robots or carts of a task, since their removal might not be detected and the controller is consequently not activated. All detected faults mainly concern misinterpretation of requirement specifications. The kind of faults that we detected underpins one of the strengths of our approach: the ability to reveal faults which are the result of a misinterpretation of the specification *(R2)*.

To answer *R3* and *R4*, we focused on the performance of test case generation and execution, investigating the abilities of the boundary interior testing approach for SO mechanisms. The results concerning the failures revealed, especially F1, F2, and F5, that the failures are more likely occur on the boundaries where SO switches between being possible and impossible; e.g., F1 was revealed when only one possible routing was left to fulfill the task, while F2 was revealed when no more routing is possible for the task. For *R4*, we used a test case generation algorithm using a *depth-first search* strategy that systematically explores the input space without respecting the boundaries of SO, unlike our proposed

Table 2. Statistical data comparing boundary-interior testing of SO mechanisms (DCCA w/o heuristics) with a simple depth-first search. The configuration that is compared is the first one of Table 1.

Metrics	Boundary-interior						Depth-first					
	F1	F2	F3	F4	F5	F6	F1	F2	F3	F4	F5	F6
#Test Cases	13	15	1	1	1,609	4	10	16	1	1	16,813	5
Time (in s)	3.12	3.91	< 1	< 1	420	0.96	2.25	3.11	< 1	< 1	7583.33	1.13

approach. The overall testing times required by the test system to reveal the failures and the number of test cases used is measured in Table 2.

At a first glance, the results indicate that the proposed approach for test case generation does not payoff as expected in most cases. That is mainly an effect of the kinds of faults we detected in the SO mechanisms which are able to be revealed with quite a lot different combinations of component faults and thus detected very early on. However, for F5 the potential of the approach especially for a bit more sophisticated faults is shown. Furthermore, it is even possible to optimize the concepts based on how the DCCA is used for reaching the boundaries. Currently, DCCA is applying a kind of depth-first search towards the states where no reconfiguration is possible anymore. Within this search, DCCA further performs optimizations according to the activation of the component faults based on monotonicity of the cut set property.

8   Related Work

The approach for testing adaptive system could be clustered into run-time and design-time approaches; both have identified non-determinism and the emergent behavior as the main challenges for testing adaptive systems.

Run-time approaches for testing take up the paradigm of run-time verification [5,12]. They shift testing into run-time to be able to observe and test, e.g., the adaptation to new situations. Camara et al. [1] use these concepts to consider fully integrated systems. Their testing approach focuses mainly on testing the non-functional properties of resilience of the adaptive system. The gained information is used as feedback for the running system. A similar approach is taken by Ramirez et al. [15], also focusing on non-functional requirements. The authors use the sampled data from a simulation to calculate a distance to the expected values derived from the goal specification of the system. This information is subsequently used to adapt the system or its requirements proactively. The run-time approaches are limited to tests of the fully integrated system and therefore are faced with problems like error masking which is very likely in such self-healing systems. In our testing approach, by contrast, we benefit from the piecemeal integration of the system for testing. Thus, it is possible to avoid error masking by testing the SO mechanism in an isolated way. Another important difference to the aforementioned work is that we use these techniques for finding failures instead of analyzing the current system state for generating feedback for adaptation. Still, we also use the basic concepts of run-time testing. The CEI allows us to split the evaluation into the three responsibilities of R-Detection, R-Solution, and R-Distribution which in turn enables us to evaluate the runs without the evaluation of complex system states on the system level.

Design-time approaches like [13,20] test the systems in a classical manner during development. All of these approaches consider some dedicated parts of the system. Consequently, it is not possible to give evidence about the correct functionality of the overall system. Zhang et al. [20] compose their tests towards fully integrated system tests, but they do not consider adaptivity or SO explicitly since they focus on testing the correct execution of plans within multi-agent systems. Nguyen [13] promotes an approach for a component test suite, but does not consider interactions between or organization of components as it would be necessary for SO.

The evaluation of the test results, i.e., the application of a test oracle for adaptive behavior is only considered by Fredericks et al. [6] and Nguyen et al. [14]. Both approaches rely on goals reflecting the requirements of the system that are somewhat loosened in order to reflect the ever-changing environment the components have to adapt to: The approaches mitigate the goals with the *RELAXed* approach or consider soft goals that do not need to hold at all times. Consequently, the decisions of the test oracle are rather fuzzy. In our approach, the definition of correct and incorrect behavior is given by the CCB that enables us to clearly decide whether a failure indeed occured.

Back-to-back testing was initially proposed by Vouk [19] and describes the concept of the co-development of a test framework and the actual system or mechanisms based on the same requirements, letting the systems compete with each other in order to reveal discrepancies and errors. Back-to-back testing is focused on functional testing of the system with a special attention on the correct interpretation of the actual requirements and their implementation. The assumption made is that two different developers resp. development teams will not make the same mistake twice, i.e., misinterpret or neglect functional requirements, and so the discrepancies between the two systems reveal potential development errors. In [17], we already showed how BtB testing could be successfully applied to *constraint programming*, since our basic ideas of testing adaptive, self-organizing system is based on constraining the SO algorithms. This paper extends these concepts from constraint programming to SO mechanisms.

Our approach for BtB testing of SO mechanism is an efficient combination of model-based techniques using the concepts of BtB testing in order to tackle the challenges of testing SOAS. To our knowledge, there is no approach extending both of these techniques to SO mechanism.

9   Conclusion and Outlook

We motivated the need for systematic testing of adaptive, self-organizing systems and purposed a systematic approach for BtB testing of SO mechanisms. The concept of BtB testing supports the challenging task of engineering SO mechanisms in a co-development manner and is able to reveal different kinds of faults concerning the functional specification of the system. The evaluation showed the utility of the approach by revealing different faults within a real development endeavor. The model-based approach presented is built upon a model of the system and its intended behavior, with the latter being based on our concepts of the CCB that enables fully automated evaluation of test runs. The test cases to be executed are derived on the basis of the system model; the test case selection strategy is based on ideas of virtual commissioning and boundary interior testing. Test case generation, execution, evaluation, and logging is fully automated and proved to be able to reveal different failures, as shown in the evaluation. The integration in the S# modeling framework allows to use our BtB testing concepts within Visual Studio, enabling model refactoring and debugging, among others.

Future work includes, among other things, the enhancement of heuristics in test case generation, enhancing the fault diagnostics, and integrating the approach into our overall framework for testing SOAS. The *heuristics for test case generation* should allow to reach the boundaries of SO mechanisms more efficiently. A first concept might be to start with bigger initial sets of component faults, e.g., to activate the component faults for all drills of all robots except of one. This leads, in a first evaluation, to better converge towards the boundaries of SO mechanisms and should reveal failures with less testing effort. *Fault diagnostic* is already possible in sense that we are able to track faults back to a part of the SO mechanism as well as to a set of activated component faults and a system configuration. However, the non-deterministic behavior of the SO mechanisms is still a challenge that we are going to address in future research. At last, the approach needs to be *integrated into an overall approach for testing SOAS* to supply a complete framework for testing the class of self-organizing resource flow systems.

Acknowledgments. This research is sponsored by the research project *Testing Self-Organizing, adaptive Systems (TeSOS)* of the German Research Foundation. Additionally, we thank our college Alexander Schiendorfer for his support with MiniZinc.

References

1. Cámara, J., de Lemos, R.: Evaluation of resilience in self-adaptive systems using probabilistic model-checking. In: Proceedings of 7th International Symposium Software Engineering for Adaptive and Self-Managing Systems (SEAMS), pp. 53–62 (2012)
2. Eberhardinger, B., Anders, G., Seebach, H., Siefert, F., Knapp, A., Reif, W.: An approach for isolated testing of self-organization algorithms. CoRR abs/1606.02442 (2016). http://arxiv.org/abs/1606.02442
3. Eberhardinger, B., Seebach, H., Knapp, A., Reif, W.: Towards testing self-organizing, adaptive systems. In: Merayo, M.G., Oca, E.M. (eds.) ICTSS 2014. LNCS, vol. 8763, pp. 180–185. Springer, Heidelberg (2014). doi:10.1007/978-3-662-44857-1_13
4. ElMaraghy, H., Monostori, L.: Variety management in manufacturing cyber-physical production systems: roots, expectations and r&d challenges. In: Procedia CIRP, vol. 17, pp. 9–13 (2014)
5. Falcone, Y., Jaber, M., Nguyen, T.-H., Bozga, M., Bensalem, S.: Runtime verification of component-based systems. In: Barthe, G., Pardo, A., Schneider, G. (eds.) SEFM 2011. LNCS, vol. 7041, pp. 204–220. Springer, Heidelberg (2011). doi:10.1007/978-3-642-24690-6_15
6. Fredericks, E.M., Ramirez, A.J., Cheng, B.H.C.: Towards run-time testing of dynamic adaptive systems. In: Proceedings of 8th International Symposium on Software Engineering for Adaptive and Self-Managing Systems (SEAMS), pp. 169–174. IEEE (2013)

7. Güdemann, M., Nafz, F., Ortmeier, F., Seebach, H., Reif, W.: A specification and construction paradigm for organic computing systems. In: Proceedings of 2nd IEEE International Conference Self-Adaptive and Self-Organizing Systems (SASO), pp. 233–242 (2008)
8. Habermaier, A., Eberhardinger, B., Seebach, H., Leupolz, J., Reif, W.: Runtime model-based safety analysis of self-organizing systems with S#. In: Proceedings of 9th IEEE International Self-Adaptive and Self-Organizing Systems Workshops (SASOW), pp. 128–133 (2015)
9. Kephart, J.O., Chess, D.M.: The vision of autonomic computing. Computer **36**(1), 41–50 (2003)
10. Lee, C.G., Park, S.C.: Survey on the virtual commissioning of manufacturing systems. J. Comput. Des. Eng. **1**(3), 213–222 (2014)
11. de Lemos, R., et al.: Software engineering for self-adaptive systems: a second research roadmap. In: de Lemos, R., Giese, H., Müller, H.A., Shaw, M. (eds.) Software Engineering for Self-Adaptive Systems II. LNCS, vol. 7475, pp. 1–32. Springer, Heidelberg (2013)
12. Leucker, M., Schallhart, C.: A brief account of runtime verification. J. Logic Algebraic Program. **78**(5), 293–303 (2009)
13. Nguyen, C.D.: Testing techniques for software agents. Ph.D. thesis, Uni. di Trento (2009)
14. Nguyen, C.D., Marchetto, A., Tonella, P.: Automated oracles: an empirical study on cost and effectiveness. In: Proceedings of Joint Meet European Software Engineering Conference and ACM SIGSOFT Symposium Foundations of Software Engineering (ESEC/FSE), pp. 136–146. ACM (2013)
15. Ramirez, A.J., Jensen, A.C., Cheng, B.H.C., Knoester, D.B.: Automatically exploring how uncertainty impacts behavior of dynamically adaptive systems. In: Proceedings of 26th IEEE/ACM International Conference Automated Software Engineering (ASE), pp. 568–571. IEEE (2011)
16. Richter, U., Mnif, M., Branke, J., Müller-Schloer, C., Schmeck, H.: Towards a generic observer/controller architecture for organic computing. In: Informatik 2006 (2006)
17. Schiendorfer, A., Eberhardinger, B., Reif, W., André, E.: Back-to-Back testing a soft constraint model for a smart exhibition space. In: Proceedings of 14th International Workshop Constraint Modelling and Reformulation (ModRef) (2015)
18. Seebach, H., Nafz, F., Steghöfer, J.P., Reif, W.: How to Design and Implement Self-organising Resource-Flow Systems, pp. 145–161. Springer, Heidelberg (2011)
19. Vouk, M.A.: Back-to-back testing. Inf. Softw. Technol. **32**(1), 34–45 (1990)
20. Zhang, Z., Thangarajah, J., Padgham, L.: Model based testing for agent systems. In: Proceedings of 8th International Conference Autonomous Agents and Multiagent Systems (AAMAS), pp. 1333–1334 (2009)

Test Generation by Constraint Solving and FSM Mutant Killing

Alexandre Petrenko[1]([⊠]), Omer Nguena Timo[1], and S. Ramesh[2]

[1] Computer Research Institute of Montreal, CRIM, Montreal, Canada
{petrenko,omer.nguena}@crim.ca
[2] GM Global R&D, Warren, MI, USA
ramesh.s@gm.com

Abstract. The problem of fault model-based test generation from formal models, in this case Finite State Machines, is addressed. We consider a general fault model which is a tuple of a specification, conformance relation and fault domain. The specification is a deterministic FSM which can be partially specified and not reduced. The conformance relation is quasi-equivalence, as all implementations in the fault domain are assumed to be completely specified FSMs. The fault domain is a set of all possible deterministic submachines of a given nondeterministic FSM, called a mutation machine. The mutation machine contains a specification machine and extends it with mutated transitions modelling potential faults. An approach for deriving a test suite which is complete (sound and exhaustive) for the given fault model is elaborated. It is based on our previously proposed method for analyzing the test completeness by logical encoding and SMT-solving. The preliminary experiments performed on an industrial controller indicate that the approach scales sufficiently well.

Keywords: FSM · Conformance testing · Mutation testing · Fault modelling · Fault model-based test generation · Test coverage · Fault coverage analysis

1 Introduction

Fault model-based testing receives constantly growing interests of both researchers and test practitioners. Fault models are defined in the literature in a variety of ways [16]. The work [10] proposes to define a fault model as a tuple of a specification, conformance relation and fault domain. In the context of testing from finite state machines, the specification is a certain type of FSM. A conformance relation is specific to the FSM type and for completely specified deterministic machines it is equivalence, while for partially specified machines it is quasi-equivalence. The fault domain is a set of implementation machines, aka mutants, each of which models some faults, such as output, transfer and transition faults.

In the traditional checking experiment theory the fault domain is the universe of all machines with a given number of states and input and output alphabets of the specification, see, e.g., [7, 8, 11–13]. Checking experiments are in fact sound and exhaustive, i.e., complete tests. However, their size for realistic specifications is often considered too big for practical applications. To us, this is a price to pay for considering

© IFIP International Federation for Information Processing 2016
Published by Springer International Publishing AG 2016. All Rights Reserved.
F. Wotawa et al. (Eds.): ICTSS 2016, LNCS 9976, pp. 36–51, 2016.
DOI: 10.1007/978-3-319-47443-4_3

the universe of all FSMs. Intuitively, choosing a reasonable subset of this fault domain might be the way to mitigate the test explosion effect. As an example, if one considers the fault domain of mutants that model output faults, a test complete for this fault model is simply a transition tour. The fault domains intermediate to these two domains have not yet received in our opinion sufficient attention.

To define a fault domain which is a subset of the universe of all FSMs, one could explicitly enumerate mutants as in program or model-based mutation testing, see, e.g., [1–3, 21] or avoid this enumeration by defining a fault domain as a set of all possible submachines of a given nondeterministic FSM, called a mutation machine [4, 6, 9]. The mutation machine contains as a submachine a specification machine, additional transitions model potential faults. Several methods were developed for test generation using this fault model [4, 6, 9, 22]. All these methods are adaptations of classical checking experiments for a fault domain defined by a mutation machine. A checking experiment is in fact a complete test suite, however, the use of the state identification approach imposes limitations on the fault model. First, the specification machine must be completely specified and reduced, so that state identifiers exist. Second, the mutation machine was defined only for such specification machines. The existing methods are not applicable for partial specification machines and mutation machines derived from them. Finally, the state identification approach does not support iterative test generation with a mutation machine allowing the tester to terminate the process when a complete test suite for the given fault model is not yet obtained, but facing the scalability problems he is forced to make a compromise between fault coverage and test length.

Addressing the above limitations, in our recent work [20], we have developed a method for analyzing the test completeness for a fault model using a mutation machine. The analysis approach is based on logical encoding and SMT-solving, it avoids enumeration of mutants while still offering a possibility to estimate the test adequacy (mutation score). This method paves a road to a test generation approach which uses the results of the analysis to find tests which kill mutants survived a current test suite and iterates until a test suite complete for a given fault model with a mutation machine is obtained or the tester decides to terminate it earlier. Elaboration of the iterative test generation approach which is based on the test completeness analysis and does not require the specification machine to be complete and reduced is the main goal of this paper.

The remaining of this paper is organized as follows. Section 2 defines a specification model as well as a fault model. In Sect. 3, we develop an approach for complete test suite generation for a given fault model with a mutation machine. Section 4 reports some results of experimental evaluation of the approach. Section 5 summarizes our contributions and indicates future work.

2 Background

2.1 Finite State Machines

A *Finite State Machine* (FSM) M is a 5-tuple (S, s_0, I, O, T), where S is a finite set of states with initial state s_0; I and O are finite non-empty disjoint sets of inputs and outputs, respectively; T is a transition relation $T \subseteq S \times I \times O \times S$, (s, i, o, s') is a transition.

M is *completely specified* (complete FSM) if for each tuple $(s, x) \in S \times I$ there exists transition $(s, x, o, s') \in T$; M is *partially specified* (partial FSM), if for some $(s, x) \in S \times I$ there is no transition, we say in this case that input x is not specified in state s. Let P_M denote the set of all pairs (s, x) for which M has no transitions.

M is *deterministic* (DFSM) if for each $(s, x) \in S \times I$ there exists at most one transition $(s, x, o, s') \in T$; if there are several transitions for some $(s, x) \in S \times I$ then it is *nondeterministic* (NFSM).

An *execution* of M from state s is a sequence of transitions forming a path from s in the state transition diagram of M. The machine M is *initially connected*, if for any state $s \in S$ there exists an execution from s_0 to s. Henceforth, we assume that all FSMs are initially connected. An execution is *deterministic* if each transition (s, x, o, s') in it is the only transition for $(s, x) \in S \times I$; otherwise, i.e., if for some transition (s, x, o, s') in the execution there exists in it a transition (s, x, o', s'') such that $o \neq o'$ or $s' \neq s''$, the execution is *nondeterministic*. Clearly, a DFSM has only deterministic executions, while an NFSM can have both.

A *trace* of M in state s is a string of input-output pairs which label an execution from s. Let $Tr_M(s)$ denote the set of all traces of M in state s and Tr_M denote the set of traces of M in the initial state. Given sequence $\beta \in (IO)^*$, the *input (output) projection* of β, denoted $\beta_{\downarrow I}$ ($\beta_{\downarrow O}$), is a sequence obtained from β by erasing symbols in O (I). Given a trace β in state s the input projection $\beta_{\downarrow I}$ is an input sequence *defined in* state s. We use $\Omega_M(s)$ to denote the set of all the input sequences defined in state s and Ω_M to denote the set of all the input sequences defined in state s_0. Clearly, if M is complete then $\Omega_M = I^*$.

We say that an input sequence *triggers* an execution of M (in state s) if it is the input projection of a trace of the execution of M (in state s).

Given input sequence $\alpha \in \Omega_M$, let $out_M(s, \alpha)$ denote the set of all output sequences which can be produced by M in response to α at state s, that is $out_M(s, \alpha) = \{\beta_{\downarrow O} \mid \beta \in Tr_M(s)$ and $\beta_{\downarrow I} = \alpha\}$.

We define several relations between states in terms of traces. Given states s_1, s_2 of an FSM $M = (S, s_0, I, O, T)$, s_1 and s_2 are *(trace-) equivalent*, $s_1 \simeq s_2$, if $Tr_M(s_1) = Tr_M(s_2)$; s_2 is *trace-included* into (is a *reduction* of) s_1, $s_2 \leq s_1$, if $Tr_M(s_2) \subseteq Tr_M(s_1)$. M is *reduced* if any pair of its states are distinguishable, i.e., for every $s_1, s_2 \in S$ there exists $\alpha \in \Omega_M(s_1) \cap \Omega_M(s_2)$ such that $out_M(s_1, \alpha) \neq out_M(s_2, \alpha)$, α is called a *distinguishing* sequence for states s_1 and s_2, this is denoted $s_1 \not\simeq_\alpha s_2$ or simply $s_1 \not\simeq s_2$.

We also use relations between machines. Given FSMs $M = (S, s_0, I, O, T)$ and $N = (P, p_0, I, O, N)$, $M \leq N$ if $s_0 \leq p_0$; $N \simeq M$ if $s_0 \simeq p_0$; $N \not\simeq M$ if $s_0 \not\simeq p_0$.

In this paper, we assume that a specification machine is a DFSM which could be complete or partial, but all the implementation machines are complete DFSMs. This implies that we should use the quasi-equivalence relation [17] as a conformance relation between implementation and specification machines. Given a DFSM $M = (S, s_0, I, O, T)$ and DFSM $N = (P, p_0, I, O, N)$, N is *quasi-equivalent* to M if M is a reduction of N.

Given a complete FSM $M = (S, s_0, I, O, T)$, a machine $N = (S', s_0, I, O, N)$ is a *submachine* of M if $S' \subseteq S$ and $N \subseteq T$. The set of all complete deterministic submachines of M is denoted $Sub(M)$. Obviously, each machine in $Sub(M)$ is a reduction of M; moreover, if M is deterministic then $Sub(M)$ contains just M.

2.2 Fault Model

We define the so-called mutation machine for a given specification machine by generalizing the definition previously given only a complete specification FSM [4, 6, 9, 20, 22] to allow the latter to be partially specified.

Definition 1. Let $A = (S, s_0, I, O, N)$ be a specification DFSM with the set of state-input pairs P_A for which A has no transitions. A complete NFSM $M = (S, s_0, I, O, T)$ is a *mutation* machine of A, if $\{(s, x, o, s') \mid (s, x) \in P_A, o \in O, s' \in S\} \subseteq T$ and A is a submachine of M.

In this definition we interpret inputs which are not specified in some states of A as don't care inputs. This implies that in a conforming implementation these inputs may cause transitions with an arbitrary output to any state in S.

The transitions T of the mutation machine can be classified as follows. The transitions in the set $\{(s, x, o, s') \mid (s, x, o, s') \in T, (s, x) \in P_A\}$ are called *don't care* transitions; we let DNC_M denote this set. The transitions in $T \cap N$ are common for M and A, these are *unaltered* transitions. Transitions in the set $T \backslash (N \cup DNC_M)$, are *mutated* transitions. Given $(s, x) \in S \times I$, we let T_{sx} denote the set of transitions from state s and input x in M. If T_{sx} is a singleton then its transition is called a *trusted* transition. The set T_{sx} is called a *suspicious* set of transitions if it is not a singleton, transitions in a suspicious set are called *suspicious*. Notice that don't care transitions are also treated as suspicious, since they can either compensate faults represented by mutated transitions and form a conforming mutant or expose wrong outputs.

We assume that all possible implementation machines for the specification machine A constitute the fault domain $Sub(M)$, the set of all deterministic submachines of the mutation machine M of A. A submachine $B \in Sub(M)$, $B \neq A$ is called a *mutant*. All mutants share all the trusted transitions, they may differ in suspicious and don't care transitions. In fact, transitions in suspicious sets are alternative and only one can be present in a deterministic mutant. Similarly, each mutant has a single transition for each pair $(s, x) \in P_A$, as all mutants are complete machines. A mutant B is *conforming* if it is quasi-equivalent to A, otherwise, it is *nonconforming*. We say that input sequence $\alpha \in \Omega_A$ *detects* or *kills* the mutant B if $B \neq_\alpha A$.

The tuple $<A, \simeq, Sub(M)>$ is a fault model [10]. For a given specification machine A a quasi-equivalence relation partitions the set $Sub(M)$ into conforming and nonconforming implementations. In this paper, we do not require the FSM A to be complete and reduced. A conforming mutant may therefore have fewer states than the specification A; on the other hand, we assume that no fault creates new states in implementations, hence mutants with more states than the specification FSM are not in the fault domain $Sub(M)$.

Consider the example in Fig. 1.

The specification machine A in Fig. 1 is a partial DFSM, where input b is not specified in state 2, hence $P_A = \{(2, b)\}$. The machine is not reduced, since state 3 is quasi-equivalent to state 2. All the existing methods for test generation using mutation machines [4, 6, 9, 22] cannot be applied for such a machine, as they are based on the assumption that the specification machine is a complete and reduced machine, as required by the state identification approach.

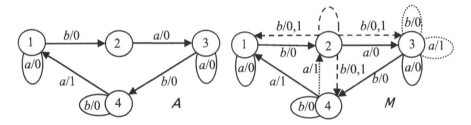

Fig. 1. A specification machine A and mutation machine M, where mutated transitions are depicted with dotted lines, don't care transitions with dashed lines; state 1 is the initial state.

The mutation machine M in Fig. 1 has three mutated transitions, one representing an output fault and the other two transfer faults. It also has 14 suspicious transitions, eight of them are don't care transitions.

The mutation machine M represents mutants as its deterministic submachines. Their number is given by the following formula:

$$|Sub(M)| = \prod_{(s,x)\in S\times I} |T_{sx}|$$

In our running example, the number of mutants is $8 \times 2 \times 2 \times 2 = 64$.

In the extreme case, considered in classical checking experiments a fault domain is the universe of all machines with at most n states, the number of states in the specification machine, and the alphabets of it. The corresponding mutation machine becomes in this case a chaos machine with all possible transitions between each pair of states. We use $Chaos(A, n)$ to denote such a mutation machine for A. The number of FSMs it represents is the product of the numbers of states and outputs to the power of the product of the numbers of states and inputs.

3   Mutation Testing

A finite set of finite input sequences $E \subset \Omega_A$ is a *test suite* for A. A test suite is said to be *complete* w.r.t. the fault model $<A, \simeq, Sub(M)>$ if for each nonconforming mutant $B \in Sub(M)$ it contains a test detecting B.

In the case where $M = Chaos(A, n)$ a complete test suite is called n-complete. This notion coincides with the classical notion of checking experiments for the fault domain consisting of FSMs with at most n states [5, 7, 10].

In the domain of program mutation testing, such a test suite is often called adequate for a program relative to a finite collection of programs (in our case the set $Sub(M)$), see, e.g., [3].

For deterministic FSMs tests that kill a given mutant FSM can be obtained from the product of the two machines, see, e.g., [1, 2, 17]. This approach can also be used to check whether a given test kills mutants, but it requires mutant enumeration.

In this work, we develop an approach for complete test suite generation for the fault model $<A, \simeq, Sub(M)>$, where A can be a partial or complete FSM not necessary reduced. It is based on mutant killing, but does not check mutants one by one, thus avoiding their full enumeration.

3.1 Distinguishing Automaton

Tests detecting mutants of the specification can be determined using a product of the specification and mutation machines obtained by composing their transitions as follows.

Definition 2 [20]. Given a specification machine $A = (S, s_0, I, O, N)$ and a mutation machine $M = (S, s_0, I, O, T)$ of A, a finite automaton $D = (C \cup \{\nabla\}, c_0, I, D, \nabla)$, where $C \subseteq S \times S$, and ∇ is an accepting (sink) state is the *distinguishing* automaton for A and M, if it holds that

- $c_0 = (s_0, s_0)$
- For any $(s, t) \in C$ and $x \in I$, $((s, t), x, (s', t')) \in D$, if there exist $(s, x, o, s') \in N$ and $(t, x, o', t') \in T$, such that $o = o'$ and $((s, t), x, \nabla) \in D$, if there exist $(s, x, o, s') \in N$ and $(t, x, o', t') \in T$, such that $o \neq o'$.

Notice that there is no outgoing transition with an input from a state of the distinguishing automata if and only if the state includes a state of A for which the input not specified.

We illustrate the definition using the specification and mutation machines in Fig. 1. Figure 2 presents the distinguishing automaton for A and M.

The accepting state defines the language L_D of the distinguishing automaton D for A and M and possesses the following properties. First, $L_D \subset \Omega_A$, then all input sequences detecting each and every mutant belong to this language.

Theorem 1. Given the distinguishing automaton D for A and M, if $B \not\simeq_\alpha A$ for some $B \in Sub(M)$, then there exists $\beta \in L_D$, such that $B \not\simeq_\beta A$ and β is a prefix of α.

Notice that for any nonconforming mutant there exists an input sequence of length at most n^2, where n is the number of states of the specification machine, since a distinguishing automaton has no more than n^2 states.

An input sequence $\alpha \in L_D$ triggers an execution in the distinguishing automaton D which is defined by an execution in the specification machine A and some execution in the mutation machine M triggered by α. The latter to represent a mutant must be deterministic. Such a deterministic execution of the mutation machine M defining an execution of the distinguishing automaton D to the sink state is called α-*revealing*. An input sequence triggering revealing executions enjoys a nice property of being able to detect mutants. Moreover all its extensions also detect at least the same mutants.

Theorem 2. [20]. Given an input sequence $\alpha \in \Omega_A$ such that $\alpha \in L_D$, an α-revealing execution includes at least one mutated transition, moreover, each mutant which has this execution is detected by the input sequence α.

Given an input sequence $\alpha \in L_D$, the question arises how all the mutants (un) detected by this input sequence can be characterized. We address this question in the next section.

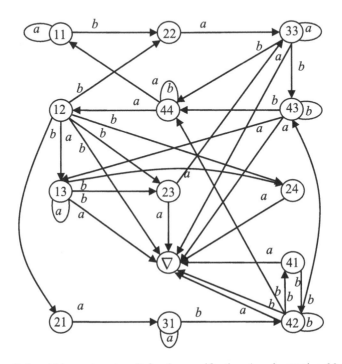

Fig. 2. The distinguishing automaton D for the specification A and mutation M machines in Fig. 1, state 11 is the initial state.

3.2   Characterisation of Mutants (Un)Detected by an Input Sequence

Consider an input sequence $\alpha \in \Omega_A$ whose prefixes trigger α-revealing executions. These executions characterize mutants detected by α, since each of them defines a distinct set of suspicious transitions involved in the execution. Based on these sets we can build a constraint on transition sets of mutants undetected by α. This can be achieved by using a distinguishing automaton constrained to a given input sequence.

Let $Pref(\alpha)$ be the set of all prefixes of α. We define a linear automaton ($Pref(\alpha)$, ε, I, D_α), such that each prefix of α is a state, and (β, x, βx) $\in D_\alpha$ if $\beta x \in Pref(\alpha)$.

Definition 3 [20]. Given a specification machine $A = (S, s_0, I, O, N)$, input sequence $\alpha \in \Omega_A$, and mutation machine $M = (S, s_0, I, O, T)$, a finite automaton $D_\alpha = (C_\alpha \cup \{\nabla\}, c_0, I, D_\alpha, \nabla)$, where $C_\alpha \subseteq Pref(\alpha) \times S \times S$, and ∇ is a designated sink state is the α-*distinguishing* automaton for A and M if it holds that

- $c_0 = (\varepsilon, s_0, p_0)$
- For any $(\beta, s, t) \in C_\alpha$ and $x \in I$, such that $\beta x \in Pref(\alpha)$, $((\beta, s, t), x, (\beta x, s', t')) \in D_\alpha$, if there exist $(s, x, o, s') \in N$, $(t, x, o', t') \in T$, such that $o = o'$ and $((\beta, s, t), x, \nabla) \in D$, if there exist $(s, x, o, s') \in N$, $(t, x, o', t') \in T$, such that $o \neq o'$.

For $\alpha = bababa$ in our running example, the α-distinguishing automaton for A and M is shown in Fig. 3.

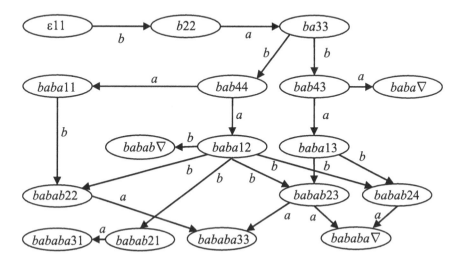

Fig. 3. The α-distinguishing automaton D_α for the specification A machine and mutation machine M in Fig. 1, where $\alpha = bababa$.

There are eleven executions of the mutation machine listed below which are defined by five executions of the α-distinguishing automaton reaching the sink state in Fig. 3. Suspicious transitions are in bold font and the others are trusted transitions. Transitions of the specification are underlined. Three executions, namely executions 9, 10, and 11, are non-deterministic. The first eight executions belong to mutants detected by $bababa$.

1. $\underline{(1,b,0,2)}\underline{(2,a,0,3)}\mathbf{(3,b,0,3)}\underline{(3,a,0,3)}$
2. $\underline{(1,b,0,2)}\underline{(2,a,0,3)}\mathbf{(3,b,0,4)}\underline{(4,a,1,2)}\mathbf{(2,b,1,2)}$
3. $\underline{(1,b,0,2)}\underline{(2,a,0,3)}\mathbf{(3,b,0,4)}\underline{(4,a,1,2)}\mathbf{(2,b,1,1)}$
4. $\underline{(1,b,0,2)}\underline{(2,a,0,3)}\mathbf{(3,b,0,4)}\underline{(4,a,1,2)}\mathbf{(2,b,1,3)}$
5. $\underline{(1,b,0,2)}\underline{(2,a,0,3)}\mathbf{(3,b,0,4)}\underline{(4,a,1,2)}\mathbf{(2,b,1,4)}$
6. $\underline{(1,b,0,2)}\underline{(2,a,0,3)}\mathbf{(3,b,0,3)}\underline{(4,a,1,2)}\mathbf{(3,b,0,3)}\underline{(3,a,1,3)}$
7. $\underline{(1,b,0,2)}\underline{(2,a,0,3)}\mathbf{(3,b,0,4)}\underline{(4,a,1,2)}\mathbf{(2,b,0,3)}\underline{(3,a,1,3)}$
8. $\underline{(1,b,0,2)}\underline{(2,a,0,3)}\mathbf{(3,b,0,4)}\underline{(4,a,1,2)}\mathbf{(2,b,0,4)}\underline{(4,a,1,2)}$
9. $\underline{(1,b,0,2)}\underline{(2,a,0,3)}\mathbf{(3,b,0,3)}\underline{(3,a,1,3)}\mathbf{(3,b,0,4)}\underline{(4,a,1,1)}$
10. $\underline{(1,b,0,2)}\underline{(2,a,0,3)}\mathbf{(3,b,0,3)}\underline{(3,a,1,3)}\mathbf{(3,b,0,4)}\underline{(4,a,1,2)}$
11. $\underline{(1,b,0,2)}\underline{(2,a,0,3)}\mathbf{(3,b,0,4)}\underline{(4,a,1,2)}\mathbf{(2,b,0,4)}\underline{(4,a,1,1)}$

Three prefixes of *bababa*, namely *baba*, *babab* and *bababa* belong to L_D and trigger α-revealing executions in the mutation machine. Any deterministic execution of the mutation machine with the input sequence *baba* is α-revealing if it uses the two suspicious transitions involved in the first execution, i.e., $(3, b, 0, 3)$ and $(3, a, 0, 3)$. We recall that trusted transitions are used in every mutant submachine. Hence, every mutant which has both these suspicious transitions is detected by *baba*. Considering all eight executions, any mutant which has any of the eight sets of suspicious transitions is nonconforming and detected by *bababa*. Conversely, any mutant undetected by *bababa* must have mutated transitions such that do not form any of the sets defined by the listed executions. This property can be formalized as a constraint on suspicious transitions using conditional operators $\{= , \neq\}$ and logical operators $\{\wedge, \vee\}$ for constraint formulas.

Given a pair $(s, x) \in S \times I$ such that T_{sx} is a suspicious set of transitions, we introduce an auxiliary variable z_{sx} which takes values from the indexes of the transitions of the mutation machine in T_{sx}.

Each α-revealing execution e of the mutation machine involving the set of suspicious transitions $\{t_1, t_2, \ldots, t_n\}$ yields a clause $c_e = ((z_{s1 \times 1} \neq t_1) \vee (z_{s2 \times 2} \neq t_2) \vee \ldots \vee (z_{snxn} \neq t_n))$ where s_i and x_i are the source state and the input of transition t_i for $1 \leq i \leq n$. The clause c_e is satisfied whenever z_{sixi} is not t_i for some $1 \leq i \leq n$. A solution of c_e excludes at least one transition in e.

In the running example, the sets of suspicious transitions indexed with an integer identifier are:

$T_{2b} = \{(2, b, 0, 2)_3, (2, b, 1, 2)_4, (2, b, 0, 1)_5, (2, b, 1, 1)_6, (2, b, 0, 3)_8, (2, b, 1, 3)_9, (2, b, 0, 4)_{10}, (2, b, 1, 4)_{11}\}$, $T_{3a} = \{\underline{(3, a, 0, 3)}_{12}, (3, a, 1, 3)_{13}\}$, $T_{3b} = \{(3, b, 0, 3)_{14}, \underline{(3, b, 0, 4)}_{15}\}$ and $T_{4a} = \{\underline{(4, a, 1, 1)}_{17}, (4, a, 1, 2)_{18}\}$. The remaining trusted transitions are indexed as follows: $\underline{(1, a, 0, 1)}_1, \underline{(1, b, 0, 2)}_2, \underline{(2, a, 0, 2)}_7, \underline{(4, b, 0, 2)}_{16}$. So we consider four variables z_{2b}, z_{3a}, z_{3b} and z_{4a} whose domains are T_{2b}, T_{3a}, T_{3b}, and T_{4a}, respectively. To simplify the presentation we use transition identifiers in constraints. The constraint formula for *bababa* consists of a preamble and eight clauses. The preamble $(z_{2b} \in T_{2b}) \wedge (z_{3a} \in T_{3a}) \wedge (z_{3b} \in T_{3b}) \wedge (z_{4a} \in T_{4a})$ specifies the domains of the variables, thus constraining the possible solutions of the conjunction of the eight clauses to transitions of the mutation machine.

$((z_{2b} \in T_{2b}) \wedge (z_{3a} \in T_{3a}) \wedge (z_{3b} \in T_{3b}) \wedge (z_{4a} \in T_{4a}) \wedge ((z_{3a} \neq 12) \vee (z_{3b} \neq 14)) \wedge ((z_{4a} \neq 18) \vee (z_{2b} \neq 4) \vee (z_{3b} \neq 15)) \wedge ((z_{4a} \neq 18) \vee (z_{2b} \neq 6) \vee (z_{3b} \neq 15)) \wedge ((z_{4a} \neq 18) \vee (z_{2b} \neq 9) \vee (z_{3b} \neq 15)) \wedge ((z_{4a} \neq 18) \vee (z_{2b} \neq 11) \vee (z_{3b} \neq 15)) \wedge ((z_{3a} \neq 13) \vee (z_{3b} \neq 14)) \wedge ((z_{4a} \neq 18) \vee (z_{2b} \neq 8) \vee (z_{3a} \neq 13) \vee (z_{3b} \neq 15)) \wedge ((z_{4a} \neq 18) \vee (z_{2b} \neq 10) \vee (z_{3b} \neq 15)))$.

Clearly, the constraint always has a solution where values of variables determine all the unaltered transitions, but to find nonconforming mutants we need a solution if it exists which has at least one mutated transition. To this end, we add the constraint $((z_{3a} \neq 12) \vee (z_{3b} \neq 15) \vee (z_{4a} \neq 17))$ excluding the solution defining the specification machine augmented with an arbitrary don't care transition, called a completed specification machine.

The final constraint formula for *bababa* is $C(bababa) = ((z_{2b} \in T_{2b} \wedge z_{3a} \in T_{3a} \wedge z_{3b} \in T_{3b} \wedge z_{4a} \in T_{4a}) \wedge ((z_{3a} \neq 12) \vee (z_{3b} \neq 14)) \wedge ((z_{4a} \neq 18) \vee (z_{2b} \neq 4) \vee (z_{3b} \neq 15)) \wedge ((z_{4a} \neq 18) \vee (z_{2b} \neq 6) \vee (z_{3b} \neq 15)) \wedge ((z_{4a} \neq 18) \vee (z_{2b} \neq 9) \vee (z_{3b} \neq 15)) \wedge ((z_{4a} \neq$

18) $\vee$ ($z_{2b} \neq 11$) $\vee$ ($z_{3b} \neq 15$)) $\wedge$ (($z_{3a} \neq 13$) $\vee$ ($z_{3b} \neq 14$)) $\wedge$ (($z_{4a} \neq 18$) $\vee$ ($z_{2b} \neq 8$) $\vee$ (z_{3a} $\neq 13$) $\vee$ ($z_{3b} \neq 15$)) $\wedge$ (($z_{4a} \neq 18$) $\vee$ ($z_{2b} \neq 10$) $\vee$ ($z_{3b} \neq 15$)) $\wedge$ (($z_{3a} \neq 12$) $\vee$ ($z_{3b} \neq 15$) $\vee$ ($z_{4a} \neq 17$))).

The constraint $C(\alpha)$ characterizing the mutants undetected by an input sequence α is the conjunction of a clause excluding all completed specification machines and the clauses generated for every α-revealing execution. Any existing constraint solver, e.g., Z3 [15], could be used for satisfiability checking. A solution of $C(\alpha)$ if it exists is an assignment of the auxiliary variables. The mutant defined by such a solution includes the transitions specified by the solution along with all the trusted transitions of the mutation machine. Any nonconforming mutant detected by α cannot be defined by any solution of $C(\alpha)$, only conforming mutants can.

Algorithm 1 presents a procedure that builds a constraint C_{TS} for a given test suite TS out of the constraints for each test in the test suite.

```
Algorithm 1. Build_Constraint
Input: TS, a test suite
       A, a specification machine
       M, a mutation machine for A
Output: C_TS, a constraint specifying mutants undetected
by tests in TS

1. C_TS = True
2. For each input sequence α ∈ TS,
     (a) Determine the α-distinguishing automaton Dα and set
         cα = True
     (b) For each α-revealing execution e of the mutation
         machine, set cα = cα ∧ ce, where ce is the disjunction
         of constraints excluding the suspicious transitions
         in e
     (c) C_TS = C_TS ∧ cα
3. Add to C_TS the constraints restricting the value of
   the variables to their domain and excluding A
4. Return C_TS
```

Theorem 3. Let C_{TS} be a constraint specifying undetected mutants by the test suite TS. TS is complete w.r.t. the fault model $<A, \approx, Sub(M)>$ if and only if C_{TS} is unsatisfiable or every solution of C_{TS} defines a conforming mutant.

In the running example, to solve the constraint formula $C(bababa)$, we use the SMT solver Z3 [15] which finds the solution $z_{2b} = 11$, $z_{3a} = 13$, $z_{3b} = 15$, $z_{4a} = 17$. The solution defines a mutant with all trusted transitions, one don't care transition $(2, b, 1, 4)_{11}$ and one mutated transition $(3, a, 1, 3)_{13}$. The mutant is presented in Fig. 4. The mutant is nonconforming, which can be verified with the help of a distinguishing automaton obtained for the specification machine and the mutant also shown in Fig. 4.

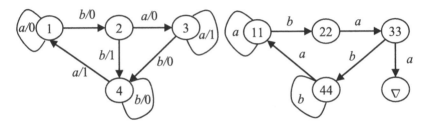

Fig. 4. A nonconforming mutant defined by a solution of the constraint for $TS = \{bababa\}$ and the distinguishing automata for the mutant and the specification A.

Notice that the solver could find another solution of the $C(bababa)$, namely, $z_{2b} = 11$, $z_{3a} = 12$, $z_{3b} = 15$, $z_{4a} = 17$ which defines a conforming mutant.

Given an initial test suite TS_{init}, the question arises how to augment TS_{init} with new input sequences to detect all nonconforming mutants. We elaborate a complete test suite generation procedure in the next section.

3.3   Complete Test Suite Generation

We are given a test suite $TS_{init} \subseteq \Omega_A$ and a fault model $<A, \simeq, Sub(M)>$. We want to add test cases to TS_{init} to obtain a complete test suite. Constraints defined in the previous section can be used to analyse the completeness of a test suite, elaborated in our previous work [20]. If the constraint for a test suite has no solution or the first solution computed by a solver defines a nonconforming mutant, we can immediately assert the incompleteness of the test suite. If however the solution defines a conforming mutant, the search continues such that the mutant will not be found again in a new round of satisfiability checking. This process iterates until no new solution is found or the generated solution defines a nonconforming mutant. A witness nonconforming mutant can be used to determine a test case which detects the mutant. A new test can kill other nonconforming mutants. Hence the constraints generated by this test should be added to the ones of the current test suite. The search terminates when the current constraint is unsatisfiable which indicates that the test suite is complete. The test generation procedure is formalized in Algorithm 2.

The algorithm has two loops. The coverage analysis loop includes statements in lines 7 to 9 and the test generation loop includes statements at lines 4 to 13. The former loop is nested in the latter. When the current test suite is not complete, the execution of the test generation loop augments (in line 4) it with a new test case and updates the constraint of the current test suite with that of the generated test case. Then the coverage analysis loop is executed checking the completeness of the updated test suite, searching for a new nonconforming mutant. To this end, constraints excluding conforming mutants defined by the found solutions are iteratively added to the current constraint. The procedure terminates when the resulting constraint is unsatisfiable, indicating that the current test suite is complete or the solver generates a solution defining a nonconforming mutant. In this case, the execution of the test generation loop augments the current test suite with a new test killing the mutant. It is determined by finding the shortest path to the sink state of the distinguishing automaton of the mutant and the specification.

```
Algorithm 2. TestSuiteGen
Inputs: TS_init, an initial test suite
        A, a specification machine
        M, a mutation machine for A
Output: TS, a complete test suite
```

1. $TS = \emptyset$
2. $C = $ True
3. $TS_{new} = TS_{init}$
4. $TS = TS \cup TS_{new}$
5. Let $C_{new} = $ **Build_Constraint**(TS_{new}, A, M) be a constraint specifying mutants undetected by TS_{new}
6. Let $C = C \wedge C_{new}$
7. Check the satisfiability of C by calling a solver
8. **if** C is "unsatisfiable" **then** terminate with "TS is a complete test suite"
9. Let N be a mutant defined by a solution of C obtained by a solver
10. **if** N is conforming **then** set $C = C \wedge C_N$ where C_N is the constraint that excludes N and **Goto** 7
11. Determine D, the distinguishing automaton of A and N
12. Let $TS_{new} = \{\alpha\}$, where $\alpha \in L_D$
13. **Goto** 4

Theorem 4. Procedure *TestSuiteGen* always terminates with a complete test suite.

Proof. The procedure *TestSuiteGen* terminates as the test generation loop terminates. It does so because a mutation machine has a finite number of submachines and the solution defining a particular mutant is generated at most once. According to Theorem 2, the computed tests are revealing input sequences. On termination of the procedure the final constraint characterizing undetected mutants excludes all conforming mutants and it is unsatisfiable. Based on Theorem 3 we have that the test suite returned by the procedure is complete.

To generate a complete test suite for the running example we consider the initial test suite $TS_{init} = \{bababa\}$, used in Sect. 3.2. Procedure *TestSuiteGen* first goes into the test generation loop which builds $C_{new} = C(bababa)$, updates TS and C to $\{bababa\}$ and $C(bababa)$ defined in Sect. 3.2. Then the coverage analysis loop finds the solution of C defining the nonconforming mutant in Fig. 4. The test baa is then generated by determining the only shortest path to the sink state in the distinguishing automaton for the specification and the mutant, so TS_{new} becomes $\{baa\}$. Then the constraint $C_{new} = C(baa) = (z_{3a} \neq 13)$ is generated in line 5, TS becomes $\{bababa,$

baa} and $C = C(bababa) \wedge C(baa)$. The solution of C defines a nonconforming mutant killed by the test $babaaba$, the input sequence of the shortest path to the sink state the distinguishing automaton for the new nonconforming mutant and the specification, then TS_{new} becomes {$babaaba$}. The constraint $C_{new} = C(babaaba) = (((z_{3a} \neq 12) \vee (z_{3b} \neq 14)) \wedge ((z_{3a} \neq 13) \vee (z_{3b} \neq 14)) \wedge ((z_{4a} \neq 18) \vee (z_{3b} \neq 15)))$ is generated; it includes one clause for each of the three α-revealing executions triggered by $babaaba$. TS becomes {$bababa, baa, babaaba$} and $C = C(bababa) \wedge C(baa) \wedge C(babaaba)$. C is satisfiable and the procedure iteratively generates only conforming mutants augmenting C each time with a constraint excluding the last conforming mutant. No additional tests are generated. The conjunction of C with the eight constraints excluding eight conforming mutants is unsatisfiable. The procedure returns a complete test suite $TS = \{bababa, baa, babaaba\}$. Notice that it generated only ten out of total 64 mutants.

The procedure *TestSuiteGen* also generates a complete test suite starting when the initial test suite contains just an empty input sequence.

In the next section we present experimental results obtained with a prototype tool.

4   Experimental Results

We have developed a prototype tool implementing the proposed method for complete test suite generation. In this section we present the tool and some experimental results using it.

4.1   Prototype Tool

The prototype tool is composed of four modules: an I/O module, a completeness checking module, a test generation module and a module for solver execution. The I/O module converts input data into an internal representation for processing and obtained results into a human-readable format. To this end, it implements an ANTLR-based parser [19] to interpret the mutation machine specified in a text format; it also parses the output of SMT solver Z3 [15] to extract a solution and builds a mutant. The completeness checking module builds α-distinguishing automata, determines revealing executions of the mutation machine and generates constraints for the solver. The test generation module iteratively calls the former module. The prototype can also be used with other SMT solvers compatible with the SMT-LIB 2.0.

For the experiments we use a desktop computer with the following settings: 3.4 Ghz Intel Core i7-3770 CPU, 16.0 GB of RAM, Z3 4.3.2, and ANTLR 4.5.1.

4.2   Test Generation for an Automotive Controller

We consider as a case study an automotive controller of the air quality system (HVAC), which we also used in our previous work [18, 20]. The functionality of the controller is to set an air source position depending on its current state and input from the environment.

Table 1. Experimental results for randomly generated mutation machines

	M	M_{+20}	M_{+100}	M_{+428}	M_{+764}	M_{+1000}
Mut. trans.	46	66	146	474	810	1046
Mutants	$6.9×10^{10}$	$3.6×10^{16}$	$9.8×10^{38}$	$7.8×10^{108}$	$4.9×10^{160}$	$3.2×10^{194}$
Tests	29	48	119	381	520	689
Seconds	0.57	0.7	1.8	8.6	58	154

The controller initially specified as a hierarchical Simulink Stateflow model is converted into an FSM with 14 states, 24 inputs and 24 × 14 = 336 transitions.

Several mutation machines were used in the experiments. The first one M_{hvac} was obtained by adding 46 mutated transitions to the specification machine (details are available in [20]). The formula in Sect. 2 gives the number of mutants $3^{12} × 2^{17} = 69,657,034,752$.

The other mutation machines were built by adding more mutated transitions to M_{hvac}. In particular, 20, 100, 428, 764 and 1000 mutated transitions were randomly added, resulting in five more mutation machines, M_{+20}, M_{+100}, M_{+428}, M_{+764} and M_{+1000}. Table. 1 presents the numbers of mutated transitions, mutants, generated tests and the computation time. Each generated mutant was non-conforming, so their number coincides with that of the tests, conforming mutants were never generated. The third column of Table. 1 represents the average values for 30 mutation machines randomly generated by adding 20 mutated transitions to M_{hvac}.

The experimental results indicate that the approach scales sufficiently well on a typical automotive controller even with the large number of mutants.

5 Conclusions

In this paper we focused on generation of a complete test suite detecting all nonconforming implementations in a fault domain defined by a mutation machine. A mutation machine is a nondeterministic FSM, interpreted as a compact representation of a set of deterministic implementations of a system represented by a partially or completely specified FSM. Each deterministic submachine of the mutation machine models an implementation.

We proposed a method for generating a complete test suite which avoids complete enumerations of nonconforming mutants. The method iteratively builds constraints specifying mutants undetected by an incomplete (possibly empty) test suite and uses a solution of constraints generated by a solver to determine an undetected mutant from which a new test case is selected and derives an augmented constraint for a next iteration step until the obtained constraint becomes unsatisfiable.

While it enumerates all conforming mutants, which exist mostly when the specification is partial or unreduced FSM, it does not generate all nonconforming ones. The experimental results with a prototype tool which uses the SMT solver Z3 indicate that the number of generated nonconforming mutants reaches only a small percentage of all mutants represented by a mutation machine.

Novelty of the contributions of this paper are as follows. The proposed approach allows one to construct checking experiments for FSMs which are not necessarily complete and reduced without using any state identification facility such as characterization sets, distinguishing sequences, and state identifiers, as opposed to traditional checking experiment approaches. Thus, we demonstrate that it is possible to construct checking experiments using logical encoding and constraint solving instead of classical methods based on state identification [4, 6, 9, 22]. Moreover, test completeness is guaranteed for a predefined subset of the universe of all FSMs with a given number of states, represented by a mutation machine. Compared to all previous work on the use of mutation machine [4, 6, 9, 20, 22], we have generalized its definition to make it applicable to partially defined specification machines. The method proposed in [22] is only applicable to mutation machines which satisfy the following assumption. If a transition of the specification machine becomes suspicious in the mutation machine then the latter has all possible (thus chaotic) suspicious transitions from the start state of the transition caused by the same input. The method also requires the specification machine be completely specified. Compared to that work, our method is applicable to arbitrary mutation machines, while the specification machine is allowed to be partially specified.

Another interesting feature of the approach is that it is iterative and allows the tester to obtain an incomplete test suite for which fault coverage can be estimated (as discussed in [20]) when facing the scalability problems he is forced to make a compromise between fault coverage and test length.

The experiments indicate that the proposed approach may scale sufficiently well, though, more experiments with industrial size specifications are needed. Our current work focuses on extending the approach to FSMs with symbolic inputs and outputs [23] and eventually to a more general type of EFSM [14].

Acknowledgements. This work is supported in part by GM, NSERC and MEIE of Gouvernement du Québec.

References

1. Pomeranz, I., Sudhakar, M.R.: Test generation for multiple state-table faults in finite-state machines. IEEE Trans. Comput. **46**(7), 783–794 (1997)
2. Poage, J.F., McCluskey, Jr., E.J.: Derivation of optimal test sequences for sequential machines. In: Proceedings of the IEEE 5th Symposium on Switching Circuits Theory and Logical Design, pp. 121–132 (1964)
3. DeMilli, R.A., Offutt, J.A.: Constraint-based automatic test data generation. IEEE Trans. Softw. Eng. **17**(9), 900–910 (1991)
4. Grunsky, I.S., Petrenko, A.: Design of checking experiments with automata describing protocols. Automatic Control and Computer Sciences. Allerton Press Inc. USA. No. 4 (1988)
5. Hennie, F.C.: Fault detecting experiments for sequential circuits. In: Proceedings of the IEEE 5th Annual Symposium on Switching Circuits Theory and Logical Design. Princeton, pp. 95–110 (1964)

6. Koufareva, I., Petrenko, A., Yevtushenko, N.: Test generation driven by user–defined fault models. In: Proceedings of the 12th International Workshop on Testing of Communicating Systems, pp. 215–233 (1999)
7. Lee, D., Yannakakis, M.: Principles and methods of testing finite-state machines - a survey. Proc. IEEE **84**(8), 1090–1123 (1996)
8. Moore, E.F.: Gedanken experiments on sequential machines. In: Automata Studies, pp. 129–153. Princeton University Press (1956)
9. Petrenko, A., Yevtushenko, N.: Test suite generation for a FSM with a given type of implementation errors. In: Proceedings of IFIP 12th International Symposium on Protocol Specification, Testing, and Verification, pp. 229–243 (1992)
10. Petrenko, A., Yevtushenko, N., Bochmann, G.V.: Fault models for testing in context. In: Gotzhein, R., Bredereke, J. (eds.) Formal Description Techniques IX, pp. 163–178. Springer, Heidelberg (1996)
11. Vasilevskii, M.P.: Failure diagnosis of automata. Cybernetics, vol. 4, pp. 653–665. Plenum Publishing Corporation, New York (1973)
12. Chow, T.S.: Testing software design modeled by finite-state machines. IEEE Trans. Softw. Eng. **4**(3), 178–187 (1978)
13. Vuong, S.T., Ko, K.C.: A novel approach to protocol test sequence generation. In: Global Telecommunications Conference, vol. 3, pp. 2–5. EEE (1990)
14. Petrenko, A., Boroday, S., Groz, R.: Confirming configurations in EFSM testing. IEEE Trans. Softw. Eng. **30**(1), 29–42 (2004)
15. de Moura, L., Bjørner, N.S.: Z3: an efficient SMT solver. In: Ramakrishnan, C.R., Rehof, J. (eds.) TACAS 2008. LNCS, vol. 4963, pp. 337–340. Springer, Heidelberg (2008)
16. Bochmann, G.V., et al.: Fault models in testing. In: Proceedings of the IFIP TC6/WG6. 1 Fourth International Workshop on Protocol Test Systems. North-Holland Publishing Co., pp. 17–30 (1991)
17. Petrenko, A., Yevtushenko, N.: Testing from partial deterministic FSM specifications. IEEE Trans. Comput. **54**(9), 1154–1165 (2005)
18. Petrenko, A., Dury, A., Ramesh, S., Mohalik, S.: A method and tool for test optimization for automotive controllers. In: ICST Workshops, pp. 198–207. IEEE (2013)
19. Parr, T.: The Definitive ANTLR 4 Reference, vol. 2. Pragmatic Bookshelf, Raleigh (2013)
20. Petrenko, A, Nguena Timo, O., Ramesh, S.: Multiple mutation testing from FSM. In: Proceedings of the 35th IFIP WG 6.1 International Conference on Formal Techniques for Distributed Objects, Components, and Systems, pp. 222–238 (2016)
21. Belli, F., Budnik, C.J., Hollmann, A., Tuglular, T., Wong, W.E.: Model-based mutation testing - approach and case studies. Sci. Comput. Programm. **120**, 25–48 (2016)
22. El-Fakih, K., Dorofeeva, R., Yevtushenko, N., Bochmann, G.V.: FSM-based testing from user defined faults adapted to incremental and mutation testing. Programm. Comput. Softw. **38**, 201–209 (2012)
23. Petrenko, A.: Checking experiments for symbolic input/output finite state machines. In: ICST Workshops, pp. 229–237. IEEE (2016)

Risk-Based Interoperability Testing Using Reinforcement Learning

André Reichstaller[1]([✉]), Benedikt Eberhardinger[1], Alexander Knapp[1],
Wolfgang Reif[1], and Marcel Gehlen[2]

[1] Institute for Software and Systems Engineering,
University of Augsburg, Augsburg, Germany
{reichstaller,eberhardinger,knapp,reif}@isse.de
[2] MaibornWolff GmbH, Munich, Germany
marcel.gehlen@maibornwolff.de

Abstract. Risk-based test strategies enable the tester to harmonize the number of specified test cases with imposed time and cost constraints. However, the risk assessment itself often requires a considerable effort of cost and time, since it is rarely automated. Especially for complex tasks such as testing the interoperability of different components it is expensive to manually assess the criticality of possible faults. We present a method that operationalizes the risk assessment for interoperability testing. This method uses behavior models of the system under test and reinforcement learning techniques to break down the criticality of given failure situations to the relevance of single system actions for being tested. Based on this risk assessment, a desired number of test cases is generated which covers as much relevance as possible. Risk models and test cases have been generated for a mobile payment system within an industrial case study.

1 Introduction

Interoperability testing of a distributed system checks whether the components of the system are able to communicate with each other and thus render requested services correctly through interaction [5]. The typically high number of possible interaction scenarios (e.g., combination of messages) makes interoperability testing a complex task. Since it seems impossible to cover all scenarios, their relevance for being tested has to be prioritized somehow. A *criticality-based test strategy* should focus the test effort on revealing faults which are expected to lead to the most critical failures [2]. However, the existence of implementation faults and the ensuing reachability of failures in real operation is unknown. Still, extending behavior models of the communicating components of the *System under Test (SuT)* with possible implementation faults, we can at least estimate the impact of a fault on the reachability of failures. The challenge is to find causal connections between the implementation faults and resulting failures.

We tackle this challenge by combining *model-based* [16] and *risk-based* testing methods [1,2] with *reinforcement learning* [15]. Our approach builds on given

F. Wotawa et al. (Eds.): ICTSS 2016, LNCS 9976, pp. 52–69, 2016.
DOI: 10.1007/978-3-319-47443-4_4

behavior models of the interacting components of the SuT, common implementation faults, and a set of the most critical failure situations, each of them described by the combination of component states and a score of its deemed effect. A failure situation is reached if all of the combined component states are active at the same point in time. None of the failures is actually reachable in the given behavior models, as the models do not describe faults. If we introduce common implementation faults into the behavior models, however, we are able to assess the *criticality* of faults, i.e., their "ability" to cause the effect of failures.

Let us imagine that a malicious developer of a component actually tries to induce the whole system to reach the maximum effect of failures in real operation by implementing the "right" component faults. These faults would be the ones to be tested for with highest priority. What he could do is to use a learning technique, such as reinforcement learning [15], on a simulated environment: He could implement his component as an intelligent agent which makes its own local decisions to achieve the global goal of reaching the most critical failures. This agent then would map received rewards to the preceding actions (either specified in the behavior model or faults) so as to assess the expected return for every possible action. The ultimate reward to be reinforced would be reaching a critical failure situation. Then the agent's learned expected return for executing a fault can be understood as the fault's criticality.

For finding those test cases which cover the most critical faults with highest priority, it seems reasonable to apply the same technique as our imaginary malicious developer. This procedure can be seen as defending the system against the faults he could inject. After the learning phase, each agent contains a function that maps its actions to their expected return, i.e., their criticality. From a *mutation testing* perspective [12], the actions representing anticipated faults can be seen as mutants of the specified actions in the behavior models. The functions of the agents weight these mutants by their criticality. Thus, test cases can now be prioritized by the criticality of the mutants they are assumed to kill. We propose a method for reducing the criticality of the mutants to the relevance of specified actions in the given behavior models for being tested. Building on this, we generate a desired number of logical test cases covering the most relevant actions. We have implemented our approach of deriving risk-optimized test cases using reinforcement learning and we have applied the method to a case study provided by an industrial partner. The case study showed, in particular, that the assessment of the criticality of actions by experts is matched by the values learned by reinforcement learning.

The remainder of this paper is structured as follows: In Sect. 2, we outline the used behavior models. Based on these models, we show in Sect. 3 how the criticality of faults can be estimated using reinforcement learning. In Sect. 4, we present our method for deriving a desired number of test cases that cover as much criticality as possible. Section 5 shows how the overall approach scales in an industrial case study in which we applied the concepts to a mobile payment system. After placing our approach in context with related work in Sect. 6, we give an outlook to future investigations in Sect. 7.

2   Test Model Specifications

We build our approach on three inputs: (1) models for the desired behavior of all local SuT components together with a precise description of their communication paradigm; (2) a fault model for implementation and communication defects spanning the fault variability space; and (3) an (expert's) estimate of critical global system situations.

2.1   Behavior SuT Models and Their Communication

Though our testing approach is not limited to a particular formalism of behavior models, for conciseness, we use in the following a rather simple model of non-deterministic finite state machines communicating over a broadcasting message bus. The execution of an assembly of such components happens in rounds in which each component chooses some currently possible action: An action is possible if all of its message dependencies have been satisfied; a component stutters if, and only if, no such action is available.

For a concrete example, consider the three components M, N and O in Figs. 1a to c. The transition $M1 \xrightarrow{a!} M2$ of M defines an action that broadcasts the message a; $N1 \xrightarrow{a?/d!} N2$ of N defines an action that broadcasts the message d when message a is received; and $O1 \xrightarrow{d?} O2$ of O defines an action that does not broadcast any message when d is received. In addition to possible broadcasts, every action defines the executing component's change in state. Figure 1d shows the composition of M, N, and O according to broadcasting communication: A local action that broadcasts a message by M leads to a local action receiving the message by N and vice versa. Furthermore, the actions $N1 \xrightarrow{a?/d!} N2$ and $M2 \xrightarrow{b?/e!} M1$ trigger the actions $O1 \xrightarrow{d?} O2$ and $O2 \xrightarrow{e?} O1$ in O, respectively. In particular, action $M1 \xrightarrow{a!} M2$ causes the global effect that the entire system will change its state to M2N2O2. By contrast, if in the next round N chooses action $N2 \xrightarrow{c!} N3$, M has to choose $M2 \xrightarrow{c?} M3$ and O has to stutter.

The composition of those *component behavior models* forms the *system behavior model*. This model shows the resulting composed actions as well as the reachable composed states forming again a (component) behavior model.

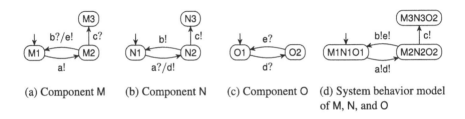

(a) Component M   (b) Component N   (c) Component O   (d) System behavior model of M, N, and O

Fig. 1. Model of the components M, N and O and their broadcasting composition.

2.2   Fault Models

The given behavior models for the SuT describe exclusively desired system behavior. The actual system behavior could, however, differ in an unknown way because of, e.g., implementation or communication faults. Since considering all imaginable faults would be quite demanding, we content ourselves with "common faults", i.e., classes of faults that are known to be frequently made. We assume the common faults to be specified in fault models defining their representation in the behavior models of the SuT. Based on them, we generate our proper *component test models* extending the given behavior models with faulty behavior using mutation.

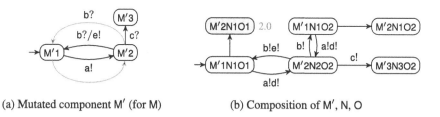

(a) Mutated component M′ (for M)   (b) Composition of M′, N, O

Fig. 2. Component test model based on the fault model of message losses and resulting system test model composing M′, N and O. Depicted in gray in (b), the system test model has been complemented by a negative situation M′2−O1 with negativity score $\nu = 2.0$.

In communicating components such as M, N and O, an exemplary common fault is the loss of messages. The associated fault model could define its representation as mutations of broadcasting transitions leaving out some messages to send. Figure 2a shows the generated test model M′ of component M for this fault model; M′1, M′2, and M′3 are just different names for M1, M2, and M3, only transitions have been added. The composition of the component test model M′, i.e., the mutated component M, and the original component behavior models N and O, shown in Fig. 2b, renders several new composed states reachable, in particular M′2N1O1, M′2N1O2, and M′N1O2. A composition involving at least one component test model is called *system test model*, as opposed to the fault-free system behavior model.

2.3   Negative Situations

By their non-deterministic nature, our test models comprise different behavior variations of the SuT, and we do not know which of them is actually implemented. Our aim is to identify those variations that would be associated with the most critical failures. However, the assessment of a failure's criticality is rather subjective and therefore hard to automate. Thus, we assume critical failures as well as a score for their criticality to be given as inputs. We represent such failures by *negative situations* described by a tuple of component states that associates each component with at most one state. Negative situations are annotated with a *negativity score* $\nu \in \mathbb{R}_{>0}$ quantifying their criticality.

In the example of components M, N, and O, a negative situation could be given by M2−O1, i.e., all those system states where component M is in state M2 and component O is in state O1; we choose $\nu = 2.0$. For the system test model, state M2 now corresponds to M′2 (see Fig. 2a) and thus all composed states of the form M′2−O1 are deemed critical. In our example (see Fig. 2b), just M′2N1O1 is reachable. Obviously, this negative situation is not reachable in the system behavior model (cf. Fig. 1). This observation matches with the fact that failures should only be reachable through faulty behavior.

3   From Failure Negativity to Fault Criticality

Let now a system test model, composed of component test models according to a fault model, and an additional set of negative situations be given. In this system test model, an action looks the more critical the higher the probability that negative situations are reached through this action and the higher the negativity scores of the reachable negative situations. Consequently, to be able to focus the test effort on revealing the most critical faults, we first have to quantify these expectations for every action. In other words, we have to map the critical failures (represented by negative situations) to those faulty and specified actions of the component test models which lead to them, and give local negativity scores to such actions. This process shows similarities to introducing decision makers, such as malicious developers, that exercise control over our models. They aim to collect the maximally possible negativity score and thus are trying to find the most critical actions.

A more formal way for modeling this task of making sequential decisions is provided by the framework of *Markov Decision Processes* (MDPs) [6]. An MDP is described by a state space S and an action space A; a map $T : S \times A \times S \rightarrow [0, 1]$ giving probabilities over state transitions, such that $T(s, a, s')$ indicates the probability that action a in state s leads o state s'; and a reward function $R : S \times A \times S \rightarrow \mathbb{R}$ denoting rewards for taking particular transitions.

In fact, we are able to express our setting as an MDP: S and A are directly constructed from the composed states and actions of the system test model. Since we do not assume that transition probabilities of the SuT are known by the tester, we suppose T for every state s and every action a to be uniformly distributed over the target states s' that are forming transitions (s, a, s') of the system test model. R reinforces transitions (s, a, s') with the negativity score of s' if s' is a negative situation, and with 0 otherwise. MDPs are meant to be partially controlled by a decision maker (often called *agent*) in the following way: in every (discrete) time step, the agent is supposed to select an action $a \in A$ that is enabled in the current state $s \in S$. This triggers a state transition according to T and offers a numerical reward signal according to R.

3.1   Solving MDPs

The task typically associated with an MDP is to find a strategy, i.e., a rule for selecting an action in any given state, that maximizes the agent's expected return (in terms of collected reward). In [15], Sutton and Barto summarize the class of so-called *reinforcement learning* methods which are designed for solving this task.

However, even though a malicious developer had to solve a reinforcement learning task for reaching a critical failure situation, ours seems different. Instead of finding a path through the system test model (or the MDP) that is supposed to offer the maximum reward, we first of all aim to assess the criticality of every action in order to eventually form a risk-optimized test suite. In terms of an MDP, we are searching for the expected returns of all actions. Fortunately, most of the reinforcement learning methods also provide us with these values. They are based on estimating value functions, i.e., mappings of states (or state-action tuples) to the expected return when being in the given state (or selecting the given action in a given state) [15]. Thus, in using one of these algorithms, we are able to estimate the actions' criticality.

Temporal difference learning, as a subclass of reinforcement learning, offers the special charm of working on sample experience and thus not requiring a model. In using a temporal difference method, we thus do not have to explicitly build the system test model which may be prohibitively large due to the number of components and possible faults. In order to exploit this advantage, we have chosen a fully decentralized approach: Within a simulation of system runs, we associate each single component of the SuT with an agent that learns the expected return of its actions. An agent's action corresponds to the simulated execution of a transition specified in the component test model. The action can be executed as soon as the specified inputs of the associated transition are present. If an action is executed, the specified messages to broadcast are sent to the other agents. In this way an agent interacts with its environment (i.e., the entirety of agents) under the rules of the system test model. The agents are synchronized by logical time steps at which each agent performs exactly one action per step. Dependencies during a time step are resolved by a scheduler which implements the chosen communication paradigm over a message bus. At the end of each time step, each agent is situated in a state defined by the associated component test model. A composed state is formed by collecting the states of every agent and each agent is reinforced according to R.

3.2   *Q*-learning

More specifically, we follow the *Q*-learning approach [18]. Each agent owns a so-called *Q*-function mapping environmental states together with actions to their expected return. We call the pair of an environmental state and an action a *decision*. After a reward R_{t+1} has been received for action a_t executed at time step t out of the environmental (global) state $\bar{s}_t$, the expected return for the decision $(\bar{s}_t, a_t)$ is updated as follows:

$$Q_{t+1}(\bar{s}_t, a_t) = Q_t(\bar{s}_t, a_t) + \alpha\big(R_{t+1} + \gamma \max_a Q_t(\bar{s}_{t+1}, a) - Q_t(\bar{s}_t, a_t)\big) \ . \qquad (1)$$

The parameters $\alpha \in\ ]0,1]$ and $\gamma \in [0,1]$ denote the *learning rate* and the *discount factor*. Decisions which have not been mapped on an expected return yet get a default assignment of 0. As one can see in Eq. 1, the expected returns – that are representing our measure of criticality – are updated with respect to a policy in which the agent chooses anytime the action with the highest criticality (represented by the max-term in 1. This *optimal policy* invokes the worst-case behavior of the component, that, as we suppose, is the most appropriate one in case of risk-based testing.

As known for *off-policy* learning [15], the evaluated policy (in our case the optimal one) is not affected by the way of generating behavior during the learning process (*behavior policy*). However, our simultaneous simulation of several agents weakens this independence, since the reachability of a negative situation may depend on decisions of multiple agents. In our running example, such a dependence can be seen at the decision of agent B for choosing action N2 $\xrightarrow{b!}$ N1 in composed state $s_1 = $ M'2N2O2. This decision could lead to different composed states depending on the selected action of agent A. Let us assume that agent A implements a behavior policy which selects each possible action with equal probability (*uniformly distributed policy*). Then, the decision for N2 $\xrightarrow{b!}$ N1 in s_1 will lead in half of the executions to $s_2 = $ M'1N1O1 and in the other half to $s_3 = $ M'1N1O2. Thus, we expect $Q($M'2N2O2, N2 $\xrightarrow{b!}$ N1$)$ in the equilibrium for (Q) (where $Q_{t+1}(\bar{s}, a) = Q_t(\bar{s}, a)$ for all $\bar{s}$ and a) to be the average of the two different outcomes $\nu(s_2) + \gamma \max_a Q(s_2, a)$ and $\nu(s_3) + \gamma \max_a Q(s_3, a)$. Table 1 shows the Q-functions of agents A, B and C for $\gamma = 0.5$ in their equilibria, assuming uniformly distributed behavior policies.

Table 1. Q-functions computed by agents for the system test model of Fig. 2b with negative situation M'2–O1, $\nu = 2.0$, and $\gamma = 0.5$.

State	Agent with action (left) and criticality (right column)					
	A for M' (see Fig. 2b)		B for N (see Fig. 1b)		C for O (see Fig. 1c)	
M'1N1O1	M'1 $\rightarrow$ M'2	2.0	N1 $\xrightarrow{a?/d!}$ N2	0.29	O1 $\xrightarrow{d?}$ O2	0.5
	M'1 $\xrightarrow{a!}$ M'2	0.5	N1 $\rightarrow$ N1	2.0	O1 $\rightarrow$ O1	2.0
M'2N2O2	M'2 $\xrightarrow{b?/e!}$ M'1	1.0	N2 $\xrightarrow{b!}$ N1	0.57	O2 $\xrightarrow{e?}$ O1	1.0
	M'2 $\xrightarrow{b?}$ M'1	0.25	N2 $\xrightarrow{c!}$ N3	0.0	O2 $\rightarrow$ O2	0.06
	M'2 $\xrightarrow{c?}$ M'3	0.0				
M'1N1O2	M'1 $\xrightarrow{a!}$ M'2	0.5	N1 $\xrightarrow{a?/d!}$ N2	0.29	O2 $\rightarrow$ O2	0.25
	M'1 $\rightarrow$ M'2	0.0	N1 $\rightarrow$ N1	0.0		

4 Deriving Tests with High Risk-Based Impact

Up to this point, we have a set of agents, each one containing a Q-function mapping decisions to criticality values. This, as an intermediate result, would enable the imaginary malicious developer of Sect. 1 to implement the most critical faults in his component; and it enables us to assess observed decisions of any of the SuT's components in real operation. However, we still want to use this learned information for generating test cases covering the most critical faults. For this purpose, two things have to be considered: (1) Positive test cases, as we exclusively consider in this paper, do only include decisions with specified actions (*specified decisions*) but are able to detect implemented decisions with mutated actions (*mutated decisions*). More precisely, we assume the test of a specified decision to detect all of its mutants, i.e., decisions with the same state but with actions that are mutants of that contained in the specified decision. Hence, we have to distinguish between a decision's criticality and a specified decision's relevance for being tested that, in fact, should even comprise the criticality values of its mutants. (2) A Q-function, as we formed it, assesses decisions with local actions (*local decisions*). A system test case, however, should specify the execution of *global decisions* involving one local decision per component.

Thus, we assess the relevance in (1) local and (2) global relevance functions whereby the latter depends on the first. System test cases then are generated and assessed using the global relevance functions.

4.1 Relevance Functions

The local relevance function r maps each specified local decision to its relevance for being tested. We define the relevance of a decision by the sum of the criticality values of its mutants. This is reasonable, since a specified decision is deemed to reveal all of its mutants if they are implemented. From a mutation-based testing perspective, the relevance can be seen as the reward for killing a set of mutants. More formally, for a specified decision $d = (\bar{s}, a)$, let $M(d)$ be the set of mutated decisions whose actions are mutants of a and whose composed state is $\bar{s}$. Then we define

$$r(d) = Q(d) + \sum_{d' \in M(d)} Q(d') \ .$$

Continuing the above example, Table 2a shows the local relevance function for agent A. The local relevance functions for agents B and C are the Q-functions of these agents as shown in Table 1, as they involve no mutated decision.

The global relevance function $\bar{r}$ maps each *possible* global decision to its relevance for being tested. A global decision $\bar{d}$ consists of one specified (local) decision per agent. A global decision is possible iff the contained local decisions can be made at the same time. Thus, the local decisions contained in a possible global decision share the same composed state and actions which satisfy the chosen communication paradigm. Since only the specified local decisions are considered, but not their mutants that would result in much more possible global decisions, the computation of the set of global decisions turns out to be feasible,

Table 2. Relevance functions on the basis of the Q-functions in Table 1.

Local decision		
State	Action	Relevance
M'1N1O1	M'1 $\xrightarrow{a!}$ M'2	2.5
M'2N2O2	M'2 $\xrightarrow{b?/e!}$ M'1	1.25
M'2N2O2	M'2 $\xrightarrow{c?}$ M'3	0.0
M'1N1O2	M'1 $\xrightarrow{a!}$ M'2	0.5

Decision name	Action	Relevance
d1	M'1N1O1 $\xrightarrow{a!d!}$ M'2N2O2	3.29
d2	M'2N2O2 $\xrightarrow{b!e!}$ M'1N1O1	2.82
d3	M'2N2O2 $\xrightarrow{c!}$ M'3N3O2	0.06
d4	M'1N1O2 $\xrightarrow{a!d!}$ M'2N2O2	1.04

(a) Local relevance function for agent A.

(b) Global relevance function on the basis of the local relevance functions in Tab. 2a.

even for rather complex models. The execution of a global decision by a test case implies the execution of all included specified (local) decisions. We define a global decision $\overline{d}$ to be as relevant as the sum of its local decisions:

$$\overline{r}(\overline{d}) = \sum_{d \in \overline{d}} r(d) \ .$$

Table 2b shows the global relevance function for our running example of agents A, B and C where we abbreviate a global decision by its resulting composed action in the system test model.

4.2   Deriving Logical Test Cases

Building on the global relevance function, we are now able to derive a *risk-optimized test suite*, i.e., a suite of a desired number of logical interoperability test cases that covers as much relevance as possible. A logical test case comprises a path through the system behavior model starting from the initial state. However, we still want to avoid computing the complete system behavior model. In fact, since the criticality and relevance values were learned by sample experience, we have no guarantee that each composed action of the system behavior model has been reached and thus assessed by the global relevance function. Hence we directly consider the graph of the global relevance function, linking the states of the assessed global decisions with their defined composed actions. Decisions that cannot be reached from the composed source state, such as $d4$ in our example, are ignored. Then, a logical test case, i.e., a sequence of global decisions in the graph of the global relevance function, covers the relevance of each comprised decision.

In practice, the number of executable and assessable test cases is typically limited by an upper bound σ, particularly for huge systems with many components. Hence, we are looking for the σ test cases covering the most relevant decisions with σ given by the tester. More formally, if $\mathcal{P}_\sigma$ is the set of all cycle-free path sets with cardinality σ and $\overline{r}(P) = \sum_{\overline{d} \in P} \overline{r}(\overline{d})$ for each $P \in \mathcal{P}_\sigma$, we aim to find $ts = \arg\max\{\overline{r}(P) \mid P \in \mathcal{P}_\sigma\}$, i.e., a test suite ts with the maximum relevance. We solve this maximization problem by (1) identifying all cycle-free

Table 3. Test case selection algorithm and test cases generated for the case study.

1: $ts \leftarrow \emptyset$
2: **while** $|ts| \leq \sigma \wedge \exists \pi \in paths\,.\,\sum_{\bar{d} \in \pi} \bar{r}(\bar{d}) > 0$ **do**
3:     **choose** $\pi \in \arg\max\{\sum_{\bar{d} \in \pi} \bar{r}(\bar{d}) \mid \pi \in paths\}$
4:     $ts \leftarrow ts \cup \{\pi\}$ ▷ (2)
5:     **for all** $\bar{d} \in \pi$ **do** $\bar{r}(\bar{d}) \leftarrow 0$ ▷ (3)
6: **return** ts

(a) Iterative test case selection

No.	Test case	Cov. relev.
1	$d1 \rightarrow d2$	6.11
2	$d1 \rightarrow d3$	0.06

(b) Test cases generated for Tab. 2b with covered relevance.

paths through the graph of the global relevance function, (2) iteratively adding test cases to the test suite, and (3) updating the values of the global relevance function after adding a test case. Table 3a implements (2) and (3) for the set *paths* identified in (1). Since the relevance values of covered global decisions are set to zero (see Table 3), the derived test suite cannot contain a path twice. Table 3b shows the test cases of a generated test suite with an upper bound $\sigma = 2$ for our running example.

The presented algorithm generally works for every graph with weighted edges. In addition to relevance values resulting from the proposed learning procedure, the tester is thus able to introduce any desired custom weights. The algorithm in Table 3a, in particular, generates test cases out of the global relevance function which exclusively comprises specified decisions. Thus, it does not suffer from the major state space blow up resulting from the inclusion of mutations. Though it repeatedly iterates through the state space, the following case study will show that this test case generation is indeed feasible, at least for moderately sized systems.

5 Evaluation Within a Mobile Payment Application

We implemented our risk-based interoperability testing procedure in a research prototype. For evaluation, we applied it to the specification of a mobile payment system provided by an industrial partner.

5.1 Inputs and Implications for an Optimal Test Suite

Mobile payment systems enable customers to pay goods or services cashless with their mobile phone. We extracted the involved components of such an application and translated them into finite state machines as inputs for our prototype. For conciseness, we thereby focused on the use case of the actual payment process. Figures 3a to f show the resulting component models: the *user interface* (typically an app on the user's mobile phone, component UI), the *cashier* (the cashier himself, C), the *cash desk* (the software deployed on the cash desk for processing the payment, CD), the *retailer system* (a central server on the retailer side, R), the *service provider* (a server handling the payment process, S), and the

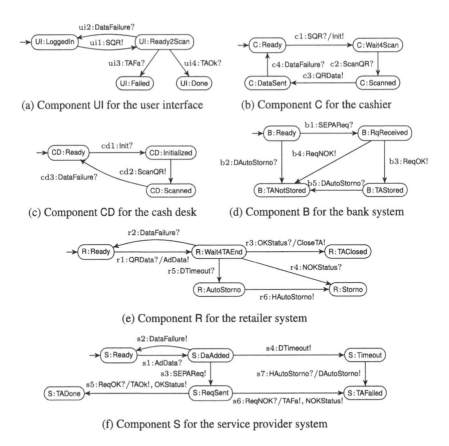

(a) Component UI for the user interface

(b) Component C for the cashier

(c) Component CD for the cash desk

(d) Component B for the bank system

(e) Component R for the retailer system

(f) Component S for the service provider system

Fig. 3. Component behavior models for the mobile payment case study.

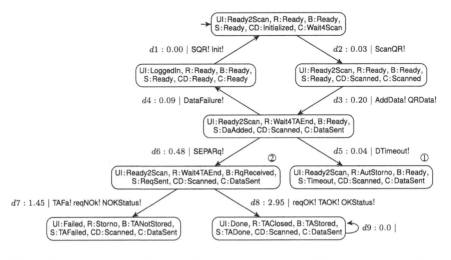

Fig. 4. Generated graph of the mobile payment system's global relevance function.

bank system (the bank's service for processing a transaction, B). Every action in the presented models is named by a prefix at the message specification, e.g., UI:LoggedIn $\xrightarrow{\text{ui1:SQR!}}$ UI:Ready2Scan. Each component exclusively consumes the messages for which it is authorized. Thus, even though the considered communication over a broadcasting message bus would not be explicitly implemented for a mobile payment system, it does not restrict the presented models in representing the intended communication behavior.

We consider situations to be critical where the retailer assumes the success of a transaction although the bank refused it. In the models, these situations can be described by those system states in which the bank is in B:TANotStored while the retailer system is in R:TAClosed. In such system states, the service provider could be either in S:TAFailed or in S:TADone. Thus, we distinguish the following two negative situations, each one annotated with an exemplary negativity score of 1.0 ("−" indicates that the corresponding component may be in arbitrary state):

1. UI:−, C:−, CD:−, R:TAClosed, S:TAFailed, B:TANotStored
2. UI:−, C:−, CD:−, R:TAClosed, S:TADone, B:TANotStored

For the purpose of this case study, we exclusively considered output faults, i.e., faults in sending messages. Thereby we identified three classes of common faults: (1) message loss, (2) sending of a wrong message, and (3) delay in sending a message. The associated fault models mutate transitions as follows: For (1), message losses, no outgoing message is sent at all. For (2), wrong messages, messages are sent which originally are defined for being sent on other transitions with the same source state as the mutated one. The messages which are defined for being sent on the mutated transition are not sent. Finally, for (3), delayed messages, specified outgoing messages on a transition t_1 are shifted to any other transition t_2 reachable from the target state of t_1. Whilst t_1 then sends no message at all, t_2 sends a random message out of all delayed messages in addition to the originally defined ones on t_2.

Considering the resulting mutants, the defined negative situations are only reachable if the bank system chooses transition b4. If the bank system sends the wrong message ReqOK on b4, the service provider has to enter S:TADone. Then, negative situation 2 occurs, if the service provider sends the specified message OKStatus. Even if the bank system sends the specified message on b4 a negative situation could occur: The service provider has to choose s6 into S:TAFailed; if it thereby sends the faulty message OKStatus, the retailer enters R:TAClosed and negative situation 1 is reached.

Thus, it can be assumed that composed actions which include r3, s5, and b4 or r3, s6, and b4 are crucial for the reachability of negative situations. These actions, which we are referencing in the following as $\{r3, s5, b4\}$ and $\{r3, s6, b4\}$, should be associated with higher relevance values than the others. The other composed actions cannot directly lead to a negative situation, and their relevance should depend on the length of the paths which are leading to $\{r3, s5, b4\}$ and $\{r3, s6, b4\}$. A risk-optimized test suite should preferably test paths leading through $\{r3, s5, b4\}$ and $\{r3, s6, b4\}$.

Table 4. Case study results: (a) Test cases generated for the global relevance function in Fig. 4 with their covered relevance. (b) Results for ten executions with different numbers of simulation runs; the right-most columns show the number of generated test suites that contain both expected test cases of (a) or at least one of them.

No.	Test case	Cov. relev.
1	$d1 \to d2 \to d3 \to d6 \to d8 \to d9$	3.68
2	$d1 \to d2 \to d3 \to d6 \to d7$	1.45
3	$d1 \to d2 \to d3 \to d4$	0.09
4	$d1 \to d2 \to d3 \to d5$	0.04

#Sim. runs	∅Neg. sit. reached	#Test suites with 2	with ≥ 1
100	0.0	0	0
1,000	0.4	0	0
5,000	1.7	2	6
10,000	2.0	7	9
100,000	33.7	10	10

(a) Test cases generated for Fig. 4.   (b) Results for different simulation runs.

5.2 Application and Results

We applied our prototype on the inputs described in Sect. 5.1. For this evaluation, we chose a fixed learning rate of $\alpha = 0.1$ and a fixed discount factor of $\gamma = 0.5$. Furthermore, for promoting exploration within the simulation procedure, all agents were reset to their initial states when (1) a negative situation was reached, (2) no negative situation was reachable anymore, or (3) the number of global decisions made since the last reset exceeded the upper bound of 100. Figure 4 shows the graph of the global relevance function generated with 100,000 simulation runs, i.e., sequences of global decisions from the agents' initial states up to the next reset. The graph contains one edge per crucial composed action: edge $d7$ contains $\{r3, s5, b4\}$, $d8$ contains $\{r3, s6, b4\}$. As expected in Sect. 5.1, their relevance is predominant. In correspondence with the system behavior model and the reset conditions mentioned above, the graph includes the following paths:

1. $d1 \to d2 \to d3 \to d4$
2. $d1 \to d2 \to d3 \to d5$
3. $d1 \to d2 \to d3 \to d6 \to d7$
4. $d1 \to d2 \to d3 \to d6 \to d8 \to d9$

Paths 1 and 2 cover the most relevant composed actions $d7$ and $d8$ and thus should be contained in a risk optimized test suite with an upper bound of 2 as test cases. Table 4a shows the actually generated test cases for the global relevance function shown in Fig. 4 together with their covered relevance. The test case order seems to be plausible—for an upper bound of 2 exactly the defined test cases would be chosen.

However, the chosen behavior strategy cannot assure that every possible combination of local decisions is covered during the simulation. Since number and kind of chosen decisions may differ, we can not even assure that different executions of the prototype will lead to the same results. In fact, because of the uniformly distributed behavior policy, it is rather unlikely to get the same absolute relevance values twice. Because of the convergence of learning, the returned values, however, should become the more representative the higher the number of executed simulation runs. To investigate the stability of the results, we executed the prototype several times with the same inputs but a different number of simulation runs, in each case ten times. Table 4b shows the frequency the expected test suite had been generated, the frequency the generated test suite at least contained one of the two expected test cases, and the average number of reached negative situations within the ten executions for the different number of simulation runs. Obviously, the average number of reached negative situations increases with the number of simulation runs. The higher the number of reached negative situations, the more often the expected test suite is generated. For 100,000 simulation runs and an average of 33.7 reached negative situations, every execution generates the expected test suite. This result implies, on the one hand, that a more focused behavior strategy could be useful. If it would lead to a higher average number of reached negative situations, the expected test suite could be generated constantly for less simulation runs. On the other hand, the proposed approach leads to acceptable results, even if the state space is not fully explored many times. Although the expected test suite had been generated only two times out of ten executions for 5,000 simulation runs, it contained 6 times at least one of the desired test cases. Such a test suite covers wide parts of the model's relevance.

6   Related Work

Our approach combines interoperability testing, risk-based testing, and test case generation with reinforcement learning.

Machine Learning. The application of *machine learning techniques* on software testing has already been identified as a fruitful perspective by Groce et al. [9]. In [8], Groce uses reinforcement learning via *adaption-based programming* for test input generation. This method rewards coverage increases during test execution to achieve a higher coverage than random testing. By contrast, our method uses reinforcement learning for assessing the criticality of possible faults before test execution. Veanes et al. [17] present a technique inspired by reinforcement learning for choosing coverage optimizing test actions in online testing, i.e., the combination of test generation and test execution in a single algorithm. They also do not consider risk estimations.

Interoperability Testing. For generating *interoperability* test cases, it is a common technique to form a system test model by the composition of several component test models. Luo et al. [11] reduce a set of *communicating non-deterministic finite state machines* to a single machine and generate test sequences from this machine. Seol et al. [13] propose a method that composes *input/output state machines* to generate interoperability test cases. Though our algorithm for generating test cases from the global relevance function implements a similar approach, it additionally takes into account the relevance of actions for being tested. In fact, in [11, 13] the number of generated test cases depends on the composed, global model's complexity, whereas our approach generates a desired number of risk-optimized test cases.

Risk-Based Testing. Building on general high-level considerations from authors such as Bach [2] or Amland [1], several methods for integrating *risk estimations* in testing evolved though at different levels of automation. Similar to our approach, several works propose the use of test models for the SuT, which are getting annotated by risk values, for deriving or even generating test cases: Kloos et al. [10] construct test models from the results of a fault tree analysis from which test cases can be generated. Bauer et al. [4] transfer the risk of annotated UML diagrams to a test model, from which test cases are derived. Zimmermann et al. [20] extend this approach by refining the test models so that from these only so-called *critical* test cases are generated. Wendland et al. [19] propose to formulate requirements for the SuT in so-called *integrated behavior trees*. These are annotated with risk values associated with certain risk levels. A risk-optimized test suite is generated from the annotated models by using test directives. In all of these approaches the risk assessment is done by experts. Also our approach builds on expert estimation, since the most critical failure situations have to be given. However, in contrast to the mentioned methods, we automatically derive the contribution of the component's actions to critical situations.

Stallbaum and Metzger [14] note that the *risk assessment* of test cases done by experts could get a critical cost factor. They propose an approach that automates the risk assessment based on requirement metrics. Such metrics refer for example to the revision frequency or the cyclomatic complexity of a use case. However, the determination of risk exposures is still done by experts. The use of metrics for risk estimation in testing was also proposed by Amland [1]. He calculates so called *risk indicators* for every function of the SuT from which the occurrence probability of failures can be estimated. The exposure of possible failures is quantified by expert estimates. No hint is given on how to derive test cases based on these considerations. Since Amland [1] assesses rather the probability and costs of possible failures than a fault criticality, his method could be used for identifying the most hazardous failures together with their deemed effect as input for our approach. Altogether, we assume that metrics are eligible for approximating the occurrence probability of faults in different parts of the system. The assessment of the criticality of faults, however, is hard to determine using code or requirement metrics. Our approach of assessing the criticality of faults by their contribution to the reachability of failures seems more reasonable. In the future, metrics-based approaches could be used to extend our approach with assumed occurrence probabilities of faults.

Probabilistic Model Checking. Not only from the strict risk-based testing perspective, the model-based test case generation is an active research topic. Fraser et al. [7] summarize methods which are using *model checkers* for this task. The fundamental idea behind this approach is to formulate logical properties on a model of the SuT in such a way that the counterexamples returned by the model checker can be interpreted as test cases. Closest to our approach are the mutation-based test case generation approaches [7]: Mutations are introduced in the inputs of the model checker according to some fault model and then logical properties are formulated for getting counterexamples representing test cases that kill the mutants. Traditional model checkers, however, only return single counterexamples for absolute properties, such as "The system will never reach a negative situation", whereas the metrics of fault criticality and action relevance imply the need for quantitative properties, such as "The system will reach a negativity score of 10 with a probability of at most 0.4". For evaluating such quantitative properties we would need to use *probabilistic model checkers* which are able to solve verification tasks on Markov-Chains and Markov-Decision-Processes [3]. In fact, we believe that our approach is implementable by such model checkers. The performance could, however, be rather unsatisfactory, since a probabilistic model checker would have to consider the system test model with all of the introduced mutants for evaluating given quantitative properties.

7   Conclusions and Future Work

We have presented a risk-based generation procedure for interoperability test cases. It extends behavior models of the SuT with possible faults and assesses them by their criticality w.r.t. reachable failures. An agent-based simulation using the technique of reinforcement learning automates wide parts of this process: Each component of the system is associated with a software agent which learns the criticality of possible faults during a parallel simulation of all agents. The global relevance function is formed by merging the learned criticality values of the agents. Afterwards, Table 3a generates a risk-optimized test suite out of the graph of the global relevance function. We applied a prototype on parts of a specification of a mobile payment system. It could be seen that the quality of results increases with the number of executed simulation runs. With 100,000 simulation runs the prototype generated constantly the expected test suite. These observations emphasize the general eligibility of the presented approach.

However, several concepts still can be optimized. More sophisticated agent behavior strategies could lead to the expected results with fewer simulation runs. The agents currently make random decisions between their possible actions thus not always hitting the worst-case behavior of the system. Letting the agents, however, always choose the decision with the highest criticality value, exploration is nearly dropped. Hence, some other strategies should be studied that balance between exploration and exploitation. We exclusively considered the worst-case behavior of the SuT, as we did not assume probabilities for choosing specified actions or for the occurrence of faults to be given. Annotating the models with such probabilities would incorporate such system behavior assumptions and lead to a kind of on-policy learning. To increase the efficiency of our algorithms, we aim to avoid calculating the set of possible global decisions from the local ones. The application of meta-heuristic techniques could further improve the scaling of the test cases generation algorithm on the global relevance function. Further case studies will be made for different system models to identify additional optimizations.

Apart from the definition of behavior models for the components we automatized every activity of the proposed approach. For further automation, these behavior models could also be generated, e.g., from common interface definitions, and the generated test cases could be transformed for a direct import into common test automation systems.

Acknowledgment. This research is partly funded by the research project *Testing self-organizing, adaptive Systems (TeSOS)* of the German Research Foundation.

References

1. Amland, S.: Risk-based testing: risk analysis fundamentals and metrics for software testing including a financial application case study. J. Syst. Softw. **53**(3), 287–295 (2000)
2. Bach, J.: Heuristic risk-based testing. Softw. Test. Qual. Eng. Mag. **11**(9), 99 (1999)
3. Baier, C., Katoen, J.P.: Principles of Model Checking. MIT Press, Cambridge (2008)
4. Bauer, T., Stallbaum, H., Metzger, A., Eschbach, R.: Risikobasierte Ableitung und Priorisierung von Testfällen für den modellbasierten Systemtest. Softw. Eng. **121**, 99–111 (2008)
5. Chen, N.: Passive interoperability testing for communication protocols. Ph.D. thesis, Université Rennes 1 (2013)
6. Feinberg, E.A., Shwartz, A.: Handbook of Markov Decision Processes: Methods and Applications, vol. 40. Springer Science & Business Media, Heidelberg (2012)
7. Fraser, G., Wotawa, F., Ammann, P.E.: Testing with model checkers: a survey. Softw. Test. Verification Reliab. **19**(3), 215–261 (2009)
8. Groce, A.: Coverage rewarded: test input generation via adaptation-based programming. In: Proceedings of the 2011 26th IEEE/ACM International Conference on Automated Software Engineering, pp. 380–383. IEEE Computer Society (2011)
9. Groce, A., Fern, A., Erwig, M., Pinto, J., Bauer, T., Alipour, A.: Learning-based test programming for programmers. In: Margaria, T., Steffen, B. (eds.) ISoLA 2012, Part I. LNCS, vol. 7609, pp. 572–586. Springer, Heidelberg (2012)
10. Kloos, J., Hussain, T., Eschbach, R.: Risk-based testing of safety-critical embedded systems driven by fault tree analysis. In: 4th International Conference on Software Testing, Verification and Validation Workshops (ICSTW), pp. 26–33. IEEE (2011)
11. Luo, G., Bochmann, G., Petrenko, A.: Test selection based on communicating non-deterministic finite-state machines using a generalized Wp-method. IEEE Trans. Softw. Eng. **20**(2), 149–162 (1994)
12. Offutt, A.J., Untch, R.H.: Mutation 2000: uniting the orthogonal. In: Wong, W.E. (ed.) Mutation Testing for the New Century. The Springer International Series on Advances in Database Systems, vol. 24, pp. 34–44. Springer, Heidelberg (2001)
13. Seol, S., Kim, M., Chanson, S.T., Kang, S.: Interoperability test generation and minimization for communication protocols based on the multiple stimuli principle. IEEE J. Sel. Areas Commun. **22**(10), 2062–2074 (2004)
14. Stallbaum, H., Metzger, A.: Employing requirements metrics for automating early risk assessment. In: Wsh. Measuring Requirements for Project and Product Success (MeReP), pp. 1–12 (2007)

15. Sutton, R.S., Barto, A.G.: Reinforcement Learning: An Introduction. MIT Press, Cambridge (1998)
16. Utting, M., Legeard, B.: Practical Model-based Testing: A Tools Approach. Elsevier, Amsterdam (2006)
17. Veanes, M., Roy, P., Campbell, C.: Online testing with reinforcement learning. In: Havelund, K., Núñez, M., Roşu, G., Wolff, B. (eds.) FATES/RV -2006. LNCS, vol. 4262, pp. 240–253. Springer, Heidelberg (2006). doi:10.1007/11940197_16
18. Watkins, C.J.C.H., Dayan, P.: Q-learning. Mach. Learn. 8(3–4), 279–292 (1992)
19. Wendland, M.F., Kranz, M., Schieferdecker, I.: A Systematic approach to risk-based testing using risk-annotated requirements models. In: 7th International Conference on Software Engineering Advances (ICSEA), pp. 636–642 (2012)
20. Zimmermann, F., Eschbach, R., Kloos, J., Bauer, T.: Risk-based statistical testing: a refinement-based approach to the reliability analysis of safety-critical systems. In: 12th European Workshop on Dependable Computing (EWDC) (2009)

A Combinatorial Approach to Analyzing Cross-Site Scripting (XSS) Vulnerabilities in Web Application Security Testing

Dimitris E. Simos[1]([✉]), Kristoffer Kleine[1],
Laleh Shikh Gholamhossein Ghandehari[2], Bernhard Garn[1], and Yu Lei[2]

[1] SBA Research, 1040 Vienna, Austria
{dsimos,kkleine,bgarn}@sba-research.org
[2] Department of Computer Science and Engineering,
University of Texas at Arlington, Arlington, TX 76019, USA
laleh.shikhgholamhosseing@mavs.uta.edu, ylei@cse.uta.edu

Abstract. Web applications typically employ sanitization functions to sanitize user inputs, independently whether this input is assumed to be legitimate, invalid or malicious. When such functions do not work correctly, a web application immediately becomes vulnerable to security attacks such as XSS. In this paper, we report a combinatorial approach to analyze XSS vulnerabilities in web applications. Our approach first performs combinatorial testing where a set of test vectors is executed against a subject application. If one or more XSS vulnerabilities are triggered during testing, we analyze the structure of each test vector to identify XSS-inducing combinations of its parameter model. If an attack vector contains an XSS-inducing combination, then the execution of this vector will successfully exploit an XSS vulnerability. Identification of XSS-inducing combinations provides insights about which kinds of user input might still be leverageable for XSS attacks and how to correct the function to provide better security guarantees. We conducted an experiment in which our approach was applied to four sanitization functions from the Web Application Vulnerability Scanner Evaluation Project (WAVSEP). The experimental results show that our approach can effectively identify XSS-inducing combinations for these sanitization functions.

Keywords: Combinatorial testing · XSS · Fault localization · Security testing

1 Introduction

Web application security is as important as ever but pervasive ubiquitous computing, bundled with 24/7 network access, makes any connected web application especially susceptible to attacks. Naturally, injection attacks are remote exploits

© IFIP International Federation for Information Processing 2016
Published by Springer International Publishing AG 2016. All Rights Reserved
F. Wotawa et al. (Eds.): ICTSS 2016, LNCS 9976, pp. 70–85, 2016.
DOI: 10.1007/978-3-319-47443-4_5

which can cause security breaches. Cross-site scripting (XSS) falls into this category and constitutes the third serious vulnerability according to the Open Web Application Security Project (OWASP) [22]. We focus on analyzing XSS vulnerabilities where we distinguish between two different types of XSS, namely reflected XSS and stored XSS. In the former case the web server response contains some data from the corresponding request, while the latter case includes data stored permanently on the server (e.g., in a database). In line of this work we are concerned only for reflected XSS vulnerabilities.

In this paper, we apply for the *first time* a fault-localization technique based on combinatorial methods to identify one or more combinations of input parameter values that would definitely trigger an XSS vulnerability for a given system under test (SUT). We refer to these combinations as XSS-inducing combinations or simply inducing combinations. If an XSS attack vector (test vector) contains an inducing combination, then the execution of this test vector against the SUT will successfully exploit an XSS vulnerability. The identification of inducing combinations provides important information about why an input filter fails to sanitize a malicious vector, which in turns helps to make necessary corrections.

Note that this is different from traditional fault localization, which is aimed at identifying the location of a fault in the source code. Sanitization functions are typically employed in web applications to sanitize invalid or malicious user inputs. XSS vulnerabilities, if they exist, are in most cases contained in these sanitization functions, which are mostly simply referred to as *filters*. Thus, the location of an XSS vulnerability in the source code is typically considered known or not difficult to be identified. However, designing and implementing rigorous and secure input filters is a very complicated and challenging task [1]. In particular, when an input filter does not work as expected, it could be difficult for one to understand why it does not work and how to correct a vulnerable filter. The results of this paper enhance the capabilities of security testers to design better attack models for web applications but at the same time guide the developers on how to improve the filtering mechanisms met in such applications.

In Sect. 2 we describe related work for web application security testing and fault localization techniques. Sections 3 and 5 reviews past achievements on combinatorial testing for web security testing and fault localization methods, respectively, that relate to this work. Section 4 discusses the test execution method used in this work. In Sect. 6 we present our methodology for analyzing XSS vulnerabilities using combinatorial based fault localization methods. An experimental evaluation that validates our approach is given in Sect. 7. Finally, Sect. 8 concludes the work and discusses directions for future work.

2   Related Work

In this section, we describe related works with respect to fault localization approaches for combinatorial testing and security testing frameworks devoted to XSS detection. For a systematic literature review on research devoted to XSS we refer to [12] while for important contributions in combinatorial testing and fault localization that relate to the work presented in this paper we refer to Sects. 3 and 5, respectively, and cited references there in.

Web Application Security Testing Frameworks. Security testing is meant to support vulnerability detection, and for this task several approaches and tools have been developed in the past. In the following, we depict the most important of them. A comparison of several penetration testing tools is given in [7,15]. The authors of these works compare commercial as well as open source penetration testing tools by testing several web applications. Security testing tools incorporating fuzzing techniques have been presented in [5,6,20]. The authors of the last two works apply evolutionary approaches and learning in order to detect potential vulnerabilities. Even though these works add towards test automation, complete automation of the security testing process remains a very active challenge. Recent works on XSS vulnerability detection include unit testing methods that can detect XSS vulnerabilities which cannot be found by static analysis tools [16] and attack patterns for black-box security testing of web applications [19].

It is evident that even though a lot of works have been devoted to XSS vulnerability detection very few of them focus on analyzing these vulnerabilities and even fewer correlate malicious vectors with sanitizing functions.

Fault Localization Techniques Based on Combinatorial Methods. Combinatorial testing has been shown to be a very effective testing strategy [13]. A t-way combinatorial test set is designed to detect failures that are triggered by combinations involving no more than t parameters. After a failure is detected, the next task is to identify the fault that causes the failure. The problem of fault localization can be divided into two sub-problems: (1) Identifying failure-inducing combinations. A combination is failure-inducing or simply inducing if its existence in a test causes the test to fail. (2) Identifying actual faults in the source code. A fault is a code defect that can be an incorrect, extra, or missing statement. As explained in Sect. 1, we are mainly interested in identifying XSS-inducing combinations. Thus, in the following, we will focus on existing approaches to identify failure inducing combinations.

Two techniques, called FIC and FIC_BS [24], take as input a single failed test from a combinatorial test set, and identify as output a minimal inducing combination that causes the test to fail. The main idea of the two techniques consists of changing, in a systematic manner, the parameter values in the failed test. A parameter value is considered to be involved in an inducing combination if changing it to a different value causes the failed test to pass. It is assumed that changing a parameter value does not introduce any new inducing combination.

The AIFL technique in [18] first identifies a set of suspicious combinations as candidates for being inducing. Second, it generates a group of tests for each failed test. After executing the newly generated tests, combinations which appeared in the passed tests are removed from the suspicious set. The IterAIFL technique is an iterative approach proposed by Wang et al. in [21]. It iteratively generates and refines suspicious set until it becomes stable.

In our earlier work, we developed a approach called BEN that identifies suspicious combinations in the same way as `AIFL` and `IterAIFL`. However, BEN produces a ranking of suspicious combinations and focuses on the most suspicious combinations. Moreover, BEN significantly differs from `AIFL` and `IterAIFL` in the way of generating new tests. A detailed description of BEN is given in Sect. 5.

Lastly, to the best of our knowledge this is the first work where combinatorial based fault localization techniques are applied to analyze security vulnerabilities.

3   Combinatorial Testing for Web Security Testing

Combinatorial testing has been successfully applied for testing (critical) software systems in large organizations [11]. It is an already proven method for black-box security testing of large-scale web software systems [2,3,7] where t-way testing was applied successfully to XSS detection. In this section, we review these key contributions in web security testing that are based on combinatorial methods and are used as a basis for analyzing XSS vulnerabilities via fault localization methods throughout this paper. For a general treatment of the field of combinatorial testing we refer the interest reader to the surveys of [4,17].

Throughout this paper, we are uniformly using a strength four ($t = 4$) test set against the SUTs for reasons explained later in this section. The underlying combinatorial model of XSS attack vectors is a refined and extended version from the works in [2,7] and is a form of input parameter model [10]. Its goal is to discretize the input space to parameters and discrete values so that these can be given to combinatorial testing tools.

The generated test vectors aim at producing valid JavaScript code when these are executed against SUTs. A description of parameters that appear in the input model has briefly been mentioned in [2,7], however we give an excerpt here, for the sake of completeness:

- The **JSO** (JavaScript Opening Tags) type represents tags that open a JavaScript code block.
- The **WS** (white space) type family represents white space characters.
- The **INT** (input termination) type represents values that terminate the original valid tags (HTML or others).
- The **EVH** (event handler) type contains values for JavaScript event handlers.
- The **PAY** (payload) type contains executable JavaScript.
- The **PAS** (payload suffix) type contains different values that should terminate the executable JavaScript payload (PAY parameter).
- The **JSE** (JavaScript end tag) type contains different forms of JavaScript end tags.

Moreover, this input model is optimized to fit to the employed test execution method (see Sect. 4). A suitable metric has been introduced in [2] to assess the quality of produced combinatorial test sets for XSS detection, called exploitation rate (ER), which measures the proportion of XSS attack vectors that were successful, e.g. the ones that exploit an XSS vulnerability, per given test set and SUT.

In particular, past work of ours has revealed that the usage of a 4-way test set (with constraints) yields satisfactory practical results for web application security testing and is justified as follows:

- In the majority of our past security testing experiments [2,3,7] we have witnessed that higher strength interaction testing yields better results w.r.t. exploitation rate. More specifically, we were able to report an increase in the exploitation rate when moving from 2-way to 3-way and 4-way testing. Also, in [2] we reported on cases where only a 4-way test set was able to successfully trigger XSS exploits for specific SUTs but none of the test sets with weaker t-way coverage properties could.
- In some of our past experiments [7], we have noticed performance issues when moving from pairwise-testing to higher interaction testing. Depending on the test execution method (see Sect. 4) (i.e. used penetration testing tool), the SUT (i.e. tested HTTP parameter of a web application) and the underlying operating system, we have seen execution times to vary greatly between repeated test runs. We further noticed SUTs to become unresponsive, as well as, increased memory usage. However, we were still able to exploit XSS vulnerabilities using a 4-way test set.
- An important finding in the post-processing of 2-way test sets used in [3] was that it revealed a surprising high percentage of 3-way and 4-way combinations covered in the successful XSS attack vectors (per test set and SUT).

These statements are in accordance with a relationship known as *interaction rule* in combinatorial testing which is based on empirical data and shows that most software faults are triggered by a single parameter value, or interactions between a small number of parameters, generally two to six [14].

4   Penetration Testing Execution Methods

In this section, we provide details about the penetration testing execution method we have used in our experimental evaluation. We give a detailed description of its procedure, functionality and test oracle, applicable when testing for XSS vulnerabilities. The described method can be applied to security testing in general, but in this paper we focus explicitly on penetration testing, e.g. exploiting XSS vulnerabilities, where the main difference (to security testing) relies on the fact that we initiate the testing procedure once the web applications are installed in an operational environment. The main difference to conventional penetration testing is that we are not interested in pinpointing *where* a vulnerability is located in the source code, but rather to analyze a known vulnerable input field in a web application in order to get insights into its structure, i.e. the necessary degree of interaction to trigger the successful exploitation of an XSS vulnerability.

Test Execution. As test execution environment we used the Burp Suite[1] which is an integrated platform for performing security testing of web applications. It is widely used by security professionals since it allows to perform many penetration testing tasks.

In our case the Intruder module of BURP was used to execute our test vectors. Intruder offers automated customized attacks against web applications, to identify and exploit all kinds of security vulnerabilities including XSS attacks. In order to test an SUT we supplied its location (server, port and URL) to Intruder and also provided the position for the input parameter. Then, our test set consisting of XSS attack vectors was loaded and executed one by one. The response (HTML) of the SUT for each test vector was recorded and supplied to the test oracle in order to determine whether an XSS vulnerability was triggered.

Test Oracle. The usual penetration testing procedure is mostly concerned with finding which parts of a web application are potentially vulnerable to an XSS attack. Here, the tester submits a request with user-controlled string in a HTTP-parameter (e.g. the user enters a string <script> in a search function and submits the query) and then examines the HTML response page from the web application whether it contains any part of the submitted string. If there are no sanitization functions invoked on the input at all, then this input field is a very probable candidate for having an XSS vulnerability. It is a common practice in security testing to rely on string matching as the underlying test oracle which is commonly referred to as *reflection oracle*. This process is repeated with all HTTP parameters in a web application. However, the reflection oracle can not decide whether an identically reflected user input string would actually be executed by a web browser. Therefore, the reflection oracle decision is not indicative of the vector actually triggering an XSS vulnerability. Thus, in relation to the detection of true XSS an oracle relying on reflection alone is not infallible as it suffers both from false positives and false negatives. In order to determine if the XSS vulnerability was indeed triggered by a test vector – meaning that we have a true XSS – the response of the web application needs to be evaluated under real-world conditions.

This necessary task can be fulfilled by employing a new test oracle, henceforward called the *execution oracle*. As indicated by the name, this oracle operates similar to a web browser and evaluates/parses the page response from a web application. The generated test vectors must be designed in such a way that their behavior is detectable by the execution oracle. Additionally, in the presented form it must be ensured that this behavior is distinct from normal intended behavior by the SUT, so that we can deduce true XSS by page-parsing anomaly detection. We have used the XSS Validator extension of BURP to fill the role of the execution oracle. The inner workings of the Validator are described below in detail. We state an important fact: Under these conditions, every vector marked as triggering by the execution oracle is indeed a test vector which triggers a true XSS vulnerability exploitation and as such the execution oracle

---

[1] http://portswigger.net/burp/.

does not produce false positives. To illustrate this point, consider the test vector `onError=alert(1)` which is reflected inside the body tag of an HTML page. Under the assumption that the web application applies no filtering to the input then this vector will be reflected without changes in the page response and the reflection oracle will flag this vector. The execution oracle however, will not flag this vector because it does not exploit the vulnerability.

An instantiation of the execution oracle can be found in the XSS Validator[2] extension to BURP. This extension enhances the test execution capabilities of BURP by adding a detection mechanism of triggered XSS vulnerabilities.

The XSS Validator receives the response from the SUT (including the reflected test vector) and renders the HTML. During rendering, JavaScript contained in the website will be executed. When it is detected that JavaScript was executed which originated from a test vector then this test vector is flagged as having triggered the XSS vulnerability.

Since the Validator extension comes with its own set of test vectors and is targeted towards the detection of XSS vulnerabilities triggered by them we modified the code to use our own test vectors and adapted the detection code to recognize behavior triggered by them (see Sect. 6.2 for more details).

5 Fault Localization Based on Combinatorial Methods

BEN [8,9] adopts a spectrum-based fault localization technique and has been applied to a Siemens test set and two programs i.e., grep and gzip. It leverages the results of the combinatorial test set and generates the ranking of statements in terms of their likelihood of being faulty. BEN consists of two major phases: (1) In phase 1, BEN identifies a combination that is very likely to be a failure-inducing combination. (2) In phase 2, BEN takes the failure-inducing combination identified in phase 1 and then produces a ranking of statements in the source code by analyzing the spectra of the small group of tests.

In this work, we only applied the first phase of BEN because we are not interested on the ranking of statements in the source code since we are following a black-box security testing approach. Therefore, we focus solely on the first phase, identifying failure-inducing combinations. BEN takes the input parameter model and a t-way combinatorial test set with execution results as input, and adopts an iterative framework to identify inducing combinations of size t or larger. At each iteration, BEN analyzes a test set F, which initially is the t-way combinatorial test set taken as input. BEN first identifies a set of t-way suspicious combinations, π, then, ranks them based on their suspiciousness, i.e., likelihood to be inducing.

Next, a small set of new tests, F', is generated. If all tests in F' that contain a suspicious combination c are failing, then c is marked as an inducing combination, and the process stops. Otherwise, all tests in F', will be added to test set F, to refine the set of suspicious combinations and their ranking. BEN continues

---

[2] https://portswigger.net/bappstore.

the two steps, i.e., rank and test generation iteratively until a t-way suspicious combination is marked as an inducing combination or a stopping condition is satisfied [9]. In the latter case, no t-way inducing combination is identified, BEN increases the size of inducing combination, and tries to identify a $(t + 1)$-way inducing combination.

Rank generation and test generation are based on two notions, suspiciousness of a combination and suspiciousness of the environment of a combination. Informally, the environment of a combination consists of other parameter values that appear in the same test case. The higher the suspiciousness of a combination, the lower the suspiciousness of its environment, the higher this combination is ranked. Moreover, new tests are generated for the most suspicious combinations. Let f be a new test generated for a suspicious combination c. Test f is generated such that it contains c and the suspiciousness of the environment for c is minimized. If f fails, it is more likely to be caused by c instead of other values in f.

This process is repeated until an inducing combination is found. Note that this process must terminate, as a failed test is by definition an inducing combination. Note that if there is a resource limitation, the user can stop the process. The top-ranked suspicious combination is reported as failure-inducing combination, in this case.

6   Methodology

In this section, we present our approach for analyzing XSS vulnerabilities using combinatorial based fault localization methods. Our methodology is comprised of two parts: First executing XSS attack vectors against SUTs and second identifying one or more combinations of input values that can trigger a successful XSS exploit. Our utter goal is to map the failure-inducing combinations found to XSS-inducing combinations. As explained in Sects. 4 and 5, respectively, we used the BURP suite for the first part and the BEN tool for the second. Further, we discuss below modifications of the BEN tool needed for XSS detection and also the necessity for a refinement of the attack model.

6.1   Modifications of BEN for XSS Detection

As explained in Sect. 5, BEN first looks for a t-way inducing combination, where t is the strength of the initial test set. Since all t-way combinations are covered by the t-way combinatorial test set, BEN guarantees to identify t-way inducing combination if such a combination exists. When there is no t-way inducing combination, BEN looks for $(t + 1)$-way inducing combination that is covered by the t-way test set.

For our experiments, we modified BEN to take the size of inducing combination as well as the t-way combinatorial test set. The user can search for an inducing combination whose size is equal to, greater or less than the strength of combinatorial test set, t. When the size of inducing combination is equal to or less than t, BEN could identify inducing combination of a requested size, if there is any. When the size of inducing combination is greater than the strength of the combinatorial test set, BEN starts looking for an inducing combination with the requested size is covered by the test set. In this case, BEN does not search for t-way inducing combination, although it may exist.

In the test generation step, a set of new tests is generated for a user-specified number of top-ranked suspicious combinations. Note that the user could specify the number of top-ranked suspicious combinations and the number of tests generated for each top-ranked combination. The more tests generated, the more effort it takes to execute them, but the more confidence we have about the identified inducing combinations. Moreover, the bigger the top-ranked set, the more effort to generate and execute the new tests, but the faster an inducing combination may be identified. This is because if an inducing combination c is included in the top-ranked set, c is identified to be an inducing combination in the first iteration. Otherwise, it may take multiple iterations for c to move up into the top-ranked set.

For our experiments, we configure BEN to generate two tests for each of the five top ranked suspicious combinations at each iteration. So, at each iteration maximum 10 new tests will be added to the test set. Note that this is a practical decision made in consideration with resource constraints.

6.2 Model Refinement

We revised our combinatorial model of XSS attack vectors from [2,7] to fit to the new execution oracle based on the Validator extension of BURP and to limit the size of the generated 4-way test set (due to the performance issues mentioned in Sect. 3), resulting in a significantly more robust and sophisticated test framework able to cast a 100 % confidence decision on triggering test cases. To this end, we changed some parameter values and removed some others such that the resulting test vectors are in line with the implementation of hooks in the Validator so we can detect triggering test vectors. Most importantly, we chose two kinds of values for the payload parameter. One kind contains a call to the built-in JavaScript `alert` function while the other defines the `src` attribute pointing to some predefined and non-existing resource. Both types of these payloads trigger detectable behavior at runtime by PhantomJS. We have also verified this kind of JavaScript is not contained in our SUTs used in the experimental evaluation.

7   Experimental Evaluation

In this section, we conduct an experimental evaluation in order to validate our methodology for analyzing XSS vulnerabilities.

7.1   Design of the Experiment

The purpose of the experiment is to have a setup where we can evaluate our methodology for analyzing XSS vulnerabilities using combinatorial based fault localization techniques. To this end we choose 4 input fields as SUTs from WAVSEP, the Web Application Vulnerability Scanner Evaluation Project[3], version 1.2. WAVSEP is a web application specifically designed to allow testing for various kinds of XSS exploits, among other vulnerabilities. In contrast with training applications for web application security testing that have been thoroughly tested in the past [12], WAVSEP offers sophisticated filter mechanisms and the majority of its SUTs can be tested for XSS vulnerabilities. In the following, we give details about the chosen input fields.

In particular, we use four input HTTP parameters as SUTs out of the WAVSEP when testing for XSS vulnerabilities. Each SUT receives over HTTP one GET parameter which is reflected on the page in different contexts. Also, the input might optionally be filtered by a SUT specific sanitization function.

SUT ID	SUT name	Reflection site
1	Tag2HtmlPageScope	`<body>$input</body>`
2	Tag2TagStructure	`<input type="text" value="$input">`
3	Event2TagScope	`<img src="$input">`
4	Event2DoubleQuotePropertyScope	`<img src="$input">`

We give an description of these four SUTs, below:

SUT 1. This SUT just outputs the received parameter without modifications into the HTML body tag. Thus, possible exploits could just inject any HTML tag without having to worry about properly terminating a preceding tag in the page.

SUT 2. This SUT outputs the received parameter without modifications into the `value` attribute of an input tag.

SUT 3. This SUT outputs the received parameter into the `src` attribute of an image tag and filters angle brackets.

SUT 4. This SUT outputs the received parameter into the `src` attribute of an image tag and filters angle brackets and single quotes.

Test Vectors. We have employed the `ACTS` combinatorial test generation tool [23] for automated test generation of test vectors. The tool is developed jointly by the US National Institute of Standards and Technology and the University of Texas at Arlington and currently has more than 1400 individual and corporate users. In line of this work, we generated a 4-way test set consisting of 6891 test vectors.

Workflow. The test vectors described above were then all executed against all four SUTs and classified as either triggering an XSS vulnerability or not. Then,

---

[3] https://github.com/sectooladdict/wavsep.

BEN was run on the abstract test set together with the positions of vectors which did trigger a vulnerability (positive vectors) one time for each SUT. In the first round BEN searched for 4-way suspicious combinations and produced a set of recommended tests. These tests were then translated to concrete attack vectors and executed again. Depending on the result, BEN classified the underlying suspicious combinations either as inducing (in the case of all recommended tests succeeding) or not.

In the case that inducing combinations were found, we instructed BEN to look for lower strength faults to confirm if the fault was a true 4-way fault or an embedded lower strength fault. In the other case, when not all recommended tests succeeded, we instructed BEN to look for 5 or 6-way inducing combinations.

7.2 Results and Analysis

Here, we present our evaluation results grouped per analyzed SUT. In particular, we evaluate our findings w.r.t. underlying vulnerabilities and also correlate failure-inducing combinations with shortcomings in the filter mechanisms.

SUT 1. The initial test execution revealed 24 test vectors to trigger the XSS vulnerability. All ten recommended tests produced by BEN for 4-way suspicious combinations did not trigger the vulnerability. Therefore, we increased the strength and searched for 5 and 6-way suspicious combinations. As all eight recommended tests from 6-way suspicious combinations triggered the vulnerability we arrived at four inducing combinations of strength 6. In Table 1 we show the composition of these recommended tests and highlight in red the inducing combinations.

In the table the common structure of the triggering vectors is clearly visible as they all start with an opening `img` tag and contain a reference to the predefined resource. The other components of the inducing combination make sure that the vector does not contain any interfering characters to ensure that the vector will be parsed correctly when reflected in the page response.

Table 1. Recommended tests with embedded 6-way inducing combinations

JSO	WS1	INT	WS2	EVH	WS3	PAY	WS4	PAS	WS5	JSE
<img	ε	␣	ε	ε	ε	src="invalid"	ε	ε	ε	\>
<img	ε	␣	ε	ε	ε	src="invalid"	ε	ε	ε	'\>
<img	ε	␣	ε	ε	ε	src="invalid"	ε	ε	ε	ε
<img	ε	␣	ε	ε	ε	src="invalid"	ε	ε	ε	<</script>
<img	ε	␣	ε	ε	ε	src="invalid"	ε	ε	ε	>
<img	ε	␣	ε	ε	ε	src="invalid"	ε	ε	ε	>>
<img	ε	␣	ε	ε	ε	src="invalid"	ε	ε	ε	</script>">
<img	ε	␣	ε	ε	ε	src="invalid"	ε	ε	ε	</script>

Since this SUT applies no filter to the input parameter the final page response will include the following HTML body when the first recommended test in the table above is submitted:

```
<body><img src="invalid"\></body>
```

This will force the application to load the resource `invalid` and thus trigger the XSS vulnerability.

SUT 2. The initial test execution revealed 3 test vectors to trigger the XSS vulnerability. Four out of ten generated recommended tests derived from 4-way suspicious combinations triggered the vulnerability. Because of this we instructed BEN to search for 5-way inducing combinations. Since all four recommended tests for 5-way suspicious combinations triggered, we found two inducing combinations. The final recommended tests and inducing combinations are summarized in Table 2.

Table 2. Recommended tests with embedded 5-way inducing combinations

JS0	WS1	INT	WS2	EVH	WS3	PAY	WS4	PAS	WS5	JSE
"><script>	␣	ϵ	␣	ϵ	␣	alert(1)	␣	ϵ	␣	</script>">
"><script>	␣	ϵ	␣	onLoad=	␣	alert(1)	␣	ϵ	␣	</script>">
"><script>	ϵ	ϵ	ϵ	ϵ	ϵ	alert(1)	ϵ	ϵ	ϵ	</script>">
"><script>	ϵ	ϵ	ϵ	onError=	ϵ	alert(1)	ϵ	ϵ	ϵ	</script>">

This SUT also does not perform any filtering of the input parameter and the page response will include the following HTML expression after the first recommended test from the table above is reflected:

```
<input type="text" value=""><script>   alert(1)   </script>">">
```

This vector, as well as the other recommended 5-way tests, triggers the XSS vulnerability because of the embedded inducing combination. First the `value` field and the `input` tag are terminated and then a new `script` environment with the payload is created. Upon rendering the payload inside the script environment is then executed.

SUT 3. In the initial test execution 228 test vectors triggered the XSS vulnerability. Based on these results, BEN recommended 10 tests using the found 4-way suspicious combinations. All of these tests triggered the vulnerability. We also instructed BEN to look for 2-way and 3-way suspicious combinations but none were found. This means that the reported 4-way inducing combinations are truly 4-way and not lower-strength inducing combinations embedded inside higher-strength combinations. The recommended tests and the inducing combinations are displayed in Table 3.

As this SUT encodes angle brackets a page response contains the following HTML part after the first recommended test is reflected:

Table 3. Recommended tests with embedded 4-way inducing combinations

JSO	WS1	INT	WS2	EVH	WS3	PAY	WS4	PAS	WS5	JSE
<<script>		">		onError=		alert(1)		'>		\>
<<script>		">		onError=		alert(1)		')		\>
<<script>		">		onError=		'alert(1)'		'>		\>
<<script>		">		onError=		'alert(1)'		')		\>
<script		">		onError=		alert(1)		')		\>
<script		">		onError=		alert(1)		<		\>
<script		">		onError=		'alert(1)'		')		\>
<script		">		onError=		'alert(1)'		<		\>
<script>		">		onError=		alert(1)		<		\>
<<script>		">		onError=		alert(1)		<		\>

```
<img src="&lt;&lt;script&gt;"&gt; onError= alert(1) '&gt; \&gt;">
```

This vector succeeds in triggering the vulnerability because it contains an inducing combination which first defines the src attribute as "<<script> " which of course is not a valid image resource. This causes the onError handler to be called which activates the payload, in this case alert(1).

SUT 4. The initial test execution showed 280 vectors to trigger the XSS vulnerability. As all ten tests recommended by BEN for 4-way suspicious combinations triggered the vulnerability five inducing combinations were found. As for SUT 3, we also instructed BEN to look for 2-way and 3-way suspicious combinations but none were found, meaning that the inducing 4-way combinations are minimal inducing combinations. The recommended tests can be found in Table 4.

Table 4. Recommended tests with embedded 4-way inducing combinations

JSO	WS1	INT	WS2	EVH	WS3	PAY	WS4	PAS	WS5	JSE
"><script>		';		onError=		alert(1)		'>		\>
"><script>		'>		onError=		alert(1)		'>		\>
"><script>		'>		onError=		alert(1)		')		\>
"><script>		ε		onError=		alert(1)		'>		\>
"><script>		ε		onError=		alert(1)		')		\>
"><script>		'>>		onError=		alert(1)		')		\>
"><script>		';		onError=		src="invalid"		'>		\>
"><script>		'>		onError=		src="invalid"		'>		\>
"><script>		'>		onError=		src="invalid"		')		\>
"><script>		ε		onError=		src="invalid"		'>		\>

To illustrate how the inducing combinations trigger the vulnerability consider the example below which shows the first recommended test vector from the above table reflected in the page response after all angle brackets and single quotes have been encoded by the SUT.

```
<img src=""&gt;&lt;script&gt; &#39;; onError= alert(1) &#39;&gt; \&gt;">
```

Here the vector succeeds in triggering the vulnerability because it first closes the `src` attribute leaving it empty. Since the empty string is not a valid resource the `onError` handler is called which in turn calls the `alert(1)` statement.

8 Conclusion and Future Work

In this paper we have presented a combinatorial approach to analyzing XSS vulnerabilities in web applications. Our approach is based on the notion of XSS-inducing combinations. An XSS-inducing combination is a combination of input parameter values whose appearance in a test vector would definitely result in a successful triggering of an XSS vulnerability at runtime when executed against the SUT. Identification of XSS-inducing combinations helps to better understand the root cause of an XSS vulnerability and provides insights about how to fix a flawed sanitization function. Our approach is developed based on our earlier work on applying combinatorial methods to security testing. In particular, our approach consists of a refinement of a combinatorial model of XSS attack vectors and a modification of a combinatorial testing-based fault localization method that are developed in our earlier works. We have reported an experiment in which our approach is applied to four sanitization functions from WAVSEP. The experimental results show that our approach can effectively identify XSS-inducing combinations and that these combinations provide significant insights about the inner working of these sanitization functions.

We plan to continue our work in the following three directions. First, we plan to conduct additional experiments for a more thorough evaluation of our approach. In particular, we plan to apply our approach to more sanitization functions that are found in real-life web applications. Second, we plan to apply our approach to other types of vulnerabilities, e.g., SQL injections. We believe that the principles embodied in our approach are general, i.e. not limited to XSS vulnerabilities. Finally, we plan to build a software tool that automates our approach with the goal to make our approach accessible to web application developers.

Acknowledgments. This work has been funded by the Austrian Research Promotion Agency (FFG) under grant 851205 and the Austrian COMET Program (FFG).

References

1. Argyros, G., Stais, I., Kiayias, A., Keromytis, A.G.: Back in black: towards formal, black box analysis of sanitizers and filters. In: Proceedings of the 37th IEEE Symposium on Security and Privacy (2016)
2. Bozic, J., Garn, B., Kapsalis, I., Simos, D., Winkler, S., Wotawa, F.: Attack pattern-based combinatorial testing with constraints for web security testing. In: Proceedings of the 2015 IEEE International Conference on Software Quality, Reliability and Security, QRS 2015, pp. 207–212 (2015)

3. Bozic, J., Garn, B., Simos, D.E., Wotawa, F.: Evaluation of the IPO-family algorithms for test case generation in web security testing. In: 2015 IEEE Eighth International Conference on Software Testing, Verification and Validation Workshops (ICSTW), pp. 1–10 (2015)
4. Brcic, M., Kalpic, D.: Combinatorial testing in software projects. In: Proceedings of the 35th International Convention, MIPRO, 2012 , pp. 1508–1513 (2012)
5. Duchene, F., Groz, R., Rawat, S., Richier, J.L.: XSS vulnerability detection using model inference assisted evolutionary fuzzing. In: Proceedings of the 2012 IEEE Fifth International Conference on Software Testing, Verification and Validation, ICST 2012, pp. 815–817. IEEE Computer Society, Washington (2012)
6. Duchene, F., Rawat, S., Richier, J.L., Groz, R.: KameleonFuzz: evolutionary fuzzing for black-box XSS detection. In: CODASPY. ACM (2014)
7. Garn, B., Kapsalis, I., Simos, D., Winkler, S.: On the applicability of combinatorial testing to web application security testing: a case study. In: Proceedings of the 2014 Workshop on Joining AcadeMiA and Industry Contributions to Test Automation and Model-Based Testing, pp. 16–21. ACM (2014)
8. Ghandehari, L.S., Lei, Y., Kung, D., Kacker, R., Kuhn, R.: Fault localization based on failure-inducing combinations. In: 2013 IEEE 24th International Symposium on Software Reliability Engineering (ISSRE), pp. 168–177. IEEE (2013)
9. Ghandehari, L.S.G., Lei, Y., Xie, T., Kuhn, R., Kacker, R.: Identifying failure-inducing combinations in a combinatorial test set. In: 2012 IEEE Fifth International Conference on Software Testing, Verification and Validation (ICST), pp. 370–379. IEEE (2012)
10. Grindal, M., Offutt, J.: Input parameter modeling for combination strategies. In: Proceedings of the 25th Conference on IASTED International Multi-Conference: Software Engineering SE 2007, pp. 255–260. ACTA Press, Anaheim (2007)
11. Hagar, J.D., Wissink, T.L., Kuhn, D., Kacker, R.N.: Introducing combinatorial testing in a large organization. Computer 48(4), 64–72 (2015)
12. Hydara, I., Sultan, A.B.M., Zulzalil, H., Admodisastro, N.: Current state of research on cross-site scripting (XSS) a systematic literature review. Inf. Softw. Technol. 58, 170–186 (2015)
13. Kuhn, D.R., Okun, V.: Pseudo-exhaustive testing for software. In: 30th Annual IEEE/NASA Software Engineering Workshop, SEW 2006, pp. 153–158. IEEE (2006)
14. Kuhn, D., Kacker, R., Lei, Y.: Introduction to Combinatorial Testing. Chapman & Hall/CRC Innovations in Software Engineering and Software Development Series. Taylor & Francis (2013)
15. van der Loo, F.: Comparison of penetration testing tools for web applications. Master's thesis, University of Radboud, Netherlands (2011)
16. Mohammadi, M., Chu, B., Lipford, H.R., Murphy-Hill, E.: Automatic web security unit testing: XSS vulnerability detection. In: Proceedings of the 11th International Workshop on Automation of Software Test, AST 2016, pp. 78–84. ACM, New York (2016)
17. Nie, C., Leung, H.: A survey of combinatorial testing. ACM Comput. Surv. 43(2), 11: 1–11: 29 (2011)
18. Shi, L., Nie, C., Xu, B.: A software debugging method based on pairwise testing. In: Sunderam, V.S., Albada, G.D., Sloot, P.M.A., Dongarra, J. (eds.) ICCS 2005. LNCS, vol. 3516, pp. 1088–1091. Springer, Heidelberg (2005). doi:10.1007/11428862_179

19. Sudhodanan, A., Armando, A., Carbone, R., Compagna, L.: Attack patterns for black-box security testing of multi-party web applications. In: Proceedings of the Network and Distributed system Security Symposium (NDSS) (2016)
20. Tripp, O., Weisman, O., Guy, L.: Finding your way in the testing jungle: a learning approach to web security testing. In: Proceedings of the 2013 International Symposium on Software Testing and Analysis, ISSTA 2013, pp. 347–357. ACM, New York (2013)
21. Wang, Z., Xu, B., Chen, L., Xu, L.: Adaptive interaction fault location based on combinatorial testing. In: 2010 10th International Conference on Quality Software (QSIC), pp. 495–502. IEEE (2010)
22. Williams, J., Wichers, D.: OWASP Top 10 2013 (2013). https://www.owasp.org/index.php/Top_10_2013
23. Yu, L., Lei, Y., Kacker, R., Kuhn, D.: Acts: a combinatorial test generation tool. In: 2013 IEEE Sixth International Conference on Software Testing, Verification and Validation (ICST), pp. 370–375 (2013)
24. Zhang, Z., Zhang, J.: Characterizing failure-causing parameter interactions by adaptive testing. In: Proceedings of the 2011 International Symposium on Software Testing and Analysis, pp. 331–341. ACM (2011)

Heuristics and Non-determinism in Testing

Controllability Through Nondeterminism in Distributed Testing

Robert M. Hierons[1], Mercedes G. Merayo[2], and Manuel Núñez[2(✉)]

[1] Department of Information Systems and Computing, Brunel University London,
Uxbridge, Middlesex UB8 3PH, UK
rob.hierons@brunel.ac.uk
[2] Departamento de Sistemas Informáticos y Computación,
Universidad Complutense de Madrid, Madrid, Spain
mgmerayo@fdi.ucm.es, mn@sip.ucm.es

Abstract. If the system under test interacts with its environment at physically distributed ports, there is a separate independent tester at each port, and there is no global clock then we are testing in the distributed test architecture. It is known that the distributed test architecture can lead to additional controllability problems in which a tester cannot know when to send an input and this has led to most test generation techniques aiming to produce controllable test cases. However, there may be no controllable test case that achieves a given objective. This paper introduces the notion of a test section, in which each tester has a fixed input sequence to apply and there is no attempt to synchronise the testers. It defines the notion of a test section being convergent and shows how convergent test sections can be used as the basis of a less restrictive form of controllability.

1 Introduction

Software testing has traditionally been represented as a process in which a single tester synchronously interacts with the system under test (SUT). However, testing does not operate in this way if the SUT has multiple physically distributed interfaces (ports) at which it interacts with its environment; one might then have one local tester at each interface. For example, when testing the implementation of a layer of a communications protocol there might be one local tester that acts as the layer above the SUT and a second local tester that sits on a different machine [4,5,21]. More generally, if the SUT has multiple ports then there might be a separate tester at each port. If these testers do not synchronise their actions and there is no global clock then we are testing in the ISO standardised distributed test architecture [14].

Research partially supported by the projects DArDOS (TIN2015-65845-C3-1-R (MINECO/FEDER)) and SICOMORo-CM (S2013/ICE-3006).

F. Wotawa et al. (Eds.): ICTSS 2016, LNCS 9976, pp. 89–105, 2016.
DOI: 10.1007/978-3-319-47443-4_6

Most work on formal testing in the distributed test architecture uses *multi-port finite state machine (FSM)* models [4,5,21] in which a transition is triggered by an input, produces up to one output at each port, and possibly changes the state. We also use this approach, of assuming that the specification is a multi-port FSM, and we use the term FSM for such models. Note, however, that some work has explored more general types of models in which, for example, a transition can be labelled by a partially-ordered multi-set of actions [1,7,18,19].

Previous work has shown that the distributed test architecture changes the nature of testing. Let us suppose that we wish to start a test sequence with input x_1 at port 1, this should lead to output y_1 at port 1 and we wish to follow this with input x_2 at port 2. We might implement this using a test case t in which the tester t_1 at port 1 applies x_1 and the tester t_2 at port 2 applies x_2. Since we are testing in the distributed test architecture, tester t_2 does not observe the input or output at port 1 and so cannot know when to supply x_2. Thus, if we use the test case t then we cannot guarantee that the inputs arrive in the correct order; this introduces non-determinism into testing even if the SUT is deterministic. This situation is normally called a *controllability problem* [4,5,21]; if a test case has no controllability problems then it is *controllable*. Controllability problems can lead to situations in which we cannot know whether a test objective has been achieved and also make it more difficult to debug a faulty system and trace failures back to requirements. As a result, almost all work in distributed testing aims to produce controllable test cases (see, for example, [4,5,13,16,21,23]).

While there are test generation algorithms that produce controllable test cases from FSMs, these have inherent limitations. In particular, one can construct an FSM M such that controllable testing can achieve very little. Consider, for example, the fragment of an FSM shown in Fig. 1. Here, the label $x_p/(y_q, y_r)$ on an arc means that the input is x_p at port p and the output is y_q at port q and y_r at port r, with $-$ denoting no output at the corresponding port. If an input sequence starts with x_2 then there is no change in state and the resultant output is at port 2 only. Thus, for a test sequence to be controllable we require that the next input is at port 2, since only the tester at port 2 observed the previous input and output. It is straightforward to see that this situation continues and so any controllable test case that starts with x_2 cannot contain x_1 and only visits state s_0. If we now consider a test case that starts with x_1, the first input takes the FSM to state s_1 and produces y_1 at port 1 only. Therefore, for a test sequence to be controllable, the next input must be at port 1. However, if we apply x_1 then the FSM returns to s_0 and produces output at port 1 only. Thus, any controllable test case that starts with x_1 cannot contain x_2 and only visits s_0 and s_1. Hence, if an FSM is of the form shown in Fig. 1 then controllable testing can only visit s_0 and s_1 irrespective of how many states the FSM has.

There are several ways in which one might try to tackle the above problem. One approach is for the testers to synchronise actions through message exchange [2,20]. When feasible, this allows controllability problems to be overcome and provides a general solution. However, this requires a network to be introduced and so can make testing more expensive. Message latency might also

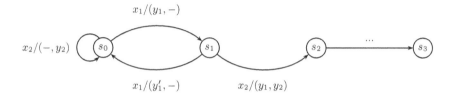

$$x_1/(y_1,-)$$

$$x_2/(-,y_2)$$ s_0 s_1 s_2 $\cdots$ s_3

$$x_1/(y_1',-)$$ $$x_2/(y_1,y_2)$$

Fig. 1. Part of an FSM where controllable testing achieves little

lead to situations in which a test case cannot be executed since it has timing constraints. A second line of work aims to allow one to reason about what can be achieved in controllable testing [8]. In particular, it is possible to construct an FSM $\chi_{min}(M)$ from the specification FSM M such that the transitions of $\chi_{min}(M)$ are those that can be executed in controllable testing and it is possible to construct a non-deterministic FSM $\chi_{max}(M)$ such that controllable testing can show that an SUT is faulty if and only if there are traces of the SUT that are not in the language defined by $\chi_{max}(M)$. One can use $\chi_{min}(M)$ and $\chi_{max}(M)$ to reason about the potential effectiveness of controllable testing. If the tester decides that controllable testing is sufficiently powerful then they can use a recently developed technique that generates a test suite that achieves as much as possible given the constraint that testing is controllable [10]. It is also possible to abandon the restriction that we use controllable test cases. However, as noted above, there are good practical reasons for using controllable test cases and it has also been shown that test generation problems, such as finding a prefix of a test case that is guaranteed to take M to a given state s, become undecidable [9].

Consider now the part of an FSM, with three ports, shown in Fig. 2. If testing starts with input x_1 then a controllable test case can then apply input at any port. There are two paths that take the FSM from s_1 to s_4: one has label $x_2/(y_1,y_2,-)x_3/(y_1,y_2',y_3')$ and the other has label $x_3/(-,-,y_3)x_2/(y_1,y_2',y_3')$. Both of these are uncontrollable: in the first case the tester at port 3 does not observe input or output from the transition with label $x_2/(y_1,y_2,-)$ and in the second case the tester at port 2 does not observe input or output from the transition with label $x_3/(-,-,y_3)$. However, if we just require that the tester at port 2 sends input x_2 and the tester at port 3 sends input x_3 then state s_4 is reached irrespective of the order in which the inputs are supplied. Thus, even though a corresponding test case is not controllable, we do know that it reaches s_4, with this situation being similar to partial order reduction (see, for example, [6]). In addition, the testers at ports 2 and 3 know when s_4 has been reached since at this point they receive particular outputs (y_2' at port 2, y_3' at port 3). Testing can thus continue with one of these testers applying an input in state s_4. In contrast, if one considers the two paths then in one case the tester at port 1 observes y_1 and in the other the tester at port 1 observes y_1y_1. If the tester at port 1 observes y_1 then there are two possible explanations and the state is either s_2 or s_4. As a result, one cannot guarantee that the tester at port 1 knows when

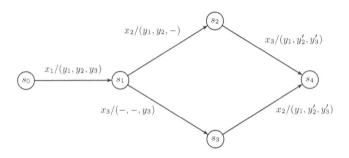

Fig. 2. Part of an FSM with controllability problems

s_4 has been reached. This paper formalises and extends these ideas, showing how one can relax controllable testing while retaining some of its benefits.

The rest of the paper is structured as follows. We start in Sect. 2 by defining FSMs and the notation used. Section 3 shows how we can relax the notion of controllability. Section 4 then considers computational complexity issues and a bounded form. Finally, Sect. 5 draws conclusions and discusses related work.

2   Preliminaries

This paper concerns the testing of a state-based system and, as such, we will reason about sequences of *inputs* and *outputs*. In testing the SUT will receive a sequence of inputs and there will be a resultant sequence of input/output pairs, called an *input/output sequence* or *trace*.

Definition 1. *We let X be the set of inputs of the SUT and Y the set of outputs of the SUT. Given $x \in X$ and $y \in Y$, the corresponding input/output pair x/y represents the SUT producing output y in response to input x.*

A trace is a (possibly empty) sequence of input/output pairs. The trace that has input/output pair x^1/y^1 followed by x^2/y^2, ..., and finally x^k/y^k will be represented using either $x^1/y^1\ x^2/y^2\ \ldots x^k/y^k$, $x^1 x^2 \ldots x^k/y^1 y^2 \ldots y^k$, or $\bar{x}/\bar{y}$ where $\bar{x} = x^1 x^2 \ldots x^k$ and $\bar{y} = y^1 y^2 \ldots y^k$.

Given a sequence $\bar{a}$ and an element a we let $a \cdot \bar{a}$ denote the sequence in which a is followed by $\bar{a}$. Given a sequence $\bar{a} = a^1 \ldots a^k$, with $k \geq 0$, we will let $pre(\bar{a}) = \{a^1 \ldots a^i | 0 \leq i \leq k\}$ denote the set of prefixes of $\bar{a}$ and we use ϵ to represent the empty sequence. Given a set A of sequences, $pre(A) = \bigcup_{\bar{a} \in A} \{pre(\bar{a})\}$.

Since a trace is a sequence of input/output pairs, all prefixes of traces are also traces and so

$$pre(x^1/y^1\ x^2/y^2\ \ldots x^k/y^k) = \{x^1/y^1\ x^2/y^2\ \ldots x^i/y^i | 0 \leq i \leq k\}$$

Work on testing from an FSM in the distributed test architecture has used multi-port FSMs. In such an FSM, there is a finite set of ports, which represent the interfaces at which the SUT interacts with its environment. We let P denote the set of (m) ports, with $\{1, \ldots, m\}$ denoting the names of the ports. If an input is received in a multi-port FSM then this triggers a transition, which can lead to a change in state and at most one output being produced at each port.

Definition 2. *A multi-port FSM M with m ports is defined by a tuple $(S, s_0, X, Y, \delta, \lambda)$ in which:*

- S *is the finite set of states of M.*
- $s_0 \in S$ *is the initial state of M.*
- $X = X_1 \cup \ldots \cup X_m$ *is the finite input alphabet of M, where for $1 \leq p \leq m$, X_p is the input alphabet at port p and for all $1 \leq p < q \leq m$ we have that $X_p \cap X_q = \emptyset$.*
- $Y = (Y_1 \cup \{-\}) \times \ldots \times (Y_m \cup \{-\})$ *is the output alphabet of M, where for $1 \leq p \leq m$, Y_p is the output alphabet at port p, $-$ denotes no output, and for all $1 \leq p < q \leq m$ we have that that $Y_p \cap Y_q = \emptyset$. In addition, the inputs and outputs are disjoint and so $X \cap \cup_{1 \leq p \leq m} Y_p = \emptyset$.*
- δ *is the (total) next state function of type $S \times X \to S$.*
- λ *is the (total) output function of type $S \times X \to Y$.*

If M receives input x when in state s then it moves to state $s' = \delta(s, x)$ and outputs an m-tuple $y = \lambda(s, x)$. This defines a transition $t = (s, s', x/y)$. We let T denote the set of transitions of M. When we refer to actions, a subscript will denote the port at which it is observed and a superscript will denote its position in a sequence.

The functions δ and λ can be extended in the usual way to deal with sequences of inputs. Specifically, given a state $s \in S$ and a sequence of inputs $\bar{x} = x^1 x^2 \cdots x^n$ we define $\delta(s, \bar{x})$ as $\delta(\delta((\cdots \delta(\delta(s, x^1), x^2) \ldots), x^{n-1}), x^n)$, that is, the state reached after following the sequence $\bar{x}$ and we define $\lambda(s, \bar{x})$ as $\lambda(s, x^1) \cdot \lambda(\delta(s, x^1), x^2) \cdot \ldots \lambda(\delta((\cdots \delta(\delta(s, x^1), x^2), \ldots), x^{n-1}), x^n)$, that is, the sequence of tuples of outputs observed after following the sequence $\bar{x}$.

A path of M is a sequence $\rho = (s_1, s_2, x_1/y_1)(s_2, s_3, x_2/y_2) \ldots (s_k, s_{k+1}, x_k/y_k)$ of consecutive transitions. We let $x_1/y_1 x_2/y_2 \ldots x_k/y_k$ denote the label of ρ.

The requirement that the alphabets at the ports are pairwise disjoint is not a restriction since one can label inputs and outputs with port numbers. We will use the term FSM for multi-port FSMs and the term single-port FSM for FSMs with one port. Note that our FSMs are deterministic: the current state and input received uniquely determine the next state and output produced. Most work on testing from single-port FSMs has concerned such deterministic machines (see, for example, [3,15,17]), as has almost all work on distributed testing from FSMs (see, for example, [4,5,13,16,21,23]).

Next we introduce notation to project the actions of an input sequence or a trace onto a port.

Definition 3. *Given a sequence $\bar{x} \in X^*$ and a port p, the projection $\pi_p(\bar{x})$ of $\bar{x}$ at port p can be inductively defined as follows:*

$$\pi_p(\bar{x}) = \begin{cases} \epsilon & \text{if } \bar{x} = \epsilon \\ \overline{x}' & \text{if } \bar{x} = x \cdot \overline{x}' \wedge x \notin X_p \\ x \cdot \pi_p(\overline{x}') & \text{if } \bar{x} = x \cdot \overline{x}' \wedge x \in X_p \end{cases}$$

Definition 4. *Let $M = (S, s_0, X, Y, \delta, \lambda)$ be an FSM with port set P such that $|P| = m$. Given an input/output sequence $\bar{z}$ and a port p, the projection $\pi_p(\bar{z})$ of $\bar{z}$ at port p can be inductively defined as follows:*

$$\pi_p(\bar{z}) = \begin{cases} \epsilon & \text{if } \bar{z} = \epsilon \\ \overline{z}' & \text{if } \bar{z} = x/(y_1, \ldots, y_m) \cdot \overline{z}' \wedge x \notin X_p \wedge y_p = - \\ x \cdot \pi_p(\overline{z}') & \text{if } \bar{z} = x/(y_1, \ldots, y_m) \cdot \overline{z}' \wedge x \in X_p \wedge y_p = - \\ y_p \cdot \pi_p(\overline{z}') & \text{if } \bar{z} = x/(y_1, \ldots, y_m) \cdot \overline{z}' \wedge x \notin X_p \wedge y_p \neq - \\ x \cdot y_p \cdot \pi_p(\overline{z}') & \text{if } \bar{z} = x/(y_1, \ldots, y_m) \cdot \overline{z}' \wedge x \in X_p \wedge y_p \neq - \end{cases}$$

We say that $\pi_p(\bar{z})$ is a local trace.

Given an input/output pair x/y, $ports(x/y) = \{p \in P | \pi_p(x/y) \neq \epsilon\}$ denotes the set of ports involved in x/y. Given transition $t = (s_i, s_j, x/y)$, $ports(t) = ports(x/y)$ and $port(x)$ denotes the port $p \in P$ such that $x \in X_p$.

Note that we have overloaded π_p and *ports*: the first one was previously used to project sequences of inputs and the second one denotes both the ports involved in an input/output pair and in a transition.

Let us suppose that the input sequence $x^1 \ldots x^k$ leads to output sequence $y^1 \ldots y^k$ when applied to M. In order for $x^1 \ldots x^k$ to be *controllable* [2,11,22] we require that the tester that applies x^i knows when to send x^i and that this is the case for all $1 < i \leq k$. If the tester at p sends x^i ($p = port(x^i)$) then it knows when to send x^i if it observed the previous transition and this is the case if either x^{i-1} is at port p or y^{i-1} has non-empty output at port p.

Definition 5. *Let $M = (S, s_0, X, Y, \delta, \lambda)$ be an FSM with port set P. Trace $x^1/y^1 \ x^2/y^2 \ldots x^k/y^k$ is controllable if $port(x^i) \in ports(x^{i-1}/y^{i-1})$ for all $1 < i \leq k$. Further, input sequence $x^1 \ldots x^k$ is controllable if $x^1 \ldots x^k/\lambda(s_0, x^1 \ldots x^k)$ is controllable and a path is controllable if its label is controllable.*

Previous work [12] showed how a directed graph $G(M)$ can be produced from FSM M such that the paths of $G(M)$, from the vertex representing the initial state of M, correspond to the controllable paths of M. The construction of $G(M)$ is based on the following concepts.

Definition 6. *Let $M = (S, s_0, X, Y, \delta, \lambda)$ be an FSM with port set P. For each state $s \in S$ and port $p \in P$ we denote by $Depart^p(s)$ the set of transitions of M whose starting state is s and whose input is at port p, that is, the set $\{(s, s', x/y) \in T | x \in X_p\}$. For each state s and set $\mathcal{P} \subseteq P$ of ports we denote by $Arrive^{\mathcal{P}}(s)$ the set of transitions whose ending state is s and that involve the set $\mathcal{P}$ of ports, that is, the set $\{(s', s, x/y) \in T | ports(x/y) = \mathcal{P}\}$.*

In order to ensure controllability, transitions belonging to $Arrive^{\mathcal{P}}(s)$ can only be followed by input at a port p if $p \in \mathcal{P}$. Thus, given transitions $\tau = (s_1, s_2, x/y)$ and $\tau' = (s_2, s_3, x'/y')$, we can follow τ by τ' without causing controllability problems if $port(x') \in ports(x/y)$. It is straightforward to see that if $\tau \in Arrive^{\mathcal{P}}(s_2)$ then we can follow τ by τ' in controllable testing if and only if there is some $p \in \mathcal{P}$ such that $\tau' \in Depart^p(s_2)$. We will use these properties to construct the desired graph.

Definition 7. *Let $M = (S, s_0, X, Y, \delta, \lambda)$ be an FSM with port set P. The graph $G(M) = (V, E)$ provides all the controllable sequences contained in M. The vertex set of $G(M)$ is defined in two steps. First, we define an auxiliary vertex set as follows:*

1. $v_{s_0}^P$ *is in* V_{aux}.
2. *For all $s \in S$ and $\mathcal{P} \subseteq P$ we include $v_s^{\mathcal{P}}$ in V_{aux} if $Arrive^{\mathcal{P}}(s) \neq \emptyset$.*

Edge set E is defined by: for each $t = (s, s', x/y) \in T$ and $v_s^{\mathcal{P}} \in V_{aux}$ with $port(x) \in \mathcal{P}$ we include in E the edge $(v_s^{\mathcal{P}}, v_{s'}^{\mathcal{P}_t}, x/y)$ where $\mathcal{P}_t = ports(x/y)$. Finally, V is the subset of V_{aux} that includes all the nodes reachable from $v_{s_0}^P$.

The notion of path (see Definition 2) can also be used with graphs: a path is a sequence of consecutive edges. The vertex $v_{s_0}^P$ (the *initial vertex*) represents the situation in which the first input has not yet been applied; this first input can be at any port. $v_s^{\mathcal{P}}$ denotes the situation in which M has reached state s and $\mathcal{P}$ is the set of ports that can receive the next input if testing is controllable.

Example 1. Consider the fragment of an FSM M with port set $P = \{1, 2, 3\}$ depicted in Fig. 3(a). Figure 3(b) shows $G(M)$. For each of the transitions that reaches a state of M, a new vertex is included in $G(M)$. For example, the state s_2 is reached by transitions $(s_1, s_2, x_2/(y_1, -, y_3))$ and $(s_0, s_2, x_3/(-, -, y_3))$. Thus, two vertexes, $V_{s_2}^{\{1,2,3\}}$ and $V_{s_2}^{\{3\}}$, respectively, are generated. The superscripts of each vertex contains the ports that are involved in the corresponding transition. The graph only contains those transitions whose input corresponds to a port included in the set associated with one of the vertices related to the outgoing state. For example, the transition $(s_1, s_2, x_2/(y_1, -, y_3))$ cannot be included in the graph because the port 2, in which the action x_2 must be applied, does not belong to the set of ports of the only vertex associated to state s_1, that is, $V_{s_2}^{\{1,3\}}$. Intuitively, a tester placed at port 2 cannot know when to apply the input x_2 because no action in the previous transition has been produced at this port. In this case we would have a controllability problem. Finally, we do not include $V_{s_2}^{\{1,2,3\}}$ because it is not reachable from $V_{s_0}^{\{1,2,3\}}$.

The following relates paths of $G(M)$ and controllable traces of M [12].

Proposition 1. *For each path ρ of M that starts at the initial state of M and has a controllable label, there is a path ρ' in $G(M)$ that starts at $v_{s_0}^P$ and has the same label. In addition, for each path ρ' of $G(M)$ that starts at $v_{s_0}^P$, there is a path ρ of M that starts at the initial state of M and has the same label.*

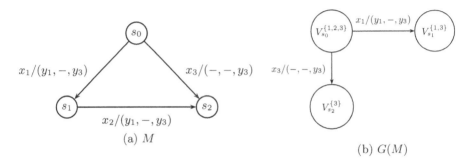

Fig. 3. Generation of $G(M)$

3   Extending the Graph $G(M)$

We have seen that an FSM might have states that cannot be reached using controllable input sequences; there might be a state s such that no vertex of the form $v_s^{\mathcal{P}}$ is reachable in $G(M)$. In this section we explain how $G(M)$ can be extended through including parts of a test that are not controllable but where the lack of controllability is not problematic. First we introduce *test sections*.

Definition 8. *Let P be a set of m ports. Given m sequences of inputs such that for all $1 \leq p \leq m$ we have that $\bar{x}_p \in X_p^*$, we say that the tuple $\bar{\bar{x}} = (\bar{x}_1, \ldots, \bar{x}_m)$ is a* test section. *Given a test section $\bar{\bar{x}} = (\bar{x}_1, \ldots, \bar{x}_m)$, we denote by $INT(\bar{\bar{x}})$ the set of interleavings of the sequences $\bar{x}_1, \ldots, \bar{x}_m$. Formally, for all $\bar{x} \in X^*$ we have that $\bar{x} \in INT(\bar{\bar{x}})$ if and only if for all $p \in P$ we have $\pi_p(\bar{x}) = \bar{x}_p$.*

We will use a double overline to denote a test section. In using a test section $\bar{\bar{x}}$, each tester simply applies its input sequence. Note that we allow empty sequences of inputs for some of the ports. We now consider conditions under which edges corresponding to test sections can be added to $G(M)$.

It is straightforward to determine which vertices of $G(M)$ can have edges labelled with a particular test section leaving them: in order to be able to apply $(\bar{x}_1, \ldots, \bar{x}_m)$ in a vertex $v_s^{\mathcal{P}}$ we require that for every $p \in P$ we have that if the tester at p is to apply input $(\bar{x}_p \neq \epsilon)$ then $p \in \mathcal{P}$.

Definition 9. *Let $M = (S, s_0, X, Y, \delta, \lambda)$ be an FSM with port set P and $\bar{\bar{x}} = (\bar{x}_1, \ldots, \bar{x}_m)$ be a test section. Let $G(M) = (V, E)$.*

Given $v_s^{\mathcal{P}} \in V$, we say that $\bar{\bar{x}}$ can be applied from $v_s^{\mathcal{P}}$ if for all $p \in P$ we have that $\bar{x}_p \neq \epsilon$ implies that $p \in \mathcal{P}$. Given states $s, s' \in S$, we say that $\bar{\bar{x}}$ is convergent *from s to s' if for all $\bar{x} \in INT(\bar{\bar{x}})$ we have that $s' = \delta(s, \bar{x})$. We also say that $\bar{\bar{x}}$ takes M from s to s'. Further, we say that $\bar{\bar{x}}$ is* convergent *from s if there exists a state s' such that $\bar{\bar{x}}$ is* convergent *from s to s'.*

Convergence requires that all interleavings of the input sequences take M from state s to s'; we do not have to control which interleaving occurs. Having reached s', we might continue testing in a controllable manner.

Proposition 2. *Let $M = (S, s_0, X, Y, \delta, \lambda)$ be an FSM with port set P, $\bar{\bar{x}} = (\bar{x}_1,$ $\ldots, \bar{x}_m)$ be a test section and $s, s' \in S$. If M is in state s, $\bar{\bar{x}}$ takes M from s to s', and from s the local tester at port p applies $\bar{x}_p$ (for all $p \in P$) then M is guaranteed to be in state s' after all inputs from $\bar{\bar{x}}$ have been received.*

If $\bar{\bar{x}}$ takes M from s to s' then there is potential to add a new edge to $G(M)$ that represents this fact. However, we then need to determine which vertex $v_{s'}^{\mathcal{P}'}$ should be reached and so the set $\mathcal{P}'$ of ports at which the next input (after the test section) can be applied. This set of ports should be the ports whose tester can determine when all of the inputs from $(\bar{x}_1, \ldots, \bar{x}_m)$ have been received. The following gives a condition under which the tester at port p can determine this.

Definition 10. *Let $M = (S, s_0, X, Y, \delta, \lambda)$ be an FSM with port set P, $\bar{\bar{x}}$ be a test section, $s \in S$ be a state of M and $p \in P$ be a port. We say that port $p \in P$ is* termination aware *when $\bar{\bar{x}}$ is applied from state s if for all $\bar{x} \in INT(\bar{\bar{x}})$ and $\bar{x}' \in pre(INT(\bar{\bar{x}})) \setminus INT(\bar{\bar{x}})$ we have $\pi_p(\lambda(s, \bar{x})) \neq \pi_p(\lambda(s, \bar{x}'))$.*

Once all inputs from $\bar{\bar{x}}$ have been received the tester at p observes a local trace of the form $\pi_p(\lambda(s, \bar{x}))$ for some $\bar{x} \in INT(\bar{\bar{x}})$; the above condition ensures that this observation cannot have been made if one or more inputs from $\bar{\bar{x}}$ have not been received. The following is clear from the previous definition.

Proposition 3. *Given FSM $M = (S, s_0, X, Y, \delta, \lambda)$ with port set P and $p \in P$, let us suppose that p is termination aware when $(\bar{x}_1, \ldots, \bar{x}_m)$ is applied from state $s \in S$. If $(\bar{x}_1, \ldots, \bar{x}_m)$ is applied from s then the tester at port p knows when all inputs from each $\bar{x}_q$ have been received.*

We can now combine the notions of convergence and termination to obtain a weaker type of controllability.

Definition 11. *Let $M = (S, s_0, X, Y, \delta, \lambda)$ be an FSM with port set P, $s, s' \in S$ be states, $\bar{\bar{x}}$ be a test section, and $\mathcal{P}, \mathcal{P}' \subseteq P$ be sets of ports. Let us suppose that $\bar{\bar{x}}$ takes M from s to s', $\mathcal{P}$ is the set of ports that are termination aware when $\bar{\bar{x}}$ is applied from state s, and $\mathcal{P}'$ is the following set of ports*

$$\mathcal{P} \cup \{p \in P | \forall \bar{x}, \bar{x}' \in INT(\bar{\bar{x}}) : \pi_p(\lambda(s, \bar{x})) = \pi_p(\lambda(s, \bar{x}'))\}$$

Then we say that $(s, \bar{\bar{x}}, s', \mathcal{P}, \mathcal{P}')$ is a semi-controllable tuple *of M. We let $Reach(M)$ be the set of semi-controllable tuples of M.*

If $(s, \bar{\bar{x}}, s', \mathcal{P}, \mathcal{P}')$ is a semi-controllable tuple then $\bar{\bar{x}} = (\bar{x}_1, \ldots, \bar{x}_m)$ is a test section with the property that if $\bar{\bar{x}}$ is applied from state s (and for all p such that $\bar{x}_p \neq \epsilon$, the tester at p knows that the state is s) then it takes M to s' and the testers in $\mathcal{P}$ are termination aware. In this definition, a port p is in $\mathcal{P}'$ if either p is termination aware or there is fixed output at p when the test section is applied. Essentially, $p \in \mathcal{P}'$ captures two scenarios that ensure that if the tester at p observes an output from a transition that is after $\bar{\bar{x}}$ then this tester can know that the output did not result from the application of the test section. We will see that this condition is important if we later wish to apply inputs at p.

Reach(M) may be infinite and so an algorithm should not include a step that generates this set. Instead, in this section we assume that there is some fixed $R \subseteq Reach(M)$; this will be a parameter of the algorithms introduced. In the next section we consider the case where we place a bound k on the size of the test sections used and so it is possible to generate the corresponding set *Reach*(M, k).

If $(s, \bar{\bar{x}}, s', \mathcal{P}, \mathcal{P}')$ is a semi-controllable tuple, $p \in \mathcal{P}$ and $\bar{\bar{x}}$ is applied from state s then the tester at p can apply an input after $\bar{\bar{x}}$ and know that this will be received in state s'. This potentially allows an input $x_p \in X_P$ to be applied in a state s' even if $G(M)$ does not have a reachable vertex of the form $v_{s'}^{\mathcal{P}''}$ with $p \in \mathcal{P}''$. In such cases, it is possible to execute additional transitions of M in testing and to know that this has been achieved despite this not being possible in controllable testing.

We will add vertices and edges based on $R \subseteq Reach(M)$; if $v_s^{\mathcal{P}}$ is a current vertex and $(s, \bar{\bar{x}}, s', \mathcal{P}, \mathcal{P}') \in R$ then there is the potential to add a new vertex and edge if $\bar{\bar{x}}$ can be applied from $v_s^{\mathcal{P}}$ (Definition 9). Before providing an algorithm, for extending $G(M)$, we will describe two additional factors that should be considered.

Example 2. Consider again the part of an FSM shown in Fig. 2. We know that (ϵ, x_2, x_3) is a test section that takes this FSM from s_1 to s_4 and also that the testers at ports 2 and 3 are termination aware. Let us suppose that we follow this test section by input x_2 at port 2 and the corresponding transition t takes the FSM to a state s_5 and produces output $(y_1, y_2, -)$. Then $ports(t) = \{1, 2\}$ and so normally one would expect to be able to apply input at either port 1 or port 2 after t. However, at this point there are two possible observations at port 1: either $y_1 y_1 y_1$ or $y_1 y_1 y_1 y_1$, depending on which path from s_1 to s_4 was followed. In addition, one of these ($y_1 y_1 y_1$) is an observation that might have been made in state s_4. Thus, the tester at port 1 need not be able to determine when s_5 has been reached if t follows the test section from s_1 to s_4.

Let us suppose that $(s, \bar{\bar{x}}, s', \mathcal{P}, \mathcal{P}') \in Reach(M)$ is used to reach s'. The example above shows that the restriction, on ports where one can apply inputs, may still be required *after* we apply an additional input x at $p \in \mathcal{P}$: even if the tester at p' observes output in response to x, the tester need not be able to know that the output was in response to x. This is because there may have been several possible observations at p' in response to a test section previously used. Naturally, there is no problem if the test section led to a fixed output sequence at port p; this is why we use $\mathcal{P}'$ in addition to $\mathcal{P}$ in tuples in *Reach*(M) (see Definition 11). Thus, if we use $(s, \bar{\bar{x}}, s', \mathcal{P}, \mathcal{P}')$ then we impose the restriction that (in the current test sequence) no future input is applied at a port outside of $\mathcal{P}'$. We will achieve this by adding a second set of ports to the label of a vertex. A vertex with label $v^{\mathcal{P}_1, \mathcal{P}_2}$ will denote the situation in which (in controllable testing) input can be applied next at any port in $\mathcal{P}_1$ and in the current test sequence we require that no further input is applied at ports outside of $\mathcal{P}_2$. The graphs we construct will have that if $v^{\mathcal{P}_1, \mathcal{P}_2}$ is a vertex then $\mathcal{P}_1 \subseteq \mathcal{P}_2$. Similar to

---

Algorithm 1. $Update(G, R)$: Updating graph G

Input $G = (V, E)$ and $R \subseteq Reach(M)$
$V' = V$
while $V' \neq \emptyset$ **do**
   Choose some $v_s^{\mathcal{P}_1, \mathcal{P}_2} \in V'$
   $V' = V' \setminus \{v_s^{\mathcal{P}_1, \mathcal{P}_2}\}$
   for all $r = (s, (\bar{x}_1, \dots, \bar{x}_m), s', \mathcal{P}, \mathcal{P}') \in R$ **do**
     $\mathcal{P}_1' = \mathcal{P} \cap \mathcal{P}_2$
     $\mathcal{P}_2' = \mathcal{P}' \cap \mathcal{P}_2$
     if $\forall 1 \leq p \leq m : (\bar{x}_p \neq \epsilon \Rightarrow p \in \mathcal{P}_1)$ **and** $v_{s'}^{\mathcal{P}_1', \mathcal{P}_2'}$ is not subsumed by V **then**
       $V = V \cup \{v_{s'}^{\mathcal{P}_1', \mathcal{P}_2'}\}$
       $V' = V' \cup \{v_{s'}^{\mathcal{P}_1', \mathcal{P}_2'}\}$
       $E = E \cup \{(v_s^{\mathcal{P}_1, \mathcal{P}_2}, (\bar{x}_1, \dots, \bar{x}_m), v_{s'}^{\mathcal{P}_1', \mathcal{P}_2'})\}$
     end if
   end for
end while
Output (V, E)

---

before, we will say that $(\bar{x}_1, \dots, \bar{x}_m)$ can be applied from $v_s^{\mathcal{P}_1, \mathcal{P}_2}$ if for all $p \in \mathcal{P}$ we have that $\bar{x}_p \neq \epsilon$ implies that $p \in \mathcal{P}_1$.

The second factor is that the addition of a new vertex $v_s^{\mathcal{P}_1, \mathcal{P}_2}$ is only useful if this provides potential for test execution that is not provided by current vertices; if it is not subsumed by the current vertices.

Definition 12. *Let* $M = (S, s_0, X, Y, \delta, \lambda)$ *be an FSM with port set* P *and let us consider a graph* $G = (V, E)$. *Given a state* $s \in S$ *and sets* $\mathcal{P}_1, \mathcal{P}_2 \subseteq P$, *we say that a vertex* $v_s^{\mathcal{P}_1, \mathcal{P}_2}$ *is subsumed by the set* V *of vertices if for all* $p \in \mathcal{P}_1$ *there exist* $\mathcal{P}_1', \mathcal{P}_2'$ *such that* $v_s^{\mathcal{P}_1', \mathcal{P}_2'} \in V$ *and* $p \in \mathcal{P}_1'$.

This definition ignores $\mathcal{P}_2$; we do this in order to limit the size of the extended graph we form (we avoid a, potentially exponential, subset construction). The factors discussed above lead to the Update function in Algorithm 1 that extends the current graph G, whose vertices are of the form $v_s^{\mathcal{P}_1, \mathcal{P}_2}$, on the basis of a set $R \subseteq Reach(M)$. Having used Algorithm 1, there may now be potential to add new edges and further vertices that correspond to controllable testing from the vertices added. This process is outlined in Algorithm 2.

The overall algorithm starts with the traditional graph $G(M)$ as defined in Definition 7 and repeatedly applies the Update and Complete functions until a fixed point is found. This process is outlined in Algorithm 3 in which $G'(M)$ is the graph G in which a vertex of the form $v_s^{\mathcal{P}}$ is renamed $v_s^{\mathcal{P}, P}$.

Example 3. Consider the (part of an) FSM M in Fig. 2. $G(M)$ is showed in Fig. 4 (non-dotted vertices and lines). Next we explain how Algorithm 3 works. Consider test section (ϵ, x_2, x_3) and $R = \{(s_1, (\epsilon, x_2, x_3), s_4, \{2, 3\}, \{2, 3\})\}$. Note that ports 2 and 3 are termination aware, because the conditions included in Definition 10 are satisfied.

Algorithm 2. $Complete(G, M)$: Completing graph G

Input $G = (V, E)$ and FSM M
$V' = V$
while $V' \neq \emptyset$ **do**
    Choose some $v_s^{\mathcal{P}_1, \mathcal{P}_2} \in V'$
    $V' = V' \setminus \{v_s^{\mathcal{P}_1, \mathcal{P}_2}\}$
    for all $p \in \mathcal{P}_1$ and $x \in X_p$ **do**
        $s' = \delta(s, x)$ and $y = \lambda(s, x)$
        $\mathcal{P}' = ports(x/y)$, $\mathcal{P}_1' = \mathcal{P}' \cap \mathcal{P}_2$
        if $v_{s'}^{\mathcal{P}_1', \mathcal{P}_2}$ is not subsumed by a vertex in V **then**
            $V = V \cup \{v_{s'}^{\mathcal{P}_1', \mathcal{P}_2}\}$
            $V' = V' \cup \{v_{s'}^{\mathcal{P}_1', \mathcal{P}_2}\}$
            $E = E \cup \{(v_s^{\mathcal{P}_1, \mathcal{P}_2}, x, v_{s'}^{\mathcal{P}_1', \mathcal{P}_2})\}$
        end if
    end for
end while
Output (V, E)

Algorithm 3. Generating the graph G

▸ Input FSM M, $G(M) = (V, E)$ and $R \subseteq Reach(M)$
$V' = \{v_s^{\mathcal{P}, \mathcal{P}} | v_s^{\mathcal{P}} \in V\}$
$E' = \{(v_s^{\mathcal{P}, \mathcal{P}}, a, v_{s'}^{\mathcal{P}', \mathcal{P}'}) | (v_s^{\mathcal{P}}, a, v_{s'}^{\mathcal{P}'}) \in E\}$
$G' = (V', E')$
repeat
    $G = G'$
    $G' = Complete(Update(G, R), M)$
until $G = G'$
Output G

The application of the update function to $G(M)$ and R creates a new vertex $V_{s_4}^{\{2,3\},\{2,3\}}$ and a new edge $(V_{s_1}^{\{1,2,3\}\{1,2,3\}}, (-, x_2, x_3), V_{s_4}^{\{2,3\},\{2,3\}})$ in the graph (see the dotted edge and vertex).

Next we consider the complexity of constructing the final graph, assuming that R is given. A vertex $v_s^{\mathcal{P}_1, \mathcal{P}_2}$ is added if it is not subsumed by the current vertices and this is the case if and only if there exists $p \in \mathcal{P}'$ such that no current vertex $v_s^{\mathcal{P}_1', \mathcal{P}_2}$ has $p \in \mathcal{P}_1'$. If $v_s^{\mathcal{P}_1, \mathcal{P}_2}$ is added then this increases the number of ports p such that there is a vertex $v_s^{\mathcal{P}_1', \mathcal{P}_2'}$ with $p \in \mathcal{P}_1'$. As a result, given state s, Algorithm 3 can add at most m vertices of the form $v_s^{\mathcal{P}_1, \mathcal{P}_2}$. Therefore, if R has already been produced then Algorithm 3 is a polynomial time algorithm. In the next section we explore the case where there are bounds on test section size and the complexity of the problem of generating $Reach(M)$ in this situation.

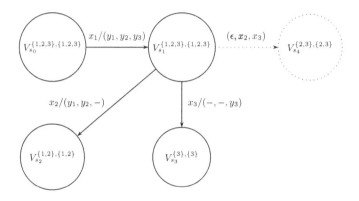

Fig. 4. Extension of $G(M)$

4   Bounding Convergent Test Sections

In the previous section we showed how $G(M)$ can be extended using test sections. In principle such test sections might be arbitrarily long but we will want to use relatively short test sections if we want testing to be efficient. Thus, in practice one might want to place upper bounds on the lengths of test sections used. The following two results provide additional motivation; they show that even the process of checking whether a test section is convergent is coNP-complete.

Theorem 1. *Let $M = (S, s_0, X, Y, \delta, \lambda)$ be an FSM, $s, s' \in S$ be states of M, and $\bar{\bar{x}}$ be a test section. The problem of deciding whether $\bar{\bar{x}}$ is convergent from s to s' is coNP-complete.*

Proof. We start by proving that the problem is in coNP. A non-deterministic Turing machine might guess an interleaving $\bar{x} \in INT(\bar{\bar{x}})$ and check whether $\bar{x}$ takes M from s to s'. Since this process takes polynomial time, a non-deterministic Turing machine can decide in polynomial time whether there is an interleaving of $\bar{\bar{x}}$ take M from s to a state other than s'. Thus, the problem of deciding whether all interleavings of $\bar{\bar{x}}$ take M from s to s' is in coNP.

We now prove that the problem is coNP-hard by relating it to the negation of the (NP-complete) Hamiltonian Path Problem (HPP). Let us suppose that we are given a directed graph G and we wish to solve the HPP, which is to determine whether there is a path that includes all vertices exactly once. Let $v_1, \ldots, v_n$ be the vertices of G. We will construct an FSM M with inputs $x_1, \ldots, x_n$ (each x_i at a separate port i) and states $s_0, s_1, \ldots, s_n, s_e$ as follows.

1. From the initial state s_0 input x_i takes M to s_i.
2. In state $s_i \neq s_e$, input x_j has the following effect:
   (a) If G contains an edge from v_i to v_j then we include a transition to s_j.
   (b) Otherwise there is a transition to the "error state" s_e.
   (c) In state s_e, all inputs lead to no change of state.
   (d) The outputs of the transitions can be chosen arbitrarily.

Now consider the test section $(x_1, \ldots, x_n)$ and its possible interleavings. The key observation is that an interleaving $\bar{x} = x_{i_1} \ldots x_{i_n}$ of $(x_1, \ldots, x_n)$ takes M from s_0 to a state other than s_e if and only if $v_{i_1} \ldots v_{i_n}$ is a path of G and such a path of G must be a Hamiltonian path of G. Thus, G has a Hamiltonian path if and only if $(x_1, \ldots, x_n)$ is not convergent from s_0 to s_e for M. Since the HPP is NP-hard, this means that it is NP-hard to check that a test section is not convergent. The result therefore follows.

Theorem 2. *Let $M = (S, s_0, X, Y, \delta, \lambda)$ be an FSM, $s \in S$ be a state of M, and $\bar{\bar{x}}$ be a test section. The problem of deciding whether $\bar{\bar{x}}$ is convergent from s is coNP-complete.*

Proof. The problem being in coNP follows from Theorem 1 and there being polynomially many states. The proof that the problem is coNP-hard follows in the same way as the proof of Theorem 1 since in the constructed FSM we have that the test section $(x_1, \ldots, x_n)$ is convergent if and only if it converges to s_e (if the final state is not s_e, for interleaving $x_{i_1} \ldots x_{i_n}$, then it is s_{i_n}).

Since we want to have efficient algorithms, we now explore the case where we place an upper bound on the size of test sections considered.

Definition 13. *Let $M = (S, s_0, X, Y, \delta, \lambda)$ be an FSM, $s, s' \in S$ be states of M, $k \geq 0$, and $\bar{\bar{x}} = (\bar{x}_1, \ldots, \bar{x}_m)$ be a test section. $\bar{\bar{x}}$ is k-convergent from s to s' if $\bar{\bar{x}}$ is convergent from s to s' and $\sum_{p=1}^{m} |\bar{x}_p| \leq k$. Further, $\bar{\bar{x}}$ is k-convergent from s if there exists a state s' such that $\bar{\bar{x}}$ is k-convergent from s to s'.*

Let $M = (S, s_0, X, Y, \delta, \lambda)$ be an FSM and $k \geq 0$. We define $Reach(M, k)$ as the following subset of $Reach(M)$

$$\left\{ (s, (\bar{x}_1, \ldots, \bar{x}_m), s', \mathcal{P}, \mathcal{P}') \in Reach(M) \,\middle|\, \sum_{p=1}^{m} |\bar{x}_p| \leq k \right\}$$

Importantly, if we place an upper bound on k, or we fix k, then the number of interleavings defined by a test section is also bounded. As a result, the process of checking which states are reached using interleavings of a test section takes polynomial time. We therefore obtain the following results.

Theorem 3. *Let $M = (S, s_0, X, Y, \delta, \lambda)$ be an FSM, $s \in S$ be a state, $k \geq 0$, and $\bar{\bar{x}}$ be a test section. If k is bounded then*

1. *Given state $s' \in S$, the problem of deciding whether $\bar{\bar{x}}$ is k-convergent from s to s' can be decided in polynomial time.*
2. *The problem of deciding whether $\bar{\bar{x}}$ is k-convergent from s can be decided in polynomial time.*

The next result follows from the fact that for bounded k the number of possible test sections, and the number of interleavings of each one, are bounded by polynomials.

Theorem 4. *Let $M = (S, s_0, X, Y, \delta, \lambda)$ be an FSM and $k \geq 0$. If k is bounded then the problem of generating $Reach(M, k)$ has polynomial time complexity.*

This shows that if we bound (or fix) k then we can compute $Reach(M, k)$ in polynomial time and so Algorithm 3 takes polynomial time. On the contrary, from Theorem 1, we have that this result does not hold if we do not bound k (unless $P = NP$). This suggests that Algorithm 3 can be applied with the entire set $Reach(M, k)$ if one wishes to restrict attention to a relatively small value of k but otherwise one might use heuristics to generate some $R \subseteq Reach(M)$.

5   Conclusions

This paper concerned testing in the distributed test architecture, where a local tester only observes events at its port, the testers do not synchronise, and there is no global clock. Almost all test generation algorithms, for testing from an FSM in the distributed test architecture, return controllable test sequences but this can be restrictive. For example, an FSM specification M may have states that cannot be reached in controllable testing. We introduced the notion of a test section, which contains a fixed input sequence for each port. We showed how test sections can be used to weaken the classical notion of controllability: rather than require that the path of the FSM specification M traversed is uniquely determined, we instead require that there is only one state of M that can be reached by a test section (the test section is convergent). Thus, the notion of a test section being convergent is similar to partial order reduction. We showed how, given a set R of convergent test sections, one can derive a directed graph G that describes what can be achieved using these test sections. In general, one cannot expect to generate all convergent test sections, since this set might be infinite. However, we found that if one bounds the size of the test sections then one can generate the complete set (that satisfies this upper bound) in polynomial time. As a result, one can also generate the graph G in polynomial time.

There are several possible lines of future work. First, it would be interesting to explore alternative conditions under which one can efficiently generate the set $Reach(M)$. There is also the potential for the approach to be generalised to allow test sections whose components are adaptive (the next input depends on the observed output) and also to non-deterministic FSMs. One might also explore notions of coverage. Finally, one might implement the proposed technique in a tool and then carry out industrial case studies.

References

1. von Bochmann, G., Haar, S., Jard, C., Jourdan, G.-V.: Testing systems specified as partial order input/output automata. In: Suzuki, K., Higashino, T., Ulrich, A., Hasegawa, T. (eds.) FATES/TestCom-2008. LNCS, vol. 5047, pp. 169–183. Springer, Heidelberg (2008). doi:10.1007/978-3-540-68524-1_13
2. Cacciari, L., Rafiq, O.: Controllability and observability in distributed testing. Inf. Softw. Technol. **41**(11–12), 767–780 (1999)

3. Chow, T.S.: Testing software design modeled by finite state machines. IEEE Trans. Softw. Eng. **4**, 178–187 (1978)
4. Dssouli, R., von Bochmann, G.: Error detection with multiple observers. In: 5th WG6.1 International Conference on Protocol Specification, Testing and Verification, PSTV 1985, pp. 483–494. North-Holland (1985)
5. Dssouli, R., von Bochmann, G.: Conformance testing with multiple observers. In: 6th WG6.1 International Conference on Protocol Specification, Testing and Verification, PSTV 1986, pp. 217–229. North-Holland (1986)
6. Godefroid, P.: Using partial orders to improve automatic verification methods. In: Clarke, E.M., Kurshan, R.P. (eds.) CAV 1990. LNCS, vol. 531, pp. 176–185. Springer, Heidelberg (1991). doi:10.1007/BFb0023731
7. Haar, S., Jard, C., Jourdan, G.-V.: Testing input/output partial order automata. In: Petrenko, A., Veanes, M., Tretmans, J., Grieskamp, W. (eds.) FATES/TestCom-2007. LNCS, vol. 4581, pp. 171–185. Springer, Heidelberg (2007). doi:10.1007/978-3-540-73066-8_12
8. Hierons, R.M.: Canonical finite state machines for distributed systems. Theor. Comput. Sci. **411**(2), 566–580 (2010)
9. Hierons, R.M.: Reaching and distinguishing states of distributed systems. SIAM J. Comput. **39**(8), 3480–3500 (2010)
10. Hierons, R.M.: Generating complete controllable test suites for distributed testing. IEEE Trans. Softw. Eng. **41**(3), 279–293 (2015)
11. Hierons, R.M., Merayo, M.G., Núñez, M.: Controllable test cases for the distributed test architecture. In: Cha, S.S., Choi, J.-Y., Kim, M., Lee, I., Viswanathan, M. (eds.) ATVA 2008. LNCS, vol. 5311, pp. 201–215. Springer, Heidelberg (2008). doi:10.1007/978-3-540-88387-6_16
12. Hierons, R.M., Ural, H.: UIO sequence based checking sequences for distributed test architectures. Inf. Softw. Technol. **45**(12), 793–803 (2003)
13. Hierons, R.M., Ural, H.: Checking sequences for distributed test architectures. Distrib. Comput. **21**(3), 223–238 (2008)
14. Joint Technical Committee ISO/IEC JTC 1. International Standard ISO/IEC 9646-1. Information Technology - Open Systems Interconnection - Conformance testing methodology, framework - Part 1: General concepts. ISO/IEC (1994)
15. Lee, D., Yannakakis, M.: Principles and methods of testing finite state machines: a survey. Proc. IEEE **84**(8), 1090–1123 (1996)
16. Luo, G., Dssouli, R., von Bochmann, G.: Generating synchronizable test sequences based on finite state machine with distributed ports. In: 6th IFIP Workshop on Protocol Test Systems, IWPTS 1993, pp. 139–153. North-Holland (1993)
17. Moore, E.P.: Gedanken experiments on sequential machines. In: Shannon, C., McCarthy, J. (eds.) Automata Studies. Princeton University Press, Princeton (1956)
18. Ponce de León, H., Haar, S., Longuet, D.: Unfolding-based test selection for concurrent conformance. In: Yenigün, H., Yilmaz, C., Ulrich, A. (eds.) ICTSS 2013. LNCS, vol. 8254, pp. 98–113. Springer, Heidelberg (2013). doi:10.1007/978-3-642-41707-8_7
19. Ponce de León, H., Haar, S., Longuet, D.: Model-based testing for concurrent systems: unfolding-based test selection. Int. J. Softw. Tools Technol. Transfer **18**(3), 305–318 (2016)
20. Rafiq, O., Cacciari, L.: Coordination algorithm for distributed testing. J. Supercomputing **24**(2), 203–211 (2003)
21. Sarikaya, B., von Bochmann, G.: Synchronization and specification issues in protocol testing. IEEE Trans. Commun. **32**, 389–395 (1984)

22. Ural, H., Whittier, D.: Distributed testing without encountering controllability and observability problems. Inf. Process. Lett. **88**(3), 133–141 (2003)
23. Ural, H., Williams, C.: Constructing checking sequences for distributed testing. Formal Aspects Comput. **18**(1), 84–101 (2006)

Parallelizing Heuristics for Generating Synchronizing Sequences

Sertaç Karahoda[1], Osman Tufan Erenay[1], Kamer Kaya[1,2],
Uraz Cengiz Türker[3], and Hüsnü Yenigün[1(✉)]

[1] Computer Science and Engineering, Faculty of Science and Engineering,
Sabanci University, Tuzla, Istanbul, Turkey
{skarahoda,osmantufan,kaya,yenigun}@sabanciuniv.edu
[2] Department of Biomedical Informatics,
The Ohio State University, Columbus, OH, USA
[3] Computer Engineering, Faculty of Engineering,
Gebze Technical University, Gebze, Kocaeli, Turkey
urazc@gtu.edu.tr

Abstract. Synchronizing sequences are used in the context of finite state machine based testing in order to initialize an implementation to a particular state. The cubic complexity of even the fastest heuristic algorithms known in the literature to construct a synchronizing sequence can be a problem in practice. In order to scale the performance of synchronizing heuristics, some algorithmic improvements together with a parallel implementation of these heuristics are proposed in this paper. An experimental study is also presented which shows that the improved/parallel implementation can yield a considerable speedup over the sequential implementation.

1 Introduction

Model Based Testing (MBT) uses formal models of system requirements to generate effective test cases. Most MBT techniques use state-based models, where the behaviour of the model is described in terms of states and state transitions. There has been much interest in testing from finite state machines (FSMs) (e.g., see [1–6]). Common to most FSM based testing methods is the need to bring the system under test (SUT) to a particular state. When there is a trusted *reset* input in the SUT, this is quite easy. However, sometimes such a reset input is not available, or even if it is available, it may be time consuming to apply the reset input. Therefore there are cases where the use of a reset input is not preferred [7–9].

A *synchronizing sequence*[1] for an FSM M is a sequence of inputs such that no matter at which state M currently is, if this sequence of inputs is applied, M

---

[1] Synchronizing sequences are also known as *reset sequences*, or *reset words*.

F. Wotawa et al. (Eds.): ICTSS 2016, LNCS 9976, pp. 106–122, 2016.
DOI: 10.1007/978-3-319-47443-4_7

is brought to a particular state. Therefore a synchronizing sequence is in fact a compound reset input, and can be used as such to simulate a reset input in the context of FSM based testing [10].

A synchronizing sequence may not exist for an FSM. However, as the size of the FSM gets larger, there almost always exists a synchronizing sequence [11]. For an FSM M with n states and alphabet size p, checking if M has a synchronizing sequence can be decided in time $O(pn^2)$ [12]. Since a synchronizing sequence will possibly be used many times in a test sequence, computing a shortest one for an FSM is of interest, but this problem is known to be NP-hard [12]. There exist a number of heuristics, called *synchronizing heuristics*, to compute short synchronizing sequences, such as GREEDY [12] and CYCLE [13] both with time complexity $O(n^3 + pn^2)$, SYNCHROP and SYNCHROPL [14] with time complexity $O(n^5 + pn^2)$, and FASTSYNCHRO [15] with time complexity $O(pn^4)$. The upper bound for the length of the synchronizing sequence that will be produced by all of these heuristics is $O(n^3)$. Although synchronizing sequences are important for testing methods, the scalability of the synchronizing heuristics has not been addressed thoroughly. For practical applications, the use of even the fastest algorithms (GREEDY and CYCLE) with cubic complexity can be a problem.

In this work we investigate the use of modern multicore CPUs to scale the performance of synchronizing heuristics. We consider the GREEDY algorithm to start with, as it is one of the two cheapest synchronizing heuristics (in practice as well [16]), known to produce shorter sequences than CYCLE [16], and has been widely used as a baseline to evaluate the quality and speed of more advanced heuristics. To the best of our knowledge, this is the first work towards parallelization of synchronizing heuristics. Although, a parallel approach for constructing a synchronizing sequence for a *partial* machines is proposed in [17], the method proposed in [17] is not exact (in the sense that it may fail to find a synchronizing sequence even if one exists) and also it is not a polynomial time algorithm.

All synchronizing heuristics consist of a preprocessing phase, followed by synchronizing sequence generation phase. As presented in this paper, our initial experiments revealed that the preprocessing phase dominates the runtime of the overall algorithm for GREEDY. Therefore for both parallelization and for algorithmic improvements of GREEDY, we mainly focus on the first phase of the algorithm. With no parallelization, our algorithmic improvements alone yield a 20x speedup on GREEDY for automata with 4000 states and 128 inputs. Furthermore, around 150x speedup has been obtained for the same class of automata, when the improved algorithm is executed in parallel with 16 threads.

The rest of the paper is organized as follows: In Sect. 2, the notation is given, and synchronizing sequences are formally defined. We give the details of Eppstein's GREEDY construction algorithm in Sect. 3. The proposed improvements and the parallelization approach together with implementation details are described in Sect. 4. Section 5 presents the experimental results and Sect. 6 concludes the paper.

2 Preliminaries

FSMs are used to describe a reactive behaviour, i.e., when an input is applied to an FSM, it produces an output as a response. However, the output sequence produced by the application of a synchronizing sequence does not play a role. Therefore, in the context of synchronizing sequences, an FSM can simply be considered as an automaton where the state transitions are only performed by the application of an input, and no output is produced.

In this work, we only consider complete deterministic automata. An *automaton* is defined by a triple $A = (S, \Sigma, \delta)$ where S is a finite set of n states, Σ is a finite set of p input symbols (or simply *inputs*) called the alphabet. $\delta : S \times \Sigma \rightarrow S$ is a transition function. If the automaton A is at a state s and if an input x is applied, then A moves to the state $\delta(s, x)$. Figure 1 shows an example automaton A with 4 states and 2 inputs.

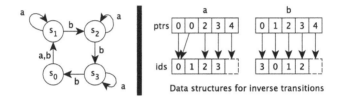

Fig. 1. A synchronizable automaton A (left), and the data structures we used to store and process the transition function δ^{-1} in memory (see Sect. 4.4 for the details). A synchronizing sequence for A is *abbbabbba*.

An element of the set $\Sigma^\star$ is called an *input sequence*. We use $|w|$ to denote the length of w, and ε is the empty input sequence. We extend the transition function δ to a set of states and to an input sequence in the usual way. We have $\delta(s, \varepsilon) = s$, and for an input sequence $w \in \Sigma^\star$ and an input symbol $x \in \Sigma$, we have $\delta(s, xw) = \delta(\delta(s, x), w)$. For a set of states $S' \subseteq S$, we have $\delta(S', w) = \{\delta(s, w) | s \in S'\}$.

We use the notation $\delta^{-1}(s, x)$ to denote the set of those states with a transition to state s with input x. Formally, $\delta^{-1}(s, x) = \{s' \in S | \delta(s', x) = s\}$.

Let $A = (S, \Sigma, \delta)$ be an automaton, and $w \in \Sigma^\star$ be an input sequence. w is said to be a *merging sequence for a set of states* $S' \subseteq S$ if $|\delta(S', w)| = 1$, and S' is called *mergable*. Any set $\{s\}$ with a single state is mergable, since ε is a merging sequence for $\{s\}$. w is called a *synchronizing sequence for A* if $|\delta(S, w)| = 1$. A is called *synchronizable* if there exists a synchronizing sequence for A. For example, the automaton given in Fig. 1 is synchronizable, since *abbbabbba* is a synchronizing sequence for the automaton. Deciding if an automaton is synchronizable or not can be performed in polynomial time based on the following result.

Proposition 1 [12,18]. *An automaton $A = (S, \Sigma, \delta)$ is synchronizable iff for all $s_i, s_j \in S$, there exists a merging sequence for $\{s_i, s_j\}$.*

For a set of states $C \subseteq S$, let $C^{\langle 2 \rangle} = \{\langle s_i, s_j \rangle | s_i, s_j \in C\}$ be the set of all *multisets* with cardinality 2 with elements from C, i.e. $C^{\langle 2 \rangle}$ is the set of all subsets of C with cardinality 2, where repetition is allowed. An element $\langle s_i, s_j \rangle \in C^{\langle 2 \rangle}$ is called *a singleton* if $s_i = s_j$, otherwise it is called *a pair*.

As Proposition 1 makes it explicit, checking the existence of merging sequences for pairs of states is needed to decide if an automaton is synchronizable. In addition, the heuristic algorithms also make use of the merging sequences for pairs. For both checking the existence of merging sequences and finding a merging sequence (in fact for finding a shortest merging sequence) for pairs of states of an automaton, one can use the notion of the pair automaton, which we define next.

Definition 1. *For an automaton $A = (S, \Sigma, \delta)$, the pair automaton $\mathcal{A}$ of A is defined as $\mathcal{A} = (S^{\langle 2 \rangle}, \Sigma, \Delta)$, where for a state $\langle s_i, s_j \rangle \in S^{\langle 2 \rangle}$ and an input symbol $x \in \Sigma$, $\Delta(\langle s_i, s_j \rangle, x) = \langle \delta(s_i, x), \delta(s_j, x) \rangle$.*

3 Eppstein's Algorithm

In this section, we explain Eppstein's GREEDY algorithm, and we present an observation on the timing profile of the algorithm. This observation guided our work on the improvements and parallelization of the algorithm, which will be explained in Sect. 4. GREEDY (and also all other synchronizing heuristics mentioned in Sect. 1) has two phases. In the first phase, a shortest merging sequence for each mergable pair of states is found. If all pairs are mergable, these merging sequences are used to construct a synchronizing sequence in the second phase.

For a pair of states s_i, s_j of an automaton $A = (S, \Sigma, \delta)$, checking the existence of a merging sequence for $\{s_i, s_j\}$, and computing a shortest merging sequence for $\{s_i, s_j\}$ can be performed in time $O(pn^2)$ by finding a shortest path from the state $\langle s_i, s_j \rangle$ of the pair automaton $\mathcal{A}$ to a singleton state in $\mathcal{A}$ using Breadth First Search (BFS). Since we will have to check the existence and find merging sequences for all pairs of states, one can instead use a *backward* BFS, seeded at singleton states of the pair automaton, as explained below.

For an automaton $A = (S, \Sigma, \delta)$, a function $\tau : S^{\langle 2 \rangle} \to \Sigma^\star$, is called *a pairwise merging function (PMF) for A*, if for all $\langle s_i, s_j \rangle \in S^{\langle 2 \rangle}$, $\tau(\langle s_i, s_j \rangle)$ is a shortest merging sequence for $\{s_i, s_j\}$ if $\{s_i, s_j\}$ is mergable, and $\tau(\langle s_i, s_j \rangle)$ is undefined if $\{s_i, s_j\}$ is not mergable. Note that PMF for an automaton A is not unique, and it is a total function iff A is synchronizable. Algorithm 1 computes such a PMF τ for a given automaton A, where initially $\tau(\langle s, s \rangle) = \varepsilon$ for the singleton states in $S^{\langle 2 \rangle}$ (line 1), and $\tau(\langle s_i, s_j \rangle)$ is considered to be "undefined" for pair states in $S^{\langle 2 \rangle}$ (line 2). The algorithm iteratively computes the values of $\tau(.)$ as it discovers shortest merging sequences for more pairs in $S^{\langle 2 \rangle}$.

Algorithm 1 keeps track of a *frontier* set F which is initialized to all singleton states at line 3. Throughout the algorithm, R represents the remaining set of pairs with $\tau(\langle s_i, s_j \rangle)$ still being undefined. In each iteration of the algorithm (lines 5–6), a BFS step is performed by using BFS_step_F2R given in Algorithm 2.

Algorithm 1. Computing a PMF $\tau : S^{\langle 2 \rangle} \to \Sigma^\star$ (F2R based)

---

    input : An automaton $A = (S, \Sigma, \delta)$
    output: A PMF $\tau : S^{\langle 2 \rangle} \to \Sigma^\star$
 1 **foreach** *singleton* $\langle s, s \rangle \in S^{\langle 2 \rangle}$ **do** $\tau(\langle s, s \rangle) = \varepsilon$;
 2 **foreach** *pair* $\langle s_i, s_j \rangle \in S^{\langle 2 \rangle}$ **do** $\tau(\langle s_i, s_j \rangle) = undefined$;
 3 $F \longleftarrow \{\langle s, s \rangle | s \in S\}$; // all singleton states of $\mathcal{A}$
 4 $R \longleftarrow \{\langle s_i, s_j \rangle | s_i, s_j \in S \wedge s_i \neq s_j\}$; // all pair states of $\mathcal{A}$
 5 **while** F *is not empty* **do**
 6 $\lfloor$ $F, R, \tau \longleftarrow$ BFS_step_F2R(A, F, R, τ);

Algorithm 2. BFS_step_F2R

---

    input : An automaton $A = (S, \Sigma, \delta)$, the frontier F, the remaining set R, τ
    output: The new frontier F', the new remaining set R', and updated function τ
 1 $F' \longleftarrow \emptyset$;
 2 **foreach** $\langle s_i, s_j \rangle \in F$ **do**
 3   **foreach** $x \in \Sigma$ **do**
 4   **foreach** $\langle s_i', s_j' \rangle$ *such that* $s_i' \in \delta^{-1}(s_i, x)$ *and* $s_j' \in \delta^{-1}(s_j, x)$ **do**
 5   **if** $\tau(\langle s_i', s_j' \rangle)$ *is undefined* **then** // $\langle s_i', s_j' \rangle \in R$
 6 $\tau(\langle s_i', s_j' \rangle) \longleftarrow x\tau(\langle s_i, s_j \rangle)$;
 7 $F' = F' \cup \{\langle s_i', s_j' \rangle\}$;

 8 let R' be $R \setminus F'$;

BFS_step_F2R constructs the next frontier F' from the current frontier F, by considering each $\langle s_i, s_j \rangle \in F$ (line 2). Lines 4–5 of BFS_step_F2R identify a pair $\langle s_i', s_j' \rangle \in R$ such that $s_i' = \delta(s_i, x)$ and $s_j' = \delta(s_j, x)$ for some $x \in \Sigma$, and lines 6–7 performs the necessary updates. Since this algorithm considers, in a sense, the *reverse* transitions of $\langle s_i, s_j \rangle$ in the frontier F to reach to pairs $\langle s_i', s_j' \rangle$ in R, we call it as "Frontier to Remaining (F2R)" BFS step.

    Algorithm 1 eventually assigns a value to $\tau(\langle s_i, s_j \rangle)$ if $\{s_i, s_j\}$ is mergable. Based on Proposition 1, A is synchronizable iff there does not exist a pair state $\langle s_i, s_j \rangle$ with $\tau(\langle s_i, s_j \rangle)$ being undefined when Algorithm 1 terminates. We can now present Eppstein's GREEDY algorithm based on Algorithm 1.

    The GREEDY algorithm keeps track of a current set C of states yet to be merged, initialized to S at line 4. A pair $\langle s_i, s_j \rangle \in C^{\langle 2 \rangle}$ is called an *active pair*. In each iteration of the while loop at line 7, an active pair $\langle s_i, s_j \rangle \in C^{\langle 2 \rangle}$ is found such that it has a shortest merging sequence among all active pairs in C (line 8). The synchronizing sequence (initialized to the empty sequence at line 6) is extended with $\tau(\langle s_i, s_j \rangle)$ at line 9. Finally, $\tau(\langle s_i, s_j \rangle)$ is applied to C to update the current set of states. When $|C| = 1$, this means that Γ accumulated at that point is a synchronizing sequence.

    The following results are shown in [12, Theorem 5]. For an automaton A with n states and p inputs, Phase 1 of GREEDY (lines 1–3) can be implemented to

---

Algorithm 3. Eppstein's GREEDY Algorithm

---

input : An automaton $A = (S, \Sigma, \delta)$
output: A synchronizing sequence Γ for A (or fail if A is not synchronizable)
1 compute a PMF τ using Algorithm 1;
2 **if** *there exists a pair $\langle s_i, s_j \rangle$ such that $\tau(\langle s_i, s_j \rangle)$ is undefined* **then**
3 $\quad \lfloor$ report that A is not synchronizable and exit;
4 **foreach** $s_i, s_j, s_k \in S$ **do** compute $\delta(s_k, \tau(\langle s_i, s_j \rangle))$;
5 $C = S$; // C will keep track of the current set of states
6 $\Gamma = \varepsilon$; // Γ is the synchronizing sequence to be constructed
7 **while** $|C| > 1$ **do** // we have two or more states yet to be merged
8 $\quad$ find a pair $\langle s_i, s_j \rangle \in C^{\langle 2 \rangle}$ with minimum $|\tau(\langle s_i, s_j \rangle)|$ among all pairs in $C^{\langle 2 \rangle}$;
9 $\quad$ $\Gamma = \Gamma \, \tau(\langle s_i, s_j \rangle)$;
10 $\quad \lfloor$ $C = \delta(C, \tau(\langle s_i, s_j \rangle))$;

---

run in time $O(pn^2)$ and Phase 2 of GREEDY (lines 4–10) can be implemented to run in time $O(n^3)$. Hence the overall time for GREEDY is $O(n^3 + pn^2)$.

We performed an experimental analysis to see how much Phase 1 (which we will call as the PMF construction phase[2]) and Phase 2 (the synchronizing sequence construction phase) of the algorithm contribute to the running time in practice for a sequential implementation. Based on these experiments, we observed that PMF construction actually dominates the running time of the algorithm (see Table 1). Hence, in order to improve the performance of GREEDY, we developed approaches for parallel implementation of PMF construction, together with some algorithmic modifications, which we explain in Sect. 4.

Table 1. Sequential PMF construction time (t_{PMF}), and overall time (t_{ALL}) for automata with $n \in \{1000, 2000, 4000\}$ states and $p \in \{2, 8, 32, 128\}$ inputs.

p	$n = 1000$			$n = 2000$			$n = 4000$		
	t_{ALL}	t_{PMF}	$\frac{t_{PMF}}{t_{ALL}}$	t_{ALL}	t_{PMF}	$\frac{t_{PMF}}{t_{ALL}}$	t_{ALL}	t_{PMF}	$\frac{t_{PMF}}{t_{ALL}}$
2	0.045	0.042	0.928	0.188	0.175	0.929	1.214	1.158	0.954
8	0.125	0.122	0.974	0.526	0.513	0.975	2.757	2.698	0.979
32	0.483	0.480	0.993	2.151	2.138	0.994	9.980	9.919	0.994
128	2.202	2.199	0.999	9.243	9.229	0.999	39.810	39.749	0.998

4   Parallelization Approach and Improvements

Algorithm 1 necessarily performs a BFS on the pair automaton $\mathcal{A}$, and a BFS forest rooted at singleton states of $\mathcal{A}$ is implicitly obtained. At the roots of

---

[2] Lines 2–3 of Phase 1 is easily handled as a part of PMF construction by checking if R is empty or not at the end of PMF construction.

the forest (i.e. in the first frontier set F) we have singleton states of $\mathcal{A}$, which corresponds to the nodes at level 0 of the BFS forest. At each iteration of the algorithm, the current frontier F has all the nodes at level k in the BFS forest. These nodes are processed by Algorithm 2 to compute the next frontier F' which are the nodes at level $k+1$ in the BFS forest. The processing of the state pairs in F are the tasks to be performed at the current level. To process a state pair, Algorithm 2 considers incoming transitions of the pair (i.e., inverse transitions) based on the δ^{-1} function (line 4). Hence, the cost of each task can be different. Furthermore, the total number of edges of the tasks in F, i.e., frontier edges, determines the cost of the corresponding level's BFS_step_F2R execution and this also varies for each level. We used OpenMP for parallel implementation and employed the dynamic scheduling policy (with batches of 512-pairs) since the task costs are not uniform.

4.1 Computing a PMF in Parallel

When Algorithm 1 is implemented sequentially, handling two consecutive iterations is seamless: using a single queue to enque and deque the frontier pairs suffices to process them in the correct order (i.e. a pair at level $k+1$ is only found after all level k pairs are found). However, with multiple threads, a barrier (a global synchronization technique) is required after each iteration. Otherwise, a pair from the next frontier can be processed before another pair in the current frontier and an incorrect PMF function τ can be computed. Here we present Algorithm 1 iteratively, and isolate the BFS_step_F2R from the main flow of the algorithm since it will be our main target for efficiency.

Algorithm 4. BFS_step_F2R (in parallel)

input : An automaton $A = (S, \Sigma, \delta)$, the frontier F, the remaining set R, τ
output: The new frontier F', the new remaining set R', and updated function τ
1 **foreach** *thread t* **do** $F'_t \longleftarrow \emptyset$;
2 **foreach** $\langle s_i, s_j \rangle \in F$ **in parallel do**
3   **foreach** $x \in \Sigma$ **do**
4   **foreach** $\langle s'_i, s'_j \rangle$ *where* $s'_i \in \delta^{-1}(s_i, x)$ *and* $s'_j \in \delta^{-1}(s_j, x)$ **do**
5   **if** $\tau(\langle s'_i, s'_j \rangle)$ *is undefined* **then** // $\langle s'_i, s'_j \rangle \in R$
6         $\tau(\langle s'_i, s'_j \rangle) \longleftarrow x\tau(\langle s_i, s_j \rangle)$;
7         $F'_t = F'_t \cup \{\langle s'_i, s'_j \rangle\}$;

8 $F' \longleftarrow \emptyset$;
9 **foreach** *thread t* **do** $F' = F' \cup F'_t$;
10 let R' be $R \setminus F'$;

To parallelize BFS_step_F2R, we partition the current frontier F among multiple threads where only a single thread processes a frontier pair as shown in Algorithm 4 (line 2). Since there is no task-dependency among the pairs, all the threads can simultaneously work. However, a race condition occurs since the next frontier set F' is a shared object in the sequential implementation.

To break dependency with a lock-free approach, in our parallel implementation, each thread t uses a local frontier array F'_t and when a new pair from the next frontier is found by thread t, it is immediately added to F'_t. When two threads find the same pair $\langle s'_i, s'_j \rangle$ at the same time, both threads insert it to their local frontiers (lines 5–7). Hence, when the local frontiers are combined at the end of each iteration (lines 8–9), the same pair can occur multiple times if no duplicate pair check is applied. In our preliminary experiments, we observed that at most one in a thousands extra pairs are inserted to F' when they are allowed. Hence, we let the threads process them since the total extra pair cost is negligible compared to the cost of checking and resolving duplicates.

4.2 Another Approach for BFS Steps

Algorithms 2 and 4 follow a natural and possibly the most common technique to construct the next frontier set F' from the current frontier set F by considering the incoming transitions. Another approach to construct the next frontier F' function, which we call "Remaining to Frontier (R2F)", is processing the remaining state pairs' edges instead of those in the frontier. As mentioned above, a state pair $\langle s_i, s_j \rangle$ stays in R, i.e., in the remaining pair set, as long as $\tau(\langle s_i, s_j \rangle)$ stays undefined. In the parallel R2F approach described by Algorithm 5, the threads process the transitions of the remaining state pairs instead of the ones in the frontier. Hence, instead of δ^{-1}, the original transition function δ is used and the pair found is checked to be in the frontier (lines 5–6). If a pair $\langle s_i, s_j \rangle$ has a transition to a pair $\langle s'_i, s'_j \rangle \in F$ (i.e., if $\langle s_i, s_j \rangle$ is in the next frontier), $\tau(\langle s_i, s_j \rangle)$ is set and the process ends (lines 7–9). Otherwise, $\langle s_i, s_j \rangle$ is kept in the remaining set (lines 10–11). Similar to parallel F2R, we use a local remaining pair array R'_t for each thread t in the lock-free parallelization of R2F.

Algorithm 5. BFS_step_R2F (in parallel)

---

    input : An automaton $A = (S, \Sigma, \delta)$, the frontier F, the remaining set R, τ
    output: The new frontier F', the new remaining set R', and updated function τ
1   **foreach** *thread* t **do** $R'_t \longleftarrow \emptyset$;
2   **foreach** $\langle s_i, s_j \rangle \in R$ **in parallel do**
3   *connected* $\longleftarrow$ **false**;
4   **foreach** $x \in \Sigma$ **do**
5          $\langle s'_i, s'_j \rangle \longleftarrow \langle \delta(s_i, x), \delta(s_j, x) \rangle$;
6   **if** $\tau(\langle s'_i, s'_j \rangle)$ *is defined* **then** // $\langle s'_i, s'_j \rangle \in F$
7             $\tau(\langle s_i, s_j \rangle) \longleftarrow x\tau(\langle s'_i, s'_j \rangle)$;
8   *connected* $\longleftarrow$ **true**;
9   **break**;
10   **if** *not connected* **then**
11        $R'_t = R'_t \cup \{\langle s_i, s_j \rangle\}$;
12   $R' \longleftarrow \emptyset$;
13   **foreach** *thread* t **do** $R' = R' \cup R'_t$;
14   **let** F' **be** $R \setminus R'$;

Algorithm 6. Computing a function $\tau : S^{\langle 2 \rangle} \to \Sigma^\star$ (Hybrid)

---

    input : An automaton $A = (S, \Sigma, \delta)$
    output: A function $\tau : S^{\langle 2 \rangle} \to \Sigma^\star$
1 **foreach** *singleton* $\langle s, s \rangle \in S^{\langle 2 \rangle}$ **do** $\tau(\langle s, s \rangle) = \varepsilon$;
2 **foreach** *pair* $\langle s_i, s_j \rangle \in S^{\langle 2 \rangle}$ **do** $\tau(\langle s_i, s_j \rangle) = undefined$;
3 $F \longleftarrow \{\langle s, s \rangle | s \in S\}$; // all singleton states of $\mathcal{A}$
4 $R \longleftarrow \{\langle s_i, s_j \rangle | s_i, s_j \in S \wedge s_i \neq s_j\}$; // all pair states of $\mathcal{A}$
5 **while** F *is not empty* **do**
6   **if** $|F| < |R|$ **then**
7       $F, R, \tau \longleftarrow$ BFS_step_F2R(A, F, R, τ);
8   **else**
9       $F, R, \tau \longleftarrow$ BFS_step_R2F(A, F, R, τ);

4.3 A Hybrid Approach to Construct the Next Frontier

Since the size of R decreases at each iteration, R2F becomes faster at each step. On the other hand, F2R is expected to be faster than R2F during the earlier iterations. Therefore it makes sense to use a hybrid approach, where either an F2R or an R2F BFS step is used depending on their respective cost for the current iteration. These observations have been used by Beamer et al. to implement a direction-optimized BFS [19]. Since the cost of each F2R/R2F iteration depends on the number of edges processed, it is reasonable to compare the number of frontier/remaining pairs' edges to choose the cheaper approach at each iteration as in [19]. When the BFS is executed on a simple graph, this strategy is easy to apply. However, by only using δ^{-1}, it takes $O(p)$ time to count a new frontier pair's edges. Overall, the counting process takes $O(pn^2)$ time which is expensive considering that the overall sequential complexity is also $O(pn^2)$. In this work, we compared the size of R and F instead of the edges to be processed. The total additional complexity due to counting is $O(n^2)$ since each pair will be counted only once.

To analyze the validity of our counting heuristic and the potential improvement due to the Hybrid approach described in Algorithm 6, we compared the size of R and F, and the corresponding execution time of each F2R/R2F execution in Fig. 2. As the figure shows, counting the pairs instead of transitions can be a good heuristic to guess the cheaper approach in our case. Furthermore, the performance difference of F2R and R2F at the each iteration shows that the proposed *Hybrid* approach can yield a much better performance.

4.4 Implementation Details

To store and utilize the $\delta^{-1}(s, x)$ for all $x \in \Sigma$ and $s \in S$, we employ the data structures in Fig. 1 (right). For each symbol $x \in \Sigma$, we used two arrays ptrs$_x$ and js$_x$ where the former is of size $n+1$ and the latter is of size n. For each state $s \in S$, ptrs$_x[s]$ and ptrs$_x[s + 1]$ are the start (inclusive) and end (exclusive)

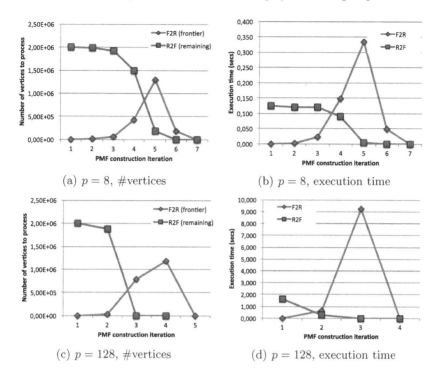

(a) $p = 8$, #vertices

(b) $p = 8$, execution time

(c) $p = 128$, #vertices

(d) $p = 128$, execution time

Fig. 2. The number of frontier and remaining vertices at each BFS level and the corresponding execution times of F2R and R2F while constructing the PMF τ for $n = 2000$ and $p = 8$ (top) and $p = 128$ (bottom).

pointers to two $\mathtt{js_x}$ entries. The array $\mathtt{js_x}$ stores the ids of the states $\delta^{-1}(s, x)$ in between $\mathtt{js_x}[\mathtt{ptrs_x}[s]]$ and $\mathtt{js_x}[\mathtt{ptrs_x}[s+1]$ - $1]$. This representation has a low memory footprint. Furthermore, we access the entries in the order of their array placement in our implementation hence, it is also good for spatial locality.

The memory complexity of the algorithms investigated in this study is $O(n^2)$. For each pair of states, we need to employ an array to store the length of the shortest merging sequence. To do that one can allocate an array of size n^2, Fig. 3 (left), and given the array index $\ell = (i - 1) \times n + j$ for a state pair $\{s_i, s_j\}$ where $1 \leq i \leq j \leq n$, she can obtain the state ids by $i = \lceil \frac{\ell}{n} \rceil$ and $j = \ell - ((i - 1) \times n)$. This simple approach effectively uses only the half of the array since for a state pair $\{s_i, s_j\}$, a redundant entry for $\{s_j, s_i\}$ is also stored. In our implementation, Fig. 3 (right), we do not use redundant locations. For an index $\ell = \frac{i \times (i+1)}{2} + j$ the state ids can be obtained by $i = \lfloor \sqrt{1 + 2\ell} - 0.5 \rfloor$ and $j = \ell - \frac{i \times (i+1)}{2}$. Preliminary experiments show that this approach, which does not suffer from the redundancy, also have a positive impact on the execution time. That being said, all the algorithms in the paper uses it and this improvement will not have change their relative performance.

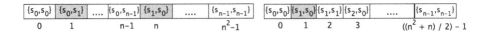

Fig. 3. Indexing and placement of the state pair arrays. A simple placement of the pairs (on the left) uses redundant places for state pairs $\{s_i, s_j\}$, $i \neq j$, e.g., $\{s_1, s_2\}$ and $\{s_2, s_1\}$ in the figure. On the right, the indexing mechanism we used is shown.

5   Experimental Results

All the experiments in the paper are performed on a single machine running on 64 bit CentOS 6.5 equipped with 64GB RAM and a dual-socket Intel Xeon E7-4870 v2 clocked at 2.30 GHz where each socket has 15 cores (30 in total). For the multicore implementations, we used OpenMP and all the codes are compiled with gcc 4.9.2 with the -O3 optimization flag enabled.

To measure the efficiency of the proposed algorithms, we used randomly generated automatons[3] with $n \in \{1000, 2000, 4000\}$ states and $p \in \{2, 8, 32, 128\}$ inputs. For each (n, p) pair, we randomly generated 20 different automatons and executed each algorithm on these automatons. The values in the figures and the tables are the averages of these 20 executions for each configuration, i.e., algorithm, n and p.

5.1   Multicore Parallelization of PMF Construction

Figure 4 shows the speedups of our parallel F2R implementation over the sequential baseline (that has no parallelism). Since F2R uses the same frontier extension mechanism with the sequential baseline, and R2F employs a completely different one, here we only present the speedup values of F2R. As the figure shows, when p is large, the parallel F2R presents good speedups, e.g., for $p = 128$, the average speedup is 14.1 with 16 threads. Furthermore, when compared to the single-thread F2R, the average speedup is 15.2 with 16 threads. A performance difference between sequential baseline and single-threaded F2R exists because of the parallelization overhead during the local queue management. Overall, we observed 10 % parallelization penalty for F2R on the average over the sequential baseline for all (n, p) pairs.

For p values smaller than 128, i.e., 2, 8, and 32, the average speedups are 5.4, 9.1, and 12.8, respectively, with 16 threads. The impact of the parallelization overhead is more for such cases since the amount of the local-queue overhead is proportional to the number of states but not to the number of edges. Consequently, when p decreases the amount of total work decreases and hence, the impact of the overhead increases. Furthermore, since the number of iterations for PMF construction increases with decreasing p, the local queues are merged more for smaller p values. Therefore, one can expect more overhead, and hence, less efficiency for smaller p values as the experiments confirm.

---

[3] For each state s and input x, $\delta(s, x)$ is randomly assigned to a state $s' \in S$.

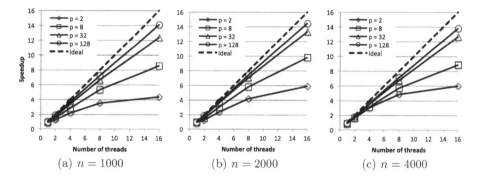

Fig. 4. The speedup of our parallel F2R PMF construction over the sequential PMF construction baseline.

Figure 5 compares the execution times of F2R, R2F and Hybrid algorithm for $n = 1000$ (top) and $n = 4000$ (bottom) states, $p \in \{2, 8, 32\}$ and $\{1, 2, 4, 8, 16\}$ threads (the results for $n = 2000$ are similar but omitted due to space limitations). For better figure scaling, the results for $p = 128$ is given in Fig. 6. An interesting observation is that F2R is consistently faster than R2F for $p = 2$, however, it is slower otherwise. This can be explained by the difference in the number of required iterations to construct PMF: when p is large, the frontier expands very quickly and the PMF is constructed in less iterations, e.g., for $n = 2000$, the PMF is generated in 16 iterations for $p = 2$, whereas only 7 iterations are required for $p = 8$. Since each edge will be processed once, the runtime of F2R always increases with p, i.e., with the number of edges. However, since the frontier expands much faster, the total number of remaining (R-)pairs processed by the R2F throughout the process will probably decrease. Furthermore, since when the frontier is large, while traversing the edge list of an R-pair, it is more probable to early terminate the traversal and add the R-pair to the next frontier earlier. Surprisingly, when p increases, these may yield a decrease in the R2F runtime (observe the change from $p = 2$ to $p = 8$ in Fig. 5). However, once the performance benefits of early termination are fully exploited, an increase on the R2F runtime with increasing p is more probable since the overall BFS work, i.e., the total number of edges, also increases with p (observe the change from $p = 8$ to $p = 32$ in Fig. 5).

Observing such performance differences for R2F and F2R on automatons with different characteristics, the potential benefit of a Hybrid algorithm in practice is more clear. As Figs. 5 and 6 show, the hybrid approach, which is just a combination of F2R and R2F, is almost always faster than employing a pure F2R or a pure R2F BFS-level expansion. Furthermore, we do not need parallelism to observe these performance benefits: the Hybrid approach works better even when a single thread is used at runtime. For example, when $n = 4000$ and $p = 128$, the Hybrid algorithm is 23 and 6 times faster than F2R and R2F, respectively. For the same automaton set, the speedups due to hybridization of the process become 14 and 4 with 16 threads on average.

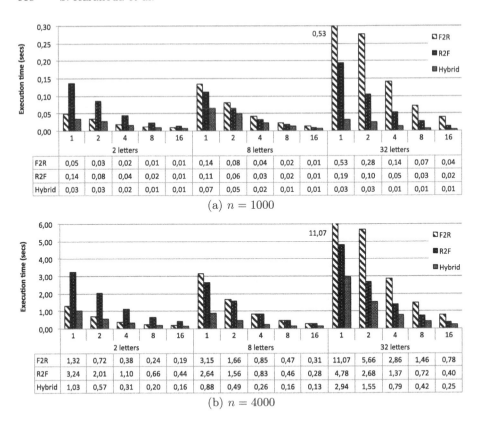

Fig. 5. Comparison of the parallel execution times of the three PMF construction algorithms: (1) F2R, (2) R2F, and (3) hybrid. The figures show the times for $n = 1000$ (top) and $n = 4000$ (bottom), $p \in \{2, 8, 32\}$, with $\{1, 2, 4, 8, 16\}$ threads (x-axis). For a better readability and figure scaling, the single-thread F2R bars with 32 inputs are allowed to exceed the max value on the y-axis.

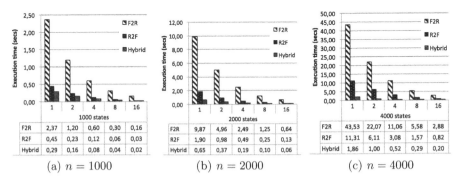

Fig. 6. Comparison of the parallel execution times of the three PMF construction algorithms: (1) F2R, (2) R2F, and (3) hybrid. The figures show the times for $n = 1000$ (left), $n = 2000$ (middle), and $n = 4000$ (bottom), $p = 128$, with $\{1, 2, 4, 8, 16\}$ threads (x-axis).

When the Hybrid algorithm is used, the speedups on the PMF generation phase are given in Fig. 7. As the figure shows, thanks to parallelism and good scaling of Hybrid (for large p values), the speedups increase when the number of threads increases. The PMF generation process becomes 95, 165, and 199 times faster when 16 threads used for 1000, 2000, and 4000 state automatons, respectively. Even with single thread, i.e., no parallelization, the Hybrid heuristic is 8, 14, and 21 times faster than the sequential algorithm.

Since we generate the PMF to find a synchronizing sequence, a more practical evaluation metric would be the performance improvement over the sequential reset sequence construction process. As Table 1 shows, for Eppstein's GREEDY

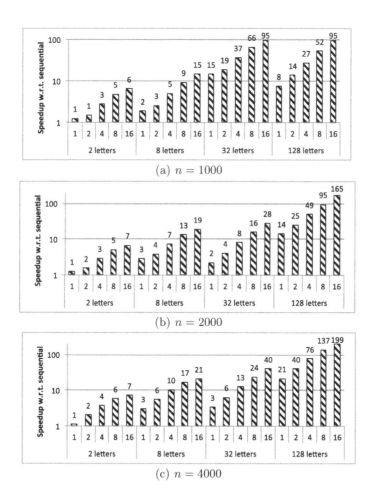

Fig. 7. The speedups of the Hybrid PMF construction algorithm with $n = 1000$ (top), 2000 (middle), 4000 (bottom) and $p \in \{2, 8, 32, 128\}$. The x-axis shows the number of threads used for the Hybrid execution. The values are computed based on the average sequential PMF construction time over 20 different automatons for each (n, p) pair.

heuristic (also for some other heuristics such as CYCLE [13]), the PMF generation phase dominates the overall runtime. For this reason, we simply conducted
an experiment where the Hybrid approach is used to construct the PMF and no
further parallelization is applied during the synchronizing sequence construction
phase. Table 2 shows the speedups for this experiment for single thread and 16
thread Hybrid executions. As the results show, even when the sequence construction phase is not parallelized, more than 50x and more than 100x improvement
is possible for $p = 32$ and $p = 128$, respectively.

Table 2. The speedups obtained on Eppstein's GREEDY algorithm when the Hybrid
PMF construction algorithm is used.

n	p (Single thread)				p (16 threads)			
	2	8	32	128	2	8	32	128
1000	1.2	1.8	13.4	7.5	4.6	10.8	58.2	83.7
2000	1.2	2.7	2.2	14.0	4.8	13.1	24.3	133.9
4000	1.1	2.9	3.3	20.7	5.5	14.8	31.7	154.0

As noted before, F2R based PMF construction has $O(pn^2)$ time complexity.
R2F based PMF construction, on the other hand, has $O(dpn^2)$ time complex-
ity (where d is the diameter of the pair automaton $\mathcal{A}$), since states of $\mathcal{A}$ in
the remaining set R will be processed at most d times. In practice, however,
R2F based construction (and Hybrid computation which also has $O(dpn^2)$ time
complexity since it performs R2F steps) can beat F2R based construction.

We did not perform an extensive study on automata with larger state numbers, since it takes too long with the sequential baseline implementation. For
example, sequential PMF generation takes around 75 min for an automaton with
32000 states and 128 letters, whereas our Hybrid implementation completes in
3 min.

6   Conclusion and Future Work

We investigated the efficient implementation and use of modern multicore CPUs
to scale the performance of synchronizing sequence generation heuristics. We
parallelized one of the well-known heuristics GREEDY. We mainly focused on
the PMF generation phase (which is employed by almost all the heuristics in the
literature), since it is the most time consuming part of GREEDY. Even with no
parallelization, our algorithmic improvements yielded a 20x speedup on GREEDY
for automatons with 4000 states and 128 inputs. Furthermore, around 150x
speedup has been obtained with 16 threads for the same automata class.

To eliminate threats to validity, we checked and confirmed that the sequence
constructed by each algorithm is indeed a synchronizing sequence. We also compared the length of the sequences constructed by the original implementation of

GREEDY and different versions of GREEDY algorithms suggested in this paper. We observed that regardless of the PMF construction approach used, for each pair $\langle s_i, s_j \rangle$, we obtain the same length $|\tau(\langle s_i, s_j \rangle)|$ for the shortest merging sequences, but the actual shortest merging sequence $\tau(\langle s_i, s_j \rangle)$ can differ, which causes around $\pm 1\%$ difference in the length of the synchronizing sequences.

As a future work, we will apply our techniques to other heuristics in the literature that are relatively slower than GREEDY but can produce shorter synchronizing sequences. For these heuristics, parallelizing only the PMF generation phase may not be sufficient since the synchronizing sequence construction part of these heuristics are much more expensive compared to GREEDY. Hence, we aim to parallelize the whole sequence generation process. Another problem we want to study is the use of cutting-edge manycore architectures such as GPUs and FPGAs to make such heuristics faster and more practical for large scale automatons.

Acknowledgements. This work is supported by TÜBİTAK Grants #114E569 and #115C018.

References

1. Chow, T.S.: Testing software design modeled by finite-state machines. IEEE Trans. Softw. Eng. **4**(3), 178–187 (1978)
2. Hennie, F.C.: Fault-detecting experiments for sequential circuits. In: Proceedings of Fifth Annual Symposium on Switching Circuit Theory and Logical Design, Princeton, New Jersey, pp. 95–110 (1964)
3. Ural, H., Wu, X., Zhang, F.: On minimizing the lengths of checking sequences. IEEE Trans. Comput. **46**(1), 93–99 (1997)
4. Hierons, R.M., Ural, H.: Reduced length checking sequences. IEEE Trans. Comput. **51**(9), 1111–1117 (2002)
5. Petrenko, A., Yevtushenko, N.: Testing from partial deterministic FSM specifications. IEEE Trans. Comput. **54**(9), 1154–1165 (2005)
6. Simão, A.S., Petrenko, A., Yevtushenko, N.: On reducing test length for FSMs with extra states. Softw. Test. Verif. Reliab. **22**(6), 435–454 (2012)
7. Hierons, R.M., Ural, H.: Generating a checking sequence with a minimum number of reset transitions. Autom. Softw. Eng. **17**(3), 217–250 (2010)
8. Schrammel, P., Melham, T., Kroening, D.: Chaining test cases for reactive system testing. In: Yenigün, H., Yilmaz, C., Ulrich, A. (eds.) ICTSS 2013. LNCS, vol. 8254, pp. 133–148. Springer, Heidelberg (2013). doi:10.1007/978-3-642-41707-8_9
9. Groz, R., Simao, A., Petrenko, A., Oriat, C.: Inferring finite state machines without reset using state identification sequences. In: El-Fakih, K., Barlas, G., Yevtushenko, N. (eds.) ICTSS 2015. LNCS, vol. 9447, pp. 161–177. Springer, Heidelberg (2015). doi:10.1007/978-3-319-25945-1_10
10. Jourdan, G.V., Ural, H., Yenigun, H.: Reduced checking sequences using unreliable reset. Inf. Process. Lett. **115**(5), 532–535 (2015)
11. Berlinkov, M.V.: On the probability of being synchronizable. In: Govindarajan, S., Maheshwari, A. (eds.) CALDAM 2016. LNCS, vol. 9602, pp. 73–84. Springer, Heidelberg (2016). doi:10.1007/978-3-319-29221-2_7

12. Eppstein, D.: Reset sequences for monotonic automata. SIAM J. Comput. **19**(3), 500–510 (1990)
13. Trahtman, A.N.: Some results of implemented algorithms of synchronization. In: 10th Journees Montoises d'Inform (2004)
14. Roman, A.: Synchronizing finite automata with short reset words. Appl. Math. Comput. **209**(1), 125–136 (2009)
15. Kudlacik, R., Roman, A., Wagner, H.: Effective synchronizing algorithms. Expert Syst. Appl. **39**(14), 11746–11757 (2012)
16. Roman, A., Szykula, M.: Forward and backward synchronizing algorithms. Expert Syst. Appl. **42**(24), 9512–9527 (2015)
17. Türker, U.C.: Parallel algorithm for deriving reset sequences from deterministic incomplete finite automata. IJFCS Int. J. Found. Comput. Sci. (submitted)
18. Natarajan, B.K.: An algorithmic approach to the automated design of parts orienters. In: FOCS, pp. 132–142 (1986)
19. Beamer, S., Asanović, K., Patterson, D.: Direction-optimizing breadth-first search. In: Proceedings of the International Conference on High Performance Computing, Networking, Storage and Analysis, SC 2012, pp. 12:1–12:10. IEEE Computer Society Press, Los Alamitos (2012)

Resolving the Equivalent Mutant Problem in the Presence of Non-determinism and Coincidental Correctness

Krishna Patel$^{(\boxtimes)}$ and Robert M. Hierons

Department of Computer Science, Brunel University,
Uxbridge, Middlesex UB8 3PH, UK
{krishna.patel,rob.hierons}@brunel.ac.uk

Abstract. In this paper, we develop a new mutation testing technique called Interlocutory Mutation Testing (IMT) that mitigates the equivalent mutant problem in the presence of coincidental correctness and non-determinism. The accuracy of IMT was evaluated; it obtained a classification accuracy of 93.33 % for non-equivalent mutants and 100 % for equivalent mutants in a non-deterministic system with coincidental correctness.

Keywords: Mutation testing · Coincidental correctness · Non-determinism · Equivalent mutant problem

1 Introduction

Mutation Testing (MT) is a technique for generating artificial faults [15], which are reasonably accurate simulations of real faults [2]. MT operates by applying a minor augmentation (referred to as a mutation) to the system under test (SUT) S_o to produce a faulty version S_m [5] called a mutant. For example, a statement $X < 5$ in S_o might be transformed into $X > 5$ in S_m.

Unfortunately, a limitation of MT is that it can produce equivalent mutants [7] — this is known as the equivalent mutant problem. An equivalent mutant is an augmentation S_m that is observationally equivalent to the SUT S_o. For example, suppose that $Math.abs(5)$ and $Math.abs(-5)$ appear on Line 1 in S_o and S_m respectively. S_m is an equivalent mutant, because the augmentation is semantically equivalent and doesn't modify the behaviour of S_o.

A study conducted by Yao et al. [24] demonstrated that the equivalent mutant problem is pervasive. Despite the fact that deducing mutant equivalence is undecidable [4], this has motivated some research into how the problem can be circumvented [11]. For example, let $S_o(I)$ and $S_m(I)$ denote the respective outputs of S_o and S_m for a given input. Many researchers typically expose S_o and S_m to a test suite to obtain a set of pairs $\langle S_o(I), S_m(I) \rangle$ and assume that S_o and S_m

© IFIP International Federation for Information Processing 2016
Published by Springer International Publishing AG 2016. All Rights Reserved
F. Wotawa et al. (Eds.): ICTSS 2016, LNCS 9976, pp. 123–138, 2016.
DOI: 10.1007/978-3-319-47443-4_8

are equivalent if the following condition holds for each pair: $S_o(I) = S_m(I)$. For ease of reference, we refer to this as the Traditional Equivalent Mutant Detection Technique (TEMDT). An example of the use of TEMDT can be found in Sadi et al. [21].

However, this assumption doesn't always hold. For example, non-deterministic behaviours may be responsible for any observed discrepancies, and may be misinterpreted as having originated from the mutation [5]. Another example includes the presence of coincidental correctness; the SUT can misbehave but still produce the expected output, which can lead to non-equivalent mutants being mistakenly classified as equivalent. Alternative techniques have been proposed to address these problems, but have limitations (see Sect. 2). Manual inspection is typically used under such circumstances [1].

In our previous work, we developed Interlocutory Testing (IT), a testing technique that suppresses coincidental correctness and can operate effectively in the presence of non-determinism [19]. This paper explores how IT can be used to alleviate the Equivalent Mutant Problem in systems with non-determinism and/or coincidental correctness. We call the approach Interlocutory Mutation Testing (IMT).

The relationship between the input and output of the SUT, in conjunction with one's knowledge/expectations about the SUT, can be used to predict aspects of the execution trace. For example, consider the Bubble Sort algorithm; *Input* and *Output* are sequences of integers. If *Input* $\neq$ *Output*, one can predict that the Swap Operator was invoked at least once. The correctness of this prediction is predicated on whether the SUT's behaviour mirrors the tester's expectations. Let f denote a fault in Bubble Sort that overwrites the value of the first element of *Input* with a random value. f can lead to situations in which *Input* $\neq$ *Output* and the swap operator was not invoked; the failure to satisfy the prediction above in such situations shows that the behaviour of the SUT does not satisfy the tester's expectations[1]. IMT exploits this observation as follows. Let S denote the SUT and M denote a mutated version of S. Suppose that M is executed with an input *MInput*, and produces an execution trace *MET* and output *MOutput*. IMT uses the relationship between *MInput* and *MOutput*, in conjunction with the tester's knowledge/expectations about S, to predict aspects of *MET*. If this prediction is incorrect then this suggests that M is not an equivalent mutant.

This paper makes the following main contributions:

1. A new technique called IMT that can classify mutants as equivalent and non-equivalent in programs with coincidental correctness and/or non-deterministic behaviours.
2. An evaluation of the accuracy of IMT.

The paper is structured as follows. We begin by presenting related work in Sect. 2. Section 3 describes our proposed technique and explains how the

---

[1] Later we will see more complicated examples in which this process can help to overcome coincidental correctness.

technique can be applied. Section 4 outlines our experimental set-up. The experiment results are presented and discussed in Sect. 5, along with threats to validity in Sect. 6. Conclusions are finally drawn in Sect. 7.

2   Related Work

2.1   The Equivalent Mutant Problem and Coincidental Correctness

Fault detection requires the execution of a faulty statement, that causes the subsequent infection of a state (to produce a failure), and propagation of an infected state to the output (so an oracle can assess it) [23]. According to Masri and Assi [14], strong coincidental correctness occurs when the first two conditions are satisfied, but the third is not, and weak coincidental correctness occurs when the first condition is satisfied, but not the third; the second condition may or may not be satisfied. Weak coincidental correctness subsumes strong coincidental correctness. In this paper, "coincidental correctness" refers to weak coincidental correctness.

In the context of mutation testing, coincidental correctness can be described as follows: Let S_o be the SUT and S_m be a non-equivalent mutant. Also let s_m denote the state in S_m after the mutated statement executes and s_o be the corresponding state in S_o. Coincidental correctness occurs if s_m and s_o map to the same output, despite the differences in code.

Masri and Assi [13] define information flow strength as the percentage of information that propagates between two program points; a higher percentage indicates greater strength. This determines the probability that an infected state will propagate to the output, which is tantamount to the likelihood of observing coincidental correctness. Masri et al. [14] conducted a series of experiments that suggested that coincidental correctness is widespread. For example, 72 % and 96.5 % of the systems they investigated had strong and weak coincidental correctness respectively and between 63.76–97.58 % of the weak information flows in six of these systems had a strength of 0.

Despite the prevalence of coincidental correctness, little research has been conducted on determining mutant equivalence in the context of coincidental correctness. To our knowledge, only one approach has been proposed. Offutt and Lee [16] extend TEMDT (see Sect. 1). They suggest additionally comparing s_o and s_m. While this can be useful in some situations it's not a universal solution e.g. its effectiveness may be limited in non-deterministic systems.

2.2   The Equivalent Mutant Problem and Non-deterministic Systems

Non-deterministic systems are becoming increasingly prevalent e.g. concurrency can lead to alternative interleavings. For example, consider a variable X that is instantiated with a value of 3. Suppose we have two threads t_1 and t_2 and that t_1 applies the following operation to X: $X = X + 1$. Further, suppose that t_2

updates the value of X to $X = X \times 2$. The order of the interleavings affects the final state of X i.e. if t_1 executes first, then $X = 8$ and if t_2 executes first $X = 7$.

This complicates the mutant classification process. Several proposals have been made to address this. For example, Carver [5] identifies two methods - Multiple Execution Testing (MET) and Deterministic Execution Testing (DET). In MET, confidence is improved by executing the original S_o and mutant S_m versions multiple times and observing their output distributions. DET involves forcing the SUT to execute deterministically by manipulating conditions e.g. a Genetic Algorithms Mutation Rate can be set to 100 % or 0 % to force deterministic execution of the Mutation Operator.

Both strategies are viable, but have limitations. For example, MET is dictated by chance; thus there is scope for misclassification [5] and non-replicability [5]. It's also expensive because it uses multiple executions. On the other hand, DET limits test case selection; thus some mutation points may not be reachable with allowable test cases. Carver [5] attempted to reduce the impact of these weaknesses by combining MET and DET.

Gligoric et al. [7] suggest executing S_o with a test case t, and then establishing whether the mutant statement in S_m could have been reached by this execution. Non-reachability implies equivalence for t. This approach is limited to the identification of equivalent mutants in unexecuted code.

Finally, Papadakis et al. [17] propose comparing S_m's object code to the object code of S_o. If S_m's object code matches S_o's object code, then we can guarantee that S_o is equivalent to S_m. However, if the comparison reveals that there are discrepancies, S_m may either be equivalent or non-equivalent to S_o. Although the approach can't correctly classify all mutants, it is inexpensive and so can be a valuable complimentary equivalent mutant classification technique.

3   Interlocutory Mutation Testing

IMT was developed to enable the classification of equivalent and non-equivalent mutants in programs that are non-deterministic and/or are susceptible to coincidental correctness. Section 3.1 introduces the technique and demonstrates how it can classify mutants despite the presence of coincidental correctness, and Sect. 3.2 shows how the technique can be extended to cope with non-determinism.

3.1   Interlocutory Mutation Testing and Coincidental Correctness

This section draws on the following running example.

The SUT is a Genetic Algorithm, which is a search optimisation technique. The SUT consists of four major components: Initial Population Generator, Crossover, Mutation, and Selection. Let Sys denote the SUT.

Consider Sys's selection operator, denoted by Sys_{so}. Sys_{so}'s $Input$ consists of a population size parameter PS, which is the maximum population size, and a $Population$, such that $Population.size() \geq PS$. Let $Population_{SOI}$ be the state of *Population* at this point in the execution trace. *Input* is processed by Sys_{so} as follows: random elements of $Population_{SOI}$ are iteratively removed until $Population.size() == PS$. Sys_{so}'s resultant *Output* is a version of the *Population* that has been subjected to this process; $Population_{SOO}$ denotes the state of *Population* at this point in the execution.

Suppose that a non-equivalent mutant, denoted by MUT, of the *Sys* was produced. The delta between MUT and *Sys* is that MUT performs an additional operation; it adds a random individual to $Population_{SOI}$ during Sys_{so}'s initialisation phase. Since Sys_{so} iteratively removes random individuals from $Population_{SOO}.size()$ until $Population_{SOO}.size() == PS$, all traces of an additional member being added to $Population_{SOI}$ might be lost by the time the execution reaches the $Population_{SOO}$ state. Thus, MUT is a coincidentally correct mutant.

Intuition. Let's consider how MUT could be correctly classified. Suppose that MUT is executed and produces a log file that details the execution trace MET. Let MUT_{so} denote MUT's selection operator. The execution trace of MUT_{so} is a subsequence of MET. Let $MInput$ and $MOutput$ be MUT_{so}'s input and output respectively. Information about MET can be revealed by assessing the relationship between $MInput$ and $MOutput$. For example, $Population_{SOI}.size() > Population_{SOO}.size()$ may be one relationship between $MInput$ and $MOutput$, and from this, we can deduce that members of *Population* were removed during the execution.

If we assume that MUT is equivalent to *Sys*, we can use our knowledge about how *Sys* behaves in this context to predict aspects of MET. To illustrate, since we know that the Selection Operator iteratively removes random members of *Population* until $Population.size() == PS$, when $Population_{SOI}.size() > Population_{SOO}.size()$, we can deduce that the *Population* must have been expanded by $Population_{SOI}.size() - Population_{SOO}.size()$ individuals before the Selection Operator was executed. Since we also know that the only function that can add additional members to a *Population* of size PS is the Crossover Operator, the following prediction about MET can be made: the Crossover Operator generated $Population_{SOI}.size() - Population_{SOO}.size()$ individuals and added them to *Population*.

Finally, this prediction can be checked against MET. Let $CrossoverN$ be the total number of members that were actually generated by the Crossover Operator during the execution i.e. as reported in MET. In continuation of the example above, this involves checking $CrossoverN == Population_{SOI}.size() - Population_{SOO}.size()$. Since an additional member is added to $Population_{SOI}$ by MUT, this predicate would evaluate to false, which indicates that the prediction was incorrect. The behaviour of MUT deviated from how *Sys* would have behaved; thus we can conclude that MUT is not equivalent to *Sys*.

Had MUT been equivalent to *Sys* (i.e. had the additional member not been added to *Population* during the initialisation of the Selection Operator), the prediction would have been correct.

The example above demonstrates that one can use the relationship between *MInput* and *MOutput* to predict properties of *MET*. Discrepancies between this prediction and *MET* indicate that *MUT* is not equivalent to *Sys*. The example also demonstrates that this approach works in the presence of coincidental correctness. This forms the intuition of our technique - Interlocutory Mutation Testing (IMT).

Technique Description. This section outlines how IMT realises the intuition described above. IMT requires that the relationship between an input and output (Input-Output pair) is associated with a prediction about the mutant's execution trace *MET*. Associating a prediction with every individual Input-Output pair would be impractical. Instead, IMT groups Input-Output pairs together using Input-Output Relationships (IORs). Certain predictions are applicable to all Input-Output pairs in such a group. Consider the earlier example; $Population_{SOI}.size() > Population_{SOO}.size()$ is an IOR (for ease of reference, we call this IOR_1), and it groups Input-Output pairs where the prediction is that the Crossover Operator produced $Population_{SOI}.size() - Population_{SOO}.size()$ members and added them to the *Population*.

The prediction that is associated with an IOR is referred to as an "Interlocutory Decision" (ID). An ID can be expressed using any method, on the proviso that it can unambiguously describe one's prediction about *MET* and be automatically compared with the execution trace *MET*. For example, as demonstrated above, IDs can be expressed as predicates e.g. $CrossoverN == Population_{SOI}.size() - Population_{SOO}.size()$ (this ID is associated with IOR_1). Alternative methods of expressing IDs are discussed in our previous work [19].

In IMT, the mutant is executed, which results in an execution trace *MET*. IMT checks whether an IOR is satisfied by an input *MInput* and output *MOutput*, which are extracted from *MET*. In continuation of the example above, $MInput = Population_{SOI}$ and $MOutput = Population_{SOO}$. If $MInput.size() > MOutput.size()$, then IOR_1 is satisfied. If the IOR is satisfied, then IMT checks that *MET* satisfies the IOR's associated IDs (e.g. in the case of IOR_1, this would involve checking $CrossoverN == Population_{SOI}.size() - Population_{SOO}.size()$). Finally, if the prediction is correct (e.g. if $CrossoverN == Population_{SOI}.size() - Population_{SOO}.size()$), then IMT reports that the mutant is possibly equivalent, otherwise it reports that the mutant is non-equivalent.

An Input-Output pair I/O is said to be valid if the SUT can produce output O in response to input I. IOR_1 doesn't cater for all valid Input-Output pairs — it's possible to observe $Population_{SOI}.size() == Population_{SOO}.size()$ in *Sys*. IOR_1 must report that its classification was inconclusive in such cases. This can be remedied by creating more IORs that cover such pairs. For example, $Population_{SOI}.size() == Population_{SOO}.size()$ can be IOR_2 and $CrossoverExecuted == false$ can be its ID.

Interlocutory Relations (IRs) are the final construct used by IMT. An IR groups multiple IORs together to enable the definition of potentially complex relationships between IORs. Such relationships can enhance their classification accuracy. To illustrate, since all valid Input-Output pairs in Sys are collectively covered by IOR_1 and IOR_2, if a situation arises where neither IOR_1 nor IOR_2 is satisfied i.e. if $Population_{SOI}.size() < Population_{SOO}.size()$, then the IR can guarantee that the Input-Output pair under consideration can not have been observed in Sys, and thus reports that the mutant is non-equivalent. We refer to this grouping of IOR_1 and IOR_2 as IR_1. Thus, an IR operates as follows: Each IOR that is associated with the IR is evaluated as described above to obtain a set of Possibly Equivalent/Non-Equivalent/Inconclusive classifications. These classifications are analysed by the IR to arrive at a final conclusion. If at least one classification is possibly equivalent and none are non-equivalent, then the final conclusion is that the mutant is equivalent, and if at least one is non-equivalent, then the final conclusion is non-equivalent. Assuming that the IR has IORs that collectively cover all valid Input-Output Pairs, the final conclusion can be non-equivalent if all classifications are inconclusive (as is the case for IR_1).

3.2 Interlocutory Mutation Testing and Non-determinism

Intuition. Consider the Tournament Selection Operator (TSO) of a Genetic Algorithm. In particular, consider the logic that determines the winner of a tournament. A tournament consists of a set of competitors $tournament = \{Competitor_1, Competitor_2, ..., Competitor_n\}$, each of which is associated with a fitness value. One $Competitor_i \in tournament$ is randomly selected to be the winner of the tournament. A competitor's chance of winning is based on their fitness value, relative to the combined fitness values of all other competitors in the tournament. Thus, even though any competitor could win, the competitor with the highest fitness will have the greatest chance of being selected as the winner. Let $winner$ denote the selected competitor. On invocation of TSO, multiple tournaments are performed $tournaments=\{\langle tournament_1, winner_1\rangle, \langle tournament_2, winner_2\rangle, \langle tournament_3, winner_3\rangle, ...\}$.

An IR, which we will refer to as TournamentPIR, may be constructed for TSO. TournamentPIR may be associated with one IOR IOR_{TPIR} that is only satisfied under the following condition: For each $\langle tournament_i, winner_i\rangle$ in $tournaments$, $tournament_i$ contains at least two competitors $Competitor_j$ and $Competitor_k$, such that $Competitor_j.getFitnessValue() \neq Competitor_k.get$ $FitnessValue()$.

Let $tournaments_{strong}$ be a subset of $tournaments$, such that for each $\langle tournament_i, winner_i\rangle \in tournaments_{strong}$, $winner_i$ was a solution with the highest fitness in $tournament_i$. Conversely, let $tournaments_{weak}$ be a subset of $tournaments$, where in each $\langle tournament_i, winner_i\rangle \in tournaments_{weak}$, $winner_i$ was a solution with the lowest fitness. IOR_{TPIR} may be associated with an ID that predicts that $tournaments_{strong}$ contains more members than $tournaments_{weak}$.

In summary, TournamentPIR predicts that $tournament_{strong}$ will contain more members than $tournaments_{weak}$ (this is the ID), when every tournament in *tournaments* contains at least two competitors with different fitness values (this is the IOR). Although it's unlikely, it's possible that $tournament_{strong}$ may validly contains fewer members than $tournaments_{weak}$. This means that TournamentPIR can misclassify an equivalent mutant as a non-equivalent mutant. We refer to such a misclassification error as a false positive.

This demonstrates that a revised evaluation method is necessary for IRs that deal with probabilistic behaviours, to reduce the incidence of false positives. We refer to IRs that use the revised evaluation method as Probabilistic IRs (PIRs). For the sake of clarity, we refer to IRs that use the evaluation method detailed above as Deterministic IRs.

The intuition behind the new evaluation method is as follows. As discussed above, certain behaviours can cause PIRs to report false positives e.g. when $tournament_{strong}$ contains fewer members than $tournament_{weak}$. The randomised properties of a system determine how frequently certain behaviours are observed. This means that all behaviours, including those that can lead to false positives will have a typical rate of occurrence. In other words, a PIR has a typical false positive rate. The proposed evaluation method is to use statistical techniques to compare a PIR's typical false positive rate to the proportion of non-equivalent classifications made by that PIR; if the proportion of non-equivalent mutant classifications is significantly higher than the false positive rate, then it's likely that the mutant is non-equivalent, otherwise, it's possible that the mutant is equivalent.

Technique Description. This section introduces the evaluation method used by PIRs to reduce the impact of false positives.

The PIR evaluation method is two-fold. The first part of the evaluation method attempts to reduce the impact of false positives for a single test case tc. Let PIR be a PIR e.g. TournamentPIR and suppose that PIR has a typical false positive rate FPR_{tc} of 30 %. FPR_{tc} can be determined by analysing the randomised properties of the SUT, extrapolated from empirical test data, or be based on the tester's expertise. PIR may be evaluated multiple times during an execution of tc. For example, TournamentPIR is evaluated each time TSO is executed, and TSO can execute multiple times if the Genetic Algorithm has been configured to perform more than one generation. Each evaluation of PIR will either yield an equivalent or non-equivalent classification. Let $R_{tc} = count(Non\_Equivalent_{tc}) \div (count(Non\_Equivalent_{tc}) + count(Equivalent_{tc}))$, where $count(Non\_Equivalent_{tc})$ and $count(Equivalent_{tc})$ represent the number of times the mutant was classified as Non-Equivalent and Equivalent respectively. Thus, R_{tc} represents the proportion of times that PIR classified the mutant as Non-Equivalent in tc. In the first part of the evaluation method, R_{tc} is compared with FPR_{tc} using Pearsons χ^2. PIR's classification of the mutant based on tc is Non-equivalent if $R_{tc} > FPR_{tc}$ and the difference is statistically significant, otherwise the classification is equivalent. $PIR_C(tc)$ denotes this classification. To illustrate, suppose that $R_{tc} = 70\%$ and PIR was evaluated 100 times; since $70\% > 30\%$ and the difference between R_{tc} and FPR_{tc} is significant, $PIR_C(tc)$

would be Non-Equivalent. Conversely, if $R_{tc} = 33\%$, the difference between R_{tc} and FPR_{tc} would not be statistically significant and $PIR_C(tc)$ would Equivalent.

As discussed above, the first part of the PIR evaluation method alleviates the impact of false positives for a single test case execution. However, because of non-determinism, it's also possible for $PIR_C(tc)$ to be a false positive. Typically, one has access to a test suite $ts = \{tc_1, tc_2, ...\}$. Each test case $tc_i \in ts$ would have been subjected to the first part of the PIR evaluation method to obtain an Equivalent or Non-Equivalent classification $TCClassifications = \{PIR_C(tc_1), PIR_C(tc_2), ...\}$. The second part of the PIR evaluation method compares the proportion of Non-Equivalent to Equivalent classifications in $TCClassifications$ to a known false positive rate for $TCClassifications$ for the PIR under consideration using Pearsons χ^2. This "known false positive rate" can be determined using the same methods as above. The results of this comparison is interpreted in the same way as in the first part of the evaluation method; the resulting classification is the PIR's final classification for the mutant.

3.3 Applying IMT

Multiple IRs. In practice, one would typically leverage multiple IRs. Each IR may classify the mutant differently. This should be interpreted as follows: The mutant should be assumed to be non-equivalent if at least one IR classifies the mutant as non-equivalent, and should be considered to be equivalent if all IRs classify the mutant as equivalent.

Assumptions. IMT assumes that an IR is encoded with accurate information about how Sys works. Unfortunately, this assumption may not hold if a real fault is in the system or IRs. To reduce the impact of this assumption, we recommend applying the IRs to Sys with a test suite. If any of the IRs indicate that the Sys is non-equivalent, then the assumption doesn't hold. In such cases, one can either modify the system and/or IRs, or remove IRs until all IRs report that Sys is equivalent. The same test suite should then be used for conducting IMT.

Constructing IRs. Let s_i and s_o denote the program's input and output respectively. One must use one's domain knowledge to develop an intuition into how s_i and s_o are related. s_i, s_o and this intuition form an IOR. Tools that partially automate the exploration of relationships between inputs and outputs may simplify this task [6]. One must then leverage one's knowledge about the SUT's implementation details to identify execution trace behaviours that should manifest in executions in which this IOR is satisfied.

UCov is a test case coverage adequacy assessment tool for regression testing [3]. Like IMT, UCov leverages execution trace behaviours to achieve its objective. However, these execution trace behaviours are used to assess the intent of a test case i.e. program behaviours that should be executed by the test case, whilst such behaviours are used by IMT to assess the intent of the SUT i.e. program behaviours that should manifest if the SUT has not been adversely affected by the mutation. Given their similarities, some of UCov's findings are relevant for IMT. For example, the aforementioned knowledge has been found to be available in the SUT's documentation [3].

Automated program analytic tools like Program Slicing [8] and Invariant Detection e.g. Daikon [9] can assist one in identifying useful execution trace behaviours. These behaviours are the IDs of IOR. This process is repeated to obtain multiple pairs $\langle IOR_i, IDs_i \rangle$, where IOR_i is an IOR and IDs_i is a set of IDs that are associated with IOR_i. Finally, one can group multiple pairs together, such that the IORs in these pairs have relationships. Identifying IORs that are amenable to such a grouping can be a natural task, because such IORs are typically highly related.

4   Experimental Set-Up

4.1   Subject Program

The subject program is a Genetic Algorithm for the Bin Packing Problem that was developed by the author based on the design of Mladen Jankovic [10] with the JAGA Genetic Algorithm API toolbox [18]. The subject program consists of 1606 source lines of code (SLOC)[2], 29 classes and 244 methods (average 8 per class). The subject was partly selected to enhance the representativeness of the experiment and also minimise experimental bias. The former is achieved because it is non-deterministic and has weak information flow strength [14] and is thus susceptible to coincidental correctness. With regards to the latter, the implementation involves multiple developers, most of which were not aware of this research.

4.2   Interlocutory Relations

We used the same 48 IRs that were used in our previous work [19]. For a comprehensive list of these IRs, please see [19]. A real fault was present in the system, so we tested the assumption outlined in Sect. 3.3. We found that the assumption holds i.e. these IRs were not sensitive to the real fault. 42 IRs are Deterministic and 6 are Probabilistic.

4.3   Mutants

MuJava [12] was used to generate 30 non-equivalent mutants. It was applied to all classes that significantly contributed to the SUT's core functionality. 11 interface classes (MuJava couldn't produce mutants for these), 2 unused classes and the test case input class were excluded. We also excluded 3 simple data

---

[2] We used the "Code Lines" metric in the Understand program [22] to compute SLOC. This metric ignores blank and comment lines.

classes and 2 abstract classes that stored a single object and only implemented getter/setter methods and/or just exposed methods that this object already has. For example, the simple data class may have an ArrayList *ArrayObj* and a method *remove(i)*, which simply calls *ArrayObj.remove(i)*. Finally, a comparator class was also excluded. Equivalent mutants and obvious mutants (i.e. mutants that resulted in system crashes or infinite loops) were also removed. We also rejected mutations of faulty code. These mutants were classified as either coincidentally correct or standard faults. Let S denote the system and M be a mutant of S. $ORACLE$ is an oracle that checks all of S's output properties (listed below). This was achieved by using $ORACLE$ on M's output. If $ORACLE$ passes, then the infected state didn't propagate to the output; thus M is coincidentally correct. We found that 15 were coincidentally correct and 15 were standard.

- Let *DataSet* be the set of items to be sorted into bins. The output O should be a permutation of *DataSet*.
- O should contain at least one bin.
- O should not contain empty bins.
- O should not contain a bin that has more items than its capacity.
- O should not have a fitness that is greater than the maximum obtainable fitness (Fitness Function Constant).

Refactoring augments source code structure, while retaining behaviour; thus refactorings are effectively equivalent mutants. AutoRefactor [20] was used to generate 30 equivalent mutants.

In summary, this experiment leverages 60 mutants in total, 30 non-equivalent and 30 equivalent.

4.4   Test Cases

We use the same test suite that was used in our previous work [19]. The test suite consists of 100 test cases that were generated by Random Testing.

5   Results and Discussion

This section reports an empirical study that measures the accuracy of IMT for non-equivalent and equivalent mutants.

5.1   Non-equivalent Mutants

IMT correctly classified 28/30 non-equivalent mutants. This suggests that IMT's classification accuracy can be high for non-equivalent mutants. Since the SUT is non-deterministic, this also demonstrates that the technique's classification accuracy for these mutants was not hampered by non-determinism. Specifically, 15/15 and 13/15 standard and coincidentally correct mutants were correctly

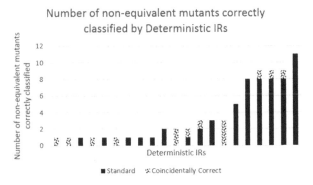

Fig. 1. Number of mutants that were correctly classified by Deterministic IRs, broken down by mutant type

classified. The difference in performance for these mutant types is not significant (Fisher's Exact Test: $p > 0.05$). This indicates that IMT can be effective for standard and coincidentally correct faults.

Recall that there are two types of IRs - Deterministic and Probabilistic IRs. These IRs are distinguished by the types of logic they are applied to — deterministic IRs are applied to aspects of the system that behave deterministically, whilst probabilistic IRs are applied to non-deterministic aspects of the system. To that end, each approach has different evaluation methods; the difference being, Probabilistic IRs leverage statistical techniques to factor out the effect of false positives that arise due to non-determinism. We therefore decided to further break down the analysis by these IR types.

Deterministic IRs correctly classified 23/30 (13/15 standard and 10/15 coincidentally correct) non-equivalent mutants. The difference in the Deterministic IR's performance for standard and coincidentally correct mutants is not statistically significant (Fisher's Exact Test: $p > 0.05$). This demonstrates that one can leverage these IRs in contexts where coincidental correctness is present, or absent. Each bar in Fig. 1 represents a Deterministic IR that correctly classified a mutant. The height of the bar denotes the number of correctly classified non-equivalent mutants. Each bar also represents the proportion of mutants that were standard or coincidentally correct. Figure 1 demonstrates that some IRs are more accurate than others for different mutants. For example, the IR represented by the third bar correctly classifies standard mutants, but not coincidentally correct mutants, and the converse is true for the IR represented by the second bar.

19/30 (14/15 standard and 5/15 coincidentally correct) non-equivalent mutants were correctly classified by Probabilistic IRs. A comparison of the performance of Deterministic and Probabilistic IRs for standard faults revealed that the difference was not statistically significant (Fisher's Exact Test: $p > 0.05$), but was for coincidentally correct faults (Fisher's Exact Test: $p < 0.05$). This suggests that Probabilistic IRs may be less effective in situations where coincidental correctness is present. However, we observed that 3 of the coincidentally

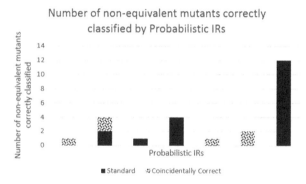

Fig. 2. Number of mutants that were correctly classified by Probabilistic IRs, broken down by mutant type

correct faults found by IMT were uniquely identified by Probabilistic IRs, which means that they can add value in situations where coincidental correctness is present. Figure 2 presents the same information as in Fig. 1, but for Probabilistic IRs; it shows the breakdown of the results; similar observations can be made to those in Fig. 1.

As discussed above, all of the IRs collectively, correctly classified 28/30 non-equivalent mutants. Deterministic IRs and Probabilistic IRs correctly classified 23 and 19 mutants respectively, which means that neither IR type correctly classified all of the mutants on their own. This demonstrates that both IR types can add value.

Interestingly, these results also suggest that there was a substantial degree of overlap in terms of the number of mutants that were correctly classified by the IRs. We therefore decided to perform a subsumption analysis to determine the smallest number of IRs that would be required to obtain the same results. We found that only 12 were necessary: AverageFitnessGeneration, ChoosingPairsOfParentsComposition, CreateRandomIndividualNewBins, CrossoverRate, DecidingWhoShouldMutateFineGrained, GAController, Mutate-Individual, PartitionChild, ReplacementOperationIntegrity, ShouldUseNewIndividual, TerminateGA, TournamentComposition. This shows that the technique can be effective with relatively few IRs.

5.2   Equivalent Mutants

Promisingly, IMT correctly classified 30/30 equivalent mutants. Since Deterministic IRs don't check non-deterministic aspects of the system, they aren't susceptible to false positives, assuming that the assumption detailed in Sect. 3.3 holds. It's therefore not surprising that they did not misclassify any equivalent mutants. Since Probabilistic IRs do check such behaviours, false positives may be possible. To that end, we extended the evaluation method used by Probabilistic IRs, as described in Sect. 3.2, to curtail the incidence of false positives.

These results illustrate that this evaluation method was successful in achieving this goal.

6   Threats to Validity

There are several threats to validity. We attempted to address these where possible e.g. randomisation was used throughout the experiment to reduce experimental bias.

Firstly, the presence of real faults may confound the results i.e. an IR may assume that misbehaviour emanating from a real fault actually originated from the mutant process. To mitigated the impact of real faults on the experiment, we only used IRs that were not sensitive to the real fault and excluded mutations of the real fault.

Each IR is associated with a logging function. These logging functions capture data about the execution trace, during the execution of the SUT. Some mutants can alter the SUT's control flow. These alterations can cause the logging functions to crash. In such situations, the IR has effectively recognised that the SUT's control flow is incorrect and has thus correctly classified the non-equivalent mutant. Our experiment did not distinguish between these crashes and system crashes, and so they were conservatively removed. Therefore, the experimental results presented in this paper for non-equivalent mutants underestimate the technique's effectiveness. However, we do not believe that this had a significant impact on the results, since the technique already correctly classifies most of the mutants.

There is also a threat to generalisability; we only used one subject program. However, the subject program had the operating environment that we were studying i.e. non-determinism and a high propensity for coincidental correctness, and was therefore suitable for assessing our research objectives. As a part of ongoing research, we are currently applying IMT to four other subject programs; the preliminary results are promising, see Sect. 7.

Finally, the results demonstrated that different IRs obtained different levels of effectiveness. Thus, the effectiveness of the technique may vary considerably, depending on one's choice of IRs. This may be a threat to repeatability.

7   Conclusion

In this paper, we proposed Interlocutory Mutation Testing, the first mutant classification technique that can be applied in the presence of coincidental correctness and/or non-determinism. The technique correctly classified 93.33 % of the non-equivalent mutants and 100 % of the equivalent mutants, which suggests that the technique is capable of producing highly accurate results. We also observed that different IRs are more effective than others for classifying different faults, which suggests that using a diverse range of IRs can be valuable.

As mentioned in Sect. 6, one of the limitations of our study is that we only considered one subject program. As a part of ongoing research, we are currently conducting IMT on four other subject programs. A brief summary of the preliminary results are as follows. We applied IMT to Dijkstra's Algorithm. IMT obtained a non-equivalent mutant classification accuracy of 93.33 %, and 100 % mutant classification accuracy for equivalent mutants; 30 non-equivalent and 30 equivalent mutants were used. 34 mutants, which include a mixture of equivalent and non-equivalent mutants, were also generated across Bubble Sort, Binary Search and Knuth-Morris-Pratt. All of these mutants were correctly classified. It is our hope that these experiments will reduce the impact of this limitation.

Another limitation of our work is the effort required to apply the technique. Our experiment leveraged 48 IRs, which may be unacceptable in some cases. In Sect. 5.1, we observed that a small proportion (12) of the IRs subsumed all of the other IRs. This demonstrates that the technique can be applied with relatively few IRs, which may be more acceptable in the aforementioned cases, if one restricts their development efforts to such IRs. Unfortunately, the results did not indicate how one might do this. We would therefore like to investigate this in future work.

In Sect. 3.3, we detailed the partially automated process that is used to develop IRs. Increasing the degrees of automation further will also reduce the effort required to use the technique and so can reduce the impact of the limitation above. Thus, for future work, we would like to explore methods of automating the development of IRs further.

In the future, we would also like to assess the impact that IMT has on one's mutant classification productivity. This would involve determining the costs that are associated with developing IRs, and the cost savings that can be obtained from leveraging the technique. As a part of ongoing work, we are currently investigating the latter.

References

1. Aichernig, B.K., Jobstl, E.: Efficient refinement checking for model-based mutation testing. In: International Conference on Quality Software (QSIC), pp. 21–30. IEEE, Xi'an (2012)
2. Androutsopoulos, K., Clark, D., Dan, H., Hierons, R.M., Harman, M.: An analysis of the relationship between conditional entropy and failed error propagation in software testing. In: Proceedings of the 36th International Conference on Software Engineering, pp. 573–583. ACM, NY (2014)
3. Assi, R.A., Masri, W., Zaraket, F.: UCov: a user-defined coverage criterion for test case intent verification. Softw. Test. Verif. Reliab. **26**(6), 1–32 (2016)
4. Budd, T.A., Angluin, D.: Two notions of correctness and their relation to testing. Acta Informatica **18**(1), 31–45 (1982)
5. Carver, R.: Mutation-based testing of concurrent programs. In: Proceedings of IEEE International Test Conference, pp. 845–853. IEEE, USA (1993)
6. Chen, T.Y., Poon, P.L., Xie, X.: METRIC: METamorphic relation identification based on the category-choice framework. J. Syst. Softw. **116**, 177–190 (2016)
7. Gligoric, M., Jagannath, V., Marinov, D.: MuTMuT: efficient exploration for mutation testing of multithreaded code. In: Proceedings of the Third International Conference on Software Testing, Verification and Validation, pp. 55–64. IEEE Computer Society, USA (2010)

8. Harman, M., Hierons, R.M.: An overview of program slicing. Softw. Focus **2**(3), 85–92 (2001)
9. Harman, M., McMinn, P., Shahbaz, M., Yoo, S.: A comprehensive survey of trends in oracles for software testing. Technical report TR-09-03, University of Sheffield (2013)
10. Jankovic, M.: Genetic Algorithm for Bin Packing Problem (2013). http://www.codeproject.com/Articles/633133/ga-bin-packing
11. Jia, Y., Harman, M.: An analysis and survey of the development of mutation testing. IEEE Trans. Softw. Eng. **37**(5), 649–678 (2011)
12. Ma, Y.S., Kwon, Y.R., Offutt, J., Li, N.: Mujava (2013). http://cs.gmu.edu/~offutt/mujava/
13. Masri, W., Assi, R.: Cleansing test suites from coincidental correctness to enhance fault-localization. In: Third International Conference on Software Testing, Verification and Validation (ICST), pp. 165–174. IEEE, Paris (2010)
14. Masri, W., Assi, R.A.: Prevalence of coincidental correctness and mitigation of its impact on fault localization. ACM Trans. Softw. Eng. Methodol, **23**(1), 1–28 (2014)
15. Offutt, A.J.: Investigations of the software testing coupling effect. ACM Trans. Softw. Eng. Methodol. **1**(1), 5–20 (1992)
16. Offutt, A.J., Lee, S.D.: How strong is weak mutation? In: Proceedings of the Symposium on Testing, Analysis, and Verification, pp. 200–213. ACM, NY (1991)
17. Papadakis, M., Jia, Y., Harman, M., Traon, Y.L.: Trivial compiler equivalence: a large scale empirical study of a simple, fast and effective equivalent mutant detection technique. In: Proceedings of the 37th International Conference on Software Engineering, pp. 936–946. IEEE, USA (2015)
18. Paperin, G.: JAGA - Java API for Genetic Algorithms (2004). http://www.jaga.org/index.html
19. Patel, K., Hierons, R.M.: Interlocutory Testing: Combating Coincidental Correctness in Testing (2015). http://people.brunel.ac.uk/csstrmh/Intt/IT.pdf
20. Rouvignac, J.N.: AutoRefactor (2015). https://marketplace.eclipse.org/content/autorefactor
21. Sadi, M.S., Kuo, F.C., Ho, J.W.K., Charleston, M.A., Chen, T.Y.: Verification of phylogenetic inference programs using metamorphic testing. J. Bioinf. Comput. Biol. **9**(6), 729–747 (2011)
22. Scitools: Understand static code analysis tool (2016). https://scitools.com/
23. Voas, J.: PIE: a dynamic failure-based technique. IEEE Trans. Softw. Eng. **18**(8), 717–727 (1992)
24. Yao, X., Harman, M., Jia, Y.: A study of equivalent and stubborn mutation operators using human analysis of equivalence. In: Proceedings of the 36th International Conference on Software Engineering, pp. 919–930. ACM, NY (2014)

On-the-Fly Construction of Adaptive Checking Sequences for Testing Deterministic Implementations of Nondeterministic Specifications

Nina Yevtushenko[1], Khaled El-Fakih[2(✉)], and Anton Ermakov[1]

[1] Tomsk State University, Tomsk, Russia
nyevtush@gmail.com, antonermak@inbox.ru
[2] American University of Sharjah, Sharjah, UAE
kelfakih@aus.edu

Abstract. A method is proposed for deriving an adaptive checking sequence for a given deterministic implementation of a nondeterministic Finite State Machine (FSM) specification with respect to the reduction relation. The implementation is non-initialized, i.e., there is no reliable reset input. In order to obtain a sequence of reasonable length, in the proposed technique, we consider specifications with adaptive distinguishing test cases and adaptive transfer sequences. In fact, we show how under these considerations we can on-the-fly derive a checking sequence where the head part establishes the one-to-one correspondence between states of the implementation and the specification and if established the second part of the sequence is constructed for checking the one-to-one correspondence between transitions of the implementation and a submachine of the specification FSM. The latter construction appropriately utilizes information from the first part to reach and check intended transitions.

Keywords: Nondeterministic finite state machines · Reduction relation · Fault model · Test derivation · Distinguishing test case · Definitely reachable states · Adaptive sequence

1 Introduction

Finite State Machine (FSM) based test derivation is widely used when deriving conformance tests in many application domains such as sequential circuits, communication protocols, web-services, etc. There are many approaches for FSM-based test derivation that are summarized in many surveys such as [2, 4, 20, 24]. In many approaches, such as in the W-method [3] and its many derivatives, both the specification and implementation FSMs are assumed to be initialized and thus, tests (input sequences or traces) are derived from a given initialized specification FSM; these tests are concatenated by a reliable reset that brings the machine to the initial state. Many other approaches do not rely on the existence of such possibly expensive resets and derive so-called checking sequences consisting of one test without resets. The reader may refer to [7–13] for some approaches and summary of existing work on deriving and reducing length of

F. Wotawa et al. (Eds.): ICTSS 2016, LNCS 9976, pp. 139–152, 2016.
DOI: 10.1007/978-3-319-47443-4_9

checking sequences for deterministic FSMs. In general, while constructing a checking sequence for deterministic FSMs, as there are no resets, one may rely on the so-called synchronizing (or homing) sequence that takes the FSM from any state to the known state in addition to an input sequence that can distinguish two different states of the machine.

Nowadays, design and analysis of non-deterministic systems is capturing a lot of attention. Nondeterminism can occur due to several reasons, such as limited observability, abstraction, etc. Accordingly, in this paper, we consider the derivation of checking sequences for observable nondeterministic FSMs. A nondeterministic machine is *observable* if for each state and input the machine can have many outgoing transitions under the input as long as different outputs are produced at these transitions. Otherwise, the machine is *non-observable*. We consider observable machines as it is known that any non-observable specification machine can be transformed into an observable one with the same behavior.

Petrenko *et al.* [14] proposed a method for deriving a checking sequence for a complete nondeterministic FSM with respect to the equivalence relation under appropriate assumptions about the specification FSM and the fault domain. The specification FSM has to have a distinguishing input sequence for which the sets of output responses at any two different states do not coincide. Since an implementation under test (IUT) can be nondeterministic, the authors also rely on the all-weather conditions assumption. In [21] the authors extended the work considering the derivation of a checking sequence with respect to the reduction relation. Resetting is still used yet only in one phase of the construction approach. Ermakov [6] presented a method for deriving an adaptive checking sequence with respect to the reduction relation under the assumption that the specification has a separating sequence, i.e., an input sequence for which the sets of output responses at any two different states are disjoint. The specification FSM has also to be deterministically connected, i.e., each state is deterministically reachable from any other state while an IUT is a complete deterministic FSM. A checking sequence is *adaptive* if the selection of the next input to be applied to an IUT depends on the outputs produced by the IUT to previously applied inputs. As in the other above approaches, the approach given in [6] also uses resetting. In this paper, we reduce the limitation considered in the above papers about the use of resets. Moreover, differently from [6] we show how to effectively use adaptive transfer and distinguishing sequences when deriving an adaptive checking sequence as such adaptive sequences can exist when there are no preset ones; in addition, such adaptive sequences can be shorter [1, 17, 19]. More precisely, we construct an adaptive checking sequence from a given non-deterministic observable FSM against a given complete deterministic IUT assuming that the specification FSM has adaptive transfer sequences as well as an adaptive distinguishing sequence (a distinguishing test case) of reasonable length. The existence of an adaptive transfer sequences means that every state of the machine is definitely reachable from any other state. We show that in this case, when testing with respect to the reduction relation, each state of the specification FSM is required to be implemented in an IUT. As usual, we also assume that the behavior of the IUT is not known, we only know that the number of states of the IUT does not exceed that of the specification. Under the above assumptions, an IUT is a reduction of the specification machine if and only if the IUT is isomorphic to a complete submachine of the specification FSM and thus, when testing it is enough to establish the one-to-one correspondence between states and transitions of the IUT and states and transitions of an appropriate submachine in the specification FSM. In other words, each transition of the IUT has to be traversed and an adaptive distinguishing sequence has to be applied for verifying the final state of the transition. This approach allows us to derive checking sequences of reasonable length when an adaptive distinguishing sequence has polynomial length with respect to the number of states of the specification FSM.

This paper is organized as followed. Section 2 includes preliminaries with related definitions. Section 3 includes the considered fault model and Sect. 4 includes the checking sequence construction method with related propositions and a simple application example. Section 5 concludes the paper.

2 Preliminaries

A *finite state machine* (FSM), or simply a *machine*, is a 4-tuple $S = \langle S, I, O, h_S \rangle$, where S is a finite nonempty set of states, I and O are finite input and output alphabets, and $h_S \subseteq S \times I \times O \times S$ is a (*behavior*) *transition relation*. FSM S is *nondeterministic* if for some pair $(s, i) \in S \times I$ there can exist several pairs $(o, s') \in O \times S$ such that $(s, i, o, s') \in h_S$. FSM S is *complete* if for each pair $(s, i) \in S \times I$ there exists $(o, s') \in O \times S$ such that $(s, i, o, s') \in h_S$. FSM S is *observable* if for each two transitions (s, i, o, s_1), $(s, i, o, s_2) \in h_S$ it holds that $s_1 = s_2$. FSM S is *initialized* if it has the designated initial state s_1, written S/s_1. Thus, an initialized FSM is a 5-tuple $\langle S, I, O, h, s_1 \rangle$. In the following, we consider observable and complete FSMs if the contrary is not explicitly stated.

A *trace* of S at state s is a sequence of input/output pairs of consecutive transitions starting from state s. Given a trace $i_1 o_1 \ldots i_k o_k$ at state s, the input projection $i_1 \ldots i_k$ of the trace is a *defined* input sequence at state s. For an observable nondeterministic FSM, if $\gamma = i_1 o_1 \ldots i_k o_k$ is a trace at a state s, then there exists a unique sequence of consecutive transitions $(s, i_1, o_1, s_1)(s_1, i_2, o_2, s_2) \ldots (s_{k-1}, i_k, o_k, s_k)$. As usual, for state s and a sequence $\gamma \in (IO)^*$ of input/output pairs, the γ-*successor* of state s is the set of all states that are reached from s by trace γ. If γ is not a trace at state s then the γ-successor of state s is empty or we simply say that the γ-successor of state s does not exist. For an observable FSM S, for any string $\gamma \in (IO)^*$, the cardinality of the γ-successor of state s is at most one. Given a subset S' of states, the γ-*successor* of S' is the union of γ-successors over all states of the set S'.

FSM S is *single-input* if at each state there is at most one defined input at the state, i.e., for each two transitions (s, i_1, o_1, s_1), $(s, i_2, o_2, s_2) \in h_S$ it holds that $i_1 = i_2$, and S is *output-complete* if for each pair $(s, i) \in S \times I$ such that the input i is defined at state s, there exists a transition from s with i for every output in O. An initialized FSM S is *acyclic* if the FSM transition diagram has no cycles. An initialized FSM S is (*initially*) *connected* if each state is reachable from the initial state. Given an input alphabet I and an output alphabet O, a *test case* TC(I, O) is an initially connected single-input output-complete observable initialized FSM $T = (T, I, O, h_T, t_1)$ with an acyclic transition graph [22]. Given a complete FSM S over alphabets I and O, a test case TC(I, O) represents an adaptive experiment with the FSM S [15].

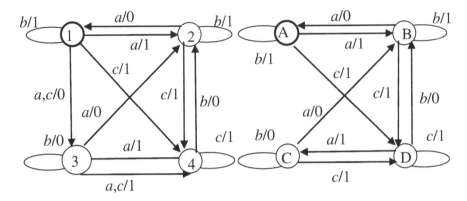

Fig. 1. (a) Specification FSM S (b) Implementation FSM P

If $|I| > 1$ then a test case is a partial FSM. A state $t \in T$ is a *deadlock* state of the FSM T if there are no defined inputs at this state. In general, given a test case T, the *length (height)* of the test case T is defined as the length of a longest trace from the initial state to a deadlock state of T and it specifies the length of the longest input sequence that can be applied to an FSM S during the experiment. A trace from the initial state to a deadlock state is a *complete* trace of a test case [23]. As usual, for complexity reasons, one is interested in deriving a test case with minimal length. A test case T is a *distinguishing* test case (DTC) for an FSM S if for every trace γ of T from the initial state to a deadlock state, γ is trace at most at one state of S. Sometimes, a distinguishing test case is called an *adaptive distinguishing sequence*.

Consider FSM S in Fig. 1a. Using the approach proposed in [18] a (adaptive) distinguishing test case can be constructed for FSM S (Fig. 2).

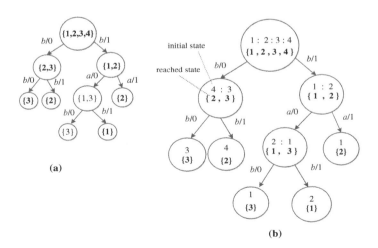

Fig. 2. (a) The distinguishing test case (b) The test case for (a) where source states are indicated

Given a complete observable FSM S = (S, I, O, h_S), state $s' \in S$ is *definitely-reachable* (*def-reachable*) from state $s \in S$ if there exists a test case $T_{s,s'}$ over I and O, initialized with the singleton $\{s\}$, and for every trace γ of $T_{s,s'}$ from the initial state to a deadlock state, the γ-successor of state s is either the empty set or $\{s'\}$.

We hereafter refer to such a test case $T_{s,s'}$ as a *def-transfer* test case from state s to state s' or as an *adaptive def-transfer sequence*.

In fact, a *def-transfer* test case is defined in [23] as an extension of a deterministic (*d*-)transfer sequence for states s and s'. All the traces of $T_{s,s'}$ take the FSM S from state s to state s'. When testing with respect to the reduction relation not each state of the specification FSM, except for the initial state, is required to be implemented in an implementation FSM P. However, if there exists a *def-transfer* test case $T_{s,s'}$ and state s is implemented in the reduction P of S then according to [23], state s' must be implemented in P.

In [23], necessary and sufficient conditions were established to check if state $s' \in S$ is definitely reachable from the initial state of the initialized FSM. Accordingly, when checking whether state s' is definitely reachable form state s, the initialized FSM S/s can be considered. Moreover, in [23] it is shown how a *def-transfer* test case $T_{s,s'}$ can be derived such that the length of $T_{s,s'}$ (if it exists) does not exceed the number of states of FSM S.

By direct inspection, one can assure that for every two different states s, s' of FSM S (Fig. 1a) there exists a *def*-transfer test case $T_{s,\,s'}$. As an example, consider $T_{1,2}$ in Fig. 3. If an IUT replies with 1 to the applied input a at state 1 then we know that the next state of the specification is state 2. If the output 0 is produced by the IUT then the specification reaches state 3 and we apply the input a again. If the IUT replies with 0 to the applied input a then we know that the next state of the specification is state 2. If the output 1 is produced by the IUT then the specification reaches state 4 and we apply an input b in order to reach state 2.

Consider the FSM in Fig. 1a. For states 2 and 1, 3 and 1, and 4 and 1, there exist deterministic transfer sequences, namely, state 1 is *d*-reachable from 2 by input sequence a, state 3 is *d*-reachable from 1 by input sequence c b a and state 4 is *d*-reachable from 1 by input sequence b a. State 2 is *d*-reachable from 3 and 4 by input sequences c b and b correspondingly, state 3 is *d*-reachable from 2 and 4 by input sequences b a and a, while state 4 is *d*-reachable from 2 and 3 by input sequence b. By direct inspection, one can assure that $T_{1,3}$ and $T_{1,4}$ can be easily derived from the machine in Fig. 3 as states 3 and 4 are deterministically reachable from state 2.

In order to check if there exists a distinguishing test case for the specification FSM S, we can use the procedures proposed in [16, 17]. If a general procedure is used then the complexity can become exponential w.r.t. the number of FSM states [5]. The complexity of the procedure proposed in [16] is polynomial but it can be applied only for so-called merging free FSMs. A complete observable FSM is *merging free* if for each two different states s_1 and s_2, every input i and every output o, the non-empty i/o successors of s_1 and s_2 do not coincide. For a merging free FSM, a distinguishing test case exists if and only if a distinguishing test case exists for each pair of different

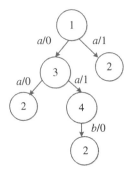

Fig. 3. A *def*-transfer test case for states 1 and 2 of the FSM in Fig. 1a

state of the FSM; the latter can be checked in polynomial time and the length of such test case is at most $n(n-1)/2$ if the FSM has n states. Then a distinguishing test case for the FSM is derived step by step starting from a single pair and adding a new state for the set of initial states at each step. In [16], it is shown that the length of such test case is $O(n^3)$. The class of merging-free FSMs is big enough; at least it contains many deterministic FSMs which are used in practical applications [9].

Hereafter we use S to denote a complete observable nondeterministic specification machine while P denotes a complete deterministic IUT.

Given complete FSMs S and P, state p of the FSM P is a *reduction* of state s of the FSM S, written $p \leq s$, if the set of traces of P at state p is a subset of that of S at state s; otherwise, p is not a reduction of state s, written $p \nleq s$. FSM P is a *reduction* of FSM S if for each state p there exists state s such that $p \leq s$.

Given complete FSM S, two different states s_1 and s_2 and an input sequence α, α is a *separating* sequence of states s_1 and s_2 if the sets $out(s_1, \alpha)$ and $out(s_2, \alpha)$ are disjoint. If α separates each pair of different states then α is a separating sequence for FSM S. For non-deterministic observable machines the tight upper bound on the length of a separating sequence of two states is known to be exponential with respect to number of FSM states [25] while for deterministic FSMs the length of an adaptive distinguishing sequence (a distinguishing test case) is polynomial [26]. Moreover, if there exists a separating sequence then there exists a distinguishing test case but the opposite is not necessarily true. When an implementation is deterministic then the observation of n different replies to a separating sequence immediately means that the IUT has at least n states. For recognizing states of an implementation, a separating sequence sometimes can be replaced by state identifiers. An input sequence α is a *state identifier* of state s of FSM S if α is a separating sequence for each pair (s, s'), $s' \neq s$. As an example, the $b\,b$ is a state identifier for states 3 and 4 of the FSM in Fig. 1a and $b\,a\,b$ is a state identifier for states 1 and 2.

Given a test case TC of a complete observable specification S, a trace that takes TC from the initial state to a deadlock state is a *complete* trace; the set *CompleteTraces*(TC) is the set of all complete traces of TC. If there exists a distinguishing test case then any two different states s_1 and s_2 of FSM S are r-distinguishable and thus, any state of any complete FSM over alphabets I and O is not a reduction of two different states of FSM S [22]. The set of input projections of all complete traces of a distinguishing test case sometimes is called a *distinguishing set*. In [22], it is shown, that given a state p of a complete FSM over alphabets I and O, for any two states s_1 and s_2 of FSM S there always exists an input sequence of the distinguishing set such that the set of output responses of P at state p is not a subset of that at both states s_1 and s_2. Moreover, given a reduction P of FSM S, not each state of S has to be implemented in P. However, according to Proposition 1, if S has both a distinguishing test case and a *def*-transfer test case for each pair of different states then each state of S has to be implemented in P and there is the one-to-one correspondence between states and transitions of P and the corresponding states and transitions of an appropriate submachine of S. The latter allows the construction of shorter tests and reduces the efforts of checking if a given FSM P is a reduction of such specification FSM.

Two FSMs over the same input and output alphabets are *isomorphic* if there exists one-to-one correspondence between their states and transitions, i.e., if there exists one-to-one mapping $f: S \rightarrow P$ such that for any input i and any state s the 4-tuple $(s, i, o, s') \in h_s$ if and only if $(f(s), i, o, f(s')) \in h_P$.

Proposition 1. Given a complete observable FSM S with n states, let S have a distinguishing test case and each pair of different states s and s' of S have a *def*-transfer test case $T_{s, s'}$. A complete observable FSM P that has at most n states is a reduction of S if and only if P is isomorphic to a submachine of S.

Proof. If P is isomorphic to a submachine of S then P is a reduction of S.

Let now P be a reduction of S, i.e., for each state p of P there exists state s of S such that $p \leq s$. When there exists a distinguishing test case *DTC* for S, states of the FSM S are r-distinguishable and thus, any state of any complete FSM over alphabets I and O is not a reduction of two different states of FSM S [23]. Moreover, if $p \leq s$ then a distinguishing test case *DTC* has a trace at state p of P that is not a trace at any other state of S. On the other hand, let state s of FSM S be implemented in P as state $p \leq s$. Any state s' is *def*-reachable from s and thus also is implemented in P as $p' \leq s'$. Therefore, each state of S is implemented in P and since P has at most n states, each state of S is implemented as a unique P state. Correspondingly, we can establish one-to-one correspondence $F_{DTC}: S \rightarrow P$ between states of FSMs S and P according to the given distinguishing test case.

Moreover, since P is a reduction of S the following holds. If there is a transition $p - i/o - p'$ where $p = F_{DTC}(s)$ and $p' = F_{DTC}(s')$ then S has a transition $s - i/o - s'$. □

Let S have a distinguishing test case *DTC*, each pair of different states s and s' of S have a *def*-transfer test case $T_{s, s'}$ and the number of states of FSM P does not exceed that of S. FSM P is *DTC-compatible* with S if there exists one-to-one correspondence $F: S \rightarrow P$ such that for each state $s \in S$ it holds that the intersection of $Tr(S/s) \cap Tr(P/p) \cap CompleteTraces(DTC)$ is not empty if and only if $p = F(s)$.

Proposition 2. Given the specification FSM S that has a distinguishing test case *DTC*, let a deterministic complete FSM P be *DTC*-compatible with S, each pair of different states s and s' of S have a *def*-transfer test case $T_{s, s'}$ and the number of states of FSM P does not exceed that of S. For each state p of P, the distinguishing test case *DTC* has a complete trace α/β that is a trace at state p; moreover, α is a state identifier of state p in P.

Proof. In fact, if there exists one-to-one correspondence between states of S and P according to the distinguishing test case *DTC*, then for each two states s and s', $s' \neq s$, there exists a prefix of an input sequence of some complete trace α/β of *DTC* such that output responses at corresponding states $p = F(s)$ and $p' = F(s')$ are different. As *DTC* is a distinguishing test case of S and FSM P is complete and deterministic, the latter means that a corresponding input projection of trace α/β is a state identifier of state p.   □

3 Fault Model for Deriving an Adaptive Checking Sequence

In FSM-based testing, it is assumed that the specification FSM describes the reference behavior while the fault domain FD contains each possible implementation FSM of the specification. In our case, the specification FSM S is complete and observable, moreover, S has a distinguishing test case and there exists a *def*-transfer test case for each pair of different states of S. The conformance relation is the reduction relation while any IUT of the FD is complete and deterministic and the number of its states does not exceed that of the specification FSM. In other words, we implicitly assume that the nondeterminism of the specification is implied by the optionality where a designer selects a better option according to some criteria. We do not rely on machines for having a reset; moreover, if the machines have a reset we still check if it is implemented correctly.

An implementation P *conforms* to the specification S if P is a reduction of S; otherwise, P is a *nonconforming* implementation. According to Proposition 1 the former means that P is isomorphic to some complete submachine of S.

An *adaptive sequence* is an input sequence when the next input of the sequence is selected based on the output of the IUT to the previous inputs. In fact, an adaptive checking sequence is a test case; however, the total length of this test case is big enough and for this reason, we do not talk about the complete test case and usually consider only a part of it that is appropriate for the implementation at hand. Correspondingly, similar to [23], we propose a technique for testing an IUT P on-the-fly but with a single input sequence; the algorithm yields the verdict *pass* if P is a reduction of a given specification FSM S and the verdict *fail* if P is not a reduction of S. Our proposed technique has two procedures. The former checks if P has the same number of states as S and establishes, based on a distinguishing test case, the one-to-one correspondence between the states of P and S if such a correspondence exists. We underline that when such correspondence can be established then an appropriate trace of the distinguishing test case is identified as a state identifier of the corresponding state in P (Proposition 2). The second procedure checks that there is one-to-one correspondence between the transitions of P and an appropriate submachine of S.

4 Deriving an Adaptive Checking Sequence

This section includes two procedures for on-the-fly constructing a checking sequence for a given IUT P from the specification FSM S with respect to the reduction relation. Given a distinguishing case DTC for the FSM S, Procedure 1 returns the verdict *fail* if P is not DTC-compatible with S; otherwise, it computes the set "state_identifier". For each state s of S, this set includes the trace of DTC executed by the IUT at the state of P corresponding to s and it also includes the state of S reached after this trace. Then Procedure 2 starting from information obtained from Procedure 1 continues deriving the checking sequence where it focuses on checking the one-to-one correspondence between transitions of P and some submachine of S.

As an application example of Procedure 1, consider the implementation FSM P in Fig. 1b and assume that at the beginning of testing P is at state C. After applying DTC (in Fig. 2a) we observe a trace $b\ b/0\ 0$ which is a trace of state 3 of S. Accordingly, $s = s_1 = 3$, $\sigma = \gamma$. After applying DTC again (at Step 1), we observe $\eta = b\ b/0\ 0$ which is a trace of state C of P. Thus, σ becomes $b\ b\ b\ b/0\ 0\ 0\ 0$, $s_2 = 3$, $s' = 3$ as the starting state of S where η is a trace of DTC, and the tuple $<3, b\ b/0\ 0, 3>$ is added to the (initially empty) set "state_identifier", $s = 3$, $\gamma = \eta = b\ b/0\ 0$, and then we go to Step 2 as the tuple $<3, b\ b/0\ 0, 3>$ is in "state_identifier".

Let $s_{new} = 4$, then $s = 4$, we then apply the transfer sequence c, observe 1, and thus have $\eta = c/1$. Then after applying the $b\ b$ of DTC to P, we observe $b\ b/0\ 1$. As $\sigma = b\ b\ b\ b\ c\ b\ b/0\ 0\ 0\ 0\ 1\ 0\ 1$ is a trace at s_1, then we go back to Step 1 where we apply $b\ a$ of DTC and observe 1 0, then s_2 becomes 1, $s' = 2$, and we add the tuple $<4, b\ b/0\ 1, 2>$ to "state_identifier". Similarly, afterwards, $s = s' = 2$, $\gamma: = \eta = b\ a$, at Step 1, we apply $b\ a\ b$ of DTC, the trace $b\ a\ b/1\ 1\ 1$ is observed and the tuple $<2, b\ a\ b/1\ 0\ 1, 1>$ is added to the set "state_identifier".

Then, at Step 2, $s_{new} = s = 1$, after applying $T_{2,1}$ (input sequence a) we observe 0 and then after applying again the input sequences $b\ a$ followed by $b\ b$ of DTC the traces $b\ a/1\ 1$ followed by $b\ b/1\ 1$ are observed and accordingly the tuple $<1, b\ a\ /1\ 1, 2>$ is added to "state_identifier". We stop as the set "state_identifier" is complete and the specification FSM reaches state 2 after the observed trace. Table 1 represents the set "state_identifier".

Table 1. The set "state_identifier" for the FSM in Fig. 1b according to the distinguishing test case in Fig. 2.

Current state of S (corresponding state in IUT)	State identifier	Output response	Next state of S (corresponding state in IUT)
1 (A)	$b\ a$	1 1	2 (B)
2 (B)	$b\ a\ b$	1 0 1	1 (A)
3 (C)	$b\ b$	0 0	3 (C)
4 (D)	$b\ b$	0 1	2 (B)

Procedure 1: Checking the *DTC*-compatibility between a deterministic IUT P and the specification S

Input: The complete and observable specification FSM S with n states that has a distinguishing test case DTC and a *def*-transfer test case $T_{s,s'}$ for each pair of different states s and s'; a complete deterministic FSM IUT P with at most n states.

Output: Verdict *fail* if P is not *DTC*-compatible with S or state s_2, trace σ, the set "state_identifier".

The set "state_identifier" is the empty set;

σ is the empty trace;

Apply *DTC* to P and observe a complete trace γ ;

    If γ is not a trace at any state of S **then**

        Return the verdict *fail* ;

    Else

        Determine state s_1 of S with the trace γ ;

        $\sigma := \gamma$;

        $s := s_1$;

Step 1.

Apply *DTC* to P and observe a complete trace η ;

$\sigma := \sigma\,\eta$;

    If σ is not a trace at state s_1 of S **then**

        Return the verdict *fail* ;

    Else

        Determine state s_2 where σ takes the FSM S from state s_1 ;

        Determine state s' of S with the trace η;

        Add the tuple $< s, \gamma, s' >$ to the set "state_identifier" ;

    If the set "state_identifier" has n tuples **then**

        End Procedure 1

    Else

        $s := s'$;

        $\gamma := \eta$;

    If the set "state_identifier" has a tuple $< s, \gamma, s_2 >$ **then**

        Go-to Step 2 ;

    Else

        Go-back to Step 1 ;

Step 2. Let s_{new} be the state of S such that "state_identifier" has no tuple with the first item s_{new} ;

$s := s_{new}$;

Apply $T_{s2,\,s}$ and observe a complete trace η ;

Apply *DTC* to P and observe a complete trace γ ;

$\sigma := \sigma\,\eta\,\gamma$;

    If σ is not a trace at state s_1 of S **then**

        Return the verdict *fail*;

    Else

    Go-back to Step 1;

According to Proposition 1, if P is a reduction of S then each state p of P has to have a corresponding state s in S such that the set of complete traces of *DTC* executed at state s has a trace executed at state p, i.e., the following proposition holds.

Proposition 3. If a trace σ observed when executing Procedure 1 is a trace of the specification FSM S, i.e., Procedure 1 does not return the verdict *fail*, then the IUT P is *DTC*-compatible with S.   □

If the verdict *fail* is produced by Procedure 1 then the IUT P is not a reduction of S. Otherwise, P is *DTC*-compatible with S and for each state s of S the set "state_identifier" includes the trace of DTC executed by the IUT at the state corresponding to s and it also includes the state of S reached after this trace.

    Moreover, if P is *DTC*-compatible with S, then due to Proposition 2, the input projection of a trace observed at state p of P is a state identifier of this state.

Procedure 2: Adaptive testing of a deterministic implementation FSM

Input: The complete and observable specification FSM S with n states that has a distinguishing test case *DTC* and a *def*-transfer test case $T_{s,s'}$ for each pair of different states; a complete deterministic FSM P that has at most n states, initial state s_1, already observed trace σ and the set "state_identifier" returned by Procedure 1 and state s_2 reached after executing Procedure 1.

Output: Verdict *pass* if and only if P a reduction of S.

The set "Transitions" is the empty set;

$s = s_2$;

Step 1.

If there exists input i such that there is no 4-tuple (s_2, i, o, s'_2) with the pair (s_2, i) in the set "Transitions" **then**

    Apply i followed by *DTC* and observe a trace η ;

    If η is not a trace at state s_2 **then**

        Return the verdict *fail* ;

    Else

        Add the transition (s_2, i, o, s') to the set "Transitions" where o is the observed output to i while s' is the current state according to the set "state_identifier";

        $\sigma := \sigma \eta$;

        $s_2 := s'$;

        Go-back to Step 1;

Else

Step 2.

If the set "Transitions" is full, i.e., the set includes an item (s, i, o, s') for every pair (s, i) **then**

    Return the verdict *pass* ;

Else

    Using transitions of the set "Transitions" determine a trace η from s_2 to state s such that for some i there is no transition (s, i, o, s') with the pair (s, i) in the set "Transitions" ;

    $\sigma := \sigma \eta$;

    $s_2 := s$;

Go-back to Step 1;

Proposition 4. Let the IUT P be *DTC*-compatible with S, i.e., there exists one-to-one correspondence $F: S \rightarrow P$ such that for each state $s \in S$ it holds that the intersection of $Tr(S/s) \cap Tr(P/p) \cap CompleteTraces(TC)$ is not empty if and only if $p = F(s)$. Given a tuple $<s, \gamma, s'>$ of the set "state_identifier", the input projection of trace γ is a state identifier of state $F(s)$ while s' is the state of S reached by γ.   □

Proposition 5. The verdict *pass* is produced by Procedure 2 if and only if the IUT P is a reduction of S.

Proof. If FSM P passes Procedure 1 then P is strongly connected, since each state of P is traversed when executing Procedure 1. For this reason, if at Step 1, the reached state has no unchecked transitions then at Step 2, in the set "Transitions" that has only already checked transitions, there is a path to a state with an unchecked transition. Procedure 2 establishes the one-to-one correspondence between transitions of FSM P and an appropriate submachine of S, since all P transitions are executed and checked for a conforming output and corresponding final state (according to DTC). Therefore, FSM P passes Procedure 2 if and only if P is isomorphic to some submachine of S and the proposition holds according to Proposition 1.   □

As an application example, consider the FSM in Fig. 1a, after applying Procedure 1, we obtain $s_1 = 3$, the trace σ, and state $s_2 = 2$ (reached after applying σ); in addition, the set "state_identifier" = {$<1, b\ a\ /1\ 1, 2>$, $<2, b\ a\ b/1\ 0, 1>$, $<3, b\ b/0\ 0, 3>$, $<4, b\ b/$ $0\ 1, 2 >$}. As $s = s_2 = 2$ and the set "Transitions" is empty, at Step 1, apply the input b at s_2 followed by $b\ a\ b$ of *DTC* and observe the trace $b\ b\ a\ b/1\ 1\ 0\ 1$ that reaches state 1 of the FSM S. Add $(2, b, 1, 2)$ to "Transitions", σ becomes that of Procedure 1 concatenated with the trace $b\ b\ a\ b/1\ 1\ 0\ 1$, and the reached state $s_2 = 1$ according to the tuple $<2, b\ a\ b/1\ 0\ 1, 1>$ of the "state_identifier". We go-back to Step 1, apply the input a followed by $b\ a\ b$ of DTC and observe $1\ 1\ 0\ 1$, reach state $s_2 = 1$, add $(1, a, 1, 2)$ to "Transitions", append σ as usual, and proceed again to Step 1. At $s_2 = 1$ apply b, then apply $b\ a$ of *DTC* and observe $1\ 1\ 1$; add $(1, b, 1, 1)$ to "Transitions" and reach state $s_2 = 2$. Again at Step 1, apply a followed by $b\ a$ and observe $0\ 1\ 1$, add $(2, a, 0, 1)$ to "Transitions". Then at the reached state $s_2 = 2$, apply c followed by $b\ b$ of *DTC*, observe $1\ 0\ 1$, add $(2, c, 1, 4)$ to "Transitions" and reach state $s_2 = 2$. Now, as all $(2, b, 1, 2)$, $(2, a, 0, 1)$, $(2, c, 1, 4)$ are in the set "Transitions", at Step 2, we consider $s = 4$ such that from the reached state $s_2 = 2$ there is the checked trace $\eta = c/1$ from 2 to 4 and for some input i there is no transition $(4, i, o, s')$ in the set "Transitions". We transfer to state 4 from state 2 by applying the input c, now s_2 becomes the reached state 4. We go-back to Step 1 where we select to apply the input a followed by applying the sequence $b\ b$ of *DTC*, observe $1\ 0\ 0$, add $(4, a, 1, 3)$ to "Transitions" and reach state $s_2 = 3$. We proceed as above till the set "Transitions" is full. The verdict *pass* is produced after completing the set "Transitions" and thus, FSM P is a reduction of the specification FSM S.

As the length of a transfer sequence when checking a new input is less than the number n of states of the FSM S, the length of a checking sequence returned by Procedure 2 is proportional to the length of a distinguishing test case. If this length is polynomial with respect to the number of S states as it happens for merging-free FSMs then the length of an adaptive checking sequence is $O(n^3)$, i.e., the length evaluation is almost similar to that for deterministic FSMs [10].

5   Conclusion

In this paper, we have proposed an adaptive strategy for testing a deterministic implementation FSM against nondeterministic observable specification FSM with respect to the reduction relation. Similar to deterministic FSMs, the strategy can be applied under appropriate restrictions upon the specification FSM and fault domain. However, we show that the requirement of the existence of a separating sequence can be replaced by the requirement of the existence of a distinguishing test case. This is useful as the existence of a distinguishing test case is more likely than that of a separating sequence and generally, the length of a distinguishing test case is less than that of a separating sequence (when both exist). In addition, the construction uses adaptive transfer sequences that reduce the length of an applied input sequence. We note that in this paper, we do not discuss any optimization procedure for deriving adaptive checking sequences; this is left for the future work. Another possible direction of a future work is the extension of the proposed work for testing nondeterministic non-initialized implementations. It could be also interesting to apply a proposed approach for deriving checking sequences for I/O automata, for example, with respect to the widely used *ioco* conformance relation that is very close to the reduction relation between FSMs.

Acknowledgment. This work was partially supported by the RSF project №. 16-49-03012.

References

1. Alur, R., Courcoubetis, C., Yannakakis, M.: Distinguishing tests for nondeterministic and probabilistic machines. In: Proceedings of the Twenty-Seventh Annual ACM Symposium on Theory of Computing, pp. 363–372 (1995)
2. Bochmann, G.V., Petrenko, A.: Protocol testing: review of methods and relevance for software testing. In: Proceedings of the ACM International Symposium on Software Testing and Analysis, pp. 109–123 (1994)
3. Chow, T.S.: Testing software design modelled by finite state machines. IEEE Trans. Softw. Eng. 4(3), 178–187 (1978)
4. Dorofeeva, R., El-Fakih, K., Maag, S., Cavalli, A., Yevtushenko, N.: FSM-based conformance testing methods: a survey annotated with experimental evaluation. Inf. Softw. Technol. 52(12), 1286–1297 (2010)
5. El-Fakih, K., Yevtushenko, N., Kushik, N.: On the reachability of the exponential upper bound of adaptive experiments for nondeterministic finite state machines (2016, submitted)
6. Ermakov, A.: Deriving checking sequences for nondeterministic FSMs. In: Proceedings of the Institute for System Programming of RAS, vol. 26, pp. 111–124 (2014). (In Russian)
7. Gonenc, G.: A method for the design of fault detection experiments. IEEE Trans. Comput. 19(6), 551–558 (1970)

8. Güniçen, C., Jourdan, G.-V., Yenigün, H.: Using multiple adaptive distinguishing sequences for checking sequence generation. In: El-Fakih, K., et al. (eds.) ICTSS 2015. LNCS, vol. 9447, pp. 19–34. Springer, Heidelberg (2015). doi:10.1007/978-3-319-25945-1_2

9. Güniçen, C., Inan, K., Türker, U.C., Yenigün, H.: The relation between preset distinguishing sequences and synchronizing sequences. Formal Aspects Comput. **26**(6), 1153–1167 (2014)

10. Hennie, F.C.: Fault-detecting experiments for sequential circuits. In: Proceedings of the Fifth Annual Symposium Switching Circuit Theory and Logical Design, pp. 95–110 (1964)

11. Hierons, R.M., Ural, H.: Reduced length checking sequences. IEEE Trans. Comput. **51**(9), 1111–1117 (2002)

12. Hierons, R.M., Ural, H.: Optimizing the length of checking sequences. IEEE Trans. Comput. **55**(5), 618–629 (2006)

13. Kohavi, Z.: Switching and Finite Automata Theory. McGraw-Hill, New York (1978)

14. Petrenko, A., Simão, A., Yevtushenko, N.: Generating checking sequences for nondeterministic finite state machines. In: Proceedings of the International Conference on Software Testing, pp. 310–319 (2012)

15. Kushik, N: Methods for deriving homing and distinguishing experiments for nondeterministic FSMs. Ph.D. thesis, Tomsk State University (2013). (In Russian)

16. Yevtushenko, N., Kushik, N.: Decreasing the length of adaptive distinguishing experiments for nondeterministic merging-free finite state machines. In: Proceedings of IEEE East-West Design & Test Symposium, pp. 338–341 (2015)

17. Kushik, N., El-Fakih, K., Yevtushenko, N.: Adaptive homing and distinguishing experiments for nondeterministic finite state machines. In: Yenigün, H., Yilmaz, C., Ulrich, A. (eds.) ICTSS 2013. LNCS, vol. 8254, pp. 33–48. Springer, Heidelberg (2013)

18. Yevtushenko, N., Kushik, N., El-Fakih, K., Cavalli, A.R.: On adaptive experiments for nondeterministic finite state machines. Int. J. Softw. Tools Technol. Transf. **18**(3), 251–264 (2016)

19. Kushik, N., Yevtushenko, N., Yenigun, H.: Reducing the complexity of checking the existence and derivation of adaptive synchronizing experiments for nondeterministic FSMs. In: Proceedings of the International Workshop on Domain Specific Model-Based Approaches to Verification and Validation (AMARETTO 2016), pp. 83–90 (2016)

20. Lee, D., Yannakakis, M.: Principles and methods of testing finite state machines-a survey. Proc. IEEE **84**(8), 1090–1123 (1996)

21. Petrenko, A., Simão, A.: Generalizing the DS-methods for testing non-deterministic FSMs. Comput. J. **58**(7), 1656–1672 (2015)

22. Petrenko, A., Yevtushenko, N.: Conformance tests as checking experiments for partial nondeterministic FSM. In: Grieskamp, W., Weise, C. (eds.) FATES 2005. LNCS, vol. 3997, pp. 118–133. Springer, Heidelberg (2006)

23. Petrenko, A., Yevtushenko, N.: Adaptive testing of deterministic implementations specified by nondeterministic FSMs. In: Wolff, B., Zaïdi, F. (eds.) ICTSS 2011. LNCS, vol. 7019, pp. 162–178. Springer, Heidelberg (2011)

24. Simao, A., Petrenko, A., Maldonado, J.C.: Comparing finite state machine test. IET Softw. **3**(2), 91–105 (2009)

25. Spitsyna, N., El-Fakih, K., Yevtushenko, N.: Studying the separability relation between finite state machines. Softw. Test. Verification Reliab. **17**(4), 227–241 (2007)

26. Lee, D., Yannakakis, M.: Testing finite-state machines: state identification and verification. IEEE Trans. Comput. **43**(3), 306–320 (1994)

Practical Applications

Mutation-Based Test Generation for PLC Embedded Software Using Model Checking

Eduard P. Enoiu[1]([✉]), Daniel Sundmark[1], Adnan Čaušević[1], Robert Feldt[2], and Paul Pettersson[1]

[1] Software Testing Laboratory, Mälardalen University, Västerås, Sweden
eduard.paul.enoiu@mdh.se
[2] Blekinge Institute of Technology, Karlskrona, Sweden

Abstract. Testing is an important activity in engineering of industrial embedded software. In certain application domains (e.g., railway industry) engineering software is certified according to safety standards that require extensive software testing procedures to be applied for the development of reliable systems. Mutation analysis is a technique for creating faulty versions of a software for the purpose of examining the fault detection ability of a test suite. Mutation analysis has been used for evaluating existing test suites, but also for generating test suites that detect injected faults (i.e., mutation testing). To support developers in software testing, we propose a technique for producing test cases using an automated test generation approach that operates using mutation testing for software written in IEC 61131-3 language, a programming standard for safety-critical embedded software, commonly used for Programmable Logic Controllers (PLCs). This approach uses the UPPAAL model checker and is based on a combined model that contains all the mutants and the original program. We applied this approach in a tool for testing industrial PLC programs and evaluated it in terms of cost and fault detection. For realistic validation we collected industrial experimental evidence on how mutation testing compares with manual testing as well as automated decision-coverage adequate test generation. In the evaluation, we used manually seeded faults provided by four industrial engineers. The results show that even if mutation-based test generation achieves better fault detection than automated decision coverage-based test generation, these mutation-adequate test suites are not better at detecting faults than manual test suites. However, the mutation-based test suites are significantly less costly to create, in terms of testing time, than manually created test suites. Our results suggest that the fault detection scores could be improved by considering some new and improved mutation operators (e.g., Feedback Loop Insertion Operator (FIO)) for PLC programs as well as higher-order mutations.

1 Introduction

Software testing is an important verification and validation activity used to reveal software faults and make sure that actual software behavior matches

F. Wotawa et al. (Eds.): ICTSS 2016, LNCS 9976, pp. 155–171, 2016.
DOI: 10.1007/978-3-319-47443-4_10

its expected behavior [2]. Safety-critical and real-time software systems implemented in *Programmable Logic Controllers* (PLCs) are used in many real-world industrial application domains. One of the programming languages defined by the *International Electrotechnical Commission* (IEC) for PLCs is the *Function Block Diagram* (FBD) language. In testing IEC 61131-3 FBD programs in the railway domain, the engineering processes of software development are performed according to safety standards and regulations [5]. As an alternative to manually testing software, a few techniques for *automated test generation* have been proposed [4,9]. While high code coverage has historically been used as a proxy for the ability of a test suite to detect faults, recent results (e.g., [17]) indicate that code coverage may not be a good measure of fault detection effectiveness. As an alternative to coverage-based test generation, mutation testing has been proposed [7,11]. In mutation testing, test cases are generated based on the concept of mutants – small syntactic modifications in the program, intended to imitate real faults. A set of test cases that can distinguish a certain program from its mutants is sensitive to faults, and it thus hypothesized to be good at detecting real faults (a hypothesis that has strong empirical support [21]). However, for domain specific languages used in embedded software development (i.e., IEC 61131-3), there is a lack of mature approaches and tools for performing mutation test generation.

In this paper, we describe and evaluate an automated mutation-based test generation approach for IEC 61131-3 embedded software. The main contributions of the paper are:

- An approach for mutation test generation of IEC 61131-3 programs using a model checker by combining all the mutants and the original program into a single combined model that is monitored dynamically.
- An evaluation of the approach in an industrial case study. The results show that mutation-adequate test suites are worse at detecting faults than manual test suites with the cost of performing mutation testing being consistently lower than the cost of manually testing IEC 61131-3 software.
- The identification of new mutation operators for mutation testing of IEC 61131-3 software. The reduction in fault detection between manual and mutation testing was attributed based on our analysis to an incomplete list of mutation operators for IEC 61131-3 software. We propose new operators simulating this kind of faults (e.g., Feedback loop Insertion Operator (FIO)).

The rest of the paper is organized as follows. Section 2 introduces PLC embedded software, automated test generation and mutation testing. Section 3 describes the approach for mutation test generation for IEC 61131-3 programs using a model checker. Section 4 explains the experimental method, while the results are provided and discussed in Sect. 5. Finally, Sect. 6 concludes the paper.

2   Background and Related Work

This paper describes a method for mutation testing for PLC embedded programs implemented in the IEC 61131-3 FBD language. In this section, we provide a background on PLC embedded software, automated test suite generation and mutation testing.

2.1 PLC Embedded Software

Safety-critical embedded systems implemented using Programmable Logic Controllers (PLCs) are used in many industrial application domains such as electric, transportation, chemical, pharmaceutical, etc. One of the programming languages defined by the *International Electrotechnical Commission* (IEC) for PLCs is the Function Block Diagram (FBD) language [16]. Programs developed in FBD are compiled into program code, which in turn is compiled into machine code by using specific engineering tools provided by PLC vendors. The motivation for using FBD as the target language in this study comes from the fact that it is the de facto standard in many industrial systems [26], such as the ones in the railway transportation domain. Programs running on a PLC execute in a loop, in which the iteration follows the *"read-execute-write"* semantics. FBD is popular because of its graphical notations and its usefulness in applications with a high degree of data flow between control components. As shown in Fig. 1, predefined logical and/or stateful blocks (i.e., SR, XOR, TOF, LT and TON in Fig. 1) and signals (i.e., connections) between blocks represent the behavior of an FBD program. The blocks are supplied by the hardware manufacturer or defined by a developer. PLCs contain particular types of blocks called timers (e.g., TON and TOF) that provide the same functions as timing relays in electrical circuits and are used to activate or deactivate a device after a preset interval of time. For more details on this programming language we refer the reader to the work of John and Tiegelkamp [20].

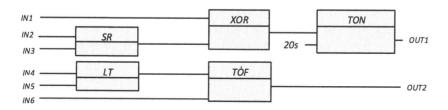

Fig. 1. An FBD program with six inputs and two outputs.

2.2 Automated Test Generation for PLC Embedded Software

In general, automated test generation has been explored in a considerable amount of work [25] in the last couple of years. Numerous techniques for automated test generation using code coverage criteria (e.g., [4,9]) have been proposed in the last decade, since test suites can be created and executed with reduced human effort and cost. However, for domain specific languages used in embedded software development, contributions have been more sparse. For IEC 61131-3 software, a few automated test generation approaches [18,28,30] have been proposed in the last couple of years, but currently there is a lack of tool support. In our previous work, we developed an automated test input generation approach and tool named COMPLETETEST [8], which automatically produces test suites for a given coverage criterion and an IEC 61131-3 program written using the FBD language. COMPLETETEST supports different code coverage criteria with the default criterion being decision coverage.

2.3 Mutation Testing

Recent work [13,17] suggests that coverage criteria alone can be a poor indication of fault detection in testing. To tackle this issue, researchers have proposed approaches for improving fault detection by using mutation analysis as a test criterion. Mutation analysis is the technique of automatically generating faulty implementations of a program for the purpose of examining the fault detection ability of a test suite [6]. A **mutant** is a new version of a program created by making a small change to the original program. The execution of a test case on the resulting mutant may produce a different output as the original program, in which case we say that the test case **kills** that mutant. The mutation score is calculated using either an output-only oracle (i.e., strong mutation [29]) or a state change oracle (i.e., weak mutation [15]) against the set of mutants. For all programs, one needs to assess the fault-finding effectiveness of each test suite by calculating the ratio of mutants killed to total number of mutants. When this technique is used to *generate* test suites rather than evaluating existing ones, it is commonly referred to as *mutation testing* or mutation-based test generation. Despite its effectiveness [21], to the best of our knowledge, no attempt has been made to propose and evaluate mutation testing for PLC embedded software written in the IEC 61131-3 FBD programming language. This motivated us to develop an automated test generation approach based on mutation testing targeting this type of software.

3   Mutation Test Generation for PLC Embedded Software

Within the last decade *model-checking* has turned out to be a useful technique for generation of test cases from models [10]. In this paper, we describe an approach to automatically generate test suites using a model checker based on mutation testing for PLC embedded software. Overall, the approach is composed of the following steps, mirrored in Fig. 2:

1. MUTANT GENERATION. This first step (described in detail in Sect. 3.1) entails systematically making small syntactic changes (mutants) to a program based on a set of predefined operators (e.g., mimicking programming errors). The output of this step is a set of replicas of the original program, each with one inserted mutant.

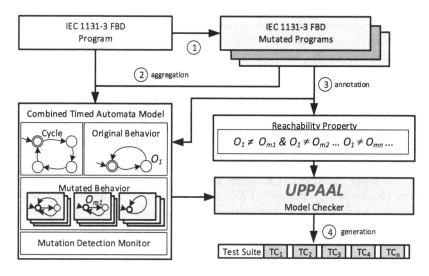

Fig. 2. Overview of mutation testing for IEC 61131-3 FBD programs.

2. MODEL AGGREGATION. The second step (described in detail in Sect. 3.2) is used for combining a program and the set of mutants into a single model. The output of this step is a model containing the original structure and behavior of the program together with all inserted mutants.
3. MUTANT ANNOTATION. The third step (described in Sect. 3.3) involves the annotation of the combined model with instrumentation instructions for the detection of each mutant. This means that the mutation detection monitor is used to record the mutant execution and detection, thus for all mutants a property is created for checking the detection of mutants.
4. TEST SUITE GENERATION. The fourth step (described in Sect. 3.4) requires the use of the UPPAAL model checker [22] to generate a set of test cases satisfying the detection of mutants by using the model checker's ability to export abstract traces witnessing a submitted property.

3.1   Mutation Generation

To facilitate mutation testing, we begin by generating mutated versions of the original program. The mutation generator parses a given program and processes the structural elements for performing mutations. In particular, for each mutation operator, the program is traversed invoking the corresponding mutation function at all possible locations, each mutation resulting in a separate mutant version of the program. For the creation of mutants, we rely on previous studies that looked at commonly occurring faults in IEC 61131-3 software [23,27]. We used these common faults in this study for establishing the following mutation operators:

- *Logic Block Replacement Operator (LRO)* replaces a logical block with another block from the same function category (e.g., replacing an XOR block with an OR block),
- *Comparison Block Replacement Operator (CRO)* replaces a comparison block with another block from the same function category (e.g., replacing a Less-Than (LT) block with a Less-or-Equal (LE) block),
- *Arithmetic Block Replacement Operator (ARO)* replaces an arithmetic block with another block from the same function category (e.g., replacing a maximum (MAX) block with a subtraction (ADD) block),
- *Negation Insertion Operator (NIO)* negates an input or output connection (e.g., an input variable IN1 becomes not (IN1)),
- *Value Replacement Operator (VRO)* replaces a value of a constant variable connected to a block (e.g., replacing a constant value ($const = 20$ s) with its boundary values (e.g., $const = 19$ s and $const = 21$ s)), and
- *Timer Block Replacement Operator (TRO)* replaces a timer block with another block from the same function category (e.g., replacing a Timer-On (TON) block with a Timer-Off (TOF) block).

These mutation operators are systematically applied to the entire program (i.e., blocks, variables, constants, connections) and thus resulting in a set of mutants, each simulating one syntactic change.

3.2   Model Aggregation

We start the model aggregation step with the translation of a program and its set of mutants to a timed automata representation. We have shown in a previous study [8] how the mapping of an IEC 61131-3 program to timed automata is implemented. Timed automata, introduced by Alur et al. [1], were chosen because there is an already existing formal semantics and tool support for simulation and model-checking using UPPAAL [22] and automated test generation using COMPLETETEST [8]. A timed automaton is a standard finite-state automaton extended with time (i.e., real-valued clocks are used for measuring time progress). A model in UPPAAL consists of a network of processes that are composed of locations. Transitions between these locations define how the model behaves. The semantics of a timed automaton A is defined in terms of a state transition system, where the state of A is defined as a pair (l, u), where l is a location (i.e. node) and u is a clock assignment. A state of A depends on its current location and on the current values of its clocks. A network of timed automata $B_0 \parallel ... \parallel B_{n-1}$ is a parallel composition of n timed automata over synchronization functions (i.e., $a!$ is correlative with $a?$). Further information on timed automata can be found in [1]. In our previous work [8] we showed that an IEC 61131-3 FBD program can be transformed to a formal representation containing both its functional and timing behavior. In this study, the model aggregation is using this already developed translation for obtaining the model needed for running mutation-based test generation. Let M be a finite set of of mutants, each of which contains one syntactic change in the original program P. The model aggregation step is applied as follows:

- Create a timed automaton P corresponding to the original FBD program, and construct the structure of the program representing the set of blocks b_n, set of signals s_m and set of variables v_p in P: $b_1 \parallel ... \parallel b_n$, $s_1 \parallel ... \parallel s_m$ and $v_1 \parallel ... \parallel v_p$.
- For each mutant m_i in M, created by changing a block, signal or variable in P, create a duplicate version of it (e.g., b_{11} is a duplicate of b_1) having a different identifier and output than the original. This duplicate version has an *interface*, consisting of a name identifier. In addition, this duplicate version contains the same inputs as the original behavior, but different output variables and internal parameters in case of a mutated block. The interface is used to access both the block behavior and its duplicated version.
- Create a supervision automaton that executes each block and its mutants according to the order of execution. The execution order N is automatically defined according to the general rules included in the IEC 61131-3 standard [16]. This predetermined order directly dictates the data dependency in a program. Basically, each mutated entity executes in parallel with its original counterpart.

As a result of the model aggregation step we consider that the combined model is a closed network of timed automata. This model, briefly shown in Fig. 2, contains four processes, two modeling the program and its mutants and the other two supervising the overall execution and monitoring the mutant detection. To show an example of an aggregated model cycle scan, different actions are executed: read(IN) for reading input variables, write(OUT) for updating the output variables, and write(OUT(m_i)) for updating the duplicated output variables corresponding to each mutant m_i. When the execution order holds, the input variables are updated and the execution continues to the next block.

3.3 Mutant Annotation

Informally, our approach is based on the idea that in order to kill all mutants of a specific program, it would be sufficient to (i) annotate the mutants in an FBD program by adding a mutation detection monitor, (ii) formulate a reachability property for the mutation score (i.e., what portion of the existing mutants have been killed), and (iii) find a path from the initial state to some state where the mutation score is 100%. Thus, using auxiliary variables, we annotate the aggregated model such that a condition describing whether a single mutant is killed or not can be expressed.

For annotation, it should be noted that there are different interpretations of how to implement mutation analysis. The most common implementation, called strong mutation deals with the comparison of the original and mutated program outputs at the end of the execution cycle. Another way is weak mutation, which compares the state of the program immediately after the execution of the mutated part of the program. As these implementations can be useful in their different interpretation of mutation analysis, our approach employed both approaches.

Weak Mutation. A mutant is *weakly* killed in an FBD program if it leads to a block output change (i.e., block infection) compared to the original program behavior. For each mutation operator we define a detection monitor that precisely describes the decision that leads to a change in block output. In model checking we require a reachability property and a mutant detection monitor that guides the search towards detection. We define this weak mutation monitor for individual mutation operators. For each mutant m_i in M, where M is the entire set of mutants, there is a weak mutation monitor $wm_i(M)$ that looks at the block output change; if $wm_i(M)$ is 1 then m_i is detected. Using a model checker, the aim of weak mutation testing is to achieve a state where all mutants are killed with respect to the block output change. For generating tests for weak mutation we represent the test obligations over a set of variables monitoring the original behavior and its mutants as a reachability property.

Strong Mutation. Weak mutation testing for an FBD program results in a test suite where an internal block is infected; however, a change in block output does not necessarily propagate to an observable program output. Using a model checker, we propose to propagate the mutated behaviors to the output of the program using additional data variables and signals and monitor the change in output using a strong mutation monitor. For each mutant m_i in M, where M is the entire set of mutants, the output of each mutant is propagated to the depended blocks until it reaches the program output. There is a strong mutation monitor $sm_i(M)$ that looks at the program output change; if $sm_i(M)$ is 1 then m_i is detected. Using a model checker, the aim of strong mutation testing is to achieve a state where all mutants are killed with respect to the program output change. In our scenario, a mutant is killed if there exists a path in the model such that a test input shows that the mutated program output differs from the output of the original program.

3.4   Test Generation

In order to generate a test suite for mutation testing of FBD programs using UPPAAL, we make use of UPPAAL's ability to generate traces witnessing a submitted reachability property. A trace produced by the model checker for a given reachability property defines the set of actions executed on an FBD program which in our case is considered the system model fbd. An example of a diagnostic trace has the following form $(fbd_0) \xrightarrow{t_1} (fbd_1) \xrightarrow{t_2} \ldots \xrightarrow{t_n} (fbd_n)$, where (fbd_k) are states of the combined model and a_k are either internal synchronization actions, time-delays or `read!`, `execute!`, and `write!` global synchronizations. Test cases are obtained by extracting from the test path the observable actions `read!` and `write!` as these actions contain updates on input and output variables. In summary, the output of this step is a set of ordered test cases containing inputs, actual outputs and timing information (i.e., the time parameter in the test suite is expressing timing constraints within one program).

4   Experimental Evaluation

In order to evaluate the proposed mutation test generation technique, we designed an industrial case study. In particular, we aimed to answer the following research questions:

– *RQ1: Does mutation adequate test suites detect more faults than tests suites manually created by industrial engineers or automatically created test suites based on decision coverage?*
– *RQ2: Are mutation adequate test suites less costly than tests suites manually created by industrial engineers or automatically created test suites based on decision coverage?*

The case study setup is shown in Fig. 3. From a high level view we started the case study by collecting: (i) a set of real industrial programs from a recently developed train control management system (TCMS), and (ii) manual test suites created for the above programs by industrial engineers. The studied programs were already thoroughly tested and are currently used in a set of operational trains. For all programs, test suites were also generated for weak mutation, strong mutation and decision coverage (as detailed below).

In order to measure fault detection, realistic faulty versions of the programs under test are required. However, the data set did not contain any information about what faults occurred during development, as Bombardier Transportation AB does not keep any such data in a format that could be directly collected post-mortem at this level of testing. To overcome this issue, several engineers from Bombardier were asked to manually create a number of faults for the programs considered in this study. We obtained faults from engineers at Bombardier Transportation manually introducing relevant faults in some of the programs considered in this study. Since mutation-based test generation is using an existing program implementation to guide the search, we automatically generate all tests suites using the seeded faults instead of the original programs. This corresponds to the realistic situation where an engineer has made a fault located in the program to be tested. In summary, we used a TCMS system containing

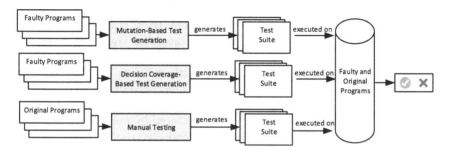

Fig. 3. Overview of the experimental setup used to perform the case study.

61 programs provided by Bombardier Transportation AB. These programs contained on average per program: 828 lines of IEC 61131-3 FBD code, 22 decisions (i.e., branches), 11 input variables and 5 output variables.

Manually Seeding Faults. For the TCMS programs, we provided four engineers working at Bombardier Transportation AB, who were not involved with the study with a document on doing fault seeding together with all the 61 programs. We asked each engineer to seed faults into the set of programs; we followed a specific fault seeding procedure using the IEC 61131-3 programming tools the engineers are using for developing the programs and instructed them to insert faults that were as realistic as possible. In particular, we instructed the engineers to insert any number of relevant faults, based on their experience, in the set of programs we provided as a TCMS project. We specifically instructed them to try to insert multiple faults in the same program one at the time and seed faults in at least ten programs from the total of 61. To avoid any misunderstanding, the fault seeding procedure document included information about the type of faults we were interested in: any fault that they might have encountered in their experience, as long as the interface (i.e., inputs and outputs) remained the same. This includes, but is not limited to, faults associated with variables, blocks, connections and constants. The fault seeding procedure resulted in 77 faults, versions of 33 (out of 61 in total) original programs containing a single fault (i.e., each fault contained one or more changes in the program). Each of the collected and generated test suites was executed on each of the faulty versions and its original counterpart so that a fault detection score could be calculated. Practically, each faulty variant contained one fault that had been manually seeded. A fault was considered to be detected by a test suite if the output from the faulty program differed from that of the original program.

Test Generation. For each faulty program, we ran mutation and decision-coverage test generation ten times using a random-depth-first search (RDFS) strategy with random seed (i.e., test suites are varying from run to run), each test generation run with a stopping time limit for the search of 10 min. The stopping criteria for the search is three-fold: achieving 100 % mutation score, reaching the time limit of 10 min, or getting a memory exception. We chose a time limit of 10 min for the sake of this experiment. In addition, we used manual test suites created by industrial engineers in Bombardier Transportation from a TCMS project delivered already to customers. Manual test suites were collected by using a post-mortem analysis of the test data available. The test suites collected in this study were based on functional specifications expressed in a natural language. Practically, we considered the original TCMS programs and for each faulty program, we executed the test suites produced by manual testing for the original program. Finally, for all test suites we collected the following measures: generation time, execution time, number of test cases and fault detection score. In order to calculate the fault detection score, each test suite was executed on both the original program and its faulty counterpart. In case the results differed between the executions, the fault was considered to be detected.

Measuring Cost. We measured the cost of performing testing focusing on the unit testing process as it is implemented in Bombardier Transportation for testing the programs selected in this case study. For the TCMS system, the creation and execution of test cases is performed by the implementer of the IEC 61131-3 software. In the cost measure, we use *the creation cost, the execution cost,* and *the result check cost.* The cost does not include the required tool preparation, the reporting and the maintenance of the test suite. We consider that all cost components related to human effort are depended to the number of test cases. The higher the number of tests cases, the higher are the respective costs. We assume this relationship to be linear with a constant factor representing the average time spend by an engineer in each cost component for a test case. Practically, we measured the costs of these activities directly as an average of the time taken by three industrial engineers (working at Bombardier Transportation implementing some of the IEC 61131-3 programs used in our case study) to perform manual testing.

5 Experimental Results and Discussion

The case study presented us with a fault detection score and a cost measurements for each of the collected test suites (i.e., manually created test suites by industrial engineers (MAN), mutation-adequate test suites (i.e., weak-mutation testing (WM), strong-mutation testing (SM)) and automatically generated test suites based on decision coverage (DC)). The overall results of this study are summarized in the form of boxplots[1] in Figs. 4 and 5.

Fault Detection. To answer RQ1 regarding the fault detection, in terms of detection of manually seeded faults, we focused on comparing all DC, WM, SM and MAN test suites. For all programs, as shown in Fig. 4, the fault detection scores obtained by manual written test suites are higher in average with 9 % and 6 % than those achieved by weak mutation and strong mutation respectively. The difference in fault detection is slightly greater between strong-mutation testing and decision coverage-adequate testing (i.e., a difference of almost 12 % on average). To understand how manual test suites achieve better fault detection than mutation-adequate test suites, we examined if the test suites are particularly weak or strong in detecting certain type of faults. We concern this analysis to what kind of faults were detected by manual testing and not by strong-mutation test generation. From a total of 77 faults, we identified eight faults (i.e., for exemplification purposes these faults are named Fault 1–8) that were not detected

---

[1] Boxes spans from 1st to 3rd quartile, black middle lines mark the median and the whiskers extend up to 1.5x the inter-quartile range and the circle symbols represent outliers.

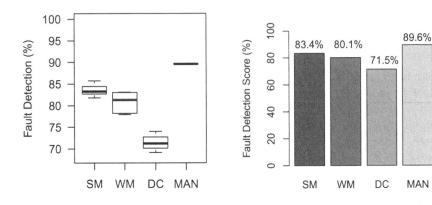

(a) Overall Fault Detection Comparison.   (b) Average Fault Detection Score.

Fig. 4. Fault detection results for manual testing (MAN), decision coverage-directed test generation (DC), weak mutation testing (WM) and strong mutation testing (SM).

by any strong-mutation test suite while being detected by manual test suites. To produce meaningful results the remaining 69 faults are not included in this fault detection analysis because there is no consistent difference between manual and strong-mutation test suites. There are some broad trends for eight faults that can be used for explaining at least the difference in fault detection between manual and strong-mutation testing. Test suites written using manual testing are able to detect all of these eight faults. Mutation test suites are achieving a poor selection of test inputs produced for detecting certain faulty behaviors; for six faults, strong mutation testing generated test suites achieving 100 % mutation score while for the remaining two faults, the model checker was unable to find a test suite detecting all mutants, given the 10 min time limit. It seems that manual testing has a stronger ability to detect these faults than mutation testing because of its inherent advantage of relying also on the specification of the program under test. For four of the faults, multiple changes in the program have been seeded (e.g., two or more blocks and variables have been replaced, deleted or inserted). For example, Fault 1 contains three changes combining three simpler faults corresponding to the application of CRO and VRO mutation operators. Fault 2 contains a combination of seeded changes corresponding to the creation of mutants using LRO and NIO mutation operators. In addition, Faults 3 and 4 contain multiple changes that were not captured by previously defined mutation operators. On the other hand, four of the faults are first order faults containing only one change in the program. A feedback loop signal connecting one of the outputs of the programs with one of the blocks was seeded in Faults 5 and 6. On the other hand, Fault 7 contains an extra logical block that was added to the original program while in Fault 8 a constant variable has been replaced to a non-boundary value. As a direct result, we discuss in Sect. 5.1 the

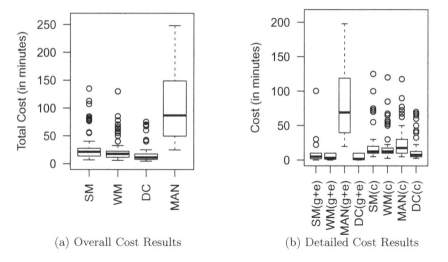

(a) Overall Cost Results   (b) Detailed Cost Results

Fig. 5. Cost measurement results for manual testing (MAN), decision coverage-directed test generation (DC), weak mutation testing (WM) and strong mutation testing (SM).

improvement of mutation-based test generation for PLC software by considering additional mutation operators not considered before in the literature [23, 27] to model possible faults.

Cost. We interviewed three engineers working on developing and manually testing TCMS software and asked them to estimate the time (in minutes) needed to create, execute and check the result of a test suite. All engineers independently provided similar cost estimations. We averaged the estimated time given by these three engineers and we calculated each individual cost using the following constants: 6.6 min for the creation of a test case, 3.3 min for the execution of a test case and 2.5 min for the checking of the result of a test case. Practically, for answering RQ2, we used these constants and the number of test cases in each test suites to represent the average time spend by an engineer to manually test each program. In addition, for mutation-based and decision coverage-directed test generation the total cost involves both machine and human resources. We calculated the cost of generating and executing a test suite by directly measuring the time required by the tool to run the test generation and the time required to execute each test case. For the cost of checking the test result we used the same average time as for manual testing (i.e. 2.5 min for the checking of the result of a test case). The resulting cost measures are reflected in Fig. 5. The cost of performing testing using mutation testing either weak or strong is consistently significantly lower than for manually created test suites; automatically generated test suites have a smaller testing cost (110 and 115 min shorter testing time on average for WM and SM respectively) than the cost of using manual test suites.

A more detailed cost measurement would be needed to obtain more confidence in the cost results obtained in this study.

5.1 Discussion

To explore the results of our study we consider the implications for future work and the extent to which mutation testing for PLC programs can be improved.

Improving Mutation Testing for PLC Programs. The results of this study indicate that fault detection scores obtained by manual test suites are better than the ones achieved by mutation testing. While comparing just strong-mutation testing with manual testing, we discovered that some of these faults are not reflected in the mutation operator list used for generating mutation adequate test suites, as described in Sect. 3.1. From our results, we highlight the need for improving the list of mutation operators used for mutation testing of PLC software by the addition of the following new mutation operators:

- *Feedback loop Insertion Operator (FIO)* is inserting a signal connecting an output variable to any block that is connected with the input variables.
- *Logical Block Insertion Operator (LIO)* is inserting a logical block between any other two logical blocks in the program.
- *Logical Block Deletion Operator (LDO)* is deleting a logical block and connecting the inputs of this block to the next logical block in the program.

In addition there are couple of already implemented mutation operators (shown in Sect. 3.1) that can be improved by considering the following operators:

- *Value Replacement Operator-Improved (VRO-I)* is replacing a value of a constant variable value connected to a block not only with its boundary values but also *with a selection of non-boundary values including 0, 1, −1.*
- *Logical Block Replacement Operator-Improved (LRO-I)* is replacing a logical block not only with logical blocks from the same category but also *with other blocks with Boolean inputs (e.g., replace an AND block with an SR block).*

By generating test suites that detect faults created based on these mutation operators, one could improve the goals of mutation testing for PLC programs. In addition, we recommend the use of higher-order mutation [19] for PLC software in order to find more complex faults.

Mutation Testing Using Model Checking. Our study is the first to consider mutation testing using model checking for PLC programs written in IEC 61131-3 FBD language. Model checking is a formal technique based on state exploration that has been applied to mutation testing by either using a process named reflection [3], by state machine duplication [24], or by explicitly evaluating the fault coverage over multiple mutants [12,14] thus creating test cases for manifesting fault propagation. The performance of this kind of approaches is depended not only on the model size but also the time spent on checking each and every mutated model or property against its original counterpart. This way of using the model checker for mutation testing can introduce unnecessary runs of the model checker and can considerably affect the feasibility of these approaches in practice. The method proposed in this study for the IEC 61131-3 FBD language is using a rather different approach for mutation testing, by combining all the mutants and the original model into a single combined model that is monitored dynamically using a model checking approach. By considering this way of utilizing the model checker one could potentially improve the cost of using mutation testing for other languages and models; the detection can be verified in a single run of the model checker for all mutated models rather than considering each individual case and thus removing the unnecessary model checking runs needed for detecting trivial mutants. This needs to be carefully considered in future studies and compared with other approaches on mutation testing using model checking.

6   Conclusions

In this paper we introduced mutation testing for PLC programs written in IEC 61131-3 programming language using a model checker. We implemented our approach in a tool and used this implementation to evaluate mutation testing on industrial programs and manually seeded faults. Our results show that mutation testing achieves lower fault detection compared to manual testing but with a significant lower cost in terms of testing time. We found out that these fault detection scores can be improved by considering some new and improved mutation operators for PLC programs as well as higher-order mutation.

Acknowledgments. This research was supported by The Knowledge Foundation (KKS) through the following projects: (20130085) Testing of Critical System Characteristics (TOCSYC), Automated Generation of Tests for Simulated Software Systems (AGENTS), and the ITS-EASY industrial research school.

References

1. Alur, R., Courcoubetis, C., Dill, D.: Model-checking for real-time systems. In: Logic in Computer Science, pp. 414–425. IEEE (1990)
2. Ammann, P., Offutt, J.: Introduction to Software Testing. Cambridge University Press, Cambridge (2008)
3. Black, P.E.: Modeling and marshaling: making tests from model checker counterexamples. In: Digital Avionics Systems, vol. 1. IEEE (2000)
4. Cadar, C., Dunbar, D., Engler, D.R.: KLEE: unassisted and automatic generation of high-coverage tests for complex systems programs. In: Symposium on Operating Systems Design and Implementation, vol. 8. USENIX (2008)
5. CENELEC: 50128: Railway Application: Communications, Signaling and Processing Systems, Software For Railway Control and Protection Systems. In: Standard. European Committee for Electrotechnical Standardization (2001)

6. DeMillo, R.A., Lipton, R.J., Sayward, F.G.: Hints on test data selection: help for the practicing programmer. IEEE Comput. **11**, 34–41 (1978)
7. Demillo, R.A., Offutt, J.A.: Constraint-based automatic test data generation. Trans. Softw. Eng. **17**(9), 900–910 (1991)
8. Enoiu, E., Čaušević, A., Ostrand, T.J., Weyuker, E.J., Sundmark, D., Pettersson, P.: Automated test generation using model checking: an industrial evaluation. J. Softw. Tools Technol. Transf. **18**(3), 335–353 (2014). Springer
9. Fraser, G., Arcuri, A.: Evosuite: automatic test suite generation for object-oriented software. In: Foundations of Software Engineering. ACM (2011)
10. Fraser, G., Wotawa, F., Ammann, P.E.: Testing with model checkers: a survey. J. Softw. Test. Verif. Reliab. **19**, 215–261 (2009). Wiley
11. Fraser, G., Zeller, A.: Mutation-driven generation of unit tests and oracles. Trans. Softw. Eng. **38**(2), 278–292 (2012)
12. Gargantini, A.: Using model checking to generate fault detecting tests. In: Gurevich, Y., Meyer, B. (eds.) TAP 2007. LNCS, vol. 4454, pp. 189–206. Springer, Heidelberg (2007)
13. Gay, G., Staats, M., Whalen, M., Heimdahl, M.: The risks of coverage-directed test case generation. Trans. Softw. Eng. **41**(8), 803–819 (2015). IEEE
14. Godskesen, J.C., Nielsen, B., Skou, A.: Connectivity testing through model-checking. In: Frutos-Escrig, D., Núñez, M. (eds.) FORTE 2004. LNCS, vol. 3235, pp. 167–184. Springer, Heidelberg (2004). doi:10.1007/978-3-540-30232-2_11
15. Howden, W.E.: Weak mutation testing and completeness of test sets. Trans. Softw. Eng. **4**, 371–379 (1982)
16. IEC: International Standard on 61131-3 Programming Languages. In: Programmable Controllers. IEC Library (2014)
17. Inozemtseva, L., Holmes, R.: Coverage is not strongly correlated with test suite effectiveness. In: International Conference on Software Engineering. ACM (2014)
18. Jamro, M.: POU-oriented unit testing of IEC 61131–3 control software. Trans. Ind. Inform. **11**, 1119–1129 (2015)
19. Jia, Y., Harman, M.: Higher order mutation testing. Inf. Softw. Technol. **51**(10), 1379–1393 (2009)
20. John, K.H., Tiegelkamp, M.: IEC 61131–3: Programming Industrial Automation Systems. Springer, Berlin (2010)
21. Just, R., Jalali, D., Inozemtseva, L., Ernst, M.D., Holmes, R., Fraser, G.: Are mutants a valid substitute for real faults in software testing? In: Foundations of Software Engineering, pp. 654–665. ACM (2014)
22. Larsen, K.G., Pettersson, P., Yi, W.: Uppaal in a nutshell. Int. J. Softw. Tools Technol. Transf. **1**, 134–152 (1997). Springer
23. Oh, Y., Yoo, J., Cha, S., Son, H.S.: Software safety analysis of FBD using fault trees. Reliab. Eng. Syst. Saf. **88**, 215–228 (2005). Elsevier
24. Okun, V., Black, P.E., Yesha, Y.: Testing with model checker: insuring fault visibility. Syst. Sci. Appl. Math. **2**(1), 77–82 (2003)
25. Orso, A., Rothermel, G.: Software testing: a research travelogue (2000–2014). In: Proceedings of the on Future of Software Engineering. ACM (2014)
26. Schwartz, M.D., Mulder, J., Trent, J., Atkins, W.D.: Control system devices: architectures and supply channels overview. In: Sandia National Laboratories Sandia Report SAND2010-5183 (2010)
27. Shin, D., Jee, E., Bae, D.-H.: Empirical evaluation on FBD model-based test coverage criteria using mutation analysis. In: France, R.B., Kazmeier, J., Breu, R., Atkinson, C. (eds.) MODELS 2012. LNCS, vol. 7590, pp. 465–479. Springer, Heidelberg (2012). doi:10.1007/978-3-642-33666-9_30

28. Simon, H., Friedrich, N., Biallas, S., Hauck-Stattelmann: automatic test case generation for PLC programs using coverage metrics. In: ETFA. IEEE (2015)
29. Woodward, M., Halewood, K.: From weak to strong, dead or alive? An analysis of some mutation testing issues. In: STVA. IEEE (1988)
30. Wu, Y.C., Fan, C.F.: Automatic test case generation for structural testing of FBD. Inf. Softw. Technol. **56**, 1360–1376 (2014). Elsevier

STIPI: Using Search to Prioritize Test Cases Based on Multi-objectives Derived from Industrial Practice

Dipesh Pradhan[1]([✉]), Shuai Wang[1], Shaukat Ali[1], Tao Yue[1,2],
and Marius Liaaen[3]

[1] Certus V&V Center, Simula Research Laboratory, Oslo, Norway
{dipesh,shuai,shaukat,tao}@simula.no
[2] University of Oslo, Oslo, Norway
[3] Cisco Systems, Oslo, Norway
marliaae@cisco.com

Abstract. The importance of cost-effectively prioritizing test cases is undeniable in automated testing practice in industry. This paper focuses on prioritizing test cases developed to test product lines of Video Conferencing Systems (VCSs) at Cisco Systems, Norway. Each test case requires setting up configurations of a set of VCSs, invoking a set of test APIs with specific inputs, and checking statuses of the VCSs under test. Based on these characteristics and available information related with test case execution (e.g., number of faults detected), we identified that the test case prioritization problem in our particular context should focus on achieving high coverage of configurations, test APIs, statuses, and high fault detection capability as quickly as possible. To solve this problem, we propose a search-based test case prioritization approach (named *STIPI*) by defining a fitness function with four objectives and integrating it with a widely applied multi-objective optimization algorithm (named Non-dominated Sorting Genetic Algorithm II). We compared *STIPI* with random search (RS), Greedy algorithm, and three approaches adapted from literature, using three real sets of test cases from Cisco with four time budgets (25 %, 50 %, 75 % and 100 %). Results show that *STIPI* significantly outperformed the selected approaches and managed to achieve better performance than RS for on average 39.9 %, 18.6 %, 32.7 % and 43.9 % for the coverage of configurations, test APIs, statuses and fault detection capability, respectively.

Keywords: Test case prioritization · Search · Configurations · Test APIs

1 Introduction

Testing is a critical activity for system or software development, through which system/software quality is ensured [1]. To improve the testing efficiency, a large number of researchers have been focusing on prioritizing test cases into an optimal execution order to achieve maximum effectiveness (e.g., fault detection capability) as quickly as possible [2–4]. In the industrial practice of automated testing, test case

© IFIP International Federation for Information Processing 2016
Published by Springer International Publishing AG 2016. All Rights Reserved.
F. Wotawa et al. (Eds.): ICTSS 2016, LNCS 9976, pp. 172–190, 2016.
DOI: 10.1007/978-3-319-47443-4_11

prioritization is even more critical because usually there is a limited budget (e.g., time) to execute test cases, and thus executing all available test cases at a given context is infeasible [1, 5].

Our industrial partner for this work is Cisco System, Norway, who develops product lines of Video Conferencing Systems (VCSs), which enable high quality conference meetings [4, 5]. To ensure the delivery of high quality VCSs to the market, test engineers of Cisco continually develop test cases to test software of VCSs under various hardware or software configurations, statuses (i.e., states) of VCSs with dedicated test APIs. A test case is typically composed of the following parts: (1) setting up test configurations of a set of VCSs under test; (2) invoking a set of test APIs of the VCSs; and (3) checking the statuses of the VCSs after invoking the test APIs to determine the success or failure of an execution of the test case. When executing test cases, several objectives need to be achieved, i.e., covering the maximum number of possible configurations, test APIs, statuses and detecting as many faults as possible. However, given a number of available test cases, it is often infeasible to execute all of them in practice due to a limited budget of execution time (e.g., 10 h), and it is therefore important to seek an approach for prioritizing the given test cases to cover maximum number of configurations, test APIs, statuses and detect faults as quickly as possible.

To address the above-mentioned challenge, we propose a search-based test case prioritization approach named *Search-based Test case prioritization based on Incremental unique coverage and Position Impact (STIPI)*. STIPI defines a fitness function with four objectives to evaluate the quality of test case prioritization solutions, i.e., Configuration Coverage (*CC*), test API Coverage (*APIC*), Status Coverage (*SC*) and Fault Detection Capability (*FDC*), and integrates the fitness function with a widely-applied multi-objective search algorithm (i.e., Non-dominated Sorting Genetic Algorithm II) [6]. Moreover, we propose two prioritization strategies when defining the fitness function in *STIPI*: (1) *Incremental Unique Coverage*, i.e., for a specific test case, we only consider the incremental unique elements (e.g., test APIs) covered by the test case as compared with the elements covered by the already prioritized test cases; and (2) *Position Impact*, i.e., a test case with a higher execution position (i.e., scheduled to be executed earlier) has more impact on the quality of a prioritization solution. Notice that both of these strategies are defined to help search to achieve high criteria (i.e., *CC*, *APIC*, *SC* and *FDC*) as quickly as possible.

To evaluate *STIPI*, we chose five approaches for the comparison: (1) Random Search (*RS*) to assess the complexity of the problem; (2) *Greedy* approach; (3) One existing approach [7] and two modified approaches from the existing literature [8, 9]. The evaluation uses in total 211 test cases from Cisco, which are divided into three sets with varying complexity. Moreover, four different time budgets are used for our evaluation, i.e., 25 %, 50 %, 75 % and 100 % (100 % refers to the total execution time of all the test cases in a given set). Notice that 12 comparisons were performed (i.e., three sets of test cases*four time budgets) for comparing *STIPI* with each approach, and thus in total 60 comparisons were conducted for the five approaches. Results show that *STIPI* significantly outperformed the selected approaches for 54 out of 60 comparisons (90 %). In addition, *STIPI* managed to achieve higher performance than RS for on average 39.9 % (configuration coverage), 18.6 % (test API coverage), 32.7 % (status coverage), and 43.9 % (fault detection capability).

The remainder of the paper is organized as follows: Sect. 2 presents the context, a running example and motivation. *STIPI* is presented in Sect. 3 followed by experiment design (Sect. 4). Section 5 presents experiment results and overall discussion. Related work is discussed in Sect. 6, and we conclude the work in Sect. 7.

2   Context, Running Example and Motivation

Figure 1 presents a simplified context of testing VCSs (Systems Under Test (SUTs)), and Fig. 2 illustrates (partial) configuration, test API and status information for testing a VCS. First, one VCS consists of one or more configuration variables (e.g., attribute *protocol* of class VCS in Fig. 2), each of which can take two or more configuration variable values (e.g., literal *SIP* of enumeration *Protocol*). Second, a VCS holds one or more status variables defining the statuses of the VCS (e.g., *NumberofActiveCalls*), and each status variable can have two or more status variable values (e.g., *NumberofActiveCalls* taking values of 0, 1, 2, 3 and 4). Third, testing a VCS requires employing one or more test API commands (e.g., *dial*), each of which includes zero or more test API parameters (e.g., *callType* for *dial*). Each test API parameter can take two or more test API parameter values (e.g., *Video* and *Audio* for *CallType*).

Figure 3 illustrates the key steps of a test case for testing VCSs. First, a test case configures one or more VCSs by assigning values to configuration variables. For example, the test case shown in Fig. 3 configures the configuration variable *protocol* with *SIP* (Line 1). Second, a test API command is invoked with appropriate values

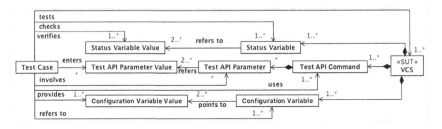

Fig. 1. A simplified context of testing VCSs

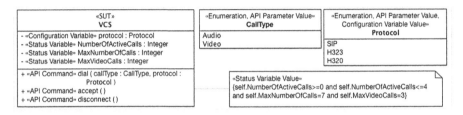

Fig. 2. Partial configuration, status and test API information for testing a VCS

```
1. protocol = SIP    //Configure the configuration variable
2. dial(Video, SIP) //Employ test API command dial and assigning
                       values to parameters: callType and protocol
3. accept               //Employ test API command with no parameters
4. assert (NumberOfActiveCalls=1,MaxNumberOfCalls=1,
              MaxVideoCalls =1) //Check values of the status variables
5. disconnect           //Employ test API command with no parameters
6. assert(NumberofActiveCalls=0) //Check status
```

Fig. 3. An excerpt of a sanitized and simplified test case

assigned to its input parameters, if any. For example, the test case in Fig. 3 invokes the test API command *dial* consisting of the two test API parameter values: *Video* for *callType* and *SIP* for *protocol*) (Line 2). Third, the test case checks the actual statuses of VCSs. For example, the test case in Fig. 3 checks the status of the VCS to see if *NumberOfActiveCalls* equals to 1 (Line 4).

In the context of testing VCSs, test case prioritization is a critical task since it is practically infeasible to execute all the available test cases within a given time budget (e.g., 5 h). Therefore, it is essential to cover maximum configurations (i.e., configuration variables and their values), test APIs (i.e., test API commands, parameters and their values) and statuses (i.e., status variables and their values), and detect faults as quickly as possible. For instance, Table 1 lists five test cases ($T_1 \ldots T_5$) with the information about configurations, test APIs and statuses. The test case in Fig. 3 is represented as T_1 in Table 1, which (1) sets the configuration variable *protocol* as *SIP*; (2) uses three test API commands: *dial* with two parameters (*callType, protocol*), *accept* and *disconnect*; and (3) checks values of three status variables (e.g., *MaxVideoCalls*).

Notice that the five test cases in Table 1 can be executed in 325 orders (i.e., $C(5,1) \times 1! + C(5,2) \times 2! + \ldots + C(5,5) \times 5!$). When there is a time budget, each particular order can be considered as a prioritization solution. Given two prioritization solutions $s_1 = \{T_5, T_1, T_4, T_2, T_3\}$, $s_2 = \{T_1, T_3, T_5, T_2, T_4\}$, one can observe that s_1 is better than s_2 since the first three test cases in s_1 can cover all the configuration variables and their values, test API commands, test API parameters, test API parameter values, status variables and status variable values, while s_2 needs to execute all the five test cases to achieve the same coverage as s_1. Therefore, it is important to seek an

Table 1. Illustrating test case prioritization*

Test case	Configuration	Test API				Status		
	Protocol	Dial		Accept	Disconnect	SV_1	SV_2	SV_3
		callType	Protocol					
T_1	SIP	Video	SIP	✔	✔	0, 1	1	1
T_2	SIP	Audio	SIP	✔	✔	0, 1	1	0
T_3	SIP	Audio	SIP	✔		1	1	0
T_4	H323	Audio	H323	✔		0, 1, 2	2	0
T_5	H320	Audio	H320	✔		1	1	1

*SV_1: *NumberOfActiveCalls*, SV_2: *MaxNumberOfCalls*, SV_3: *MaxVideoCalls*.

efficient approach to find an optimal order for executing a given number of test cases to achieve high coverage of configurations, test APIs and statuses, and detect faults as quickly as possible, which forms the motivation of this work.

3 *STIPI*: Search-Based Test Case Prioritization Based on Incremental Unique Coverage and Position Impact

This section presents the problem representation (Sect. 3.1), four defined objectives, fitness function (Sect. 3.2) and solution encoding (Sect. 3.3).

3.1 Basic Notations and Problem Representation

Basic Notations. We provide the basic notations as below used throughout the paper.

$T = \{T_1, T_2 \ldots T_n\}$ represents a set of n test cases to be prioritized.

$ET = \{et_1, et_2 \ldots et_n\}$ refers to the execution time for each test case in T.

$CV = \{cv_1, cv_2 \ldots cv_{mcv}\}$ represents the configuration variables covered by T. For each cv_i, CVV_i refers to the configuration variable values: $CVV_i = \{cvv_{i1} \ldots cvv_{icvv}\}$. $mcvv$ is the total number of unique values for all the configuration variables, which can be calculated as: $mcvv = \left| \left(\bigcup_{i=1}^{mcv} CVV_i \right) \right|$.

$AC = \{ac_1, ac_2 \ldots ac_{mac}\}$ represents a set of test API commands covered by T. For each ac_i, AP_i denotes the test API parameters: $AP_i = \{ap_{i1} \ldots ap_{iap}\}$. map is the total number of unique test API parameters, calculated as: $map = \left| \left(\bigcup_{i=1}^{mac} AP_i \right) \right|$. For each ap_i, AV_i refers to the test API parameter values: $AV_i = \{av_{i1} \ldots av_{iav}\}$. mav is the total number of unique test API parameter values, i.e., $mav = \left| \left(\bigcup_{i=1}^{map} AV_i \right) \right|$.

$SV = \{sv_1, sv_2 \ldots sv_{msv}\}$ represents a set of status variables covered by T. For each sv_i, SVV_i refers to the status variable values: $SVV_i = \{svv_{i1} \ldots svv_{isvv}\}$. $msvv$ is the total number of unique status variable values, calculated as: $msvv = \left| \left(\bigcup_{i=1}^{msv} SVV_i \right) \right|$.

$Effect = \{effect_1 \ldots effect_{neffect}\}$ defines a set of effectiveness measures.

$S = \{s_1, s_2 \ldots s_{ns}\}$ represents a set of potential solutions, such that $ns = C(n, 1) \times 1! + C(n, 2) \times 2! + \ldots + C(n, n) \times n!$. Each solution s_j consists of a set of prioritized test cases in T: $s_j = \{T_{j1} \ldots T_{jn}\}$, where $T_{ji} \in T$ refers to the test case with the execution position i in the prioritized solution s_j. Note that it is possible for the maximum number of test cases in s_j (i.e., jn) to be less than the total number of test cases in T, since only a subset of T is prioritized during limited budget (e.g., time).

Problem Representation. We aim to prioritize the test cases in T in two contexts: (1) 100 % time budget and (2) less than 100 % time budget (i.e., time-aware [1]). Therefore, we formulate the test case prioritization problem as follows: (a) search a solution s_k with nk test cases from the total number of ns solutions in S to obtain the highest effectiveness; and (b) a test case T_{jr} in a particular solution (e.g.,s_j) with a higher position p has more influence for *Effect* than the test case with a lower position q.

(1) With 100 % time budget:

$$\forall_{i=1 \, to \, n \, effect} \forall_{j=1 \, to \, ns} \, Effect \, (s_k, \, effect_i) \geq Effect\left(s_j, effect_i\right)$$
$$\vee \, effect_i\left(T_{jr}, p\right) > \forall_{q \geq (p+1)} effect_i(T_{jr}, q).$$

where $effect_i\left(T_{jr}, p\right)$ and $effect_i\left(T_{jr}, q\right)$ refer to the effectiveness measure i for a test case T_{jr} at position p and q, respectively for a particular solution s_j. $Effect(s_k, effect_i)$ and $Effect(s_j, effect_i)$ returns the effectiveness measure i for solutions s_k, s_j respectively.

(2) With a time budget tb less than 100 % time budget:

$$\forall_{i=1 \, to \, neffect} \forall_{j=1 \, to \, ns} \, Effect \, (s_k, \, effect_i) \geq Effect \, \left(s_j, \, effect_i\right)$$
$$\vee \sum_{l=1}^{nk} ET_l \leq tb, effect_i\left(T_{jr}, p\right) > \forall_{q \geq (p+1)} effect_i(T_{jr}, q).$$

3.2 Fitness Function

Recall that we aim at maximizing the overall coverage for configuration, test API and status, and detect faults as quickly as possible (Sect. 2). Therefore, we define four objective functions for the fitness function to guide the search towards finding optimal solutions, which are presented in details as below.

Maximize Configuration Coverage (CC). *CC* measures the overall configuration coverage of a solution s_j with jn number of test cases, which is composed of Configuration Variable Coverage (*CVC*) and Configuration Variable Values Coverage (*CVVC*). We can calculate *CVC* and *CVVC* for s_j as: $CVC_{s_j} = \frac{\sum_{i=1}^{jn} UCV_{T_{ji}} \times \frac{n-i+1}{n}}{mcv}$, $CVVC_{s_j} = \frac{\sum_{i=1}^{jn} UCVV_{T_{ji}} \times \frac{n-i+1}{n}}{mcvv}$, where mcv and $mcvv$ represent the total number of unique Configuration Variables (*CV*) and Configuration Variable Values (*CVV*) respectively covered by the total test cases in T (e.g., in Table 1 $mcvv = 3$). Moreover, we propose two prioritization strategies for calculating *CVC* and *CVVC*. The first one is *Incremental Unique Coverage*, i.e., $UCV_{T_{ji}}$ and $UCVV_{T_{ji}}$ representing the number of incremental unique *CV* and *CVV* covered by T_{ji} (Sect. 3.1). For example, in Table 1, for one test case prioritization solution $s_1 = \{T_5, T_1, T_4, T_2, T_3\}, UCVV_{T_5}$ is 1 since T_5 is in the first execution position and covers one *CVV* (i.e., *H320*). $UCVV_{T_1}$ and $UCVV_{T_4}$ are at the second and third position, and cover one *CVV* each (i.e., *SIP*, *H323*). However, $UCVV_{T_2}$ and $UCVV_{T_3}$ are 0, since they are already covered by $UCVV_{T_1}$. This strategy is defined since test case prioritization in our case concerns how many configurations, test APIs, and statuses can be covered rather than how many times they can be covered. The second prioritization strategy is *Position Impact*, which is calculated as $\frac{n-i+1}{n}$, where n is the total number of test cases, and i is a specific execution position in a prioritization solution. Thus, test cases with higher execution positions have higher impact on the quality of a prioritization solution, which fits the scope of test case prioritization that aims at achieving higher criteria as quickly as possible. For instance, using this strategy, $CVVC$ for s_1 is: $CVVC_{s_1} = \frac{1\times\frac{5}{5}+1\times\frac{4}{5}+1\times\frac{3}{5}+0\times\frac{2}{5}+0\times\frac{1}{5}}{3} = 0.8$. Moreover, CC for s_j is represented as: $CC_{s_j} = \frac{CVC_{s_j}+CVVC_{s_j}}{2}$. A higher value of CC shows a higher coverage of configuration.

Maximize Test API Coverage (APIC). $APIC$ measures the overall test API coverage of a solution s_j with jn number of test cases. It consists of three sub measures: Test API Command Coverage (ACC), Test API Parameter Coverage (APC), and Test API parameter Value Coverage (AVC). ACC, APC and AVC can be calculated as below:

$$ACC_{s_j} = \frac{\sum_{i=1}^{jn} UAC_{T_{ji}} \times \frac{n-i+1}{n}}{mac}, APC_{s_j} = \frac{\sum_{i=1}^{jn} UAP_{T_{ji}} \times \frac{n-i+1}{n}}{map}, AVC_{s_j}$$
$$= \frac{\sum_{i=1}^{jn} UAV_{T_{ji}} \times \frac{n-i+1}{n}}{mav}.$$

Similarly, the same two strategies (i.e., *Incremental Unique Coverage* and *Position Impact*) are applied for calculating ACC, APC and AVC, where $UAC_{T_{ji}}$, $UAP_{T_{ji}}$ and $UAV_{T_{ji}}$ denotes the number of unique test API commands (AC), test API parameters (AP), and test API parameter values (AV) respectively covered by T_{ji} (Sect. 3.1). They are measured similar as for $UCVV_T$ in $CVVC$. mac, map, and mav refer to the total number of unique AC, AP, and AV covered by the total number of test cases as explained for $mcvv$ in $CVVC$. The $APIC$ for s_j is represented as: $APIC_{s_j} = \frac{ACC_{s_j}+APC_{s_j}+AVC_{s_j}}{3}$. A higher value of $APIC$ shows a higher coverage of test APIs.

Maximize Status Coverage (SC). SC measures the total status coverage of a solution s_j. It consists of two sub measures: Status Variable Coverage (SVC) and Status Variable Value Coverage ($SVVC$), calculated as follow: $SVC_{s_j} = \frac{\sum_{i=1}^{jn} USV_{T_{ji}} \times \frac{n-i+1}{n}}{msv}$, $SVVC_{s_j} = \frac{\sum_{i=1}^{jn} USVV_{T_{ji}} \times \frac{n-i+1}{n}}{msvv}$. Similarly, $USV_{T_{ji}}$ and $USVV_{T_{ji}}$ are the number of unique Status Variables (SV) and Status Variable Values (SVV) respectively covered by T_{ji} (Sect. 3.1), which are measured similar as $UCVV_T$ in $CVVC$. msv and $msvv$ represent the total number of unique SV and SVV respectively measured similar as for $mcvv$ in $CVVC$. The SC for s_j is represented as: $SC_{s_j} = \frac{SVC_{s_j}+SVVC_{s_j}}{2}$, with a higher value indicating a higher status coverage, and therefore representing a better solution.

Maximize Fault Detection Capability (FDC). In the context of Cisco, FDC is defined as the detected number of faults for test cases in a solution s_j [4, 5, 10–12]. The FDC for a test case T_{ji} is calculated as: $FDC_{T_{ji}} = \frac{Number\ of\ times\ that\ T_{ji}\ found\ a\ fault}{Number\ of\ times\ that\ T_{ji}\ was\ executed}$. Notice that the FDC of T_{ji} is calculated based on the historical information of executing T_{ji}. For example, if tc_i was executed 10 times, and it detected fault 4 times, the FDC for tc_i is 0.4. We calculate FDC for a solution s_j as: $FDC_{s_j} = \frac{\sum_{i=1}^{jn} FDC_{T_{ji}} \times \frac{n-i+1}{n}}{mfdc}$. $FDC_{T_{ji}}$ denotes the *FDC* for a T_{ji}, *mfdc* represents the sum of all *FDC* of test cases, and a higher value of *FDC* implies a better solution. Notice that we cannot apply the *incremental unique coverage* strategy for calculating FDC_{s_j} since the relations between faults and test cases are not known in our case (i.e., we only know whether the test cases can detect faults after executing it for a certain number of times rather than having access to the detailed faults detected).

3.3   Solution Representation

The test cases in *T* are encoded as an array $A = \{v_1, v_2 \ldots v_n\}$, where each variable v_i represents one test case in *T*, and holds a unique value from 0 to 1. We prioritize the test cases in *TS* by sorting the variables in *A* in a descending order from higher to lower, such that 1 is the highest, and 0 is the lowest order. Initially, each variable in *A* is assigned a random value between 0 and 1, and during search our approach returns solutions with optimal values for *A* guided by the fitness function defined in Sect. 3.2. In terms of time-aware test case prioritization (i.e., with a time budget less than 100 %), we pick the maximum number of test cases that fit the given time budget. For example, in Table 1 for $TS = \{T_1 \ldots T_5\}$ with *A* as $\{0.6, 0.2, 0.4, 0.9, 0.3\}$ and the execution time (recorded as minutes) as $ET = \{4, 5, 6, 4, 3\}$, the prioritized test cases are $\{T_4, T_1, T_3, T_5, T_2\}$ based on our encoding way for test case prioritization. If we have a time budget of 11 min, the first two test cases (in total 8 min for execution) are first added to the prioritized solution s_j, and there are 3 min left, which is not sufficient for executing T_3 (6 min). Thus, T_3 is not added into s_j, and the next test case is evaluated to see if the total execution time can fit the given time budget. T_5 with 3 min will be added into s_j, since the inclusion of T_5 will not make the total execution time exceed the time budget. Therefore, the new prioritized solution will be $\{T_4, T_1, T_5\}$.

Moreover, we integrate our fitness function with a widely applied multi-objective search algorithm named Non-dominated Sorting Genetic Algorithm (NSGA-II) [6, 13, 14]. The tournament selection operator [6] is applied to select individual solutions with the best fitness for inclusion into the next generation. The crossover operator is used to produce offspring solutions from the parent solutions by swapping some of the parts (e.g., test cases in our context) of the parent solutions. The mutation operator is applied to randomly change the values of one or more variables (e.g., in our context, each variable represents a test case) based on the pre-defined mutation probability, e.g., 1/(total number of test cases) in our context.

4   Empirical Study Design

4.1   Research Questions

RQ1: Is *STIPI* effective for test case prioritization as compared with *RS* (i.e., random prioritization)? We compare *STIPI* with *RS* for four time budgets: 100 % (i.e., total execution time of all the test cases in a given set), 75 %, 50 % and 25 %, to assess the complexity of the problem such that the use of search algorithms is justified.

RQ2: Is *STIPI* effective for test case prioritization as compared with four selected approaches, in the contexts of four time budgets: 100 %, 75 %, 50 % and 25 %?

RQ2.1: Is *STIPI* effective as compared with the Greedy approach (a local search approach)?

RQ2.2: Is *STIPI* effective as compared with the approach used in [7] (named as *A1* in this paper)? Notice that we chose *A1* since it also proposed a strategy to give higher importance to test cases with higher execution positions.

RQ2.3: Is *STIPI* effective as compared with the modified version of the approach proposed in [8] (named as *A2* in this paper)? We chose *A2* since it combines the Average Percentage of Faults Detected (*APFD*) metric and NSGA-II for test case prioritization without considering time budget. We modified it by defining Average Percentage of Configuration Coverage (*APCC*), Average Percentage of test API Coverage (*APAC*) and Average Percentage of Status Coverage (*APSC*) (Sect. 4.3) for assessing the quality of prioritization solutions for configurations, test APIs and statuses.

RQ2.4: Is *STIPI* effective as compared with the modified version of the approach in [9] (named as *A3* in this paper)? We chose *A3* since (1) it combines the *ADFD* with cost (*APFD_c*) metric and NSGA-II for addressing time-aware test case prioritization problem. We revised *A3* by defining Average Percentage of Configuration Coverage with cost (*APCC_c*), Average Percentage of test API Coverage with cost (*APAC_c*) and Average Percentage of Status Coverage with cost (*APSC_c*). For illustration, we provide a formula for Average Percentage of Configuration Variable Value Coverage with cost (*APCVVC_c*) that is a sub-metric for *APCC_c* as:

$$APCVVC_c = \frac{\sum_{i=1}^{mcvv}(\sum_{k=TCVV_i}^{jn} et_k - \frac{1}{2}et_{TCVV_i})}{\sum_{k=1}^{jn} et_k \times mcvv}.$$ For a solution s_j with jn test cases, $TCVV_i$ is the first test case from s_j that covers CVV_i (i.e., the ith configuration variable value), $mcvv$ is the total number of unique configuration variable value, and et_k is the execution time for k^{th} test case. Notice that the detailed formulas for $APCC_c$, $APAC_c$ and $APSC_c$ can be consulted in our technical report in [15].

We also compare the running time of *STIPI* with all the five chosen approaches, since *STIPI* is invoked very frequently (e.g., more than 50 times per day) in our context, i.e., the test cases require to be prioritized and executed often. Therefore, it would be practically infeasible if it takes too much time to apply *STIPI*.

4.2   Experiment Tasks

As shown in Table 2 (*Experiment Task* column), we designed two tasks (T_1, T_2) for addressing *RQ1–RQ2*. The task T_1 is designed to compare *STIPI* with *RS* for the four time budgets (i.e., 100 %, 75 %, 50 % and 25 %) and three sets of test cases (i.e., 100, 150 and 211). Similarly, the task T_2 is designed to compare *STIPI* with the other four test case prioritization approaches, which is divided into four sub-tasks for comparing *Greedy*, *A1*, *A2* and *A3*, respectively.

Table 2. Overview of the experiment design

RQ	Experiment task		# test cases	Time budget %	Evaluation metric (*EM*)	Quality indicator	Statistical test
1	T_1: STIPI vs. RS		100 150 211	100 25, 50, 75	APCC, APAC, APSC $APCC_p$, $APAC_p$, $APSC_p$, MFDC	– –	Vargha and Delaney $\hat{A}_{12}$ Mann-Whitney U test
2	$T_{2.1}$	STIPI vs. Greedy		100 25, 50, 75	APCC, APAC, APSC $APCC_p$, $APAC_p$, $APSC_p$, MFDC	– –	
	$T_{2.2}$	STIPI vs. A1		100 25, 50, 75	APCC, APAC, APSC $APCC_p$, $APAC_p$, $APSC_p$, MFDC	Hypervolume (HV)	
	$T_{2.3}$	STIPI vs. A2		100 25, 50, 75	APCC, APAC, APSC $APCC_p$, $APAC_p$, $APSC_p$		
	$T_{2.4}$	TIPI vs. A3		100 25, 50, 75	APCC, APAC, APSC $APCC_p$, $APAC_p$, $APSC_p$		

Moreover, we employed 211 real test cases from Cisco for evaluation by dividing it into three sets with varying complexity (*#Test Cases* column in Table 2). For the first set, we used all the 211 test cases. For the second set, we used 100 random test cases from the 211 test cases. Finally, for the third set, we used the 150 test cases by choosing 111 test cases not selected in the second set (i.e., 100) and 39 random test cases from the second set. Notice that the goal for using three test case sets is to evaluate our approach with test datasets with different complexity.

4.3   Evaluation Metrics

To answer the *RQ*s, we defined in total seven *EMs* (Table 3). Six are used to assess how fast the configurations, test APIs and statuses can be covered: (1) Average Percentage Configuration Coverage (*APCC*), (2) Average Percentage test API Coverage (*APAC*), (3) Average Percentage Status Coverage (*APSC*), (4) Average Percentage Configuration Coverage that penalizes missing configuration ($APCC_p$), (5) Average Percentage test API Coverage that penalizes missing test API ($APAC_p$) and (6) Average Percentage Status Coverage with penalization for missing status ($APSC_p$). We defined *APCC, APAC* and *APSC* for test case prioritization with 100 % time budget based on the *APFD* metric [8, 16]. For example, for a solution s_j with jn test cases and total number of test cases n from T (a given number of test cases), TCV_1 is the first test case from s_j that covers CV_1 for the sub metric *APCVC* in Table 3 (Sect. 3.1). Notice that n and jn are equal when there is 100 % time budget.

When there is a limited time budget, it is possible that not all the configurations, test APIs and statuses can be covered. Therefore, we defined $APCC_p$, $APAC_p$, and $APAC_p$ to give penalty to missing configurations, test APIs, and statuses for time-aware prioritization (i.e., 25 %, 50 % and 75 % time budget) based on the variant of *APFD*

Table 3. Different metrics for evaluating the approaches*

EC	Time budget %	EM	Sub metric Name	Sub metric Formula	Formula
Con	100	APCC	APCVC	$1 - \frac{TCV_1 + TCV_2 + ... + TCV_{mcv}}{n \times mcv} + \frac{1}{2n}$	$APCC = \frac{APCVC + APCVVC}{2}$
			APCVVC	$1 - \frac{TCVV_1 + TCVV_2 + ... + TCVV_{mcvv}}{n \times mcvv} + \frac{1}{2n}$	
	25 50 75	$APCC_p$	$APCVC_p$	$1 - \frac{\sum_{cv=1}^{mcv} reveal(cv,s_j)}{jn \times mcv} + \frac{1}{2jn}$	$APCC_p = \frac{APCVC_p + APCVVC_p}{2}$
			$APCVVC_p$	$1 - \frac{\sum_{cvv=1}^{mcvv} reveal(cvv,s_j)}{jn \times mcvv} + \frac{1}{2jn}$	
API	100	APAC	APACC	$1 - \frac{TAC_1 + TAC_2 + ... + TAC_{mac}}{n \times mac} + \frac{1}{2n}$	$APAC = \frac{APACC + APAPC + APAVC}{3}$
			APAPC	$1 - \frac{TAP_1 + TAP_2 + ... + TAP_{map}}{n \times map} + \frac{1}{2n}$	
			APAVC	$1 - \frac{TAV_1 + TAV_2 + ... + TAV_{mav}}{n \times mav} + \frac{1}{2n}$	
	25 50 75	$APAC_p$	$APACC_p$	$1 - \frac{\sum_{ac=1}^{mac} reveal(ac,s_j)}{jn \times mac} + \frac{1}{2jn}$	$APAC_p = \frac{APACC_p + APAPC_p + APAVC_p}{3}$
			$APAPC_p$	$1 - \frac{\sum_{ap=1}^{map} reveal(ap,s_j)}{jn \times map} + \frac{1}{2jn}$	
			$APAVC_p$	$1 - \frac{\sum_{av=1}^{mav} reveal(av,s_j)}{jn \times mav} + \frac{1}{2jn}$	
Stat	100	APSC	APSVC	$1 - \frac{TSV_1 + TSV_2 + ... + TSV_{msv}}{n \times msv} + \frac{1}{2n}$	$APSC = \frac{APSVC + APSVVC}{2}$
			APSVVC	$1 - \frac{TSVV_1 + TSVV_2 + ... + TSVV_{msvv}}{n \times msvv} + \frac{1}{2n}$	
	25 50 75	$APSC_p$	$APSVC_p$	$1 - \frac{\sum_{sv=1}^{msv} reveal(sv,s_j)}{jn \times msv} + \frac{1}{2jn}$	$APSC_p = \frac{APSVC_p + APSVVC_p}{2}$
			$APSVVC_p$	$1 - \frac{\sum_{svv=1}^{msvv} reveal(svv,s_j)}{jn \times msvv} + \frac{1}{2jn}$	
FDC	25,50,75	MFDC	-	-	$MFDC = \frac{\sum_{j=1}^{jn} FDC_{T_j}}{\sum_{k=1}^{n} FDC_{T_k}} \times 100\%$

*EC: Evaluation Criteria, Con: Configuration, API: Test API, Stat: Status.

metric used for time-aware prioritization [1, 16]. For example, for a solution s_j with jn test cases $reveal(cv, s_j)$ gives the test case from s_j that covers cv for $APCVC_p$ in Table 3. If s_j does not contain a test case that covers cv, $reveal(cv, s_j) = jn + 1$. Notice that in our context, we only have information about how many times in a given period (e.g., a week) a test case was successful in finding faults. Therefore, it is not possible to use the *APFD* metric to evaluate *FDC*. Hence, we defined a metric: Measured Fault Detection Capability (*MFDC*) to measure the percentage of fault detected for time budget of 25 %, 50 % and 75 %.

4.4 Quality Indicator, Statistical Tests and Parameter Settings

When comparing the overall performance of multi-objective search algorithms (e.g., NSGA-II [6]), it is common to apply quality indicators such as hypervolume (*HV*). Following the guideline in [10], we employ *HV* based on the defined *EM*s to address *RQ2.2*–*RQ2.4* (i.e., tasks $T_{2.2}$–$T_{2.4}$ in Table 2). *HV* calculates the volume in the objective space covered by members of a non-dominated set of solutions (i.e., Pareto front) produced by search algorithms for measuring both convergence and diversity [17]. A higher value of *HV* indicates a better performance of the algorithm.

The Vargha and Delaney $\hat{A}_{12}$ statistics [18] and Mann-Whitney U test are used to compare the EMs (T_1 and T_2), and HV ($T_{2.2}$–$T_{2.4}$), as shown in Table 2 by following the guidelines in [19]. The Vargha and Delaney $\hat{A}_{12}$ statistics is a non-parametric effect size measure, and Mann-Whitney U test tells if results are statistically significant [20]. For two algorithms A and B, A has better performance than B if $\hat{A}_{12}$ is greater than 0.5, and the difference is significant if p-value is less than 0.05.

Notice that STIPI, A1, A2 and A3 are all combined with NSGA-II. Since tuning parameters to different settings might result in different performance of search algorithms, standard settings are recommended [19]. We used standard settings (i.e., population size = 100, crossover rate = 0.9, mutation rate = 1/(number of test cases)) as implemented in jMetal [21]. The search process is terminated when the fitness function has been evaluated for 50,000 times. Since A2 does not support prioritization with a time budget, we collect the maximum number of test cases that can fit a given time budget.

5   Results, Analyses and Discussion

5.1   RQ1: Sanity Check (STIPI vs. RS)

Results in Tables 4 and 5 show that on average STIPI is higher than RS for all the EMs across the three sets of test cases. Moreover, for the three test sets using four time budgets, STIPI managed to achieve higher performance than RS for on average 39.9 % (configuration coverage), 18.6 % (test API coverage), 32.7 % (status coverage), and 43.9 % (FDC). In addition, results of the Vargha and Delaney statistics and the Mann Whitney U test show that STIPI significantly outperformed RS for all the Ems since all the values of $\hat{A}_{12}$ are greater than 0.5 and all the p-values are less than 0.05.

Table 4. Average values of the EMs with 100 % and 75 % time budget*

# T	100 % time budget							75 % time budget						
	EM	RS	Gr	A1	A2	A3	STI	EM	RS	Gr	A1	A2	A3	STI
100	CC	0.7	0.76	0.75	0.77	0.75	0.77	CC_p	0.63	0.71	0.73	0.74	0.73	0.74
150		0.68	0.84	0.8	0.79	0.75	0.79		0.60	0.81	0.69	0.72	0.73	0.77
211		0.74	0.83	0.83	0.85	0.81	0.85		0.67	0.76	0.79	0.80	0.79	0.81
100	AC	0.83	0.74	0.85	0.85	0.84	0.86	AC_p	0.78	0.70	0.83	0.82	0.84	0.83
150		0.78	0.64	0.83	0.86	0.85	0.86		0.72	0.57	0.75	0.81	0.83	0.84
211		0.82	0.67	0.85	0.89	0.89	0.89		0.77	0.56	0.83	0.87	0.87	0.88
100	SC	0.73	0.65	0.76	0.82	0.76	0.82	SC_p	0.67	0.60	0.73	0.79	0.79	0.81
150		0.74	0.62	0.8	0.85	0.83	0.85		0.68	0.56	0.71	0.80	0.81	0.83
211		0.78	0.64	0.79	0.85	0.82	0.85		0.72	0.56	0.79	0.84	0.85	0.86
100	-	-	-	-	-	-	-	MF	0.78	0.79	0.91	-	-	0.89
150	-	-	-	-	-	-	-		0.79	0.80	0.70	-	-	0.87
211	-	-	-	-	-	-	-		0.77	0.63	0.91	-	-	0.90

*T: Test Case, Gr: *Greedy*, CC: *APCC*, AC: *APAC*, SC: *APSC*, CC_p: *APCC$_p$*, AC_p: *APACp*, SC_p: *APSCp*, MF: *MFDC*, STI: *STIPI*.

Table 5. Average values of the *EMs* with 25 % and 50 % time budget*

EM	# T	25 % time budget						50 % time budget					
		RS	Gr	A1	A2	A3	STIPI	RS	Gr	A1	A2	A3	STIPI
$APCC_p$	100	0.37	0.30	0.55	0.51	0.62	0.66	0.52	0.65	0.65	0.67	0.70	0.73
	150	0.35	0.59	0.52	0.45	0.66	0.71	0.50	0.81	0.74	0.63	0.72	0.74
	211	0.42	0.43	0.63	0.56	0.69	0.71	0.52	0.53	0.65	0.67	0.70	0.73
$APAC_p$	100	0.56	0.26	0.70	0.61	0.74	0.70	0.71	0.61	0.79	0.77	0.81	0.81
	150	0.50	0.35	0.59	0.55	0.74	0.75	0.64	0.54	0.76	0.74	0.81	0.82
	211	0.58	0.33	0.71	0.65	0.77	0.75	0.71	0.52	0.79	0.81	0.85	0.85
$APSC_p$	100	0.42	0.14	0.59	0.55	0.70	0.66	0.57	0.51	0.68	0.72	0.76	0.76
	150	0.44	0.33	0.54	0.53	0.73	0.74	0.52	0.53	0.65	0.67	0.70	0.73
	211	0.48	0.24	0.66	0.62	0.78	0.77	0.63	0.52	0.74	0.78	0.84	0.85
MFDC	100	0.30	0.06	0.55	-	-	0.50	0.54	0.45	0.77	-	-	0.78
	150	0.30	0.19	0.40	-	-	0.63	0.55	0.74	0.75	-	-	0.76
	211	0.29	0.09	0.52	-	-	0.44	0.53	0.48	0.75	-	-	0.76

5.2   *RQ2*: Comparison with the Selected Approaches

We compared *STIPI* with *Greedy*, *A1*, *A2* and *A3* using the statistical tests (Vargha and Delaney statistics and Mann Whitney U test) for the four time budgets (25 %, 50 %, 75 % and 100 %), and the three sets of test cases (i.e., 100, 150, 211). Results are summarized in Fig. 4. For example, the first bar (i.e., *Gr*) in Fig. 4 refers to the comparison between *STIPI* and *Greedy* for the 100 % time budget where $A = STIPI$ and $B = Greedy$. $A > B$ means the percentage of *EMs* for which *STIPI* has significantly better performance than *Greedy* $(\hat{A}_{12} > 0.5 \,\&\&\, p < 0.05), A < B$ means the opposite $(\hat{A}_{12} < 0.5 \,\&\&\, p < 0.05)$, and $A = B$ implies there is no significant difference in performance $(p \geq 0.05)$.

RQ2.1 (STIPI vs. Greedy). From Tables 4 and 5, we can observe that the average values of *STIPI* are higher than *Greedy* for 93.3 % (42/45)[1] *EMs* across the three sets of test cases with the four time budgets. Moreover, from Fig. 4, we can observe *STIPI* performed significantly better than *Greedy* for an average of 93.1 % for the four time budgets (i.e., 88.9 % for 100 %, 91.7 % for 75 %, 91.7 % for 50 %, and 100 % for 25 % time budget). Detailed results are available in [15].

RQ2.2 (STIPI vs. A1). Based on Tables 4 and 5, we can see that *STIPI* has a higher average value than *A1* for 82.2 % (37/45) *EMs*, and *STIPI* performed significantly better than *A1* for an average of 76.4 % *EMs* across the four time budgets, while there was no difference in performance for 14.6 % from Fig. 4. Figure 5 shows that for *HV*, *STIPI* outperformed *A1* for all the three sets of test cases with the four time budgets, and such better results are statistically significant. Detailed results are in [15].

---

[1] An *EM* has one average value for one set of test case with one time budget (Tables 4 and 5). Thus, for 100 % time budget with 3 *EMs* there are 9 values, and 45 average values for 4 time budgets and 4 EMs for other 3 time budgets.

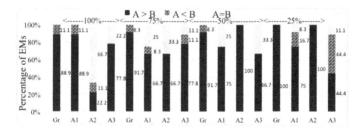

Fig. 4. Results of comparing *STIPI* with *Greedy*, *A1*, *A2* and *A3* for *EMs*

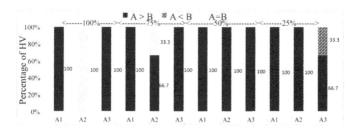

Fig. 5. Results of comparing *STIPI* with *A1*, *A2* and *A3* for *HV*

RQ2.3 (STIPI vs. A2). *RQ2.3* is designed to compare *STIPI* with the approach *A2* (Sect. 4.1). Table 4 shows that the two approaches had similar average for *EMs* with 100 % time budget. Moreover, for 100 % time budget, there was no significant difference in the performance between *STIPI* and *A2* in terms of *EMs* and *HV* (Figs. 4 and 5). However, when considering the time budgets of 25 %, 50 % and 75 %, *STIPI* had a higher performance for 96.3 % (26/27) *EMs* (Tables 4 and 5). Furthermore, the statistical tests in Figs. 4 and 5 show that *STIPI* significantly outperformed *A2* for an average of 88.9 % *EMs* and *HV* values across the three time budgets (25 %, 50 %, 75 %), while there was no significant difference for 11.1 %.

RQ2.4 (STIPI vs. A3). Based on the results (Tables 4 and 5), *STIPI* held a higher average values for 75 % (27/36) *EM* values for the four time budgets and three sets of test cases. For 100 %, 75 %, and 50 %, we can observe from Fig. 4 that *STIPI* performed significantly better than *A3* for an average of 74.1 % *EMs*, while there was no significant difference for 22.2 %. For the 25 % time budget, there was no statistically significant difference in terms of *EMs* for *STIPI* and *A3*. However, when comparing the *HV* values, *STIPI* significantly outperformed *A3* for an average of 91.7 % across the four time budgets and three sets of test cases.

Notice that 12 comparisons were performed when comparing *STIPI* with each of the five selected approaches (i.e., three test case sets * four time budgets), and thus in total 60 comparisons were conducted. Based on the results, we can observe that *STIPI* significantly outperformed the five selected approaches for 54 out of 60 comparisons (90 %), which indicate that *STIPI* has a good capability for solving our test case prioritization problem. In addition, *STIPI* took an average time of 36.5, 51.6 and 82 s (secs) for the three sets of test cases. The average running time for the five chosen approaches are: (1) RS: 18, 24.7 and 33.2 s; (2) *Greedy*: 42, 48 and 54 ms; (3) *A1*: 35.7, 42.8 and 65.5 s; (4) *A2*: 35.2, 42.2 and 55.4 s; and (5) *A3*: 8.9, 33.4 and 41.2 s. Notice that there is no practical difference in terms of the running time for the approaches except *Greedy*, however the performance of *Greedy* is significantly worse than *STIPI* (Sect. 5.2), and thus *Greedy* cannot be employed to solve our test case prioritization problem. In addition, based on the domain knowledge of VCS testing, the running time in seconds is acceptable when deployed in practice.

5.3   Overall Discussion

For *RQ1*, we observed that *STIPI* performed significantly better than *RS* for all the *EM*s with the three sets of test cases under the four time budgets. Such an observation reveals that solving our test case prioritization problem is not trivial, which requires an efficient approach. As for *RQ2*, we compared *STIPI* with *Greedy*, *A1*, *A2* and *A3* (Sect. 4.1). Results show that *STIPI* performed significantly better than *Greedy*. This can be explained that *Greedy* is a local search algorithm that may get stuck in a local space during the search process, while *STIPI* employs mutation operator (Sect. 4.4) to explore the whole search space towards finding optimal solutions. In addition, *Greedy* converted our multi-objective optimization problem into a single-objective optimization problem by assigning weights to each objective, which may lose many other optimal solutions that hold the same quality [22], while *STIPI* (integrating NSGA-II) produces a set of non-dominated solutions (i.e., solutions with equivalent quality).

When comparing *STIPI* with *A1*, *A2* and *A3*, the results of *RQ2* showed that *STIPI* performed significantly better than *A1*, *A2* and *A3* by 83.3 % (30/36). Overall *STIPI* outperformed the five selected approaches for 90 % (54/60) comparisons. That might be due to two main reasons: (1) *STIPI* considers the coverage of incremental unique elements (e.g., test API commands) when evaluating the prioritization solutions, i.e., only the incremental unique elements covered by a certain test case are taken into account as compared with the already prioritized test cases; and (2) *STIPI* provides the test cases with higher execution positions more influence on the quality of a given prioritization solution. Furthermore, *A2* and *A3* usually work under the assumption that the relations between detected faults and test cases are known beforehand, which is sometimes not the situation in practice, e.g., in our case, we are only aware how many execution times a test case can detect faults rather than having access to the detailed faults detected. However, *STIPI* defined *FDC* to measure the fault detection capability (Sect. 3.2) without knowing the detailed relations between faults and test cases, which may be applicable to the similar other contexts when the detailed faults cannot be accessed. It is worth mentioning that the current practice of Cisco do not have an efficient approach for test case prioritization, and thus we are working on deploying our approach in their current practice for further strengthening *STIPI*.

5.4   Threats to Validity

The *internal validity* threat arises due to using search algorithms with only one configuration setting for its parameters as we did in our experiment [23]. However, we used the default parameter setting from the literature [24], and based on our previous experience [5, 10], good performance can be achieved for various search algorithms with the default setting. To mitigate the *construct validity* threat, we used the same stopping criteria (50,000 fitness evaluations) for finding the optimal solutions. To avoid *conclusion validity threat* due to the random variations in the search algorithms, we repeated the experiments 10 times to reduce the possibility that the results were obtained by chance. Following the guidelines of reporting the results for randomized algorithms [19], we employed the Vargha and Delaney test as the effect size measure and Mann-Whitney test to determine the statistical significance of results. First *external validity* threat is that one may argue the comparison performed only included RS, *Greedy*, one existing approach and two modified versions of the existing approaches, which may not be sufficient. Notice that we discussed and justified why we chose these approaches in Sect. 4.1, and it is also possible to compare our approach with other existing approaches, which requires further investigation as the next step. Second *external validity* threat is due to the fact that we only performed the evaluation using one industrial case study. We need to mention that we conducted the experiment using three sets of test cases with four distinct time budgets based on the domain knowledge of VCS testing.

6 Related Work

In the last several decades, test case prioritization has attracted a lot of attention and considerable amount of work has been done [1–3, 8]. Several survey papers [25, 26] present results that compare existing test case prioritization techniques from different aspects, e.g., based on coverage criteria. Followed by the aspects presented in [25], we summarize the related work close to our approach and highlight the key differences from the following three aspects: coverage criteria, search-based prioritization techniques (which is related with our approach) and evaluation metrics.

Coverage Criteria. Existing works defined a number of coverage criteria for evaluating the quality of prioritization solutions [2, 3, 26] such as branch coverage and statement coverage, function coverage and function-level fault exposing potential, block coverage, modified condition/decision coverage, transition coverage and round trip coverage. As compared with the state-of-the-art, we proposed three new coverage criteria driven by the industrial problem (Sect. 3.2): (1) Configuration coverage (*CC*); (2) Test API coverage (*APIC*) and (3) Status coverage (*SC*).

Search-Based Prioritization Techniques. Search-based techniques have been widely applied for addressing test case prioritization problem [3–5, 10]. For instance, Li et al. [3] defined a fitness function with three objectives (i.e., Block, Decision and Statement Coverage) and integrated the fitness function with hill climbing and GA for test case prioritization. Arrieta et al. [7] proposed to prioritize test cases by defining a two-objective fitness function (i.e., test case execution time and fault detection capability) and evaluated the performance of several search algorithms. The authors of [7] also proposed a strategy to give higher importance to test cases with higher positions (to be executed earlier). A number of research papers have focused on addressing the test case prioritization problem within a limited budget (e.g., time and test resource) using search-based approaches. For instance, Walcott et al. [1] proposed to combine selection (of a subset of test cases) and prioritization (of the selected test cases) for prioritizing test cases within a limited time budget. Different weights are assigned to the selection part and prioritization part when defining the fitness function followed by solving the problem with GA. Wang et al. [5] focused on the test case prioritization within a given limited test resource budget (i.e., hardware, which is different as compared with the time budget used in this work) and defined four cost-effectiveness measures (e.g., test resource usage), and evaluated several search algorithms (e.g., NSGA-II).

As compared with the existing works, our approach (i.e., *STIPI*) defines a fitness function that considers configurations, test APIs and statuses, which were not addressed in the current literature. When defining the fitness function, *STIPI* proposed two strategies, which include (1) only considering the unique elements (e.g., configurations) achieved; and (2) taking the impact of test case execution orders on the quality of prioritization solutions into account, which is not the case in the existing works.

Evaluation Metrics (*EMs*). *APFD* is widely used in the literature as an *EM* [2, 3, 8, 16]. Moreover, the modified version of *APFD* (i.e., $APFD_p$) using time penalty [1, 16] is usually applied for test case prioritization with a time budget. Other metrics were also defined and applied as *EMs* [9, 26] such as Average Severity of Faults Detected, Total Percentage of Faults Detected and Average Percentage of Faults Detected per Cost ($APFD_c$). As compared with the existing *EMs*, we defined in total six new *EMs* driven by our industrial problem for configurations, test APIs and statuses (Table 3), which include: (1) *APCC*, *APAC*, and *APSC*, inspired by *APFD*, when there is 100 % time budget; and (2) $APCC_p$, $APAC_p$, and $APSC_p$ inspired by $APFD_p$, when there is a limited time budget (e.g., 25 % time budget). Furthermore, we defined the seventh *EM* (*MFDC*) to assess to what extent faults can be detected when the time budget is less than 100 % (Table 3). To the best of our knowledge, there is no existing work that applies these seven *EMs* for assessing the quality of test case prioritization solutions.

7   Conclusion and Future Work

Driven by our industrial problem, we proposed a multi-objective search-based test case prioritization approach named *STIPI* for covering maximum number of configurations, test APIs, statuses, and achieving high fault detection capability as quickly as possible. We compared *STIPI* with five test case prioritization approaches using three sets of test cases with four time budgets. The results show that *STIPI* performed significantly better than the chosen approaches for 90 % of the cases. *STIPI* managed to achieve a higher performance than random search for on average 39.9 % (configuration coverage), 18.6 % (test API coverage), 32.7 % (status coverage) and 43.9 % (*FDC*). In the future, we plan to compare *STIPI* with more prioritization approaches from the literature using additional case studies with larger scale to further generalize the results.

Acknowledgements. This research is supported by the Research Council of Norway (RCN) funded Certus SFI. Shuai Wang is also supported by the RFF Hovedstaden funded MBE-CR project. Shaukat Ali and Tao Yue are also supported by the RCN funded Zen-Configurator project, the EU Horizon 2020 project funded U-Test, the RFF Hovedstaden funded MBE-CR project and the RCN funded MBT4CPS project.

References

1. Walcott, K.R., Soffa, M.L., Kapfhammer, G.M., Roos, R.S.: Timeaware test suite prioritization. In: Proceedings of 2006 International Symposium on Software Testing and Analysis, pp. 1–12 (2006)
2. Rothermel, G., Untch, R.H., Chu, C., Harrold, M.J.: Test case prioritization: an empirical study. In: Proceedings of International Conference on Software Maintenance (ICSM 1999), pp. 179–188 (1999)
3. Li, Z., Harman, M., Hierons, R.M.: Search algorithms for regression test case prioritization. IEEE Trans. Softw. Eng. (TSE) **33**, 225–237 (2007)
4. Wang, S., Buchmann, D., Ali, S., Gotlieb, A., Pradhan, D., Liaaen, M.: Multi-objective test prioritization in software product line testing: an industrial case study. In: International Software Product Line Conference, pp. 32–41 (2014)
5. Wang, S., Ali, S., Yue, T., Bakkeli, Ø., Liaaen, M.: Enhancing test case prioritization in an industrial setting with resource awareness and multi-objective search. In: ICSE, pp. 182–191 (2016)
6. Deb, K., Pratap, A., Agarwal, S., Meyarivan, T.: A fast and elitist multiobjective genetic algorithm: NSGA-II. TSE **6**, 182–197 (2002)
7. Arrieta, A., Wang, S., Sagardui, G., Etxeberria, L.: Test case prioritization of configurable cyber-physical systems with weight-based search algorithms. In: Genetic and Evolutionary Computation (GECCO), pp. 1053–1060 (2016)
8. Rothermel, G., Untch, R.H., Chu, C., Harrold, M.J.: Prioritizing test cases for regression testing. TSE **27**, 929–948 (2001)
9. Elbaum, S., Malishevsky, A., Rothermel, G.: Incorporating varying test costs and fault severities into test case prioritization. In: Proceedings of International Conference on Software Engineering (ICSE), pp. 329–338 (2001)
10. Wang, S., Ali, S., Yue, T., Li, Y., Liaaen, M.: A practical guide to select quality indicators for assessing pareto-based search algorithms in search-based software engineering. In: ICSE, pp. 631–642 (2016)
11. Wang, S., Ali, S., Gotlieb, A.: Cost-effective test suite minimization in product lines using search techniques. J. Syst. Softw. **103**, 370–391 (2015)
12. Wang, S., Ali, S., Gotlieb, A.: Minimizing test suites in software product lines using weight-based genetic algorithms. In: Proceedings of 15th Annual Conference on Genetic and Evolutionary Computation, pp. 1493–1500 (2013)
13. Sarro, F., Petrozziello, A., Harman, M.: Multi-objective software effort estimation. In: ICSE, pp. 619–630 (2016)
14. Wang, S., Ali, S., Yue, T., Liaaen, M.: UPMOA: an improved search algorithm to support user-preference multi-objective optimization. In: International Symposium on Software Reliability Engineering (ISSRE), pp. 393–404 (2015)
15. Technical report (2016-06): https://www.simula.no/publications/stipi-using-search-prioritize-test-cases-based-multi-objectives-derived-industrial

16. Lu, Y., Lou, Y., Cheng, S., Zhang, L., Hao, D., Zhou, Y., Zhang, L.: How does regression test prioritization perform in real-world software evolution? In: Proceedings of 38th ICSE, pp. 535–546 (2016)

17. Nebro, A.J., Luna, F., Alba, E., Dorronsoro, B., Durillo, J.J., Beham, A.: AbYSS: adapting scatter search to multiobjective optimization. IEEE Trans. Evol. Comput. **12**, 439–457 (2008)

18. Vargha, A., Delaney, H.D.: A critique and improvement of the CL common language effect size statistics of McGraw and Wong. J. Educ. Behav. Stat. **25**, 101–132 (2000)

19. Arcuri, A., Briand, L.: A practical guide for using statistical tests to assess randomized algorithms in software engineering. In: 33rd International Conference on Software Engineering (ICSE), pp. 1–10 (2011)

20. Mann, H.B., Whitney, D.R.: On a test of whether one of two random variables is stochastically larger than the other. Ann. Math. Stat. **18**, 50–60 (1947)

21. Durillo, J.J., Nebro, A.J.: jMetal: a Java framework for multi-objective optimization. Adv. Eng. Softw. **42**, 760–771 (2011)

22. Konak, A., Coit, D.W., Smith, A.E.: Multi-objective optimization using genetic algorithms: a tutorial. Reliab. Eng. Syst. Safety **91**, 992–1007 (2006)

23. De Oliveira Barros, M., Neto, A.: Threats to validity in search-based software engineering empirical studies. Technical report 6, UNIRIO-Universidade Federal do Estado do Rio de Janeiro (2011)

24. Arcuri, A., Fraser, G.: On parameter tuning in search based software engineering. In: Cohen, M.B., Ó Cinnéide, M. (eds.) SSBSE 2011. LNCS, vol. 6956, pp. 33–47. Springer, Heidelberg (2011)

25. Yoo, S., Harman, M.: Regression testing minimization, selection and prioritization: a survey. Softw. Test. Verif. Reliab. **22**, 67–120 (2012)

26. Catal, C., Mishra, D.: Test case prioritization: a systematic mapping study. Softw. Qual. J. **21**, 445–478 (2013)

From Simulation Data to Test Cases for Fully Automated Driving and ADAS

Christoph Sippl[1,2]([✉]), Florian Bock[2], David Wittmann[3], Harald Altinger[1], and Reinhard German[2]

[1] Audi Electronics Venture GmbH, Sachsstr. 20, 85080 Gaimersheim, Germany
{christoph.sippl,harald.altinger}@audi.de
[2] Department of Computer Science 7, Friedrich-Alexander-University, 91058 Erlangen, Germany
{florian.inifau.bock,reinhard.german}@fau.de
[3] Chair of Automotive Technology, Technical University of Munich, Boltzmannstr. 15, 85748 Garching, Germany
wittmann@ftm.mw.tum.de

Abstract. Within this paper we present a new concept on deriving test cases from simulation data and outline challenging tasks when testing and validating fully automated driving functions and Advanced Driver Assistance Systems (ADAS). Open questions on topics like virtual simulation and identification of relevant situations for consistent testing of fully automated vehicles are given. Well known criticality metrics are assessed and discussed with regard to their potential to test fully automated vehicles and ADAS. Upon our knowledge most of them are not applicable to identify relevant traffic situations which are of importance for fully automated driving and ADAS. To overcome this limitation, we present a concept including filtering and rating of potentially relevant situations. Identified situations are described in a formal, abstract and human readable way. Finally, a situation catalogue is built up and linked to system requirements to derive test cases using a Domain Specific Language (DSL).

Keywords: Virtual validation · ADAS · Fully automated vehicles · Simulation · Test case generation · DSL

1 Introduction

Today's driver assistance functions and emergency systems help to avoid accidents and support the driver in critical situations. As the system boundaries are clearly defined, test cases can easily be specified. On the contrary, Advanced Driver Assistance Systems (ADAS) and fully automated vehicles ensure safety and comfort while driving in a normal mode. Here, defining all relevant test cases poses problems for developers due to the large amount of dynamic objects, including pedestrians and cyclists in urban traffic as well as the variety of priority rules and traffic guidance. So far, comprehensive test concepts and structured

© IFIP International Federation for Information Processing 2016
Published by Springer International Publishing AG 2016. All Rights Reserved
F. Wotawa et al. (Eds.): ICTSS 2016, LNCS 9976, pp. 191–206, 2016.
DOI: 10.1007/978-3-319-47443-4_12

test case generation, such as Equivalence Class Partitioning (ECP), Boundary Value Analysis (BVA) and Predicate Testing improve the efficiency of software testing as stated by Eo *et al.* [1], but are not well-suited to identify all possible and relevant situations for fully automated vehicles and ADAS.

Therefore, simulation-based development and new concepts for virtual validation are needed, instead of testing new driving functions with the help of many thousands of test kilometres. There are already numerous tools for simulation-based function development and testing, thus driving simulators with realistic, environment-sensitive behaviour of road users (e.g. pedestrians, cyclists and cars) can be used to generate a huge amount of data. This data contain new situations, which are relevant for testing certain driving functions. An automatic identification of these situations and the comparison with an existing set of situations in the test suite improve the overall test coverage of fully automated driving functions and ADAS. Manual inspection and filtering of the relevant situations or describing test cases is not recommended with respect to time and budget.

2   Related Work

In general, test cases are described by analysing the obligatory system requirements. In case of ADAS and fully automated driving functions, this can be done by evaluating data, produced by model-based simulation or empirically collected data. Zofka *et al.* [2] presented an innovative data-driven method and a concept contrary to previous approaches in order to create critical traffic situations from recorded sensor data. This concept allows reconstruction and parametrization of real world traffic scenarios. These reconstructed test scenarios can be re-simulated by deviating parameters in order to evaluate and test ADAS components. This approach may modify already observed and identified situations, but cannot detect completely unknown events.

Prior Schuldt and Menzel [3] presented a method to assign test cases automatically to X-in-the-loop simulation techniques using quality criteria. In [4], a modular virtual test repository is presented to reduce the number of required test cases for validation of driving functions by systematic test case generation with consistent test coverage. This approach improves the overall test process by using simulation techniques and provides evaluation methods. However, using this method, generated test cases are derived from predefined parameters which have impact on the system specification and requirements, scenario catalogues and existing guidelines and standards. Thus, complex and not yet identified situations are not taken into account. Stellet *et al.* [5] summed up challenging tasks on testing fully automated vehicles and ADAS and worked out, why automated driving functions cannot be tested by defining system level criteria. Stellet *et al.* argue, that "such concepts are too simplistic for future continuously intervening automated driving functions". In their work, a number of research questions are pointed out that remain unanswered to date. One of these questions is: "How to overcome the dilemma of testing the entire complexity of real-world traffic?"

To ensure consistent terminology regarding the terms *scene, situation* and *scenario* we follow the definitions given by Ulbrich *et al.* in [6]. They reflected various definitions and pointed out their understanding of the terms with regard to fully automated driving. Reduced to the key facts and following the definition given in [6], the terms are described as below:

Scene. "A scene describes a snapshot of the environment including the scenery and dynamic elements, as well as all actors' and observers' self-representations, and the relationships among those entities [...]"

Situation. "A situation is the entirety of circumstances, which are to be considered for the selection of an appropriate behavior pattern at a particular point of time. It entails all relevant conditions, options and determinants for behavior. A situation is derived from the scene by an information selection and augmentation process based on transient [...] as well as permanent goals and values. Hence, a situation is always subjective by representing an element's point of view."

Scenario. "A scenario describes the temporal development between several scenes in a sequence of scenes. Every scenario starts with an initial scene. Actions and events as well as goals and values may be specified to characterize this temporal development in a scenario. Other than a scene, a scenario spans a certain amount of time."

Aim of This Work. This paper drafts a concept to derive system test cases for black box testing from simulation data. In the first step of this concept, an environment-sensitive behaviour simulation generates a large quantity of data. Then, the simulation data is pre-filtered in order to identify traffic situations, in which dynamic objects may affect the target vehicle. Upon our knowledge, standalone criticality metrics experience limitations and might not be adequate for a reasonable rating according virtual test and validation of fully automated driving functions and ADAS. Thus, the pre-filtered data are rated by a new factor to extract relevant situations. This new factor can be parametrised by developer specifications or use case specific targets. Then, identified situations are described formally and in an abstract way to build up a situation catalogue. System requirements are linked to the situation catalogue to define test criteria and derive a test suite from evaluated simulation results using a Domain Specific Language. The situation catalogue linked to systems requirements represent the input stimuli for system testing of fully automated vehicles and ADAS. The generated test cases can be used during typical development stages e.g. Software in the Loop (SiL), Hardware in the Loop (HiL), etc. A common simulation environment might be Virtual Test Drive [7].

3   Traffic Conflict Techniques for Fully Automated Driving

Traffic Conflict Techniques (TCT) have come a long way since they were intro-duced in the late 1950s. Several studies have been conducted to evaluate traffic conflicts and criticality metrics have been developed and extensively discussed since the late 1970s. Amundsen and Hydn [8] defines a conflict as "an observa-tional situation in which two or more road users approach each other in space and time to such an extent that a collision is imminent if their movements remain unchanged". Time-To-Collision (TTC) [9] and Post-Encroachment-Time (PET) [10], Deceleration-To-Safety-Time (DST) [11] and various modifications of TTC and PET like Gap-Time (GT), the Proportion of Stopping Distance (PSD), Time-To-React, Time-To-Maneuver and Initially-Attempt-Post-Encroachment-Time (IAPT) became effective measurements for the rating of traffic conflicts and the development of Collision-Avoidance-System (CAS) and Pre-Crash Sys-tems (PCS). They are also used in the field of accident research. Rodemerk's [12] general criticality criterion represents a collision risk in potential collision areas, using motion prediction models and the knowledge of the course of the roadway. Common to all these metrics, they only calculate, whether a collision or a conflict zone occurs if participating objects do not change their path or speed. A rating of the traffic situation thus, can only be processed if there is an imminent conflict or accident.

Fully automated vehicles and ADAS have to process situation analysis and interpretation. An adequate interpretation is done by taking all relevant dynamic objects into account. Identifying these situations to process situation analysis and interpretation, they have to be detected and rated much earlier than known criticality metrics can provide. So, situations which may look harmless or initially pose no danger might also be interesting for interpretation, due to environment reasons and missing or vague traffic guidance. To be able to develop appropri-ate strategies for fully automated driving, it is necessary to analyse complex traffic situations at a time, when surrounding objects and their influence to the target vehicle cannot be assessed by conflict and criticality metrics. Analysing apparently uncritical, but complex traffic situations is inevitably to quantify a situation as a whole and further information regarding the environment, objects and traffic regulations have to be taken into account. A factor to calculate the influence of surrounding objects and all relevant attributes of a situation to the target vehicle due to its future actions can be used for a suitable situation interpretation. This is indispensable for fully automated driving and ADAS, especially in urban space. In addition, such a criterion enables new techniques to identify situations in simulation data as well as real traffic data, which will not be detected using well known conflict and criticality metrics. Junghans and Saul [13] shows methods to detect atypical situations and actions like U-turn, driving wiggling lines and traffic violations. As Detzer et al. [14] mentions "atyp-ical situations refer to incident, which differ from the usual case, but most of all present a danger to road users", the situations Junghans and Saul are able to detect are caused by driving actions and decisions of human drivers, that in fully automated vehicle are not allowed to happen.

4   Concept

To derive test cases for fully automated driving and ADAS, we propose a multilayer concept as pictured in Fig. 1. This concept shows necessary steps from an environment-sensitive behaviour simulation, an extraction of relevant situations through to the derivation of executable test cases. As seen in Fig. 1, step 1 shows an environment-sensitive behaviour simulation which generates a large amount of data. In the next step, the generated data are filtered and individual situations are rated to extract relevant situations for fully automated driving and ADAS. Extracted situations are described formally and in a textual, human understandable way, cf. step 3. In the fourth step, a situation catalogue is build up with the help of the textual description. The situations of the catalogue get linked to the formal scenario description. This enables an automated re-simulation of individual situations afterwards. Using the situation catalogue and system requirements, a test catalogue including tags to the formal description of the situation catalogue can be derived as presented in step 5 of Fig. 1. The final step of this concept is, extracting executable test cases automatically. Figure 1, step 6 shows a linking to the formal scenario description. Having the tagging of the derived test cases to the formal description, an automated simulation of the test cases can be done. From an automation perspective, Step 1 to 4 can be easily automated with respect to parameter specification (filters, etc.) which need to be performed manually. The automation level of step 5 will depend on the level of formalism used within requirements documents. From a todays practitioners perspective this will be manual work. Step 6 might be automated using various templates. In the following, the steps are described in detail and open challenges are given.

4.1   Environment-Sensitive Behaviour Simulation

The first step of this concept is the generation of simulation data using a probabilistic environment-sensitive behaviour simulation. A belonging scenario description consists of a logical database for the environment description (e.g.

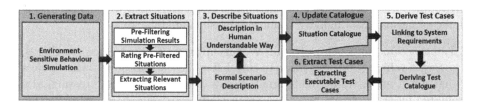

Fig. 1. Concept for deriving test cases from simulation data.

roads with their type and lanes, lane marking, traffic signs, etc.), dynamic elements (e.g. pedestrians, cyclists, vehicles, traffic lights), goals and values for dynamic objects and actions and events (cf. Ulbrich *et al.* [6]). A scenario description can exist in different formats such as XML or HTML files. All participating objects pursue individual goals controlled by behaviour models close to reality. The scenario description, the behaviour models for the dynamic objects and the logical database for the road network represent the input for the simulation and the presented method.

A target vehicle continuously moves along defined routes and further dynamic objects react situationally according to each other and to the target vehicle. Regarding the use case and implemented functions, the subject vehicle is also able to react situational. Thus, this simulation method with realistic, environment-sensitive behaviour models tries to model the complexity of real-world traffic and generates data. These data include probabilistic relevant, not known situations which have to be tested to ensure full and consistent validation of highly connected and automated vehicles. This simulation will be operated continuously and generates data by executing the dynamic elements plans (actions, paths, events, etc.). As the simulation continues, new situations will occur, which do not need to be scripted in advance and might represent a realistic scenario. Thus, randomly generated data might be too extensive to be analysed manually.

It is possible to include a driving simulator to this environment-sensitive behaviour simulation. This enables human interactions while the simulation process. Thus, driving studies in a virtual environment can be done and generated data can be evaluated afterwards. This overcomes limitations of behaviour models and a wider range of variations of included situations can be achieved.

The outcome of the simulation run contains states, positions and circumstances of every dynamic object and element for every frame. Depending on the development process and granularity of the used model and functions for the ego vehicle, the simulation results may also contain sensor views, output of control units or bus messages. This can be achieved by linking for example a HiL simulator. These extracted simulation results then are processed by the following steps of this concept.

Exemplary Situation. In order to acquire a feel for the conceptual approach, we have taken out an exemplary traffic situation in urban space. Throughout, this situation will be picked up in the following to exemplify specific steps. The environment-sensitive behaviour simulation is not restricted to simulate urban traffic scenarios. Also highway traffic can be simulated.

Exemplary Situation: Urban Traffic. We presuppose a X-intersection (cf. Fig. 2). The target vehicle (object 1) plans to turn left while the oncoming traffic (object 2) has got a green traffic light signal. Beside that, a pedestrian crossing, also regulated by traffic lights has got a green traffic light signal too. A pedestrian (object 3), located on a pedestrian walk leading to the pedestrian crossing, moves straight forward to the crossing.

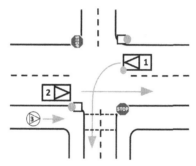

Fig. 2. Exemplary situation which is of importance for situation interpretation and cannot be detected by well known criticality metrics in case of certain circumstances. (Color figure online)

Open Challenges. As this environment-sensitive behaviour simulation is able to produce data, there are some open questions to be answered. To get a better representation of reality and improve the following overall process, a verification has to be done, whether an adequate number and variations of scenes were generated. A verification can be done in two ways, via logging and checking afterwards or online analysis. If an online analysis is done, the simulation has to provide editing specific parameters while it is running. To guarantee a wide range of relevant situations in the simulation results, it would be conceivable to include variations during the simulation process. This can be done by automated editing the behaviour models while the simulation runs or define periodic recurring elements on specific points of the environment and different states of the behaviour models. Also a challenging task is the reset and roll back of individual elements during the simulation process, if they run into crashes or deadlocks.

4.2 Extracting Relevant Situations

Pre-filtering. For fully automated vehicles, relevant situations contain all objects, elements and circumstances that may affect the vehicle in its trajectory planning. As strategy to apply situation analysis and plan future actions, we suggest the concept of manoeuvre spaces. Manoeuvre spaces describe abutting areas divided by stopping lines and logical points, where traffic guidance requires an analysis and interpretation of the situations and, if necessary, an adaptation of the driving actions. Manoeuvre spaces result from existing stopping lines at intersections and lane junctions caused by traffic guidance and logical stopping points resulting from "turning while conditional compatibility". Required information therefore can be extracted from the used logical datasets (e.g. OpenDrive [15], RoadGraph [16]). For an example, we extracted manoeuvre spaces for a simulated complex intersection (cf. Fig. 3). The source format was an XODR-file following the OpenDrive specification. The visualisation was done by using Unity 3D[1].

---

[1] Unity 3D is a game and graphic development platform to build high-quality 2D and 3D games and visualisations [17].

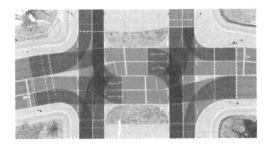

Fig. 3. Extracted manoeuvre spaces (grey surfaces) for a simulated intersection.

After extracting manoeuvre spaces in a defined area or radius around the subject vehicle, the localisation and association to the traffic lanes is necessary. The objective of the localisation and mapping to its corresponding traffic lane is to calculate, which lanes are reachable and following the lane of the target vehicle, if traffic regulations are going to be upheld. This can be expected, because fully automated vehicles have to act rule-consistently. Furthermore, as fully automated vehicles already know their actual route, only traffic lanes along the planned route have to be taken into account.

Simultaneously, all dynamic objects and elements have to be extracted and included. After that, the detected objects will be mapped to their related traffic lane or (traffic) surface, similar to the mapping of the subject vehicle to its traffic lane. Then, for every object an estimation for future trajectories or future occupied areas will be calculated. This is done by using motion prediction models (cf. [18–23]). Using motion prediction models afterwards, instead of using the implemented behaviour model for simulation, for pre-filtering has got advantages. Motion prediction models give different results than simulation behaviour models. Behaviour models take their surrounding and circumstances into account and plan their actions situationally. Motion prediction models estimate possible trajectories and future occupied areas on the basis of observed behaviour and give multiple estimated actions, assessed by a probability value. Due to use case or developer requirements, motion prediction models should be able to be adapted, e.g. how they take traffic light states and traffic regulations into account.

In conjunction with a defined temporal forecast, one can figure out potential overlapping zones with the computed manoeuvre spaces of the subject car. By having this information, the current scene can be reduced to its relevant objects according to a defined temporal forecast. The filtered situation now represents the relevant dynamic objects for the target vehicle and in which future manoeuvre it might be influenced by other objects.

The pre-filtering parameters can be edited by the developer in a configuration file. Using this, specific requirements or use cases can be included and different types of situations can be identified. It is possible, taking only pedestrians, other vehicles or cyclists into account or reduce the simulation results due to specific traffic routes or environments like intersections, pedestrian crosswalks, acceleration lanes, traffic light regulations, etc. It is also possible to filter individual situations, e.g. targets vehicles camera field of view. Situations can be found, where e.g. a defined number of pedestrians are in the field of view of the camera or dynamic objects have a defined orientation to the target vehicle.

Rating Traffic Situations. The influence of identified relevant objects to the target vehicle is calculated by extracting the information when overlapping manoeuvre spaces will be reached by the target vehicle. The extracted time will be adapted to the estimated motions of the dynamic objects and a *probability of occupancy* can be calculated. The exact definition and calculation of the probability of occupancy will be part of a future publication. So, every manoeuvre space gets a probability for being occupied by a dynamic object when the target car approaches. A calculated high probability of occupancy for a manoeuvre space at a specific point of time does not imply, that this manoeuvre space was crossed by a dynamic object in the further simulation process. It merely indicates, that this situation would have been of importance for the situation analysis and interpretation at a certain point of time. By having a probability and the extracted time when the target vehicle will reach the manoeuvre space, developers have the possibility to filter the simulation data due to a temporal forecast or a pre-defined probability of occupancy will be exceeded. To pick up the thought of an evaluation framework, the probability of occupancy can be expanded by including worst case assumptions like traffic rule violation and atypical behaviour. Furthermore, the probability of occupancy can be linked or expanded by already known criticality metrics, if a collision course exists by estimated trajectories of the dynamic objects.

Exemplary Situation: Identify the Situation. Known criticality metrics cannot rate the exemplary situation (cf. Sect. 4.1, Fig. 2), if the target vehicle is standing or driving with a certain speed, because an imminent collision does not exist. This situation, is of importance for situation interpretation, because of various ways to challenge this traffic situation and plan future actions. For example, the target vehicle waits until the oncoming traffic has passed, then continues the planned route with enough speed to pass the pedestrian walk, before the pedestrian reaches the crosswalk. Another possibility is to wait until both objects (2 and 3) have passed. Applying motion prediction models and the concept of manoeuvre spaces, this situation will be identified as relevant. Concerning the used motion prediction model, the estimated trajectory of the pedestrian (object 3) will cross the planned trajectory of the target vehicle (object 1). Also the oncoming traffic (object 2) will intersect the planned trajectory of the target vehicle. For this situation a high probability of occupancy will be calculated and the situation will be automatically detected.

Executing Relevant Situations. After pre-filtering and rating situations according to the use case or developer specifications, relevant situations have to be extracted. Therefore, the probability of the occupancy (and possibly a linked criticality metric) can be seen as a search criterion, which has to be parametrized by the developer. So, situations which exceed a defined value of probability or criticality can be found and extracted from a huge amount of simulation results. In order to get the outset of the situation, the related scene has to be reduced to its relevant objects and circumstances. Decisions of actions of the participating objects (cf. Ulbrich *et al.* [6]) have to be taken into account.

Open Challenges. As the concepts allows filtering and extracting relevant situations for interpretation, there are still some limitations. If multiple dynamic objects in one situation are viewed on their own and might be rated as "not relevant", certain circumstances of these objects and their combination might be relevant for situation interpretation. Also a specific sequence of events, like atypical behaviour, might become interesting for situation analysis. An open task is to extend the suggested concept, to be able to detect such situations or sequences of events.

4.3   Describing Executed Situations

Formal Situation Description. After the extraction of relevant situations from simulation data, the situations have to be described formally to enable further automated processing like comparison to other situations. A formal description for situations consists of the sum of its elements, its corresponding concretised parameters and the sequence of events. A formal description language may follow a scheme like the one given by Geyer *et al.* in [24].

Exemplary Situation: Formal Description. As an example for a formal description of the exemplary situation we used a XML based format. Because this example should demonstrate how a formal description can be done, the description of the situation is reduced to the key facts:

```
<!DOCTYPE FORMAL DESCRIPTION SITUATION #1>
<infrastructure>
    <trafficlight name="tl1" type="simple"
        pos="45,25,4" state="green"/>
    <trafficlight name="tl2" type="advanced"
        pos="-45,20,4" state="green"/>
    <trafficsign type="stop" pos="45,-25,3"/>
    <trafficsign type="stop" pos="-45,25,3"/>
</infrastructure>
<dynamic>
    <person name="p1" pos="-45,-30,2" direction="2" speed="1.5"/>
    <car name="car1" pos="50,20,2" direction="3" speed="20"/>
    <car name="car2" pos="-50,-20,2" direction="2" speed="10"/>
</dynamic>
```

Abstract Situation Description. To be better understandable by humans, we recommend a textual description generated from the formal scenario description (cf. Fig. 1, step 3). An advantage of a textual description of a relevant situation is, that additional information (e.g. obstacle in lane, vehicles in front in the same lane, traffic light states, ...) in plain text can be added. This textual description is tagged with the formal scenario description. So, predefined scenario element sets (e.g. traffic jam, cut in object, pedestrian crosswalks) for re-simulation, readable in an easy way for developer, can be executed. Using scenario based development, intended system behaviour for re-simulation and test cases can directly be derived, based on the abstract situation description in combination with the tagged formal scenario description.

Exemplary Situation: Textual Description. After generating the formal description, a textual and human understandable description of the identified situation can be extracted automatically. For an example, a textual description of the exemplary situation may look like the following:

```
TEXTUAL DESCRIPTION SITUATION #1:
Crossing situation with
    2 traffic lights,
    2 road signs,
    2 cars,
    1 person.
Lane 1 consists of
    2 traffic lights at (45,25,4|-45,20,4)
        with the states (green|green).
    2 cars at (50,20,2|-50,-20,2)
        with direction (4|2+3) and speed (20|10).
Lane 2 consists of
    2 road signs (stop|stop) at (45,-25,3|-45,25,3).
A person at (-45,-30,2)
    with direction (2) and speed (1.5)
    is crossing lane 2.
```

Beside extracting the formal and abstract description out of the simulation results, it is possible to generate an illustration of the identified situation (cf. Fig. 4 for our exemplary situation). Therefore, the logical database is used to generate the infrastructure representation. Dynamic objects and elements, including their positions, then can be embedded.

Situation Catalogue. Using the abstract, textual and human understandable description, a situation catalogue can be build up (cf. Fig. 1, step 4). As the situation catalogue should be dynamically extendible, new situations have to be compared with the existing set of situations. For this purpose, the tagged formal description can be used for automated comparison and evaluation of the catalogue. We also suggest a classification of the collected situations by driving

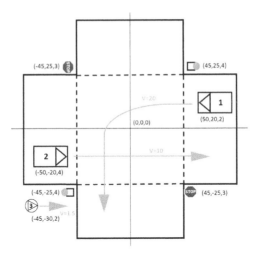

Fig. 4. Generated illustration of the exemplary situation using the logical database and the formal description.

actions, developer specific demands or use cases. Uncertainty in classifying a situation can be handled by identifying corresponding elements, parameters and events of the formal description. The built up situation catalogue claims what a system for automated driving has to manage.

Open Challenges. Establishing formal and abstract description languages and building up a suitable situation catalogue implies some open and challenging tasks. A situation can be described by ambiguous possibilities and in different ways. A sufficient large description language has to be found to display all necessary information. On the contrary, a description language has to be of manageable scale and variety, to assure efficient search, classification and evaluation of situations. In consequence, an appropriate selection of the abstraction level and choice of relevant elements and parameters is inevitable.

4.4 Build up Test Catalogue

Linking to System Requirements. To maintain a certain degree of traceability, links between each situation listed in the situation catalogue and the related system requirements have to be created and documented. This enables the user to view the requirements which are relevant for a specific situation, as well as to filter all situations covering a particular set of requirements. Additionally, situations or requirements with no established links can be identified to guarantee the integrity of the system. Textual requirements are either written in a natural language or in a formal way. Especially in the automotive domain, a natural language is often chosen as primary solution, because the specifier can stick to familiar descriptions and phrases. Formal styles are much more laborious to get used to. A link between the requirements and the situation catalogue can be established in form of a requirement identifier reference embedded in the situation description and the tool-supported tracing of these connections.

Exemplary Situation: Requirement. System requirements to handle the exemplary situation may have the following form:

```
REQUIREMENTS FOR SITUATION #1:
#1: If Ego turns left, the system has to give way to
    oncoming traffic.
#2: If Ego turns into a lane, the system has to give
    way to crossing pedestrians and cyclists.
#3: In give way situations, the system has to stop in front of
    relevant conflict zones until a safe passing is possible.
```

Deriving Test Cases. After establishing the links, test cases have to be created to be able to test the system. This can be done by hand, which requires the test engineer to review and understand the requirements and the situations, which is prone to errors and misinterpretations. A better solution is to partly automatize the test case creation. In our case, both the requirements and the situation catalogue are textual, which advices a textual generation technique.

A *Domain-Specific Language (DSL)* is a programming language limited to a specific domain and capable of automatically generating diverse textual and graphical artefacts (cf. Fig. 5). Such artefacts include, for example, diagrams, models and even source code in different general purpose languages (e.g. C++). Although DSLs can be graphical as well, the textual nature of our source documents leads to a textual DSL as optimal solution.

This textual DSL can directly use syntax and semantics of the situation catalogue and the system requirements. An automatic interpretation of both documents is possible, although it might be challenging. The feasibility of this automatism has to be examined in detail and will be part of a future publication. The advantage of this approach is the maintenance of the readability for humans and the usage of already specified patterns. The DSL then aggregates all relevant information out of the situations and requirements and generates predefined artefacts. The main type of artefact in our case are the test cases extracted

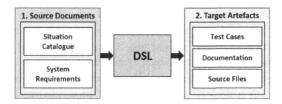

Fig. 5. DSL workflow for test case generation.

out of the situations, which then can be used in manual and automated system testing. Additionally, the test cases and the related results can be reintegrated, tagged and included in other environment-sensitive behaviour simulations. This can be done automatically, due to the fact that the derived test cases from the situation catalogue are tagged with a formal description.

Exemplary Situation: Executable Test Case. Using the extracted descriptions and the system requirement, test cases for all relevant objects of the situation can be generated automatically. The range of the parameters can differ depending on predefined legal or technical constraints. For our exemplary situation, the test case may have the following form and range of parameters:

```
TEST CASE #1, SITUATION #1:
RANGE OF PARAMS:
     p1: speed=[0;8]
   car1: speed=[0;30]
   car2: speed=[0;50]
EXPECTED SYSTEM BEHAVIOUR:
   The system should turn left on lane 2.
TEST CRITERIA:
   Does the target vehicle give way to the vehicle and pedestrian?
```

Open Challenges. Our presented concept derives test cases, but no real test oracle. The comparison of the system behaviour to the extracted test criteria can be potentially automated, but will not be considered here. A further issue that needs to be solved, is how an automated valuation method can be set up. Up today a human test expert has to rate every situation. A first implementation of a test oracle might be to define a passed test case as preventing a collision with other objects.

5 Conclusion and Future Work

We discussed well known criticality metrics regarding their usability in the field of rating traffic situations and pointed out, why their use for fully automated vehicles and ADAS is not sufficient. Fully automated vehicles and ADAS have to analyse and interpret traffic situations at every point of time. Thus, relevant situations have to be identified to ensure full testing and validation. Virtual simulation methods are getting more important and are producing a large quantity of data. The challenge thereby is to be able to execute relevant situations and derive test cases. As a solution, we suggest a multilayer model concept to filter simulation data, rate relevant situations, transfer them to a situation catalogue and derive executable test cases. Using DSLs, situations can be presented in a formal and textual, human understandable way and linked to system requirements. This enables a throughout automation for deriving test cases from simulation data. To demonstrate the benefit of this approach, an exemplary situation was taken out and picked up consistently to exemplify specific steps of this concept. Figure 1 presents a good overview to our approach.

Future work will contain an exact definition of the probability of occupancy and its parametrization. Further parameters like traffic rule violation and atypical behaviour are going to be included, to cover more specific developer requirements and get a more detailed rating of the situation executing framework. Beside that, we are working on an appropriate formal and abstract description capable of building up the situation catalogue and using a DSL to automatically link the requirements and derive executable test cases.

References

1. Eo, J.S., Choi, H.R., Gao, R., Lee, S., Wong, W.E.: Case study of requirements-based test case generation on an automotive domain. In: 2015 IEEE International Conference on Software Quality, Reliability and Security - Companion, pp. 210–215. IEEE Press (2015)
2. Zofka, R.M., Kuhnt, F., Kohlhaas, R., et al.: Data-driven simulation and parametrization of traffic scenarios for the development of advanced driver assistance systems. In: 18th International Conference on Information Fusion, pp. 1422–1428. IEEE Press, Washington DC (2015)
3. Schuldt, F., Menzel, T.: Eine Methode für die Zuordnung von Testfällen für automatisierte Fahrfunktionen auf X-in-the-Loop Verfahren im modularen virtuellen Testbaukasten. In: 10. Uni-DAS e.V. Workshop Fahrerassistenzsysteme 2015, pp. 1–12. Uni-DAS e.V., Walting (2015)
4. Schuldt, F., Lichte, B., Maurer, M., Scholz, S.: Systematische Auswertung von Testfällen für Fahrfunktionen im modularen virtuellen Testbaukasten. In: 9. Uni-DAS e.V. Workshop Fahrerassistenzsysteme 2014, pp. 169–179. Uni-DAS e.V., Walting (2014)
5. Stellet, J., Zöllner, J.M., Schumacher, J., et al.: Testing of advanced driver assistance towards automated driving: a survey and taxonomy on existing approaches and open questions. In: 2015 IEEE 18th International Conference on Intelligent Transportation Systems, pp. 1455–1462. IEEE Press (2015)
6. Ulbrich, S., Menzel, T., Reschka, A., et al.: Defining and substantiating the terms scene, situation, and scenario for automated driving. In: 2015 IEEE 18th International Conference on Intelligent Transportation Systems, pp. 982–988. IEEE Press, Las Palmas (2015)
7. Vires Simulationstechnologie GmbH: Virtual Test Drive User Manual (2014). https://www.vires.com/docs/VIRES_VTD_Overview_201403.pdf
8. Amundsen, F., Hydn, C. (eds.): Proceedings of the First Workshop on Traffic Conflicts. Institute of Transport Economics Oslo and LTH Lund (1977)
9. Hayward, J.C.: Near miss determination through use of a scale of danger. Highw. Res. Rec. **384**, 24–34 (1972). (The Pennsylvania State University, Pennsylvania)
10. Allen, B.L., Shin, B.T., Cooper, P.J.: Analysis of traffic conflict collisions. Transp. Res. Rec. **667**, 67–74 (1978). (National Research Council, Washington D.C.)
11. Hupfer, C.: Deceleration to safety time (DST) - a useful figure to evaluate traffic safety. In: ICTCT Conference Proceedings of Seminar 3, Department of Traffic Planning and Engineering, Lund (1997)

12. Rodemerk, C., Habenicht, S., Weitzel, A., et al.: Development of a general criticality criterion for the risk estimation of driving situations and its application to a maneuver-based lane change assistance system Claas. In: IV. IEEE Intelligent Vehicles Symposium, pp. 264–269. IEEE Press, Alcala de Henares (2012)
13. Junghans, M., Saul, H.: Chances for the evaluation of the traffic safety risk at intersections by novel methods. In: VII. Russisch-Deutsche Konferenz für Verkehrssicherheit, pp. 60–67. Sankt Petersburg (2014)
14. Detzer, S., Junghans, M., Kozempel, K., Saul, H.: Analysis of traffic safety for cyclists - an automatic detection of critical traffic situations of cyclists. In: 20th International Conference on Urban Transport and the Built Environment, pp. 491–503. WIT Press, Portugal (2014)
15. Dupuis, M., et al.: OpenDRIVE Format Specification, Rev. 1.4 (2015)
16. Knaup, J., Homeier, K.: RoadGraph - graph based environmental modelling and function independent situation analysis for driver assistance systems. In: 13th International IEEE Annual Conference on Intelligent Transportation Systems, pp. 428–432. IEEE Press, Madeira Island (2010)
17. Unity Technologies Website. http://unity3d.com/
18. Bonnin, S., Weisswange, T.H., Kummert, F., Schmuedderich, J.: Pedestrian crossing prediction using multiple context-based models. In: 2014 IEEE 17th International Conference on Intelligent Transportation Systems (ITSC), pp. 378–385. IEEE Press, Qingdao (2014)
19. Meyer-Delius, D., Sturm, J., Burgard, W.: Regression-based online situation recognition for vehicular traffic scenarios. In: 2009 IEEE/RSJ International Conference on Intelligent Robots and Systems, IROS 2009, pp. 1711–1716. IEEE Press, St. Louis (2009)
20. Schneider, N., Gavrila, D.M.: Pedestrian path prediction with recursive Bayesian filters: a comparative study. In: Weickert, J., Hein, M., Schiele, B. (eds.) GCPR 2013. LNCS, vol. 8142, pp. 174–183. Springer, Heidelberg (2013)
21. Ziebart, B., Ratliff, N., Gallagher, G., Peterson, K.: Planning-based prediction for pedestrians. In: Proceedings of the 2009 IEEE/RSJ International Conference on Intelligent Robots and Systems, pp. 3931–3936. IEEE Press, St. Louis (2009)
22. Rehder, E., Kl, H., Stiller, C.: Planungsbasierte Fußgängerprädiktion. In: 10. Uni-DAS e.V. Workshop Fahrerassistenzsysteme, pp. 129–138, Uni-DAS e.V., Walting (2015)
23. Quintero, R., Parra, I., Llorca, D.F., Sotelo, M.A.: Pedestrian path prediction based on body language and action classification. In: 2014 IEEE 17th International Conference on Intelligent Transportation Systems (ITSC), pp. 679–684. IEEE Press, Qingdao (2014)
24. Geyer, S., Baltzer, M., Franz, B., et al.: Concept and development of a unified ontology for generating test and use-case catalogues for assisted and automated vehicle guidance. IET Intell. Transp. Syst. **8**, 183–189 (2014)

Short Contributions

Searching Critical Values for Floating-Point Programs

Hélène Collavizza, Claude Michel, and Michel Rueher[✉]

University of Nice–Sophia Antipolis, I3S/CNRS BP 121,
06903 Sophia Antipolis Cedex, France
{helene.collavizza,claude.michel,michel.rueher}@unice.fr

Abstract. Programs with floating-point computations are often derived from mathematical models or designed with the semantics of the real numbers in mind. However, for a given input, the computed path with floating-point numbers may significantly differ from the path corresponding to the same computation with real numbers. As a consequence, developers do not know whether the program can actually produce very unexpected outputs. We introduce here a new constraint-based approach that searches for test cases in the part of the over-approximation where errors due to floating-point arithmetic could lead to unexpected decisions.

1 Introduction

In numerous applications, programs with floating-point computations are derived from mathematical models over the real numbers. However, computations on floating-point numbers are different from calculations in an idealised semantics[1] of real numbers [8]. For some values of the input variables, the result of a sequence of operations over the floating-point numbers can be significantly different from the result of the corresponding mathematical operations over the real numbers. As a consequence, the computed path with floating-point numbers may differ from the path corresponding to the same computation with real numbers. This can entail wrong outputs and dangerous decisions of critical systems. That's why identifying these values is a crucial issue for programs controlling critical systems.

Abstract interpretation based error analysis [3] of finite precision implementations computes an over-approximation of the errors due to floating-point operations. The point is that state-of-the-art tools [6] may generate numerous false alarms. In [16], we introduced a hybrid approach combining abstract interpretation and constraint programming techniques that reduces the number of false alarms. However, the remaining false alarms are very embarrassing since we cannot know whether the predicted unstable behaviors will occur with actual data.

---

[1] That's to say, computations as close as possible to the mathematical semantics of the real numbers; for instance, computations with arbitrary precision or computer algebra systems.

© IFIP International Federation for Information Processing 2016
Published by Springer International Publishing AG 2016. All Rights Reserved
F. Wotawa et al. (Eds.): ICTSS 2016, LNCS 9976, pp. 209–217, 2016.
DOI: 10.1007/978-3-319-47443-4_13

More formally, consider a program P, a set of intervals I defining the expected input values of P, and an output variable x of P on which depend critical decisions, e.g., activating an anti-lock braking system. Let $[\underline{x}_\mathbb{R}, \overline{x}_\mathbb{R}]$ be a sharp approximation over the set of real numbers $\mathbb{R}$ of the domain of variable x for any input of P. $[\underline{x}_\mathbb{F}, \overline{x}_\mathbb{F}]$ stands for the domain of variable x in the over-approximation computed over the set of floating-point $\mathbb{F}$ for input values of I. The range $[\underline{x}_\mathbb{R}, \overline{x}_\mathbb{R}]$ can be determined by calculation or from physical limits. It includes a small tolerance to take into account approximation errors, e.g. measurement, statistical, or even floating-point arithmetic errors. This tolerance – specified by the user – defines an acceptable loss of accuracy between the value computed over the floating-point numbers and the value calculated over the real numbers. Values outside the interval $[\underline{x}_\mathbb{R}, \overline{x}_\mathbb{R}]$ can lead a program to misbehave, e.g. take a wrong branch in the control flow.

The problem we address in this paper consists of verifying whether there exist *critical values* in I for which the program can actually produce a result value of x inside the suspicious intervals $[\underline{x}_\mathbb{F}, \underline{x}_\mathbb{R})$ and $(\overline{x}_\mathbb{R}, \overline{x}_\mathbb{F}]$. To handle this problem, we introduce a new constraint-based approach that searches for test cases that hit the suspicious intervals in programs with floating-point computations. In other words, our framework reduces this test case generation problem to a constraint-solving problem over the floating-point numbers where the domain of a critical decision variable has been shrunk to a suspicious interval. A constraint solver – based on filtering techniques designed to handle constraints over floating-point numbers – is used to search values for the input data. Preliminary results of experiments on small programs with classical floating-point errors are encouraging.

The CPBPV_FP, the system we developed, outperforms generate and test methods for programs with more than one input variable. Moreover, these search strategies can prove in many cases that no critical value exists.

2   Motivating Example

Before going into the details, we illustrate our approach on a small example. Assume we want to compute the area of a triangle from the lengths of its sides a, b, and c with Heron's formula:

$$\sqrt{s * (s - a) * (s - b) * (s - c)}$$

where $s = (a + b + c)/2$. The C program in Fig. 1 implements this formula, when a is the longest side of the triangle.

The test of line 5 ensures that the given lengths form a valid triangle.

Now, suppose that the input domains are $a \in [5, 10]$ and $b, c \in [0, 5]$. Over the real numbers, s is greater than any of the sides of the triangle and squared_area cannot be negative. Moreover, squared_area cannot be greater than 156.25 over the real numbers since the triangle area is maximized for a right triangle with

```
 1 /* Pre—condition :  a ≥ b and a ≥ c */
 2 float heron(float a, float b, float c) {
 3   float s, squared_area;
 4   squared_area = 0.0f;
 5   if (a <= b + c) {
 6     s = (a + b + c) / 2.0f;
 7     squared_area = s*(s-a)*(s-b)*(s-c);
 8   }
 9   return sqrt(squared_area);
10 }
```

Fig. 1. Heron

$b = c = 5$ and $a = 5\sqrt{2}$. However, these properties may not hold over the floating-point numbers because absorption and cancellation phenomena can occur[2].

Tools performing value analysis over the floating-point numbers [6,15] approximate the domain of `squared_area` to the interval $[-1262.21, 979.01]$. Since this domain is an over-approximation, we do not know whether input values leading to `squared_area` < 0 or `squared_area` > 156.25 actually exist. Note that input domains –here a $\in$ [5,10] and b, c $\in$ [0,5]– are usually provided by the user.

Assume the value of the tolerance[3] ε is 10^{-5}, the suspicious intervals for `squared_area` are $[-1262.21, -10^{-5})$ and $(156.25001, 979.01]$. CPBPV_FP, the system we developed, generated test cases for both intervals:

- a $= 5.517474$, b $= 4.7105823$, c $= 0.8068917$, and `squared_area` equals -1.000 $0001 \cdot 10^{-5}$;
- a $= 7.072597$, b $=$ c $= 5$, and `squared_area` equals 156.25003.

CPBPV_FP could also prove the absence of test cases for a tolerance $\varepsilon = 10^{-3}$ with `squared_area` $> 156.25 + \varepsilon$.

In order to limit the loss of accuracy due to cancellation [8], line 7 of Heron's program can be rewritten as follows:

```
squared_area = ((a+(b+c))*(c-(a-b))*(c+(a-b))*(a+(b-c)))/16.0f;
```

However, there are still some problems with this optimized program. Indeed, CPBPV_FP found the test case a $= 7.0755463$, b $= 4.350216$, c $= 2.72533$, and `squared_area` equals $-1.0000001 \cdot 10^{-5}$ for interval $[-1262.21, -10^{-5})$ of `squared_area`. There are no more problems in the interval $(156.25001, 979.01]$ and CPBPV_FP did prove it.

---

[2] Let's remind that absorption in an addition occurs when adding two numbers of very different order of magnitude, and the result is the value of the biggest number, i.e., when $x + y$ with $y \neq 0$ yields x. Cancellation occurs in $s - a$ when s is so close to a that the subtraction cancels most of the significant digits of s and a.

[3] Note that even this small tolerance may lead to an exception in statement 9.

3   Framework for Generating Test Cases

This section details the framework we designed to generate test cases reaching suspicious intervals for a variable x in a program P with floating-point computations.

The kernel of our framework is FPCS [1,12–14], a solver for constraints over the floating-point numbers; that's to say a symbolic execution approach for floating-point problems which combines interval propagation with explicit search for satisfiable floating-point assignments. FPCS is used inside the CPBPV bounded model checking framework [5]. CPBPV_FP is the adaptation of CPBPV for generating test cases that hit the suspicious intervals in programs with floating-point computations.

The inputs of CPBPV_FP are: P, an annotated program; a critical test ct for variable x; $[\underline{x}_\mathbb{F}, \underline{x}_\mathbb{R})$ or $(\overline{x}_\mathbb{R}, \overline{x}_\mathbb{F}]$, a suspicious interval for x. Annotations of P specify the range of the input variables of P as well as the suspicious interval for x. The latter assertion is just posted before the critical test ct.

To compute the suspicious interval for x, we approximate the domain of x over the real numbers by $[\underline{x}_\mathbb{R}, \overline{x}_\mathbb{R}]$, and over the floating-point numbers by $[\underline{x}_\mathbb{F}, \overline{x}_\mathbb{F}]$. These approximations are computed with RAICP [16], a hybrid system that combines abstract interpretation and constraint programming techniques in a single static and automatic analysis. The current implementation of RAICP is based upon the abstract interpreter FLUCTUAT [6], the constraint solver over the reals REALPAVER [10] and FPCS. The suspicious intervals for variable x are denoted $[\underline{x}_\mathbb{F}, \underline{x}_\mathbb{R})$ and $(\overline{x}_\mathbb{R}, \overline{x}_\mathbb{F}]$.

CPBPV_FP performs first some pre-processing: P is transformed into DSA-like form[4]. If the program contains loops, CPBPV_FP unfolds loops k times where k is a user specified constant. Loops are handled in CPBPV and RAICP with standard unfolding and abstraction techniques[5]. So, there are no more loops in the program when we start the constraint generation process. Standard slicing operations are also performed to reduce the size of the control flow graph.

In a second step, CPBPV_FP searches for executable paths reaching ct. For each of these paths, the collected constraints are sent to FPCS, which solves the corresponding constraint systems over the floating point numbers. FPCS returns either a satisfiable instantiation of the input variables of P, or $\emptyset$.

As said before, FPCS [1,12–14] is a constraint solver designed to solve a set of constraints over floating-point numbers without losing any solution. It uses $2B$-consistency along with projection functions adapted to floating-point arithmetic [1,13] to filter constraints over the floating-point numbers. FPCS also provides stronger consistencies like kB-consistencies, which allow better filtering results.

The search of solutions in constraint systems over floating numbers is trickier than the standard bisection-based search in constraint systems over intervals of

---

[4] DSA stands for Dynamic Single Assignment. In DSA-like form, all variables are assigned exactly once in each execution path.

[5] In bounded model checking, k is usually increased until a counter-example is found or until the number of time units is large enough for the application.

real numbers. Thus, we have also implemented different strategies combining selection of specific points and pruning. Details on theses strategies are given in the experiments section.

CPBPV_FP ends up with one of the following results:

- a test case proving that P can produce a suspicious value for x;
- a proof that no test case reaching the suspicious interval can be generated: this is the case if the loops in P cannot be unfolded beyond the bound k (See [5] for details on bounded unfolding) ;
- an inconclusive answer: no test case could be generated but the loops in P could be unfolded beyond the bound k. In other words, the process is incomplete and we cannot conclude whether P may produce a suspicious value.

4   Preliminary Experiments

We experimented with CPBPV_FP on six small programs with cancellation and absorption phenomena, two very common pitfalls of floating-point arithmetic. The benchmarks are listed in the first two columns of Table 1.

First two benchmarks concern the heron program and the optimized_heron program with the suspicious intervals described in the Sect. 1.

Program slope (see Fig. 2) approximates the derivative of the square function $f(x) = x^2$ at a given point x_0. More precisely, it computes the slope of a nearby secant line with a finite difference quotient: $f'(x_0) \approx \frac{f(x_0+h)-f(x_0-h)}{2h}$. Over the real numbers, the smaller h is, the more accurate the formula is. For this function, the derivative is given by $f'(x) = 2x$ which yields exactly 26 for $x = 13$. Over the floats, FLUCTUAT [6] approximates the return value of the slope program to the interval $[0, 25943]$ when $h \in [10^{-6}, 10^{-3}]$ and $x_0 = 13$.

```
float slope(float x0, float h) {
    float x1 = x0 + h; float x2 = x0 - h;
    float fx1 = x1*x1; float fx2 = x2*x2;
    float res = (fx1 - fx2) / (2.0*h);
    return res;
}
```

Fig. 2. Approximation of the derivative of x^2 by a slope

Program polynomial in Fig. 3 illustrates an absorption phenomenon. It computes the polynomial $(a^2+b+10^{-5})*c$. For input domains $a \in [10^3, 10^4]$, $b \in [0, 1]$ and $c \in [10^3, 10^4]$, the minimum value of the polynomial over the real numbers is equal to 1000000000.01.

simple_interpolator and simple square are two benches extracted from [9]. The first bench computes an interpolator, affine by sub-intervals while the second is a rewrite of a square root function used in an industrial context.

```
float polynomial(float a, float b, float c) {
  float poly = (a*a + b + 1e-5f) * c;
  return poly;
}
```

Fig. 3. Computation of polynomial $(a^2 + b + 10^{-5}) * c$

All experiments were done on an Intel Core 2 Duo at 2.8 GHz with 4 GB of memory running 64-bit Linux. We assume C programs handling IEEE 754 compliant floating-point arithmetic, intended to be compiled with GCC without any optimization option and run on a x86_64 architecture managed by a 64-bit Linux operating system. Rounding mode was to the nearest, i.e., where ties round to the nearest even digit in the required position.

4.1 Strategies and Solvers

We run CPBPV_FP with the following search strategies for the FPCS solver:

- std: standard prune &bisection-based search used in constraint-systems over intervals: splits the selected variable domain in two domains of equal size;
- fpc: splits the domain of the selected variable in five intervals:
  - Three degenerated intervals containing only a single floating point number: the smallest float l, the largest float r, and the mid-point m;
  - Two open intervals (l, m) and (m, r);
- fp3s: selects 3 degenerated intervals containing only a single floating point number: the smallest float l, the largest float r, and the mid-point m. Hence, fp3s is an incomplete method that might miss some solutions.

For all these strategies, we select first the variables with the largest domain and we perform a 3B−consistency filtering step before starting the splitting process.

We compared CPBPV_FP with CBMC [4] and CDFL [7], two state-of-the-art software bounded model checkers based on SAT solvers that are able to deal with floating-point computations. We also run a simple generate & test strategy: the program is run with randomly generated input values and we test whether the result is inside the suspicious interval. The process is stopped as soon as a test case hitting the suspicious interval is found.

4.2 Results

Table 1 reports the results for the other strategies and solvers. Since strategy fpc3s is incomplete, we indicate whether a test case was found or not. Column s? specifies whether a test case actually exists. Note that the computation times of CBMC and CDFL include the pre-processing time for generating the constraint systems; the pre-processing time required by CPBPV is around 0.6 s but CPBPV is a non-optimised system written in java.

Table 1. Results of the different solvers and strategies on the benchmarks

Name	Condition	CDFL	CBMC	std	fpc	fpc3s	s?
heron	$area < 10^{-5}$	3.874 s	0.280 s	>180	0.705	0.022 (n)	y
	$area > 156.25 + 10^{-5}$	> 180 s	34.512 s	22.323	7.804	0.083 (n)	y
optimized_heron	$area < 10^{-5}$	7.618 s	0.932 s	>180	0.148	0.022 (n)	y
	$area > 156.25 + 10^{-5}$	> 180 s	>180 s	8.988	30.477	0.101 (n)	n
slope with $h \in [10^{-6}, 10^{-3}]$	$dh < 26.0 - 1.0$	2.014 s	1.548 s	0.021	0.012	0.012 (y)	y
	$dh > 26.0 + 1.0$	1.599 s	0.653 s	0.055	0.011	0.011 (y)	y
	$dh < 26.0 - 10.0$	0.715 s	1.108 s	0.006	0.006	0.007 (n)	n
	$dh > 26.0 + 10.0$	1.025 s	1.080 s	0.006	0.006	0.006 (n)	n
polynomial	$r < 10^9 + 0.0099999904 - 10^{-3}$	0.170 s	0.295 s	0.022	0.006	0.006 (y)	y
simple_interpolator	$res < -10^{-5}$	0.296 s	0.264 s	0.018	0.012	0.012 (y)	y
simple_square	$S > 1.453125$	--	1.079 s	0.012	0.012	0.012 (n)	n

5 Discussion

5.1 Results Analysis

The generate & test strategy behaves quite well on programs with only one input variable when a test case exists but it is unable to find any test case for programs with more than one input variable. More precisely, it found a test case in less than 0.008 s for the 6 suspicious intervals of program slope and for program simple_interpolator. The generate & test strategy failed to find a test within 180 s in all other cases. Of course, this strategy cannot show that there is no test case reaching the suspicious interval; so, it is of little interest here.

Strategy fpc is definitely the most efficient and most robust one on all these benchmarks. Note that CBMC and CDFL could neither handle the initial, nor the optimized version of program heron in a timeout of 20 min whereas FPCS found solutions in a reasonable time.

These preliminary results are very encouraging: they show that CPBPV_FP is effective for generating test cases for suspicious values outside the range of acceptable values on small programs with classical floating-point errors. More importantly, a strong point of CPBPV_FP is definitely its refutation capabilities.

Of course, experiments on more significant benchmarks and on real applications are still necessary to evaluate the full capabilities and limits of CPBPV_FP.

5.2 Related and Further Work

The goals of software bounded model checkers based on SAT solvers are close to our approach. The point is that SAT solvers tend to be inefficient on these problems due to the size of the domains of floating-point variables and the cost of bit-vector operations [7]. CDFL [7] tries to address this issue by embedding an abstract domain in the conflict driven clause learning algorithm of a SAT solver.

SAT solvers often use bitwise representations of numerical operations, which may be very expensive (e.g., thousands of variables for one equation in CDFL). Brain et al. [2,11] have recently introduced a bit-precise decision procedure for the theory of floating-point arithmetic. The core of their approach is a generalization of the conflict-driven clause-learning algorithm used in modern SAT solvers. Their technique is significantly faster than a bit-vector encoding approach. Note that the constraint programming techniques used in our approach are better suited to generate several test cases than these SAT-based approaches. The advantage of CP is that it provides a uniform framework for representing and handling integers, real numbers and floats. A new abstract-interpretation based robustness analysis of finite precision implementations has recently been proposed [9] for sound rounding error propagation in a given path in presence of unstable tests.

A close connection between our floating-point solvers and the two above-mentioned approaches is certainly worth exploring.

A second direction for further work concerns the integration of our constraint-based approach with new abstract-interpretation based robustness analysis of finite precision implementations for sound rounding error propagation in a given path in presence of unstable tests.

Acknowledgments. This work was partially supported by ANR COVERIF (ANR-15-CE25-0002).

References

1. Botella, B., Gotlieb, A., Michel, C.: Symbolic execution of floating-point computations. Softw. Test. Verif. Reliab. **16**(2), 97–121 (2006)
2. Brain, M., D'Silva, V., Griggio, A., Haller, L., Kroening, D.: Interpolation-based verification of floating-point programs with abstract CDCL. In: Fähndrich, M., Logozzo, F. (eds.) Static Analysis. LNCS, vol. 7935, pp. 412–432. Springer, Heidelberg (2013)
3. Chen, L., Miné, A., Cousot, P.: A sound floating-point polyhedra abstract domain. In: Ramalingam, G. (ed.) APLAS 2008. LNCS, vol. 5356, pp. 3–18. Springer, Heidelberg (2008)
4. Clarke, E., Kroning, D., Lerda, F.: A tool for checking ANSI-C programs. In: Jensen, K., Podelski, A. (eds.) TACAS 2004. LNCS, vol. 2988, pp. 168–176. Springer, Heidelberg (2004)
5. Collavizza, H., Rueher, M., Van Hentenryck, P.: A constraint-programming framework for bounded program verification. Constr. J. **15**(2), 238–264 (2010)
6. Delmas, D., Goubault, E., Putot, S., Souyris, J., Tekkal, K., Védrine, F.: Towards an industrial use of FLUCTUAT on safety-critical avionics software. In: Alpuente, M., Cook, B., Joubert, C. (eds.) FMICS 2009. LNCS, vol. 5825, pp. 53–69. Springer, Heidelberg (2009)
7. D'Silva, V., Haller, L., Kroening, D., Tautschnig, M.: Numeric bounds analysis with conflict-driven learning. In: Flanagan, C., König, B. (eds.) TACAS 2012. LNCS, vol. 7214, pp. 48–63. Springer, Heidelberg (2012)
8. Goldberg, D.: What every computer scientist should know about floating point arithmetic. ACM Comput. Surv. **23**(1), 5–48 (1991)

9. Goubault, E., Putot, S.: Robustness analysis of finite precision implementations. In: Shan, C. (ed.) APLAS 2013. LNCS, vol. 8301, pp. 50–57. Springer, Heidelberg (2013)

10. Granvilliers, L., Benhamou, F.: Algorithm 852: RealPaver: an interval solver using constraint satisfaction techniques. ACM Trans. Math. Softw. **32**(1), 138–156 (2006)

11. Haller, L., Griggio, A., Brain, M., Kroening, D.: Deciding floating-point logic with systematic abstraction. In: Formal Methods in Computer-Aided Design, FMCAD, pp. 131–140. IEEE (2012)

12. Marre, B., Michel, C.: Improving the floating point addition and subtraction constraints. In: Cohen, D. (ed.) CP 2010. LNCS, vol. 6308, pp. 360–367. Springer, Heidelberg (2010)

13. Michel, C.: Exact projection functions for floating-point number constraints. In: 7th International Symposium on Artificial Intelligence and Mathematics (2002)

14. Michel, C., Rueher, M., Lebbah, Y.: Solving constraints over floating-point numbers. In: Walsh, T. (ed.) CP 2001. LNCS, vol. 2239, pp. 524–538. Springer, Heidelberg (2001)

15. Ponsini, O., Michel, C., Rueher, M.: Refining abstract interpretation based value analysis with constraint programming techniques. In: Milano, M. (ed.) CP 2012. LNCS, vol. 7514, pp. 593–607. Springer, Heidelberg (2012)

16. Ponsini, O., Michel, C., Rueher, M.: Verifying floating-point programs with constraint programming and abstract interpretation techniques. Autom. Softw. Eng. **23**(2), 191–217 (2016)

UTTOS: A Tool for Testing UEFI Code in OS Environment

Eder C.M. Gomes[1], Paulo R.P. Amora[1(✉)], Elvis M. Teixeira[1],
Antonio G.S. Lima[1], Felipe T. Brito[1], Juliano F.C. Ciocari[2],
and Javam C. Machado[1]

[1] Department of Computer Science, Federal University of Ceará, Fortaleza, Brazil
{eder.clayton,paulo.amora,elvis.teixeira,gerbson.lima,felipe.timbo,
javam.machado}@lsbd.ufc.br
[2] Hewlett-Packard Inc., Porto Alegre, Brazil
juliano.ciocari@hp.com

Abstract. Unit tests are one of the most widely used tools to assure a minimal level of quality and compliance during development. However, they are not used in many projects where development takes place at low-level contexts. The main reason is that unit test development itself demands more time and becomes expensive in this context and tools that assist test creation are rare or absent. In UEFI development this scenario matches the reality of most teams and unit testing as well as other testing techniques are often not used. To address this fault we propose UTTOS, a tool that parses EDKII build configuration files, mocks the UEFI-specific functions for C development and enables UEFI test suite code to run in the operating system. We show that UTTOS is able to run the test suit in the operating system and save development time.

Keywords: UEFI · Unit test · C · Code coverage · Embedded systems

1 Introduction

Testing has being often considered the crucial phase in the process of creating high quality software systems and most development frameworks include functionality to assist the use of some automatic testing strategy. In low level systems such as embedded systems, BIOS and device drivers development the situation is much less well established. Here, requirements are often fixed by protocol specification. This decreases complexity and most testing is basically checking for conformity to the protocols. On the other hand automated testing is not generally easy here since the code is targeted to run in devices different from the developer's workstation often through the use of cross compiling. Tools to assist the generation of automatic tests are rare in such platforms.

UEFI (Unified Extensible Firmware Interface) is the current specification for the interface between the platform firmware and the operating system, it is meant

F. Wotawa et al. (Eds.): ICTSS 2016, LNCS 9976, pp. 218–224, 2016.
DOI: 10.1007/978-3-319-47443-4_14

to eventually replace the BIOS (Basic Input Output System) and addresses many of it's limitations. First of all, the BIOS development is made in assembly language thus the complexity of keeping it modularized and maintainable was a big issue, BIOS runs on 16 bit mode so the amount of memory usable is very limited. In UEFI there is a call stack and most of the development is done in C, also the execution environment is 32bit or 64bit depending on the processor architecture. These features make it a much richer platform with many application possibilities, therefore going beyond the basic task of initializing the hardware and calling the OS loader [12,14].

UEFI also enables OEMs (Original Equipment Manufacturer) to bundle applications and drivers with the machine itself then providing a minimal OS-like environment. But with the greater flexibility provided by UEFI and the variety of software that is being written to that platform comes complexity, and then the need for robust development and quality assurance practices. The issue at hand is that the DXE (Driver Execution Environment) code is targeted to run in the pre-boot phases, so it is usually written and compiled in a workstation then run in the target machine in order to be tested and then brought back to the developers workstation to be validated and debugged.

It is possible to identify two alternatives to use automated test strategies for UEFI software: to develop or use testing tools that run in the DXE or develop tools to mimic the DXE by mocking its basic functions. We favour the second approach in order to run the code in to be tested in the OS context, thus overcoming the lack of test tools available by enabling DXE code to be run in the OS by using unit tests with the external dependencies, such as the functions in the boot services table, mocked.

Since the code is run in the OS, developers and testers have access to many other tools that exist to help them ensure code quality, such as code coverage and other tools that are not available in UEFI environment.

Contributions. In this paper we discuss a tool that enables unit tests for UEFI code to run as standard operating system programs and show a case study with a compliant driver to evaluate it's benefits. During the discussion of the driver implementation ideas about how to use the test suit to minimize the number of times a developer needs to rewrite the machine's flash memory and protocol conformity.

Section 2 describes the state-of-the-art techniques for unit testing of DXE code. It shows that the existing techniques are not extensible, and do not allow for further code metrics. In Sect. 3, the proposed tool and the way it works is explained. Section 4 describes the case study and presents results. Finally, Sect. 5 concludes this paper and proposes future work.

2   Related Work

There are several works advocating the use of unit testing in the development of software [3,7,8]. While in UEFI there are no specific unit test tools, there are validation tools for firmwares and drivers such as PI SCT [11] provided by the UEFI open source community, FWTS [1] and Chipsec [4]. All of these run functional tests.

The field that most closely resembles tasks accomplished in UEFI development is that of embedded systems development, mainly because of the use of C and the fact that many operating system services may not be available. In that context there are some tools that try to make test-driven development more pleasant, Unity [13] for example, provides several assertion macros to guide unit test development for C modules. CMock [13] parses the included header files and checks for function declarations to provide mocked or stub implementations of them, this allows one to remove the dependencies on the functionality of third party modules avoiding effects of their behaviour in the results of the tests. Ceedling [13] is a build management system that integrates those tools and allow custom configurations through its project descriptor file.

EDKII (EFI Development Kit) [10] module development uses the following structure: At first, a package is created. Inside the package are the platform descriptor file (.dsc), responsible for describing all the dependencies used by the modules in the platform. The declaration file (.dec) contains all the include paths used by the modules, as well as GUID declarations for protocol communication. Then, each module inside the package, be it an application or driver, has its descriptor file (.inf), which contains information about the module such as compiled source codes, libraries, dependencies and protocol GUIDs published or consumed, separated into sections, such as [Packages], [Guids] and [Protocols].

According to Saadat, H. [9], hardware diagnostics are not effective in detecting code errors, therefore, UEFI code must be tested from a software perspective. Also, it is mentioned that only one test tool may be insufficient to cover all the phases in UEFI, which is why a combination of tools must be used.

There are some groups interested in testing embedded systems code during development and UEFI code as well. However, the UEFI approach to unit testing still uses the UEFI environment, making the use of debbugers and other OS specific tools impossible. Our solution, called UTTOS, aims to execute the code in the OS, mocking UEFI specific dependencies, thus allowing unit tests to be run in the same development environment and enabling use of other tools, like code coverage tools.

3   The UTTOS Solution

It is possible to write unit tests that run in UEFI through the use of CuTestLib [5] or some other similar tool. However, the fact that the firmware run in a process-less, single threaded fashion poses a number of limitations. If there is a problem with a statement and the code breaks in a way that should generate a segmentation fault in an OS context, the firmware is likely to just freeze, leaving the test developer without any feedback or clue to what happened. This is an issue that may happen to even more sophisticated test approaches that involve transmission of test results over network or serial port.

Those limitations and the extra complexity needed to achieve simple tasks like writing test results to a screen or to a file in the firmware level makes good practices like test-driven development often impractical or even absent in many projects.

To avoid these problems, we propose an UEFI Test Tool for Operating Systems (UTTOS). UTTOS addresses this issue by enabling code that was written to the EDKII platform and meant to run in the DXE context to be compiled and executed as an ordinary executable in the operating system of the developer platform. The unit tests generated in this fashion are much more flexible as they enable the test developer to use the full stack of debugging tools that are available for C. If there is a segmentation fault, for example, the developer can make use of the core dump generated by the operating system and a debugger, like GDB, without any specialized hardware-aided solution.

UTTOS strategy for running EDKII in the operating system runtime consists of looking for dependencies declared in the descriptor of the module being compiled, that is our UEFI driver or application, and then generates stub versions of the EDKII specific functions. The developer is responsible for configuring the expected arguments and return values of these functions for each test suite. This effort is not repetitive since the most used functions can be reused.

The main tool used by UTTOS is Ceedling, that tracks dependencies and have a configuration file feature-rich enough to permit customization of the whole process. Ceedling itself makes use of a few other open source tools, namely: CMock for mocking and Unity for test creation. UTTOS acts in the beginning of the process parsing the EDKII build files and generating the Ceedling configuration accordingly. And as we are in an operating system environment we also include Gcov for coverage evaluation.

A more detailed view of the UTTOS workflow is described in Fig. 1. It first parses the module descriptor file and gathers information about the dependencies and the consumed resources. The resources in a UEFI firmware are identified by a Globally Unique Identifier (GUID). In the process of constructing the dependency tree, the descriptor files and declaration files (.dec extension) of other modules are read to gather all the required headers, include paths and GUIDs

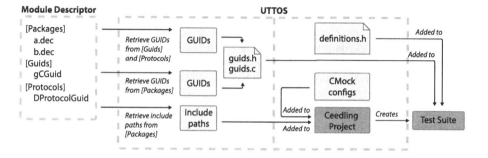

Fig. 1. Workflow of UTTOS, from module descriptor to test suites.

used by the current module. From this procedure, two files, guids.h and guids.c are output for use in the test suite compilation.

The next step is the generation of a Ceedling project where the module descriptor is located. The project is created using Ceedling's default configurations for a C project. After this, the Ceedling project descriptor is modified by UTTOS, that adds the include paths for the dependencies, the source files to be built, the suitable compiler options and the instructions to CMock on which functions have to be mocked.

The final step is the placing of the generated files inside the created test suite to allow correct code compilation. The test suite is generated with two stub functions for setup and clean up. At this stage, it is ready to use. Ceedling manages the test suite and its dependencies, assuring transparent use of the UEFI code. If further configuration is needed, the project is customizable after UTTOS executes.

With the suite ready to be executed, the user can add individual test cases with custom assertions and control flows. The user can also specify the expected parameter and return values for the mocks created by CMock to strengthen the tests coverage further. Ceedling also monitors suite execution and reports formatted results, allowing the developer to ensure quickly that the written code is working.

4   Case Study

As a case study, a simple UEFI DXE driver fully compliant with the UEFI Driver Model was developed. The driver installs a protocol and an associated GUID to the UEFI runtime that provides a service for UEFI applications to convert roman numbers in string format to a regular C integer type. Because one of the most interesting scenarios that requires testing in the context of driver development is the process of providing a new protocol, we decided to go with an algorithm that, although simple, provides a good number of test cases as there are a number of possibilities for invalid roman numbers.

The driver was developed under the EDKII version 2.6 source tree in a Debian GNU/Linux 8 machine using the GCC compiler version 4.9.

This process starts by creating a set of functions called the Driver Binding Protocol [2]. These functions are responsible for querying all the nodes of the UEFI service database checking if any of these corresponds to a device that the driver can control. This query process is performed by the Supported function and it has to return a success status for a device that is suitable for the driver and an unsupported status otherwise. If such a device is found, the Start function is called to initialize the driver data structures and the device itself.

If for some reason the user wants to remove the driver from the environment, the driver binding protocol also provides the Stop function, that is responsible for releasing all the resources that were allocated by Start, and for the removal of any protocol installed by the driver and their respective GUIDs. Stop makes sure the services provided by the driver will not appear to be available to applications after it is unloaded.

In UEFI, all the available memory is shared as a single address space to all drivers and applications. Therefore, an error in any of these functions is likely to freeze the whole system. Consequently, all these steps must be previously validated before one takes the job of rewriting the firmware of the machine to check if the driver works as expected. Here is where the ability to run unit tests in the developer's workstation as a prior step shows it's value, since most of the trivial mistakes can be avoided before actually touching the target hardware.

The Gcov [6] utility was used to evaluate the code coverage of the tests performed. Gcov is another python tool that translates the symbols generated by GCC to human readable results allowing a nice html format to be output.

Directory: .		Exec	Total	Coverage
Date: 2016-06-02	Lines:	71	75	94.7 %
Legend: low: < 75.0 % medium: >= 75.0 % high: >= 90.0 %	Branches:	71	40	95.0 %

File	Lines		Branches	
source/RomanConvertDriver.c	88.2%	30/34	88.9%	16/18
source/Validation.c	100.0%	41/41	100.0%	22/22

Fig. 2. Code coverage report of the implemented driver.

Figure 2 shows the test coverage results for our case study. It can be seen that most of the control flows were covered. The results of the individual test cases were all positive and they have successfully assured that the driver binding process would occur without errors when embedded in the machine's firmware. This is important in the sense that it allows the developer to be concerned with the driver's functionality correctness straight from the first firmware writing, and not with these initial service and protocol setup that often takes a considerable time in real world projects.

In comparison with the approach of testing the code in DXE environment directly, the first major benefit observed is that ones does not have to rewrite the firmware in the flash memory so many times to test code, a process that is time consuming and decreases flash memory life time. Additionally, code coverage measuring tools are one of many that are not available in the DXE phase so these results would not the easily achieved today.

5 Conclusion and Future Works

In this paper, we proposed UTTOS, a tool that makes use of a set of OS-based test tools to test UEFI code. It adapts the test framework to be able to run UEFI code as a regular operating system executable with that UEFI specific functions mocked. A case study was also conducted, with the implementation of an example driver in order to test the whole process of driver installation, production usage and removal to simulate as close as possible the reality of device driver development.

In the development time it was observed a decrease in the need for rewriting the machine's firmware and the ability to focus in functionality rather than in protocols conformity which can in practice be, using UTTOS, considered to be boilerplate code.

During the experiments, we were able to not only create unit tests, but to make use of code coverage, as we were running the code in an OS-based environment. This would not be possible by running the code only in UEFI DXE phase.

For future works, it is intended to integrate this tool with an IDE. Support for other code metrics, such as cyclomatic complexity and nesting depth can also be considered.

Acknowledgements. This publication is the result of a project promoted by the Brazilian Informatics Law (Law No. 8248 of 1991 and subsequent updates) and was developed under the Cooperation Agreement 11/2016 between Federal University of Ceara and HP Brazil Industry and Trade Electronic Equipment Ltda. This research was also partially supported by LSBD/UFC.

References

1. Canonical: Firmware Test Suite 16.01.00 (2016). https://wiki.ubuntu.com/FirmwareTestSuite. Accessed 23 May 2016
2. Corporation, I.: Uefi driver writer's guide (2013). https://github.com/tianocore/tianocore.github.io/wiki/UEFI-Driver-Writers-Guide. Accessed 01 June 2016
3. Greening, J.W.: Test Driven Development for Embedded C, 1st edn. Pragmatic Bookshelf, Raleigh (2011)
4. Intel Corporation: CHIPSEC: Platform Security Assessment Framework 1.2.2 (2015). http://www.intelsecurity.com/advanced-threat-researchchipsec.html. Accessed 23 May 2016
5. Jalis, A.: CuTest: C Unit Testing Framework 1.5 (2013). http://cutest.sourceforge.net. Accessed 23 May 2016
6. Ledru, S., Cai, K., Woydziak, L., Schumacher, N., Hart, W.: Gcovr (2014). http://gcovr.com. Accessed 23 May 2016
7. Myers, G.J., Sandler, C., Badgett, T.: The Art of Software Testing, 3rd edn. Wiley, Hoboken (2011)
8. Pressman, R.S., Maxim, B.: Software Engineering: A Practitioner's Approach, 8th edn. McGraw-Hill Education, New York (2014)
9. Saadat, H.: Design and development of an automated regression test suite for UEFI (2014)
10. Tianocore: Edk2 code repository (2016). https://github.com/tianocore/edk2. Accessed 01 June 2016
11. UEFI Forum: Platform Initialization Self Certification Test 2.4B (2015). http://www.uefi.org/testtools. Accessed 23 May 2016
12. UEFI Forum: UEFI Specification 2.6 (2016). http://www.uefi.org/specifications. Accessed 23 May 2016
13. VanderVoord, M., Karlesky, M., Williams, G.: ThrowTheSwitch.org (2016). http://www.throwtheswitch.org/tools. Accessed 23 May 2016
14. Zimmer, V., Rothman, M., Marisetty, S.: Beyond BIOS: Developing with the Unified Extensible Firmware Interface, 2nd edn. Intel Press, Mountain View (2010)

Towards Model Construction Based on Test Cases and GUI Extraction

Antti Jääskeläinen[⊠]

Department of Pervasive Computing, Tampere University of Technology,
PO Box 553, 33101 Tampere, Finland
antti.m.jaaskelainen@tut.fi

Abstract. The adoption of model-based testing techniques is hindered by the difficulty of creating a test model. Various techniques to automate the modelling process have been proposed, based on software process artefacts or an existing product. This paper outlines a hybrid approach to model construction, based on two previously proposed methods. The presented approach combines information in pre-existing test cases with a model extracted from the graphical user interface of the product.

Keywords: Model extraction · Model-based testing · Software testing

1 Introduction

Model-based testing is a testing methodology that automates the generation of tests as well as their execution. In a typical approach, the tester first creates a formal model (such as a state machine) that depicts the behaviour of the system under test (SUT). The model is then explored by an automated tool in order to generate a sequence of actions to be used as a test. Models can also be used to otherwise support the testing process, such as in inspections.

A significant drawback of model-based testing is the skill and effort required in modelling. Creating a model that covers all the relevant aspects of the SUT, does so correctly, and is otherwise suitable for test generation, is no small task.

Various methods for easing or partially automating the modelling process have been proposed. Models can be generated from different artefacts of the software process, or the artefacts used directly as test models. Suitable candidates include specifications [10] and pre-existing test cases [9,14]. Alternatively, models can be extracted from an existing product, either the source code [4,13,15], the structure and functionality of the graphical user interface (GUI) [1,6,11,12], or other known behaviour [7,8]. Many of these methods also use the results of the generated tests to further hone the model.

This paper outlines a hybrid model construction method based on test cases and information extracted from the GUI. Information on the correct behaviour of the SUT in specific states is found in the test cases, and the states can be combined based on information gleaned from the GUI. In this way, weaknesses of

F. Wotawa et al. (Eds.): ICTSS 2016, LNCS 9976, pp. 225–230, 2016.
DOI: 10.1007/978-3-319-47443-4_15

each method can be compensated for with the strengths of the other. Hopefully, the new method could reduce the effort required to produce a useful test model.

The rest of the paper is structured as follows: Sect. 2 presents the two model construction methods that act as the basis for the new approach, which is outlined in Sect. 3. Section 4 considers the potential benefits of the approach. Finally, Sect. 5 concludes the paper with a more general discussion.

2   Automated Model Construction

The approach of this paper builds on two previously presented methods for constructing models to describe the SUT. The first is based on combining test cases into a model, the second on examining the GUI of the system.

2.1   Synthesis from Test Cases

The model synthesis process proposed in [9] is based on pre-existing test cases that are linear sequences of automatically executable steps (*keywords*), and consists of five phases: First, keywords used in test cases are identified and classified. Second, part of the information in the test cases (such as input data) is separated into variables. Third, an initialization sequence for the test model is prepared. Fourth, important states in the test cases are identified manually. Finally, the actual merging of the test cases takes place.

In the merging phase, the linear state sequences of the test cases are combined into a more complex model by merging some of the states with each other. The previously identified common states in the test cases are trivially merged. However, states in different test cases may also be combined if they are reached by the same sequence of keywords, which suggests that the cases are in fact handling the same part of the SUT. Separating input data into variables allows states to be combined even if the stored inputs would actually leave the system in different states, as the data can be combined back into the model afterward.

Although this method works, it relies on a significant amount of manual effort. In particular, the separation of variables requires significant work and skill [9]. Also, the tester has to confirm the merges between the test cases manually, as the state sequence method may generate false positives [9]. Thus, the practicality of the method as presented is questionable.

2.2   Extraction from GUI

As an example of methods that extract a model out of a GUI we consider Murphy, a tool that examines the GUI of an application, tries out different functions, and builds a model to describe its observations [1]. It can use various methods to access the GUI, or *crawl* through it. The publicly available version [5] provides crawlers that use Windows APIs or cycle through GUI controls with the tabulator key. The constructed model is a graph with a node for each observable state of the application.

Murphy starts out at desktop, and launches the application with a predefined command. These two application states, not running and just launched, form the two first nodes in the constructed graph. In each GUI state, Murphy maps out the controls found in it. Then it proceeds to try out a control, such as clicking a button, and considers the resulting state of the GUI. A given state of the application is identified by the controls that can be found in its GUI, while ignoring the data such as the contents of text labels. Based on these, Murphy will either create a transition to an existing node or add a new node to the graph. Extraction can be performed in multiple runs starting from the desktop, with the results combined into a single graph.

Visual inspection of the extracted models can be very helpful in finding errors, and the models can support manual testing of the application [2]. They can also be used for automated regression testing by comparing the extracted models between different versions of the application or using an extracted sequence as a smoke test for the next version [2]. That said, their usefulness for test generation is limited: they can make no difference between an erroneous feature and a correct one, and contain no verifications of the system state beyond finding the expected controls in the GUI. Also, specific input data has to be added into the extraction script manually, as it cannot be inferred from the GUI.

3   Combined Methodology

Both approaches described above have their drawbacks. In the test case synthesis method, the test cases provide detailed information of what can and should happen in different situations, but constructing a model out of them is difficult. In the GUI extraction method, a graph to describe the SUT can be constructed with little manual effort, but its understanding of the SUT is limited. But what if the two were combined?

If we have a ready set of test cases when we begin the extraction process, then we can track the actions taken in the GUI within the cases. For each node of the constructed graph, we will have a set of test cases that reach the corresponding SUT state at a specific point of their execution. Then, we can examine the next steps in those cases for information on the current state of the SUT and the actions available in it. The process could work as follows:

1. Before extraction, establish a correspondence between the keywords within the test cases and actions supported by the extraction crawler. This is trivial if the two use the same mechanism for accessing the GUI, and should be doable with any mechanisms that understand the structure of a GUI. Also, make note of any keywords used to verify the state of the SUT without changing it.
2. At the beginning of an extraction run, start with the full set of test cases at their initial states. When the extractor performs an action, examine the cases to see if they would execute the corresponding keyword next, skipping past any keywords that do not change the state of the SUT. Advance these cases past that keyword, and discard the other cases in the set. Make a note that this node can be reached by the remaining test cases at their current stage.

3. At each node, examine the test cases that can reach it. Any verifications performed by the test cases at this node can be added into the model. Also, the next keywords in the cases should be executable in the GUI, even if the crawler fails to find a corresponding control. In particular, test data in the cases, such as the parameter of a *type text* keyword, can be used as an input.

This process produces a model that incorporates and combines both the information extractable from the SUT and that present in the test cases. It may even contain functionality present in neither, if the test cases provide the crawler access to a part of the GUI it could not reach on its own.

4 Potential Applications

Combining the test case synthesis and GUI extraction methods as described above offers several potential benefits. Either of the test cases or the extracted model can be used to support a testing approach based on the other. The resulting model can also act as a basis for a manually maintained test model.

If the testing process is based on test cases, their coverage can be increased with the information extracted from the GUI. With the extracted information, it is possible to tell when two test cases reach the same SUT state, or when a test case loops back into a state it has already visited. By using the model for test generation, it is possible to reach a state by a keyword sequence taken from one test case and continue with a sequence from another, even if such a combination does not occur in any of the original cases. A model that loops back into itself at several points can be particularly useful in robustness testing: properly directed, a test run can continue indefinitely without simply repeating a single sequence of keywords over and over.

Conversely, in a testing process based on the extracted model, the test cases can improve the quality of that model. They can improve model coverage by supplying performable actions that cannot be identified in the GUI, and in particular by providing realistic test data. Also, the verifications in the test cases improve the ability of the model to detect errors.

Finally, the constructed model can support a move to proper model-based testing, where the tests are generated from the model. Creating a test model can be a daunting task, especially if a fairly complete product already exists, so that the model cannot be developed incrementally as new features are added. In this situation, a method for automatically constructing a preliminary model can be helpful, even though some augmentation and refactoring is likely to be required. A model extracted purely from the GUI can already be useful here, but the increased coverage and verifications added by the test cases can take this support further.

5   Discussion

The previous sections have outlined a method for constructing models based on information in test cases and the GUI of the SUT. The resulting models can be used to improve test coverage in a testing approach based on test cases, or to better support static analysis and exploratory techniques. The method is language-independent, and only requires the SUT to have a GUI that can be handled by test automation. Obviously, it assumes the existence of some manually created test cases, and is thus primarily suited for testing approaches that will have those anyway. Practical experience will be required to see whether writing test cases specifically for this method could be worthwhile.

As presented here, the GUI extraction part of the process is based on the Murphy tool. However, there is nothing tool-specific in the approach itself, and other tools can be used, as well. The basic requirement is that the tool can distinguish different GUI events from each other, so that they can be matched with those occurring in the test cases. The test cases must naturally have a similar level of abstraction.

At this point, a prototype tool for the methodology is under development. The prototype can be used to estimate the practicality of the approach, although it will likely be unable to handle complex applications due to the limitations in the crawler component of the freely available version of Murphy [5]. For industrial use, integration with a professional quality test execution tool will be required.

There is likely also room for improvement in the methodology presented here. For example, it may be possible to factor out inputs from the test cases so that we could produce separate models for the control graph and saved data. Detecting the input data as identical output later on should be simple, but potential effects of data on the control graph could be more difficult to identify, and modified versions of the data impossible to recognize without domain knowledge. Likewise, it remains to be seen whether the Murphy approach of ignoring data in the GUI when identifying states is the best solution for the new method.

If the test cases have been created using action words and keywords [3], it might be possible to import these two tiers of abstraction into the constructed model. Presenting the model at a higher level of abstraction could make analysing it significantly easier, and produce a better basis for a full-fledged test model.

Acknowledgements. Funding by Ulla Tuominen Foundation is gratefully acknowledged.

References

1. Aho, P., Suarez, M., Kanstrén, T., Memon, A.M.: Industrial adoption of automatically extracted GUI models for testing. In: Chaudron, M., Genero, M., Abrahão, S., Pareto, L. (eds.) Proceedings of the 3rd International Workshop on Experiences and Empirical Studies in Software Modelling (EESSMod 2013), CEUR-WS, vol. 1078, pp. 49–54. CEUR Workshop Proceedings, October 2013

2. Aho, P., Suarez, M., Kanstrén, T., Memon, A.M.: Murphy tools: utilizing extracted GUI models for industrial software testing. In: O'Conner, L. (ed.) Proceedings of the 7th International Conference on Software Testing, Verification and Validation Workshops (ICSTW 2014), pp. 343–348. IEEE Computer Society, Los Alamitos (2014)

3. Buwalda, H.: Action figures. In: Software Testing and Quality Engineering Magazine, pp. 42–47, March/April 2003

4. Dallmeier, V., Knopp, N., Mallon, C., Hack, S., Zeller, A.: Generating test cases for specification mining. In: Proceedings of the 19th International Symposium on Software Testing and Analysis (ISSTA 2010), pp. 85–96. ACM, New York, July 2010

5. F-Secure: GitHub - F-Secure/murphy (2014). https://github.com/F-Secure/murphy. Accessed June 2016

6. Grilo, A.M.P., Paiva, A.C.R., Faria, J.P.: Reverse engineering of GUI models for testing. In: Proceedings of the 5th Iberian Conference on Information Systems and Technologies (CISTI 2010), pp. 1–6. IEEE Computer Society, Los Alamitos, June 2010

7. Hagerer, A., Hungar, H., Niese, O., Steffen, B.: Model generation by moderated regular extrapolation. In: Kutsche, R.-D., Weber, H. (eds.) FASE 2002. LNCS, vol. 2306, pp. 80–95. Springer, Heidelberg (2002). doi:10.1007/3-540-45923-5_6

8. Hungar, H., Margaria, T., Steffen, B.: Test-based model generation for legacy systems. In: Proceedings of the 2003 International Test Conference (ICT 2003), vol. 2, pp. 150–159. IEEE Computer Society, Los Alamitos, September–October 2003

9. Jääskeläinen, A., Kervinen, A., Katara, M., Valmari, A., Virtanen, H.: Synthesizing test models from test cases. In: Chockler, H., Hu, A.J. (eds.) HVC 2008. LNCS, vol. 5394, pp. 179–193. Springer, Heidelberg (2009). doi:10.1007/978-3-642-01702-5_18

10. Ma, C., Du, C., Zhang, T., Hu, F., Cai, X.: WSDL-based automated test data generation for web service. In: Kawada, S. (ed.) Proceedings of the International Conference on Computer Science and Software Engineering (CSSE 2008), pp. 731–737. IEEE Computer Society, Los Alamitos (2008)

11. Memon, A., Banerjee, I., Nagarajan, A.: GUI ripping: reverse engineering of graphical user interfaces for testing. In: van Deursen, A., Stroulia, E., Storey, M.A.D. (eds.) Proceedings of the 10th Working Conference on Reverse Engineering (WCRE 2003), pp. 260–269. IEEE Computer Society, Los Alamitos (2003)

12. Memon, A.M.: An event-flow model of GUI-based applications for testing. Softw. Test. Verif. Reliab. (STVR) 17(3), 137–157 (2007)

13. Silva, J.C., Silva, C., Gonçalo, R.D., Saraiva, J., Campos, J.C.: The GUISurfer tool: towards a language independent approach to reverse engineering GUI code. In: Proceedings of the 2nd ACM SIGCHI Symposium on Engineering Interactive Computing Systems (EICS 2010), pp. 181–186. ACM, New York, June 2010

14. Xie, T., Notkin, D.: Mutually enhancing test generation and specification inference. In: Petrenko, A., Ulrich, A. (eds.) FATES 2003. LNCS, vol. 2931, pp. 60–69. Springer, Heidelberg (2004). doi:10.1007/978-3-540-24617-6_5

15. Yang, W., Prasad, M.R., Xie, T.: A grey-box approach for automated GUI-model generation of mobile applications. In: Cortellessa, V., Varró, D. (eds.) FASE 2013. LNCS, vol. 7793, pp. 250–265. Springer, Heidelberg (2013). doi:10.1007/978-3-642-37057-1_19

Set-Based Algorithms for Combinatorial Test Set Generation

Ludwig Kampel and Dimitris E. Simos(⊠)

SBA Research, Vienna, Austria
{lkampel,dsimos}@sba-research.org

Abstract. Testing is an important and expensive part of software and hardware development. Over the recent years, the construction of combinatorial interaction tests rose to play an important role towards making the cost of testing more efficient. Covering arrays are the key element of combinatorial interaction testing and a means to provide abstract test sets. In this paper, we present a family of set-based algorithms for generating covering arrays and thus combinatorial test sets. Our algorithms build upon an existing mathematical method for constructing independent families of sets, which we extend sufficiently in terms of algorithmic design in this paper. We compare our algorithms against commonly used greedy methods for producing 3-way combinatorial test sets, and these initial evaluation results favor our approach in terms of generating smaller test sets.

Keywords: Combinatorial testing · Independent families of sets · Set-based algorithms

1 Introduction

In modern software development testing plays an important role and therefore requires a large amount of time and resources. According to a report of the National Institute of Standards in Technology (NIST) [1], faults in software costs the U.S. economy up to $59.5 billion per year, where these costs could be reduced by $22.2 billion, provided better software testing infrastructure. Another report from NIST [11] shows that failures appear to be caused by the interaction of only few input parameters of the system under test (SUT). Combinatorial testing guarantees good input-space coverage, while reducing the resources needed for testing. In particular, it is a t-wise testing strategy whose key ingredient is a Covering Array (CA), a abstract mathematical object that provides coverage of all t-way interactions of a certain amount of input parameters, reducing the amount of tests that need to be executed. For their use in practice, the columns of CAs are identified with the input parameters of the SUT, where each entry in a certain column is mapped to a value of the corresponding parameter [12].

© IFIP International Federation for Information Processing 2016
Published by Springer International Publishing AG 2016. All Rights Reserved
F. Wotawa et al. (Eds.): ICTSS 2016, LNCS 9976, pp. 231–240, 2016.
DOI: 10.1007/978-3-319-47443-4_16

This way each row of the CA translates to a certain parameter value setting of the input model of the SUT which can be used as a test. Translating each row of a CA in this way, one obtains a *concrete test set* hence a CA can be regarded as an *abstract combinatorial test set*. To reduce further the amount of resources needed for testing, one is interested to construct optimal CAs (e.g. arrays of a minimal size that provide maximal coverage). This software testing problem is tightly coupled with hard combinatorial optimization problems for CAs (shown to be NP-hard [17]).

Contribution. In this paper, we use a set-based method for constructing CAs based on independent families of sets (IFS) from [7]. There exists an equivalence between these two combinatorial objects which allowed us to use the two discrete structures interchangeably in terms of algorithmic design. In particular, we extend this set-based method with balancing properties that can impose restrictions on the cardinality of the appearing intersections. This (among other concepts) enabled us to define different building blocks that give rise to a family of algorithms based on IFSs (and consequently also for CAs). Furthermore, as a proof of concept we compared our algorithms against a widely used combinatorial strategy (the so-called IPO-strategy [15]) which bares similarities with our approach for constructing and extending CAs. Our initial results outperform this strategy for 3-way testing, generating better sized covering arrays.

Structure of the Paper. In Sect. 2 we give some preliminaries for CAs, where we also review related algorithms and problems for the former objects. Afterwards, in Sect. 3 we describe a set-based method for constructing CAs and extend it with concepts necessary for devising an algorithmic concept later on Sect. 4, in which we also propose a variety of algorithms for generating CAs. Subsequently, in Sect. 5 we compare our algorithms against IPO-strategy greedy techniques for constructing CAs and comment on the evaluated results. Finally, Sect. 6 concludes the work and discusses future directions of work.

2   Problems and Algorithms for Covering Arrays

In this section we give a short overview of the needed definitions, as well as of related problems, related algorithms and work in general. In the following we frequently use the abbreviation $[N]$ for a set $\{1, \ldots, N\} \subseteq \mathbb{N}$ and also A^C denotes the complement $[N] \backslash A$ of A in $[N]$. The definitions given below are slightly different phrased as those given in [5], and can also be found in [13].

2.1   Preliminaries for Covering Arrays

Definition 1 (t-Independent Family of Sets). *A t-independent family of sets, IFS$(N; t, k)$, is a family $(A_1, \ldots, A_k)$ of k subsets of $[N]$, with the property that for each choice $\{i_1, \ldots, i_t\} \subseteq [k]$ of t different indices, for all $j \in [t]$ and for all $\bar{A}_{i_j} \in \{A_{i_j}, A_{i_j}^C\}$ it holds that $\bigcap_{j=1}^{t} \bar{A}_{i_j} \neq \emptyset$. The parameters t and k are called, respectively, the strength and the size of the IFS.*

We say that a family of sets is *t-independent* if it is an $IFS(N;t,k)$ for some value of N and k. Without loss of generality we only consider IFS over a underlying set $[N]$ with $N \in \mathbb{N}$.

Table 1. The sets A_1, A_2, A_3, A_4 and B are considered as subsets of $[12]$. We identify them with their binary indicator vectors, i.e. vectors in $\{0,1\}^{12}$ that have 1 in position i if, and only if i is element of the corresponding set, and 0 otherwise.

$$A_1 = \{6,7,8,9,10,11\} \leftrightarrow (0,0,0,0,0,0,1,1,1,1,1,0)^T = a_1$$
$$A_2 = \{1,2,3,6,7,8\} \leftrightarrow (1,1,1,0,0,1,1,1,0,0,0,0)^T = a_2$$
$$A_3 = \{1,2,4,6,9,10\} \leftrightarrow (1,1,0,1,0,1,0,0,1,1,0,0)^T = a_3$$
$$A_4 = \{1,2,5,7,9,11\} \leftrightarrow (1,1,0,0,1,0,1,0,1,0,1,0)^T = a_4$$
$$B = \{1,2,5,8,9,10\} \leftrightarrow (1,1,0,0,1,0,0,1,1,1,0,0)^T = b$$

Example 1. From Table 1 the family $\mathcal{A} = (A_1, A_2, A_3, B)$ is an $IFS(12;3,4)$, i.e. if we choose 3 sets of $\mathcal{A}$ or independently their complements, their intersection is nonempty. For example, $A_1 \cap A_3^C \cap B = \{8\} \neq \emptyset$ and $A_1 \cap A_2 \cap A_3^C = \{7,8\} \neq \emptyset$.

Definition 2 (Binary t-Covering Array). *A $N \times k$ binary array M, denoted in column form as $M = (\mathbf{m_1}, \ldots, \mathbf{m_k})$, is a binary t-covering array, $CA(N;t,k)$, if M has the property that for each $\{i_1, \ldots, i_t\} \subseteq [k]$, the corresponding $t \times N$ sub array $(\mathbf{m_{i_1}}, \ldots, \mathbf{m_{i_t}})$ of M cover all binary t-tuples $\{0,1\}^t$, i.e. these tuples have to appear at least once as a row of the sub array $(\mathbf{m_{i_1}}, \ldots, \mathbf{m_{i_t}})$. In some cases M is also called a binary covering array of strength t.*

Remark 1. Covering arrays of fixed non-binary alphabet with size u are denoted with $CA(N;t,k,u)$ in the literature (e.g. see [5]). When $u = 2$ is clear from the context we simply use the notation introduced as above.

As the similarity of the former definitions of these combinatorial objects implies, there is a close relation between the two of them. For example, it is known that every $CA(N;t,k)$ is equivalent to an $IFS(N;t,k)$ (see for example [5,13], Remark 10.5).

Example 2. From Table 1 we take the vectors a_1, a_2, a_3 and b to form the array

$$A = (a_1, a_2, a_3, b) = \begin{pmatrix} 0\,0\,0\,0\,0\,1\,1\,1\,1\,1\,1\,0 \\ 1\,1\,1\,0\,0\,1\,1\,1\,0\,0\,0\,0 \\ 1\,1\,0\,1\,0\,1\,0\,0\,1\,1\,0\,0 \\ 1\,1\,0\,0\,1\,0\,0\,1\,1\,1\,0\,0 \end{pmatrix}^T ,$$

which is equivalent to the IFS given in Example 1. The defining property of an IFS translates to the defining property of a binary CA. In this case, within each three selected columns of (a_1, a_2, a_3, b), each binary 3-tuple appears at least once. Therefore the given array A is a $CA(12; 3, 4)$. On the other hand, the IFS in Example 1 can be uniquely reconstructed from the array A, interpreting its columns as indicator vectors of subsets of [12].

Definition 3. *The smallest number of rows N such that a binary $CA(N; t, k)$ exists is defined as $CAN(t, k) := min\{N : \exists\ CA(N; t, k)\}$.*

Definition 4. *The largest number k such that a $IFS(N; t, k)$ exists is defined as $CAK(N; t) := max\{k : \exists\ IFS(N; t, k)\}$.*

For an overview of the vast amount of theoretical and computational problems that arise in the theory of CAs we refer to [4,9]. Especially the problem of determining binary CAs with minimum amount of rows turns out to be NP-hard (see [17]).

2.2 Algorithms for Covering Arrays

The notorious difficulty of constructing optimal CAs has been the subject of many algorithmic approaches. The most related ones to our work are greedy methods such as AETG [2] and IPO [15]. AETG employs a randomized, greedy, one row at a time extension strategy. The IPO-strategy is to grow the covering array in both dimensions. Horizontal growth adds one column to the current array by its cells with entries in a greedy manner. Vertical extension is performed, by adding rows until the array is once again a CA. Adjusting the parameters of the IPO-strategy has been the subject of [8]. Finally, in [7] a method is proposed that produces exponentially sized IFS one set at a time. In terms of CAs this comes down to a *one column at a time* construction of a binary CA. As this method plays a pivotal role in our work, we further describe it in Sect. 3.

Due to space limitations, for other related works we refer the interested reader to a recent survey [18].

3   A Set-Based Method for Constructing CAs

In this section we elaborate on a set-based method for constructing CAs and extend it with concepts necessary for devising an algorithmic concept later on in Sect. 4.

Before the description of the method, we have to define some terms needed. It is well known that Orthogonal Arrays of index one are optimal CAs [5], i.e. within each selection of t columns each binary t-tuple appears exactly once.

Also when constructing a CA with as few rows as possible, one tends to not cover certain t-tuples multiple times; rather the target would be to cover as few t-tuples as possible more than once. Lets consider the case of a CA $(\mathbf{a_1}, \dots, \mathbf{a_r})$, where only few t-tuples appear more than once within a certain choice $\mathbf{c} = (\mathbf{a_{i_1}}, \dots, \mathbf{a_{i_t}})$ of t columns of that array. Since for each $(t-1)$-tuple $(u_1, \dots, u_{t-1})$ there are exactly two binary t-tuples, that start with $(u_1, \dots, u_{t-1})$, namely

$(u_1, \ldots, u_{t-1}, 0)$ and $(u_1, \ldots, u_{t-1}, 1)$. We know that within $(a_{i_1}, \ldots, a_{i_{t-1}})$ each $(t-1)$-tuple appears at least twice, and only few of them appear more than twice. Of course, this argument holds for each choice of $(t-1)$ columns of $\mathbf{c}$.

Remark 2. Note as well that this argumentation can be iterated. From these thoughts we design a necessary condition when a column is allowed to be added to the current array. In particular, we want to ensure a minimum amount of *balance* among the columns of the array in the regard just described.

In light of the previous remark, we introduce the notion of α-balance.

Definition 5. *Let* $\mathcal{A} = (A_1, \ldots, A_k)$ *be a family of sets* $A_i \subseteq [N]$ $\forall i \in [k]$ *and* $\alpha = (\alpha_1, \ldots, \alpha_s) \in \mathbb{N}^s$, $s \le k$. *We say that* A *is* α *-balanced, if*

$$\forall i \in [s] \ \forall \{j_1, \ldots, j_i\} \subseteq [k] \ \forall \bar{A}_{j_r} \in \{A_{j_r}, A_{j_r}^C\} : \left| \bigcap_{r=1}^{i} \bar{A}_{j_r} \right| \ge \alpha_i. \tag{1}$$

Note that if a family of sets is $(\alpha_1, \ldots, \alpha_s)$-balanced and $\alpha_s \ge 1$ then it is also s-independent.

Definition 6. *Let* $B \subseteq [N]$, $\mathcal{A} = (A_1, \ldots, A_k)$ *be a family of sets* $A_i \subseteq [N]$ $\forall i \in [k]$ *and* $\alpha = (\alpha_1, \ldots, \alpha_s) \in \mathbb{N}^s$. *We say that* B α-balanced with respect to $\mathcal{A}$, if *the family* $(A_1, \ldots, A_k, B)$ *of sets is* α-balanced.

Example 3. Consider the family $\mathcal{F} = (A_1, A_2, A_3, A_4)$, constructed from the sets of Table 1. This family is a $(6,3)$-balanced family of sets, i.e. each set, as well as its complement, has at least cardinality 6, and all intersections of any two sets of $\mathcal{F}$ (complements might be involved) have at least cardinality 3 (e.g. $A_1 \cap A_3^C = \{7, 8, 11\} \ge 3$). B is an example for a set that is not $(6,3)$-balanced w.r.t. $\mathcal{F}$, since $A_3^C \cap B = |\{5, 8\}| = 2 < 3$.

4 A New Family of IFS Algorithms

In this section, we propose a variety of algorithms, IFS-ORIGIN, IFS-GREEDY and IFS-SCORE, based on independent families of sets. We call this class of algorithms collectively a family of IFS-Algorithms. In particular, we formalized and extended in terms of a combinatorial algorithmic design the method described earlier. Our design is comprised of the following five *building blocks*: *store, select, admissible, extend* and *update* which we state below.

- *Store:* The *store* is a data structure that serves as a resource, from which the sets to build the target IFS are chosen. It may be static, or dynamic.
- *Select:* A procedure that returns one element of the *store*, e.g. randomly or via a scoring function.
- *Admissible:* This procedure decides whether a certain element is allowed to be added to the current IFS or not under certain admissible criteria which can be based for example on the concept of α-balance.

- *Extend:* A procedure that extends the IFS at hand.
- *Update:* The procedure which updates the *store* in case latter is dynamic.

In the following we frequently use $F_2(N) := \{A \subseteq [N] | N \notin A \wedge |A| = \lceil N/2 \rceil\}$, which is a 2-independent family of sets of maximal size (cf. [10]). A comprehensive overview of the proposed algorithms via their building blocks, is given below in Table 2.

Table 2. Composition of the IFS-family algorithms.

Building blocks	Algorithm		
	IFS-ORIGIN	IFS-GREEDY	IFS-SCORE
Store	F_2	F_2	F_2
Select	SELECTRANDOM	SELECTNEXT	SELECTSCORE
Admissible	ADMISSIBLE$_\alpha$	ADMISSIBLE$_\alpha$	ADMISSIBLE
Extend	EXTEND	EXTEND	EXTEND
Update	UPDATE$_\alpha$	-	UPDATE

4.1 IFS-Origin

Firstly we give a short algorithmic description of the method proposed in [7] and extended in Sect. 3. We refer to it and its implementation as IFS-ORIGIN. The algorithm takes as input the size N of the underlying set and the strength t of the to be constructed IFS. The initial STORE, S_0, is set to be equal to $F_2(N)$ and the initial IFS, A_1, is set to be a random element of the STORE. This random initialization is justified because picking a different initial element boils down to permuting the first $[N-1]$ elements of $[N]$, which also respects Definition 1, and keeps $F_2(N)$ invariant under such permutations. From now on in each step i the IFS-ORIGIN traverses through the whole STORE S_{i-1} given at that time, updating it by removing all non-ADMISSIBLE$_\alpha$ (ADMISSIBLE$_\alpha$ checks for α-balance and t-independence) elements from it, which yields S_i. For the admissibility check the algorithm requires a vector $\alpha_{1 \times (t-1)}$, which encodes the desired balance of i-tuples for $i = 1, \ldots, t-1$. Thereafter, now that S_i is left with only ADMISSIBLE$_\alpha$ elements, a random element is chosen and added to the IFS at hand, yielding A_{i+1}. The algorithm terminates when the STORE is empty.

4.2 IFS-Greedy

When being familiar with IFS-ORIGIN described above, one will realize, that this version, as was originally given in [7] lacks of a method to decide which of the elements in the remaining STORE should be added to the current array. In particular, this is done via a random pick, which in retrospect makes the UPDATE of the STORE, which leaves the STORE with only ADMISSIBLE$_\alpha$ elements inside, unnecessary. The newly proposed IFS-GREEDY version bypass this decision problem by simply taking the next found ADMISSIBLE$_\alpha$ element of the STORE, having the advantage that the STORE has never to be updated. The initialization stays the same as in IFS-ORIGIN. After that IFS-GREEDY traverses the STORE only once, adding the first element that is ADMISSIBLE with respect to the already chosen ones and α (recall Definition 6). The STORE never gets updated.

4.3   IFS-Score

The overall structure of IFS-SCORE is the same as that of IFS-ORIGIN, but different building blocks SELECTSCORE and ADMISSIBLE are defined. To circumvent the problem of IFS-ORIGIN of picking a *random element* from the updated STORE, we calculated a score for each element of the STORE, that reflects α-balance, and add the one (or one of those, since ties may occur) with the least score. Each element is initialized with a score of zero and in the i-th step of the algorithm we calculate again a score for each element of the current STORE, S_{i-1}, as before. This has also the advantage that IFS-SCORE does not require α. Since we compute a score for each element, we already encounter the tuple balance of (A_i, b) to our selection and we do not need to previously dictate via α how often certain i-tuples have to appear. Therefore IFS-SCORE is the only algorithm in the proposed IFS-family that does *not* require an input of α. Consequently, in an element of the STORE passes the decision criterion of ADMISSIBLE, if and only if (A, b) is t-independent.

5   Results

As a proof of concept of our algorithmic design (cf. Section 4) we compared our implementations of the IFS-family of algorithms for $t = 3$ to two of the most commonly used greedy algorithms of the IPO-family, namely IPOG [14] and IPOG-F [6]. In addition, we evaluate our results versus the *current* best known upper bounds for $CAK(N; 3)$ (retrieved from [3], via $CAK(N; t) = max\{k \,|\, CAN(k, t) \le N\}$, cf. [13]), that are combined results of algorithms and methods that are partly described in [18]. To the best of our knowledge the algorithms of the IPO-family are the only ones that generate CAs using a horizontal extension step similar to the one proposed in the IFS-family of algorithms.

Table 3 shows the amount of columns a binary CA of strength 3 can attain by either the respective algorithm compared or according to [3]. Table 3 starts with $N = 8$, since there are at least eight rows needed to cover all eight binary 3-tuples. It shows that the IFS-family of algorithms improves significantly over IPOG and IPOG-F in almost every case presented, as well that IFS-GREEDY and IFS-SCORE improve over IFS-ORIGIN. It is also worth pointing out that during our computations we obtained larger families, when running IFS-ORIGIN and IFS-GREEDY on more restrictive α-vectors than running them on less restrictive α-vectors. We believe the concept of admissibility via α-balance (and its requirement per different IFS algorithms) makes the difference versus IPOG and

IPOG-F, since these algorithms lack of a balancing strategy during horizontal extension. Regarding our results, we want to highlight that IFS-SCORE is able to deliver almost the same size of output IFS as IFS-GREEDY without the need of an α-vector as input. On the other hand, IFS-SCORE is more complex than IFS-GREEDY and even IFS-ORIGIN due to score computations.

The values for IPOG-F in Table 3 are taken from [16]. For the experimental evaluation we run IPOG locally as it is implemented in ACTS, a CA generation tool provided by NIST [19]. For the input values of N in Table 3, IPOG and IPOG-F were considerably faster than all three of our algorithms. We think that the extra computations are fully justified, since the IFS-family of algorithms outperforms IPOG and IPOG-F, in 14 out of the 18 documented cases in terms of output size of produced IFS (or columns of produced CAs respectively) and achieves the same size values in the other four. Especially, if we consider that in our experiments the main objective was to compare to the best bounds provided by greedy algorithms.

Table 3. Comparison of the amount of columns attained on N rows by different CA algorithms (larger is better). Information for the best lower bound for $CAK(N; t)$ where $t = 3$ is provided by Colbourn Tables [3]. The superscripts denote the α-vector that was used as input for the computation that yields the output IFS, where a $= (4, 2)$, b $= (6, 3)$, c $= (8, 4)$, d $= (10, 5)$.

N	IPOG-F	IPOG	IFS-ORIGIN	IFS-GREEDY	IFS-SCORE	Colbourn Tables
8	4	4	4^a	4^a	4	4
9	4	4	4^a	4^a	4	4
10	4	4	4^a	5^a	5	5
11	5	4	4^a	5^a	5	5
12	5	6	11^b	11^b	11	11
13	5	6	6^b	11^b	11	11
14	6	6	6^b	11^b	11	11
15	6	6	7^b	11^b	11	12
16	7	7	8^c	14^c	14	14
17	9	7	10^c	14^c	14	16
18	11	8	12^c	17^c	16	20
19	12	8	13^c	17^c	16	22
20	13	10	11^d	19^d	19	23
21	15	10	15^c	19^c	19	25
22	16	12	18^c	21^c	21	26
23	16	13	19^c	23^c	22	30
24	19	13	23^d	26^d	25	38
25	21	14	24^c	28^a	26	44

6   Conclusion and Future Work

In this paper, we present a family of set-based algorithms for covering arrays, which can be regarded as abstract combinatorial test sets, based on independent families of sets. Our algorithmic design is modular thanks to a variety of building blocks which can give rise to even more algorithms than the ones presented. As a proof of concept of our approach we compared the implementations of the proposed family against state of the art greedy algorithms that are also used in practice for 3-way testing. This initial evaluation shows, that our approach improves significantly, in terms of size, over the existing greedy algorithm, which translates to smaller test sets. As future work, we plan to enhance the functionality of our algorithms via extending it to produce combinatorial test sets over non-binary alphabets as well as conduct more experiments for test sets that can be used for higher strength interaction testing.

Acknowledgments. This work has been funded by the Austrian Research Promotion Agency (FFG) under grant 851205 and the Austrian COMET Program (FFG).

References

1. The economic impacts of inadequate infrastructure for software testing. U.S. Department of Commerce, National Institute of Standards and Technology (2002)
2. Cohen, D.M., Dalal, S.R., Fredman, M.L., Patton, G.C.: The AETG system: an approach to testing based on combinatorial design. IEEE Trans. Softw. Eng. **23**(7), 437–444 (1997)
3. Colbourn, C.J.: Table for CAN(3, k, 2) for k up to 10000. http://www.public.asu.edu/~ccolbou/src/tabby/3-2-ca.html. Accessed 25 Apr 2016
4. Colbourn, C.J.: Combinatorial aspects of covering arrays. Le Matematiche (Catania) **58**, 121–167 (2004)
5. Colbourn, C.J., Dinitz, J.H.: Handbook of Combinatorial Designs. CRC Press, Boca Raton (2006)
6. Forbes, M., Lawrence, J., Lei, Y., Kacker, R., Kuhn, D.R.: Refining the in-parameter-order strategy for constructing covering arrays. J. Res. Nat. Inst. Stand. Technol. **113**, 287–297 (2008)
7. Freiman, G., Lipkin, E., Levitin, L.: A polynomial algorithm for constructing families of k-independent sets. Discret. Math. **70**(2), 137–147 (1988)
8. Gao, S.W., Lv, J.H., Du, B.L., Colbourn, C.J., Ma, S.L.: Balancing frequencies and fault detection in the in-parameter-order algorithm. J. Comput. Sci. Technol. **30**(5), 957–968 (2015)
9. Hartman, A., Raskin, L.: Problems and algorithms for covering arrays. Discret. Math. **284**(13), 149–156 (2004)
10. Kleitman, D.J., Spencer, J.: Families of k-independent sets. Discret. Math. **6**(3), 255–262 (1973)
11. Kuhn, D., Kacker, R., Lei, Y.: Practical combinatorial testing. In: NIST Special Publication pp. 800–142 (2010)
12. Kuhn, D., Kacker, R., Lei, Y.: Introduction to Combinatorial Testing. Chapman & Hall/CRC Innovations in Software Engineering and Software Development Series. Taylor & Francis, New York (2013)

13. Lawrence, J., Kacker, R.N., Lei, Y., Kuhn, D.R., Forbes, M.: A survey of binary covering arrays. Electron. J. Comb. **18**(1), P84 (2011)
14. Lei, Y., Kacker, R., Kuhn, D.R., Okun, V., Lawrence, J.: IPOG-IPOG-D: efficient test generation for multi-way combinatorial testing. Softw. Test. Verif. Reliab. **18**(3), 125–148 (2008)
15. Lei, Y., Tai, K.C.: In-parameter-order: a test generation strategy for pairwise testing. In: 1998 3rd IEEE International Proceedings of High-Assurance Systems Engineering Symposium, pp. 254–261. IEEE (1998)
16. NIST: Table for CA(3, k, 2). National Institute of Standards and Technology. http://math.nist.gov/coveringarrays/ipof/tables/table.3.2.html. Accessed 25 Apr 2016
17. Seroussi, G., Bshouty, N.H.: Vector sets for exhaustive testing of logic circuits. IEEE Trans. Inf. Theor. **34**(3), 513–522 (1988)
18. Torres-Jimenez, J., Izquierdo-Marquez, I.: Survey of covering arrays. In: 2013 15th International Symposium on Symbolic and Numeric Algorithms for Scientific Computing (SYNASC), pp. 20–27. IEEE (2013)
19. Yu, L., Lei, Y., Kacker, R.N., Kuhn, D.R.: Acts: a combinatorial test generation tool. In: 2013 IEEE 6th International Conference on Software Testing, Verification and Validation (ICST), pp. 370–375. IEEE (2013)

Automated Localisation Testing in Industry with Test*

Mireilla Martinez[1], Anna I. Esparcia[1], Urko Rueda[1(✉)], Tanja E.J. Vos[2], and Carlos Ortega[3]

[1] Universidad Politecnica de Valencia, Camino de vera s/n, Valencia, Spain
{mimarmu1,aesparcia,urueda,tvos}@pros.upv.es
[2] Open Universiteit, Valkerburgerweg 177, Heerlen, The Netherlands
tanja.vos@ou.nl
[3] Indenova, Carrer Dels Traginers 14, Valencia, Spain
cortega@indenova.com
http://www.testar.org

Abstract. Test* is a testing tool that automatically and dynamically generates, executes and verifies test sequences based on a tree model that is derived from the software User Interface through assistive technologies. Test* is an academic prototype that we continuously try to transfer to companies to get feedback about its applicability. In this paper we report on one of these short experiences of using Test* in industry at the Valencian company Indenova. We applied the tool to check the localisation quality of a secure web platform that encapsulates a set of applications as services.

Keywords: Automated testing · Localisation · Technology transfer

1 Introduction

In previous work [4] we have presented an approach to automated testing of software applications from their User Interface (UI). Test*[1] automatically and dynamically generates test sequences which are executed and verified to reveal quality issues of the software under test. The tool is based on a tree model that is derived from the UI through the Operating System' Accessibility API[2]. From that API we can get access to the set of widgets that compose the UI of the target application (e.g. buttons, text-fields, menu bars) and the properties of each widget that characterise their appearance in the screen (e.g. screen position, size, whether it is enabled or not). From the UI model Test* is able to compute

---

[1] Previously known as TESTAR or Testar, and available as open source at http://www.testar.org.
[2] https://msdn.microsoft.com/en-us/library/windows/desktop/ff486375(v=vs.85).aspx.

© IFIP International Federation for Information Processing 2016
Published by Springer International Publishing AG 2016. All Rights Reserved
F. Wotawa et al. (Eds.): ICTSS 2016, LNCS 9976, pp. 241–248, 2016.
DOI: 10.1007/978-3-319-47443-4_17

a set of feasible actions (user events like left clicks and typing texts) to automate the interaction, so do the testing, with the software interface. No test cases are recorded and the tree model is dynamically inferred for every state[3], this implies that tests will run even when the GUI changes. This reduces the maintenance problem that threatens other GUI testing techniques like Capture and Replay [3] or Visual testing [1].

The Test* tool has been developed in the context of the EU FITTEST project that finished in 2014. First, it was evaluated in experimental conditions using different real and complex software applications like MS Office suite (running it 48 hours we detected 14 crash sequences). Subsequently, and with the purpose of getting a better understanding about the applicability of the tool in an industrial environment, we continuously try to apply Test* in companies to get feedback about its applicability and help companies to obtain solutions to the problems they face. In [5] results are described of transferring and evaluating the tool within 3 different companies on 2 desktop applications and one web application. In this paper we report on yet another short experience of using Test* in industry at the Valencian company Indenova[4].

2   Test*

To automate test generation, execution and verification, Test* performs the steps as is shown in Fig. 1: (1) start the SUT (System Under Test); (2) obtain the GUI's *State* (a widget tree[5]); (3) derive a set of sensible actions that a user could execute in a specific SUT's state (i.e. clicks, text inputs, mouse gestures); (4) select one of these actions (random or using some search-based optimisation criteria); (5) execute the selected action (through Java Robot[6] class); (6) apply the available oracles to check (in)validness of the new UI state. If a fault is found, stop the SUT (7) and save a re-playable sequence of the test that found the fault. If not, keep on testing if more actions are desired within the test sequence.

Using Test*, you can start testing immediately from the UI without the traditional requirement of specifying test cases, which are commonly provided manually with some degree of tool support. Based on the information gathered from the Accessibility API tests are generated by selecting an action to execute in the UI (e.g. left click a button with the title "Ok"). The action selection mechanism mainly drives how the test cases are generated, which can be performed randomly (select any suitable action for the current UI) or using a more advanced approach to increase the effectiveness of tests like the work in [2]. Without specifying anything, Test* can detect the violation of general-purpose system requirements through implicit oracles like those stating that the

---

[3] The Graphical User Interface at a particular time.

[4] www.indenova.com/.

[5] Test* uses the Operating System's Accessibility API, which has the capability to detect and expose a GUI's widgets, and their corresponding properties like: display position, widget size, title, description, etc.

[6] https://docs.oracle.com/javase/8/docs/api/java/awt/Robot.html.

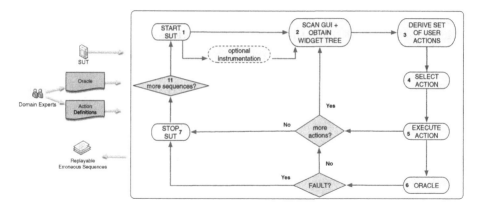

Fig. 1. Test* testing flow

SUT should not crash, the SUT should not find itself in an unresponsive state (freeze) and the GUI state should not contain any widget with suspicious words like *error*, *problem*, *exception*, etc.

This is a very attractive feature for companies because it enables them to start testing immediately and refine the tests as we go.

3   Indenova and the SUT eSigna

Indenova is a Valencian ICT company that provides ERP (Enterprise Resource Planning) solutions for companies. Their initial clients are based in Spain. But throughout the years, Indenova has gained new clients in Latin America. Testing at Indenova is mainly manual and basically done at the system acceptance test level. Written requirements are used for the design of system test suites. They would like to have more tests automated, but currently in the company there is a lack of time and people with knowledge about test automation.

Becoming aware of Test* Indenova is very interested to see how they can start test automation, so they provided access to their eSigna product. It is a web platform that securely integrates and provides access to applications as services enabling users to perform specific processes inside their organisations. Thus, eSigna is a base component in which concrete services can be plugged-in as required by each particular project. Those services are independent from each other, but they are interconnected to share information in real time.

4   The Industrial Experience

During the investigation we have measured the following *effectiveness and efficiency* aspects of Test* for testing the localisation quality of eSigna:

1. Number of failures (wrongly translated words) observed after executing Test* on eSigna

2. Time needed to set-up the test environment and get everything running
3. Lines Of Code (LOC) and time needed for UI actions definition, oracles design and stopping criteria setup.
4. Time for running Test* to reveal localisation issues on eSigna.

The project has been carried out in a fashion that allowed us to perform iterative development of Test*. The process included the following steps which were repeated several times to yield the final setup:

1. Planning: Implementation of Test Environment, consisting of planning and implementing the technical details of the test environment for Test*, as well as the anticipating and identifying potential fault patterns in the Error Definition.
2. Implementation: Consisting of implementing the Test* protocol consisting of: Oracles to implement the detection of the errors defined in the previous step; Action Definition to define the action set from which Test* selects; and the Implementation of stopping criteria that determine when sufficient testing has been done by Test*.
3. Testing and Evaluation: Run the tests.

4.1   Planning the Testing: What Do We Want to Test

One of the immediate problems that Indenova faces with eSigna, localisation to Latin America community, fits perfectly with Test* capabilities. The tool enables not only to detect stability problems for free, like crashes and exceptions, but it also allows to systematically analyse the UI in the search of wrongly translated texts.

As previously indicated, the initial clients from Indenova were from Spain, but gradually they have expanded to Spanish speaking South American countries. One of the problem encountered is that there are differences between the Castilian Spanish spoken in Spain and the different Latin American Spanish. Although it is not a problem of not being able to understand what is meant, some of the clients from Columbia and Peru just have complained about the usage of Castilian words. For example:

English	Castilian Spanish	Latin American Spanish
Mobile phone	Móvil	Celular
Holiday	Festivo	Feriado
Computer	Ordenador	Computadora

Since the implementation is not based on dictionaries and the Castilian Spanish is hard-coded, there is no other way than test the application to find the words that need to be changed for the other countries. This is a tedious and boring job.

4.2   Implementing the Test* protocol

Test* has the flexibility to adapt its default behaviour for specific needs. We will describe next how did we setup the tool to automatically verify localisation problems on *eSigna* product. We refer to the steps in the testing flow (Fig. 1):

1. START SUT - Set *eSigna* activation: it will tell Test* how to start/run the application. Being a web application, it consists of a command line *BROWSER URL* where *BROWSER* is the path and executable of an available web browser (i.e. Internet Explorer) and *URL* the entry point for the *eSigna* web application.
2. DERIVE SET OF USER ACTIONS - Set suitable actions: from the space of candidate actions that the user could perform over the product UI we are interested in (1) actions that will enable an automatic login to *eSigna* and (2) actions which are not interesting for our localisation verifying objective (i.e. web browser actions, a logout button, an administration panel in *eSigna*, etc.)
3. SELECT ACTION - Set test algorithm: the tool provides several strategies to generate a test (e.g. picking a random action each time). We are interested in exercising as much of the UI as possible to verify any potential localisation issues. We selected the Q-Learning algorithm from previous work [2].
4. ORACLE - Set localisation oracles: verifying the localisation correctness of *eSigna* for a target language can be straightforward performed by defining a list of taboo words that should not appear in the UI. This list can be easily defined in Test* UI through Java regular expressions (i.e. .*[mM][óo]vil.*—.*[fF]estivo.*—.*[oO]rdenador.*).
5. FAULT?/more actions? - Set the stopping criteria: the tool offers different approaches to stop a test, including a fixed time for execution, a fixed length for the number of UI actions to be executed or a self-made stopping criteria through a Java based protocol class (check next point). We made use of the last option to establish that we have tested enough when no more new UI is being exercised by our tests.
6. Advanced setup editing the tool' test protocol: Test* provides a Java class composed of a method for each task in the testing cycle presented in Fig. 1. Concretely, we implemented the automated login inside the task *START SUT*, non-interesting actions filtering inside the task *DERIVE SET OF USER ACTIONS* and the stopping criteria in the *more actions?* check point.

Once Test* was setup for automated localisation verification we just had to wait for the tool test reports. Following the testing flow of Test* it would first activate eSigna, perform an automated login and repeat a cycle of <*select and execute action, verify localisation problems, check stopping criteria*>.

4.3   Testing and Evaluation

Our context multilingual scenario consisted of one target language, *Latin American Spanish*, as this was the first concern on eSigna testing with Test*. We account in Table 1 (LOC = Lines Of Code; time in minutes) for metrics that measure the effort required for our solution on automated verification of localisation issues.

Setting up Test* for eSigna is an easy process that consists on providing the command line that would activate the product. Actions configuration would require some effort though as we would like Test* to perform automated tests without user intervention. Thus, we first need to analyse eSigna authentication process to provide the proper actions once the product has been activated. Additionally, we wanted to maintain our tests in relevant UI parts of eSigna, for example disabling/filtering non interesting actions like closing the browser, log-out of eSigna, etc. Yet, 35 lines of code and 10 min were enough for Test* to perform automated tests over eSigna. We acknowledge that future enhancements on Test* would enable a more efficient configuration of actions (we used version 1.1a of the tool).

Table 1. Efficiency

Setup environment	Actions		Oracles		Stop criteria		Test run
Time	LOC	Time	LOC	Time	LOC	Time	Time
1	35	10	0	5	9	2	>60

Oracles did not require any lines of code, but just a regular expression with the full list of unwanted localised product words (e.g. Móvil, Festivo, Ordenador). From Indenova, we acquired a full list of more than 30 words that the Latin American community had issued to the company in the past. This list contained wrongly used Spanish words (e.g. Móvil instead of Celular). Thus, we defined the regular expression for the words in the list that would enable Test* to check the quality of eSigna with respect to its localisation.

The stopping criteria was easily implemented taking into account how much of the UI was being exercised (user events) by the test. We named this *UI space exploration*, where the full UI space is composed of every particular and different[7] screen window that the application might show to the user. We forced to stop the tests when no more UI space was being explored by the last 100 executed actions. In other words, when there was no new UI window already exercised by the test.

Finally, using the configuration just described we let Test* run a test for almost an hour. The tool was able to report localisation issues on 2 words from the list in the first 5 min of execution. Both words were confirmed by the company as they were already aware that they were incorrectly localised. Other words were not reported, but Indenova indicated that such words were not part of

---

[7] Two windows are considered different if there is almost (a) one widget not present in both windows or (b) a widget with different properties (e.g. text or size)) in each window.

the product. We also observed that new UI space was explored after an hour of execution, which could reveal additional issues in the localised product. We expect a direct relation between the UI space exploration (coverage) and the effectiveness achieved on localisation verification of software products, but this should be analysed in a further study.

We would like to make some final considerations. We acknowledge that the verification of localisation issues has been traditionally performed using other alternatives, for example through text finding utilities like *grep* command on Linux hosts or a general purpose text editor with file searching features. A main efficiency problem of these approaches is that we cannot safely distinguish between texts used in the source code, and text that is mainly appearing in the UI: users will never complain on texts that they do not see in the User Interface.

Moreover, more complex products like eSigna might make more difficult to check localisation issues when the source code is spread over several (virtual) machines (perhaps targeting different operative systems), databases, or even legacy systems. In this sense, Test* provides a central setup place from which products localisation can be verified.

Additionally, we decided to stop our tests after an hour of execution tough we could have allowed it to run for longer. If checking localisation issues is performed manually by a human (interacting with the UI) then Test* is helpful once it is setup correctly, as it can operate without human supervision. Although Test* is a general purpose testing tool, we have presented how it can be used to verify that a software product has the quality levels expected by a company like inDenova.

5 Conclusions and Further Work

We have presented a short experience of transferring an academic prototype from the university to the industry, for testing software applications at the UI level. Indenova is a Valencian ICT company that provides ERP solutions to other companies. We applied the prototype Test* for testing localisation issues in eSigna product, which targets the Latin American countries. eSigna is a secure web platform composed of integrated web services.

The automation level achieved by the prototype and its potential for testing software products made Indenova consider the integration of Test* into their testing processes. They used the prototype for performing smoke testing, which would provide early feedback of the quality of developed product versions.

As further work, we will improve localisation testing in the prototype by including dictionaries. We would also like to further investigate the effectiveness of the presented localisation testing solution, concretely its relation to the test' UI space coverage.

Acknowledgement. This work was partly funded by the SHIP project (EACEA/ A2/UHB/CL 554187) and the PERTEST project (TIN2013-46928-C3-1-R). Test* was funded by the EC within the context of the FITTEST project, ICT-2009.1.2 no. 257574 (2012–2015).

References

1. Alegroth, E., Nass, M., Olsson, H.H.: Jautomate: a tool for system- and acceptance-test automation. In: 2013 IEEE Sixth International Conference on Software Testing, Verification and Validation (ICST), pp. 439–446, March 2013
2. Bauersfeld, S., Vos, T.: A reinforcement learning approach to automated GUI robustness testing. In: Fast Abstracts of the 4th Symposium on Search-Based Software Engineering (SSBSE 2012), pp. 7–12. IEEE (2012)
3. Nguyen, B.N., Robbins, B., Banerjee, I., Memon, A.M.: GUITAR: an innovative tool for automated testing of GUI-driven software. Autom. Softw. Eng. **21**(1), 65–105 (2014)
4. Rueda, U., Vos, T.E.J., Almenar, F., Martínez, M.O., Esparcia-Alcázar, A.I.: TESTAR: from academic prototype towards an industry-ready tool for automated testing at the user interface level. In: Canos, J.H., Gonzalez Harbour, M. (eds.) Actas de las XX Jornadas de Ingeniería del Software y Bases de Datos (JISBD 2015), pp. 236–245 (2015)
5. Vos, T.E.J., Kruse, P.M., Condori-Fernández, N., Bauersfeld, S., Wegener, J.: Testar: tool support for test automation at the user interface level. Int. J. Inf. Syst. Model. Des. **6**(3), 46–83 (2015)

Distribution Visualization for User Behavior Analysis on LTE Network

Masaki Suzuki[1(✉)], Quentin Plessis[1], Takeshi Kitahara[1], and Masato Tsuru[2]

[1] KDDI R&D Laboratories Inc., 2-1-15 Ohara, Fujimino-shi, Saitama, Japan
{masaki-suzuki,qu-plessis,kitahara}@kddilabs.jp
[2] Kyushu Institute of Technology, 680-4 Kawazu, Iizuka-shi, Fukuoka, Japan
tsuru@cse.kyutech.ac.jp

Abstract. In order to seamlessly provide high quality communication services, mobile network operators (MNOs) tackle to promptly respond to a degradation of the communication quality when it occurs. MNOs are facing a difficulty to detect the degradation without any error messages or nonconformity. For the first step of the study, we implemented a Self-Organizing Map (SOM)-based visualization system to analyze the users' behavior in evolved packet core based on state transitions estimated by capturing LTE C-Plane signals. We show a case study of analyzing actual LTE signals using the implemented system, which demonstrates that we can intuitively see the unexpected characteristic of users' behavior from the results.

Keywords: LTE · C-Plane analysis · Self-Organizing Map (SOM)

1 Introduction

Mobile network operators (MNOs) are responsible for providing high quality of communication services. It is very important for them to monitor the communication quality. For this purpose, MNOs tackle to immediately detect the degradation of the communication quality when any incidents occur. The existing approaches are generally either the log-based or the conformance-based. In the log-based approaches, a system monitors messages and system logs of equipment in the LTE network [1]. The system detects hardware errors and link errors. On the other hand, in the conformance-based approaches, a system detects unfamiliar sequence of messages referring the specifications of 3GPP standard. However, there exists a degradation of the communication quality occurring without any error messages or nonconformity. For instance, ping-pong handover is a general phenomenon in mobile networks, which causes inefficient network performance and communication quality [2, 3]. When one User Equipment (UE) which is moving close to the fringe between multiple evolve node Bs (eNBs) and connecting to one of them, it handovers from one eNB to another eNB, then it often immediately connects back to the former eNB. In the case where the UE stays around the fringe, it sometimes repeatedly handovers from/to these eNBs. In this situation, there exists no evolved packet core (EPC) equipment errors. However, this phenomenon still causes unnecessary control messages in EPC and degrades the

F. Wotawa et al. (Eds.): ICTSS 2016, LNCS 9976, pp. 249–255, 2016.
DOI: 10.1007/978-3-319-47443-4_18

communication quality. In such a case, MNOs hardly detect the degradation unless customers report the problem to them.

For the first step to study detecting the degradation without any errors, MNOs have to know how users behave in EPC. In order not to lose the generality, the users' behavior analysis should be exhaustive and comprehensive. However, since EPC signals through various interfaces between function nodes in EPC are mixture of different protocols and IDs, it is difficult to trace users' behavior sequentially.

In this paper, we report a preliminarily implemented system that captures and analyzes C-Plane signals in EPC, quantifies users' behavior, and visualizes the distribution of users' behavior. Then we introduce a case study with the actual C-Plane signals and a typical example for cluster of degraded situation of users' behavior.

2 Related Works

There exist several studies about users' behavior analysis in mobile networks. In [4], the authors analyze signaling storms based on radio resource control (RRC) protocol. In order to detect anomaly and malicious users' behavior causing signaling storms, [4] firstly models and analyzes the patterns of signals in RRC protocol. Then, it identifies the specific patterns. In [5], the authors focus on retrieving radio access information from S1-MME and S11 interfaces. As an example, the authors summarize the time transition of the duration of radio access bearer establishment.

To the best of our knowledge, there exists no study analyzing or visualizing users' behavior in EPC. Therefore, for the first step of research, we tackle to visualize users' behavior based on C-Plane signals in EPC.

3 Implementation

In order to analyze users' behavior in EPC, we implement a distribution visualization system in an actual LTE network which is standardized by 3GPP [6]. Figure 1 briefly depicts the LTE architecture regarding to C-Plane signals. In our implementation, we focus on the signals through S1-MME, S10 and S11 interfaces. They are a mixture of S1 application protocol (S1AP) and Evolved general packet radio service tunneling protocol for control plane (GTPv2-C). Figure 2 shows the architecture of our implementation. Firstly, the capture server captures signals. Secondly, the signal analyzer extracts users' state transition from capture files. Thirdly, the statistics monitor quantify users' behavior based on users' state transition. Finally, the distribution visualizer draws users' behavior distribution using self-organizing map (SOM).

3.1 Capture of C-Plane Signals and Signal Analysis

The process in our implementation starts with the capture of the signals. The implemented system groups the signals by user, then constructs signal sequences by user. After that, it extracts specific patterns of signal sequences. Note that, the implemented

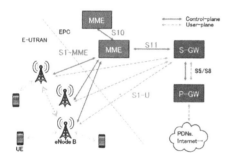

Fig. 1. LTE architecture.

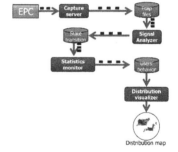

Fig. 2. System architecture.

system does not identify the specific user. It can only distinguish users using a temporary assigned identifier. Since the temporary identifier is valid for a certain duration of time, the implemented system can trace users' behavior for a short time. Thus the implemented system cannot follow any specific user for a long time, e.g. several hours or longer.

Based on the signal sequences, the system constructs a state transition graph. The state transition graph consists of 5 elements as follows. The input is specific patterns of signaling messages extracted from S1AP and GTPv2-C signals. The states are defined according to 3GPP standard, and determined by the combination of current state and input. In the system, the initial and final state of the transition are ignored since, in actual LTE networks, the initial state should always be the same state and the final state should not be naturally defined. Tables 1 and 2 show the lists of states and examples of state transition respectively.

Table 1. States in the system

State	Description	State	Description
0	UNKNOWN	13	ACTIVATION
1	IDLE	14	START_WIFI
2	INITIAL_CONTEXT_SETUP	15	END_WIFI
3	S1_HO_INITIATION	16	TAU
4	S1_HO_ALLOCATION	17	THREEG_HD
5	S1_HO_ALLOCATED	18	CALL
6	S1_HO_BEING_CARRIED_OUT	19	ACTIVE_ENTER
7	S1_HO_SUCCEEDED	20	ACTIVE_LEAVE
8	S1_HO_ALLOCATION_FAILED	21	SETUP_BEARER
9	S1_HO_PREPARATION_FAILED	22	RELEASED_BEARER
10	S1_HO_CANCELLED	23	INACTIVE
11	X2_HANDOVER_SUCCEEDED	24	X2_HANDOVER_INITIATION
12	X2_HANDOVER_FAILED	25	LEFT_MEASURED_AERA

Table 2. Examples of state transition

Current state	Next state	Description	Procedure code
X2 HO succeeded	X2 HO initiated	PATH SWITCH REQUEST ACKNOWLEDGE	3 DL SUCCESS
S1 HO allocation	S1 HO allocated	HANDOVER REQUEST ACKNOWLEDGE	1 UL SUCCESS
S1 HO allocation	S1 HO allocation failed	HANDOVER FAILURE	1 UL UNSUCCESS
S1 HO prep. failed	S1 HO initiated	HANDOVER REQUIRED	0 UL
S1 HO allocated	S1 HO in progress	HANDOVER COMMAND	0 DL SUCCESS
Inactive	Idle	UE CONTEXT RELEASE COMPLETE (inactivity)	23 UL SUCCESS
Idle	Tracking are update	INITIAL UE MESSAGE (TAU)	12 UL
Idle	Activation	INITIAL UE MESSAGE	12 UL
X2 HO initiated	X2 HO succeeded	PATH SWITCH REQUEST	3 UL
Initial context setup	Inactive	UE CONTEXT RELEASE REQUEST (inactivity)	23 UL
Activation	Initial context setup	INITIAL CONTEXT SETUP RESPONSE	9 UL SUCCESS
S1 HO alloc. failed	S1 HO allocation	HANDOVER REQUEST	1 DL
Tracking are update	Idle	UE CONTEXT RELEASE COMPLETE	23 UL
Tracking are update	Initial context setup	INITIAL CONTEXT SETUP RESPONSE	9 UL SUCCESS
S1 HO in progress	S1 HO succeeded	HANDOVER NOTIFY	2 UL
S1 HO initiated	S1 HO allocation	HANDOVER REQUEST	1 DL
S1 HO initiated	S1 HO cancelled	HANDOVER CANCEL ACKNOWLEDGE	4 DL
S1 HO initiated	S1 HO preparation failed	HANDOVER PREPARATION FAILURE	0 DL UNSUCESS
S1 HO cancelled	S1 HO initiated	HANDOVER REQUIRED	0 UL

3.2 Statistics Monitor

After that, the implemented system calculates statistics values in order to quantify the behavior of each user based on his/her state transition. In the implementation, in order to characterize the continuous-time state transition of a user, we adopt the state transition probability matrix $(p(n,m))$ as well as the average and the variation coefficient of the dwell time $(t^{(i)}(n,m))$ at state n in a transition from state n to state m. The probability $p(n,m)$ from state n to state m is calculated in Eq. 1,

$$p(n,m) = \frac{\text{the number of state transition from } n \text{ to } m}{\text{the number of state transition from } n \text{ to } any\ states}. \tag{1}$$

The dwell time $t^{(i)}(n,m)$ is calculated by state transition as in Eq. 2,

$$t^{(i)}(n,m) = t_n^{(i)} - t_m^{(i)}, \tag{2}$$

where, $t_m^{(i)}$ and $t_n^{(i)}$ is the arrival time at state m and n in i-th state transition from state m to n respectively. To gather these values, we describe users' behavior with a multi-dimensional vector. As respecting the definition of states, number of possible state transition is 600. Since we adopt 3 different statistics values, users' behavior described in a 1,800-dimensional space in our implementation.

3.3 Distribution Visualizer

In order to visualize the distribution in a multi-dimensional space, the distribution visualizer uses the self-organizing map (SOM) [7]. SOM is an artificial neural network using unsupervised learning to construct a two-dimensional space representing a multi-dimensional space. We can intuitively see the distribution of the users' behavior by mapping the distribution in a multi-dimension into a two-dimension.

According to the SOM algorithm, the distribution visualizer firstly define the vector space based on the entire input data. Secondly, the distribution visualizer plots the quantified user's behavior in an n-dimensional space one by one. Then it transforms the distribution into a two-dimensional space. In the process of the transformation, it draws regular grid of circles (namely, units) in the two-dimensional space. Each unit represents principal components and each plot is located in the closest circle so that the more the behaviors are similar, the closer they are located. The visualizer highlight the specific condition of users in the case where they are labeled in advance and we can compare different conditions of users intuitively.

4   Case Study

In order to validate the result of the implemented system and assess its usefulness, we visualize users' behavior based on 24 h of the actual anonymized C-Plane signals in a large urban area in Japan. In this case study, we intuitively identify the fundamental characteristics of specific users who had experienced ping-pong handovers and labeled in advance. Firstly, the signal analyzer parses the captured signals and constructs signal sequences by users. Then, it extracts state transitions. Figure 3 depicts the state transition diagram. In the figure, the indexes of the nodes are the indexes of the states in Table 1 and the width of edges are the probability of state transition ($p(n,m)$). For the readability, we ignore the edges which $p(n,m)$ is less than 0.10 in the figure. According to the state transitions, the statistics monitor quantifies the users' behavior in terms of p (n,m), the mean value and variation coefficient of dwell time ($t^{(i)}(n,m)$).

We define the input space using the entire 24 h of input data. We prepare 100 units to describe the input space in the 2-dimensional space and the indexes of units are numbered in a left-to-right and bottom-to-top fashion as described in Fig. 4. Figure 5 depicts distribution maps of 0 am, 6 am, 12 pm and 6 pm in the day. In each unit, we plot users' behavior of each hour in gray color. Then we highlight users' who had experienced ping-pong handovers in the period of time in red color.

According to the figures, the number of visualized users are varied by time and the distribution of users are different especially between 0 am and 6 am. The highlighted

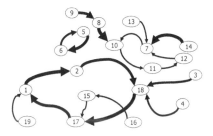

Fig. 3. State transition diagram.

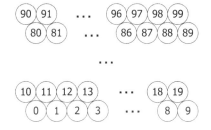

Fig. 4. Indexes of units.

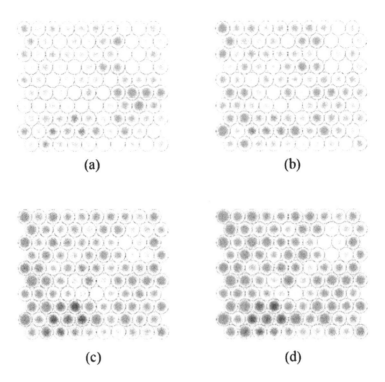

(a)   (b)

(c)   (d)

Fig. 5. Distribution maps of (a) 0 am (b) 6 am (c) 12 pm and (d) 6 pm. (Color figure online)

users, however, located in similar units. Focusing on those unit 2, 3, 13, 14, 15, 23 and 24, the components of them commonly include variation coefficient of $t^{(i \in \Omega)}(11, 24)$, p $(11, 24)$, $p(11, 23)$, $p(2, 24)$. Since ping-pong handovers mean frequent handovers, it is quite understandable those users are likely to belong to those units which include transition from 11 to 23 or 24. However, the visualized results indicate a phenomenon that a number of users who experience ping-pong handovers also start X2 handover right after the initial context setup, which is unexpected by MNOs. Our system enables to highlight the unknown characteristics of ping-pong handovers.

5   Conclusion and Future Works

In order to analyze the users' behavior in EPC, we implemented the visualization system for user's behavior distribution. We draw the distribution maps using implemented system with the actual C-Plane data. As future works, we will deeply analyze users' behavior based on multi-hop transitions of states.

References

1. Agrawal, N.: On the design of element management system for node Bs in a 3G wireless network. In: Proceedings of IEEE International Conference on Personal Wireless Communications, pp. 51–55, 15–17 December 2002
2. Li, S., Cheng, F., Yuan, Y., Hu, T.: Adaptive frame switching for UMTS UL-EDCH - Ping-Pong avoidance. In: Vehicular Technology Conference, vol. 5, pp. 2469–2473, 7–10 May 2006
3. Kim, T.-H., Yang, Q., Lee, J.-H., Park, S.-G., Shin, Y.-S.: A mobility management technique with simple handover prediction for 3G LTE systems. In: Proceedings of Vehicular Technology Conference, pp. 259–263, 30 September 2007–3 October 2007
4. Gorbil, G., Abdelrahman, O.H., Pavloski, M., Gelenbe, E.: Modeling and analysis of RRC-based signalling storms in 3G networks. In: IEEE Transactions on Emerging Topics in Computing, vol. 4, no. 1, pp. 113–127, January–March 2016
5. Wang, J., Zhou, W., Wang, H., Chen, L.: A control-plane traffic analysis tool for LTE network. In: Sixth International Conference on Intelligent Human-Machine Systems and Cybernetics (IHMSC), pp. 218–221 (2014)
6. 3rd Generation Partnership Project, General Packet Radio Service (GPRS) Enhancements for Evolved Universal Terrestrial Radio Access Network (E-UTRAN) access, TS 23.401. Release Dec 2014
7. Kohonen, T.: The self-organizing map. In: Proceedings of the IEEE, vol. 78, no. 9, pp. 1464–1480, September 1990

Author Index

Printed in the United States
By Bookmasters